Children's
Dreams

Children's Dreams

Notes from the Seminar
Given in 1936–1940

by C. G. Jung

Edited by Lorenz Jung and Maria Meyer-Grass
Translated by Ernst Falzeder with the collaboration of Tony Woolfson

PHILEMON SERIES

Published with the support of the Philemon Foundation
This book is part of the Philemon Series of the Philemon Foundation

PRINCETON UNIVERSITY PRESS
PRINCETON AND OXFORD

First published in Switzerland under the title *Seminare: Kinderträume* © Walter-Verlag 1987

English translation © 2008 by Princeton University Press

Published by Princeton University Press, 41 William Street, Princeton, New Jersey 08540

In the United Kingdom: Princeton University Press, 3 Market Place, Woodstock, Oxfordshire OX20 1SY

Library of Congress Cataloging-in-Publication Data

Jung, C. G. (Carl Gustav), 1875–1961.
[Kinderträume. English]
Children's dreams: notes from the seminar given in 1936–1940 / by C. G. Jung; edited by Lorenz Jung and Maria Meyer-Grass; translated by Ernst Falzeder with the collaboration of Tony Woolfson.
    p.   cm.
Includes bibliographical references and indexes.
ISBN 978-0-691-13323-2 (hardcover: alk. paper)
1. Children's dreams—Congresses. 2. Children's dreams—Case studies—Congresses. 3. Dreams—Congresses. 4. Archetype (Psychology)—Congresses. 5. Psychoanalysis—Congresses.
6. Jung, C. G. (Carl Gustav), 1875–1961—Congresses.
I. Meyer-Grass, Maria. II. Title.
BF1099.C55J8613 2008
154.6′3083-dc22

                                                    2007019555

British Library Cataloging-in-Publication Data is available

This book is published with the support of the Philemon Foundation and is part of the Philemon Series of the Philemon Foundation.
philemonfoundation.org

This book has been composed in Goudy

Designed by Lorraine Betz Doneker

Printed on acid-free paper. ∞

press.princeton.edu

Printed in the United States of America

10 9 8 7 6 5 4 3

Contents

Note to the English Edition

Between 1936 and 1940, C. G. Jung presented a seminar on children's dreams and old works on dream interpretation at the Eidgenössische Technische Hochschule (Swiss Federal Institute of Technology) in Zurich. In 1987, these were published in German by Walter Verlag, edited by Lorenz Jung and Maria Meyer-Grass in a 680-page volume. For the English edition, it was decided to publish the work in two volumes, placing the seminars on children's dreams in one volume and the seminars on old works on dream interpretation in a second volume, to preserve thematic continuity. Footnotes originally made by the participants of the seminars have been left standing; those by the editors of the German edition are indicated by "(ed.)." Additional editorial footnotes by the translator, Ernst Falzeder, have been added, and are indicated by "(trans.)." The translation and additional editorial work have been funded by the Philemon Foundation, a nonprofit organization dedicated to raising funds for the publication of C. G. Jung's unpublished works (www.philemonfoundation.org). The Board of the Philemon Foundation would like to thank its donors for their generous support, which has made this volume possible.

Sonu Shamdasani
General Editor, Philemon Series
Reader in Jung History,
Wellcome Trust Centre for the History of
Medicine at University College, London

Acknowledgments

My thanks go to Steven Martin, Sonu Shamdasani, and Tony Woolfson for their invaluable support and help, as well as to the community of the translators forum at http://dict.leo.org/forum/. Ulrich Hoerni of the C. G. Jung Erbengemeinschaft went through parts of the draft and made helpful suggestions. Thanks to Madeleine B. Adams and Sara Lerner of Princeton University Press for the excellent collaboration.

Ernst Falzeder
Translator

Preface

The present edition is the first supplement to C. G. Jung's *Collected Works*, comprising the minutes of the four seminars on children's dreams, with additional explanatory editorial notes.

From 1933 onward, C. G. Jung gave lectures at the Eidgenössische Technische Hochschule (ETH) in Zurich, on individuation, on dreams, and on analytical psychology in general (see the Jung bibliography in the index volume of the *Collected Works*). In 1935, he was appointed titular professor of psychology at the department of *Freifächer* (elected subjects) (XII). In the following years, he gave various lectures and seminars at this university, including the four seminars on children's dreams, with discussions of selected literature on dreams, reprinted here. These discussions of fundamental questions concerning the human psyche are of extraordinary importance, not only because of their relevance to the history of science, but also for an understanding of the practical application of Jung's method of *amplification*. For this reason they represent a good introduction to analytical psychology—in which dream interpretation plays a central role—for readers who have so far concerned themselves only occasionally with psychological problems. Thus, C. G. Jung stated: "The purpose of this seminar is to practice on the basis of the material." This goal, the easily understandable language, and the apparent simplicity of the children's dreams particularly facilitate the reader's understanding.

The views on the psychology of the individual and on collective problems of our culture expressed in these seminars have so far been available only to a very limited number of persons. First, admission to the seminar classes depended on C. G. Jung's permission, in order to allow discussions in a relatively small group of people; and second, the subsequently compiled minutes were distributed only to the seminar participants. Thus, an embargo originally preceded each of the four seminar reports: "This seminar report is intended exclusively for the use of the participants of the seminar and the subscribers only. It must not be circulated, lent, or borrowed. No parts of it may be quoted or printed without the specific permission of Professor Jung." These restrictions were to ensure professional discretion. In addition, Jung had concerns about publishing certain contributions in their original form. As we will explain in the introduction, it was only much later that C. G. Jung allowed wider circulation of the seminars.

The completion of the present edition was only made possible by the work the original editors of the seminar proceedings devoted to recording and editing the notes. Without their commitment this valuable material would probably have been lost. We owe thanks to Hans H. Baumann, Kurt Binswanger, Marie-Louise von Franz, Liliane Frey, Aniela Jaffé, and Rivkah Kluger-Schärf. We are especially indebted to Marie-Louise von Franz and Elisabeth Rüf for their support and expert advice in the preparation of this edition, as well as to William McGuire for providing us with pertinent correspondence. We also thank the numerous contributing participants in the seminar, who have kindly given their permission for the reprint. Special thanks go to the psychology fund of the ETH and the Dr. Donald C. Cooper Funds for their financial support of the printing.[1]

In the spoken word recorded in this material, now accessible to a broader public, we are able to see C. G. Jung in a different light than in his written works, in which this side is not so apparent. Here, his human side, his humor, and his satirical vein come to fore as he takes a closer look at others and at himself. The—sometimes unguarded—irony with which he does this bears special witness to his lively and straightforward temperament. The reader is reminded again and again, in a pleasantly provocative manner, that the seminar's subject is not just a sterile theory, but the actual, lived reality of the child, and thus life as such. We all know this reality because its symbols affect each of us.

Fall 1986

Lorenz Jung
Maria Meyer-Grass

[1] [For the German edition only].

Introduction by the Editors

C. G. Jung did not find the time, in the midst of writing his immense body of work, to review the four seminar reports assembled here for their scientific correctness. He was convinced, however, that such editing would be necessary; he considered his own statements, as well as those of the participants of the seminars, to be, above all, oral contributions to the discussion, which would need to be elaborated more carefully and precisely when printed, in order to stand up to criticism. The most subjective factors may often influence the spoken word, and the inevitably subjective recording of the statements does not ensure that what is recorded is in fact always *exactly* what was originally meant. Despite these reservations, much later, toward the end of his life, he agreed to have the numerous seminars on various subjects published as an appendix to his *Gesammelte Werke* (GW). On 24 May 1956, he wrote to Gerhard Adler, a member of the Anglo-American editorial team of the *Collected Works*: "I completely agree to have the 'seminar notes'[1] published as an appendix to the complete edition of my works, and I ask you . . . to see to it that the necessary excisions, or corrections, of any possible factual mistakes be made. . . . If possible, however, the style should not be altered." On another occasion, he wished to have the following note printed at the beginning of the seminar notes:

> I am well aware of the fact that the text of these seminars contains a certain number of errors and other shortcomings, which would make corrections necessary. Unfortunately, I was not able to carry out this work myself. I therefore ask the reader to read these reports with the

[1] This expression in English in the original (trans.).

xiii

necessary critical eye, and to use them with caution. Apart from that, thanks to the representational art [of the chroniclers], they give a lively and faithful image of reality as it was at that time. (May 1954)

C. G. Jung may have been prompted to make these remarks by his wish to enable the reader to form an independent judgment, and at the same time to draw the reader's attention to the fact that some of the statements should not be generalized, but rather scrutinized with benevolent criticism.

Our present edition of the seminars on children's dreams is in accordance with C. G. Jung's wish to leave the texts as much as possible in their original straightforwardness. A completely verbatim report of the discussions, however, is neither possible, for the reasons mentioned earlier, nor was it aimed at; we rather tried to eliminate some of the obvious mistakes and misunderstandings in the records that were made after the fact. Whenever possible, the illustrations used at the time were used as the templates for those in this book.

In what follows we will briefly discuss the history of the four seminar reports. At the beginning of each of the meetings of the seminar, which lasted for about two academic (fifty-minute) hours, a dream interpretation or a book report was presented. These materials had been assigned to the participants by C. G. Jung at the beginning of the semester. Then the topic was amplified in a sometimes circuitous discussion. Some participants took down more or less accurate notes of the discussion, which were compiled at the end of the semester. In later years, the stenographic records by Rivkah Kluger-Schärf were of inestimable value for the editorial work. Even if the *exact* wording could not always be established, the style of the spoken word could be preserved to a very great extent.

We learn from the preface to the first recorded seminar, given in 1936/37, written and edited by Hans H. Baumann, Kurt Binswanger, Marie-Louise von Franz, Liliane Frey, and Rivkah Schärf, that the publication "was decided on by the collaborators only at the end of the semester, with Professor C. G. Jung's assent": "It was made at the request of numerous friends of his psychology. The text is based, therefore, on notes in long- and shorthand, which were not meant to be used for a proper publication. Nevertheless, we think we have given, together with Professor Jung, a complete and faithful rendition of the commentaries." In 1935/36, before this class, the dream series of a boy had been discussed, which is reprinted in the appendix of the present edition, because there are repeated references to it in the following texts. Unfortunately, no further notes about those discussions are extant. We have also included a number of papers on the dream literature from antiquity up to modern times.[2] They provide an overview of the prevalent ideas on the topic of dreams in different epochs. We also include the discussion of a work that has still not been translated from Latin, *De Somniis* by Caspar Peucer.

The second seminar, given in 1938/39, was edited by Liliane Frey and Rivkah Schärf. That semester C. G. Jung presented a detailed introduction to the method of dream interpretation. We consider it to be so fundamental that we have placed it, disregarding chronology, at the beginning of the present volume. Although C. G. Jung repeatedly talked about dream interpretation at the beginnings of the subsequent seminars, no such introduction is extant from the first semester.

Liliane Frey and Aniela Jaffé edited the third seminar, given in 1939/40, on the basis of the notes of Rivkah Schärf. Here, as in the seminars of the other years, we added the missing papers of the participants whenever they were available.

The fourth and last report was written as late as 1975, and was privately printed by Rivkah Kluger-Schärf and Marie-Louise von Franz, in keeping with the original restrictions. In the foreword to their extraordinarily precise edition, the editors write:

> For a long time already, the undersigned have had the desire to publish this seminar, which contains, apart from the discussion and interpretation of children's dreams, the interpretation of dreams of the Renaissance scholar Girolamo Cardano, the visions of St. Perpetua, and the well-known dream of the 'Swinging Ax' of Dr. Hubbard. . . .

---

[2] All papers and discussions on the dream literature are collected in volume 2 of the English edition (see Note to the English Edition in this volume) (trans.).

To be able to present the texts by Cardanus and their interpretation with as much unity as possible, we had to sacrifice the chronological sequence of the seminar meetings. . . . A difficulty was presented by the papers of the participants of the seminar, some of which were no longer available. In these cases, the dreams on which the papers were based were replaced by short summaries or reconstructions with the help of the commentaries.

For reasons of unity and textual consistency, in the present edition we had to rearrange and make certain adaptations in the four original sets of seminar notes. Where changes in chronology were made, this is duly noted. All dates of the seminars, whenever extant, were added. All of the original footnotes were included; we have added notes of our own whenever this seemed useful for a better understanding. In these, the most important concepts of analytical psychology are briefly explained, although for a deeper understanding of the exact meaning of such terms we refer the reader to the numerous added cross-references to C. G. Jung's *Collected Works* (*CW*) or his memoirs, *Memories, Dreams, Reflections* (*MDR*). References to the volumes of *CW* are not by page numbers, but by the paragraph numbers of the passage in question. Whenever additional changes or omissions imposed themselves, they are indicated and explained at the place they were made, either by "ed." or by square brackets "[. . .]." For these corrections, and for many doubtful phrases, it was partly possible, in the interest of faithfulness to the original, to make use of the original notes of the seminar. For better recognizability, all dreams and longer quotations are italicized. An index has been added to facilitate work with this volume.

Without doubt, the four seminars on children's dreams are of great importance within the scope of Jung's complete works because they offer a rich introduction to the *practice* of Jungian dream interpretation. We find a particularly impressive application of the theory of the archetypes, because the personal context largely fades into the background in children's dreams, most of them remembered only in adulthood, and because archetypal images and situations come to the fore, owing to the child's greater proximity to the collective unconscious. In addition, the views expressed in the seminars are an important contribution, not only to the psychology of the individual, but also to the problems of modern society and to the questions of the basic religious needs of human beings. Finally, these records—snapshots, we might call them—are of interest for the history of science, because they bear witness to the development of important ideas and notions of Jung's analytical psychology.

Children's
Dreams

1

On the Method of Dream Interpretation
(Professor Jung)

Professor Jung: In this seminar[1] we will deal primarily with the dreams of children. In addition, some books about the significance of dreams will be discussed.

All of the dreams with which we will concern ourselves have been contributed by the participants. In most cases they were remembered by adults from their childhood, and were not obtained from the children themselves. This poses a difficulty as, in the case of *remembered* dreams, we can no longer ask the children themselves but have to resort to other means in order to enrich the dream material and to understand the dream. But we are also in a difficult situation when we record dreams from children *directly*. We must always reckon with the possibility that the child does not supply any information at all or, for instance, does not have associations because of being frightened by the dream. Furthermore, it lies in the nature of the earliest dreams of childhood that one usually does not get related associations: they are a manifestation of a part of the unconscious, standing alien in time. These *early* dreams in particular are of the utmost importance because they are dreamed out of the depth of the personality and, therefore, frequently represent an anticipation of the later destiny. Subsequent dreams of children become more and more unimportant, except when the dreamer is destined for a special fate. During pu-

---

[1] Session of 25 October 1938.

berty and until the twentieth year, dreams become more important again, then they lose importance, and finally they carry more and more weight again after the thirty-fifth year. This does not apply to all persons, but to the majority of cases. I would like to ask you to search your own memory if you can still remember the first dream of your life. Many remember dreams from their fourth year, others even from the third year. Maybe you could also ask your acquaintances and friends if they remember their first dreams. You should then also note what you know about the later lives of the dreamers, and also what you know about their families—if you know them—and whether you happened to notice any peculiarities among these.

Before starting our discussion of the individual dreams, I would like to make a few remarks on the *method of dream interpretation.*

As you know, the dream is a natural phenomenon. It does not spring from a special intention. One cannot explain it with a psychology taken from *consciousness.* We are dealing with a particular way of functioning independent of the human ego's will and wishes, intention or aim. It is an unintentional occurrence, just like everything occurring in nature. So we also cannot assume that the sky gets clouded only to annoy us; it simply is as it is. The difficulty is, however, to get a *handle* on that natural occurrence.

It seems best to be as unprejudiced as possible when we let things influence us. Yet anything we have to say about the event is still our *interpretation.* We are in the same situation as any natural scientist, who also deals with phenomena that do not reveal their meaning and conformity with a natural law. Any meaning given to what happens comes from *us.* We are facing the difficult task of translating natural processes into psychical language. To this end we have to use auxiliary and approximate terms for want of others, and make hypotheses. . . . But there always remains the doubt whether we have truly succeeded in giving a picture of what happens. One could, of course, argue that all of this has no meaning at all. If anything is subjective anyway, then one could as well say that nature does not conform to laws, that there is chaos. It is, however, a question of temperament whether to assume a meaning, even if one may not understand it yet, or to prefer saying: "All of this has no meaning anyway." But one can

2

also be of the opinion that, although each interpretation may always be a human assumption about what is happening, one can still try to find out the truth about it. Yet we can never be sure to achieve that aim. This uncertainty can partly be overcome, however, by inserting a meaning into other equations and then checking whether the results of these equations are in accordance with that meaning. We can thus make an assumption about the meaning of one dream, and then see whether this attribution of a meaning also explains another one, that is, if it is of more general significance. We can also make control tests with the help of *dream series*. I would actually prefer to deal with children's dreams in dream series because when we investigate dreams in series, we most often find confirmation or corrections of our original assumptions in the following dreams. In dream series, the dreams are connected to one another in a meaningful way, as if they tried to give expression to a central content from ever-varying angles. To touch this central core is to find the key to the explanation of the individual dreams. It is not always so easy, however, to delimit a dream series. It is a kind of monologue taking place under the cover of consciousness. This monologue is heard, so to speak, in the dream, and sinks down during the periods when we are awake. But in a way the monologue never ends. We are quite probably dreaming all the time, but consciousness makes so much noise that we no longer hear the dream when awake. If we succeeded in making a complete list [of the unconscious processes], we could see that the whole describes a certain line. It is a very difficult task when done thoroughly.

The way we explain dreams is primarily a *causal* one. We are inclined to explain nature in such a way. Here this method meets enormous difficulties, however, because we can explain in a strictly causal way only when the necessity of a correlation between cause and effect can be proven. But this clear relation can be found, above all, in so-called inanimate nature. Whenever phenomena can be isolated and subjected to experiments, when, in other words, uniform conditions can be established, strict attributions of cause and effect can be made. In the case of biological phenomena, however, we are hardly able to ascertain a disposition that would lead, of necessity, to certain effects. For here we are facing such complex material, such a di-

3

versity and complexity of conditions, that no *unequivocal* causal connections can be maintained. Here the term *conditional* is much more appropriate, that is, such and such conditions can lead to such and such effects. It is an attempt to replace strict causality with an interwoven action of conditions, to extend the unequivocal connection between cause and effect with a connection open to many interpretations. Thus causality as such is not abolished, but only adapted to the multilayered material of life. We have to take into account that the psyche, like all biological phenomena, is of a goal-oriented, purposive nature. This does not at all contradict the previously mentioned opinion that the dream is something unintentional. There we laid stress on the fact that natural phenomena occur unconsciously, independent of consciousness. This does not preclude the developing forms of the psyche from being determined by *unconscious purposiveness*. We cannot but assume that the fundamental nature has always been there already, and that everything that occurs is only a purposive unfolding of this primal disposition. Even things that seem to be completely unpurposive in the psychical or biological fields can be examined as to their possible purposiveness. Ancient medicine, for instance, thought that fever is, in all circumstances, a symptom of illness to be fought against. Modern medicine knows that it is a complicated and purposive defense phenomenon, and not the *noxa* that causes the illness. In working with dreams, too, we have always to keep in mind this aspect of inner purposiveness of what is happening. In this sense, we may talk about the *unconscious goal orientation* of the dream process, in noting that these are not conscious goals, not intentions like those of consciousness, but purposive automatisms that, like cell reactions, cannot be other than purposive.

❀ ❀ ❀

The dream is no unequivocal phenomenon. There are several possibilities of giving a meaning to a dream. I would like to suggest to you four definitions, which are more or less an extract of the various meanings I have come across that dreams can have.

1. The dream is the unconscious reaction to a *conscious situation*. A certain conscious situation is followed by a reaction of the uncon-

4

scious in the form of a dream, whose elements point clearly, whether in a complementary or a compensatory way, to the impression received during the day. It is immediately obvious that this dream would never have come into being without the particular impression of the previous day.

2. The dream depicts a situation that originated in a *conflict* between consciousness and the unconscious. In this case, there is no conscious situation that would have provoked, more or less without doubt, a particular dream, but here we are dealing with a certain spontaneity of the unconscious. To a certain conscious situation the unconscious adds another one, which is so different from the conscious situation that a conflict between them arises.

3. The dream represents that tendency of the unconscious that aims at a *change of the conscious attitude*. In this case, the counterposition raised by the unconscious is stronger than the conscious position: the dream represents a gradient from the unconscious to consciousness. These are very significant dreams. Someone with a certain attitude can be completely changed by them.

4. The dream depicts unconscious processes showing *no relation* to the conscious situation. Dreams of this kind are very strange and often very hard to interpret because of their peculiar character. The dreamer is then exceedingly astonished at why he is dreaming this, because not even a conditional connection can be made out. It is a spontaneous product of the unconscious, which carries the whole activity and weight of the meaning. These are dreams of an overwhelming nature. They are the ones called "great dreams" by the primitives. They are like an oracle, "somnia a deo missa."[2] They are experienced as illumination.

Dreams of this last kind also appear before the breakout of mental illness or of severe neuroses, in which suddenly a content breaks through by which the dreamer is deeply impressed, even if he does not understand it. I remember such a case from before the [First] World War:

[2] Latin: "Dreams sent by God" (ed.).

I was visited by an old man, a professor of canon law at a Catholic university. He made a dignified impression, like the old Mommsen.[3] He had business to do with me and, when this had been dealt with, said to me, "I have heard that you are also interested in dreams?" I told him, "This is part of my business." I sensed that his soul was consumed by a dream, which he then actually recounted. He had had this dream many years before, and it preoccupied him again and again.

He is on a mountain-pass road, winding along a precipice. Below there is a canyon. The road is secured against the canyon by a wall. The wall is made of Parian marble[4] with its antique yellowish tinge, as he notices at once. At this moment he sees a strange figure dancing downward on the wall, a naked woman with the legs of a chamois, a "fauna." She then jumps down into the precipice and disappears. Then he awakens.

This dream preoccupied him immensely. He had already told it to many people.

⁂ ⁂ ⁂

Another dream is from a thirty-year-old man, who consulted me because of neurasthenia, which had set in quite suddenly; he had been a prince's tutor and had had a nervous breakdown in this hard duty. I was intrigued by the fact that this neurasthenia—usually already present before in these cases, and then only getting worse over time—should have set in so suddenly. I asked him what happened at the time when he got the vertigo and the pains. At first he said that nothing special had occurred. I asked him about his dreams during that period. Then it surfaced that he had had a strange dream, whereupon the illness broke out.

He is going for a walk on a dune and suddenly discovers black shards on the ground. He lifts them; they are prehistoric pieces. He goes home,

[3] Theodor Mommsen (1817–1903), influential German historian and jurist, winner of the Nobel Prize for Literature in 1902, and author of *Römische Geschichte* [*Roman History*] and *Römisches Staatsrecht* [*Roman Constitutional Law*] (ed. and trans.).

[4] Páros, island in the Aegean Sea, famous in ancient Greece for its semitransparent marble used for sculpture (trans.).

6

fetches a spade, begins to dig up the ground, and discovers a whole prehistoric settlement, weapons and tools, stone axes, and so on. He is immensely fascinated and awakens sweating with excitement.

The dream recurred, and then the patient broke down. He was a young Swiss.

In psychotherapeutic treatment, certain elements can appear already weeks or months or years earlier, not yet connected at all to consciousness; these are direct products of the unconscious.

As you notice, I differentiate dream processes according to how the reactions of the unconscious stand in relation to the conscious situation. One can detect the most various transitions, from a reaction of the unconscious determined by the elements of consciousness, to a spontaneous manifestation of the unconscious. In the latter case, the unconscious proves to be a creative activity, in which it lets contents ascend into consciousness that have not yet been present there.

One usually assumes that the content of the dream stands in relation to consciousness, assuming that, for instance, conscious psychical contents are associatively linked to unconscious ones. This is what gave rise to the theory that the dream has to be explained solely out of consciousness, and that the unconscious as such is a derivative of consciousness. But this is not so; actually, the exact opposite is the case: *the unconscious is older than consciousness.* Primitive man lives to a great extent in unconsciousness, and we too, by the way, spend a third of our lives in the unconscious: we dream or doze. The unconscious is what is originally given, from which consciousness rises anew again and again. Consciousness, being conscious,[5] is work that exhausts us. One is able to concentrate only for a relatively short time, therefore, only to fall back into the unconscious state again; one lapses into dreams or unintentional associating. It is, in Faust's words: "Formation, Transformation, / Eternal minds in eternal recreation."[6] Thus there are dreams in whose contents no relation to con-

---

[5] In the original: *Bewußt-Sein*, a play on "consciousness" (*Bewußtsein*) and "being conscious" (*bewußt sein*) (trans.).

[6] Goethe, *Faust 2*, lines 6287–88 (trans.).

sciousness can be detected, and whose whole activity is located in the unconscious. Everything—the motive of the dream and its activity—springs from the unconscious and cannot be derived from consciousness. When you want to "force" such a dream and make it into a derivative of consciousness, you simply violate the dreaming of the dream, resulting in complete nonsense.

Dream processes follow from several causes and conditions. There are about five different possible sources:

1. They can stem from *somatic sources*: bodily perceptions, states of illness, or uncomfortable body postures. They can be bodily phenomena that, for their part, are caused themselves by quite unconscious psychical processes. The ancient dream interpreters made a great deal of the somatic source of stimuli, and this explanation is still frequently found today. Experimental psychology still takes the view that dreams always have to originate in something somatic. This is the well-known view of the dream: one ate too much before going to bed, lay on one's back or on one's belly, and therefore had that dream.

2. Other *physical stimuli*, not from one's own body but from the environment, can have effects on the dream: sounds, stimuli from light, coldness, or warmth.

I would like to give you an example from the French literature: Someone is dreaming: *He is in the French Revolution. He is persecuted and finally guillotined. He awakes when the blade is sliding down.* This is when a part of the frame of the canopy fell on his neck. So he must have dreamed the whole dream at the moment when the frame went down.

Examples of this kind have often led to the opinion that such a dream, in which one has a clear sense of time, takes place in a very short time-span.

I remember, for instance, such a dream from my own adolescence. As a university student I had to get up at half past five in the morning, because the botany lecture started at seven o'clock. This was

8

very tough for me. I always had to be awakened; the maid had to pound at the door until I finally woke up. So, once I had a very detailed dream.

"I was reading the newspaper. It said that a certain tension between Switzerland and foreign countries had arisen. Then many people came and discussed the political situation; then there came another newspaper, and again it contained new telegrams and new articles. Many people got excited. Again there were discussions and scenes in the streets, and eventually mobilization: soldiers, artillery. Canons were fired—now the war had broken out"—but it was the knocking on the door. I had the clear impression that the dream had lasted for a very long time and come to a climax with the knocking.

As evidence for the view that dreams have no temporal dimension but take place only at the moment of the acoustic stimulus, it might be helpful to quote the extremely complex perceptions of a person at the moment of a fall.

During the few seconds of his fall in the mountains, the well-known Swiss geologist Heim[7] saw his whole life in review.

The same is told in the story of a French admiral. He fell into the water and nearly drowned. In this short moment, the images of his whole life passed before his eyes.

It has to be stressed, however, that such moments are of an immense intensity. You can have an *overall view* in them that is not successive at all. During sleep there is no such intensity. That is the problem. That is why such cases give no explanation for the lack of a temporal dimension in dreams.

To be frank, I always think of another possibility, which is of course equally quixotic: that there is something going on in the realm of the unconscious with the *notion of time*, that time comes apart a little in the unconscious, that is, the unconscious always remains beside the passing of time and perceives things that do not yet exist. In the un-

[7] Albert Heim (1849–1937), Swiss geologist, known for his studies of the Swiss Alps, and professor at the University of Zurich (ed. and trans.).

conscious, everything is already there from the beginning. So, for example, one often dreams of a motif that plays a role only the next day or even later. The unconscious does not care about our time or the causal interrelation of things. This can also be observed in dream series. The series does not form a chronological, consecutive order in the sense of our temporal order. That is why it is so difficult to tell what comes first and what later. If one tried to characterize the nature of dreams, one could say that they do not form a chronological series as in a b c d, with b following from a, and c from b. We rather have to suppose an unrecognizable center from which the dreams emanate. This idea can be illustrated as in the figure.

Because dreams enter into consciousness *one after the other*, we conceive them with the help of the temporal category and relate them to one another in a causal way. It cannot be excluded, however, that the true order of the first dream enters into consciousness only much later. The seemingly chronological series is, as it were, not the true series. If we conceive of it this way, we make a concession to our concept of time. There are dream sequels into which another motif suddenly inserts itself, only to be left later to make room for an earlier motif. The actual arrangement of dreams is a radial one: the dreams radiate from a center, and are only later subjected to the influence of our time. In the final analysis, they are arranged around a *center of meaning*.

In the unconscious we have, after all, to reckon with other categories than in consciousness; this is similar to quantum physics, where facts are altered by the act of observation, as, for example, in the observation of the atomic nucleus. It seems that difficult laws apply in the microphysical world of the atom than in the macrophysical world. In this respect, there is a certain parallelism between the unconscious and the microphysical world. The unconscious could be compared to the atomic nucleus.

In everyday life, too, it can be observed how the unconscious *anticipates* things. Often these are quite harmless things without any further importance, as for instance the following phenomena: you walk on the street and believe you see an acquaintance. It is not he, but later he does come by. Such strange "near-miss perceptions" are very frequent. But they are so insignificant and carry so little weight that one usually overlooks them, thinking, "Such a coincidence!" But there are also quite fabulous examples.

> I have experienced such an example with a friend at the university. He was a natural scientist. His father had promised him a trip to Spain if he did well on an exam. Right before the exam he had a dream that he told me on the spot.
>
> *He is in a Spanish town and follows a street to a square into which several streets lead, and which is defined by a cathedral. He strolls across the square and turns right, as he first wants to have a look at the cathedral from the side. As he is turning into that street, a carriage with two Isabella horses is coming. Then he wakes up.*
>
> The dream made such an impression on him, he told me, because the image was of such great beauty and brilliance.
>
> Three weeks later, after his exam, he traveled to Spain. From there I received the news that the dream had come true. In a Spanish town he came to such a square. At once he remembered the dream, and said to himself: "Now, if the horses in the side street also came true!" He went into the side street—and the horses were there! He was an absolutely reliable man, is now in a position in the civil service, and was otherwise never known for such things but, on the contrary, for his proverbial dryness and sobriety. I have not heard anything similar from him again.

This case is not exceptional. There are numerous experiences of this kind. When you treat many patients with neuroses, you can frequently make such observations; over time you realize their typical character and can alert people beforehand that something will happen. In these cases I usually say, "Attention now, something's going to happen!" The following dream is an example:

A female patient of middle age. For some time, her dreams dealt with a certain problem. Suddenly there comes a dream, with no connection to anything else:

She was alone in a house. Evening fell. She went through the house to close all windows. Then she remembered a back door that she also had to lock. She went to the door and saw that it had no lock. She wondered what to do and started to look for pieces of furniture or boxes to put in front of the door. While she was doing this, it grew ever darker, ever more uncanny. All of a sudden the door flew open, and in shot a black bullet, right into the middle of her body. She woke up with a scream.[8]

It was the house of an aunt living in America. She had been there once, twenty years earlier. After a quarrel, the family was completely torn apart, and with this aunt in particular she was on absolutely bad terms. She had not seen her for twenty years nor kept in touch with her at all. She did not know if that aunt still lived in that house or, for that matter, if she was still alive. I inquired of the patient's sister about the correctness of this information, and she corroborated it. I told the patient to write up this dream and its date. Three weeks later a letter arrived from America saying that this aunt had died. And she had died on the very day on which the patient had had that dream. This is a typical dream.

Such effects—of whatever kind—often have the character of shots. I remind you of the famous "witches' shot."[9] The same ideas can be found among the North American Indians: the medicine man can "shoot" you with something—for example, a so-called icicle— to make you ill. Similar ideas are found in an English book about the mystic Anna Kingsford.[10] She believed that she had the same capa-

---

[8] Jung quoted this dream also in his review of the work of Macrobius; see volume 2 of the English edition (ed.).

[9] *Hexenschuß* = literally, "witch's shot"; a sudden onset of lumbago (trans.).

[10] Edward Maitland, *Anna Kingsford: Her Life, Letters, Diary and Work.*

bilities and would be able to achieve such effects. The yogis in Tibet are said to be able to exert evil influence on others.[11] What they send out is of an oblong shape. It is beyond our knowledge what is at work here, but the *consensus gentium* speaks of it.[12] The Tibetans certainly know nothing about English literature, nor my patient anything about Tibet. But there must exist a *common source* for this assumption, and it must lie in a peculiar psychical factor that we cannot explain for the time being. I am all against superciliously ascending the throne of scepticism and declaring it a swindle. What interests me is that everywhere these things are said to be so. This idea is as common and widespread as, for instance, the one that the dead do not know they are dead, and have to be enlightened about it to find rest. Independent of one another, these ideas are found among spiritualists and primitives, and in Tibetan texts. In the *Bardo Thödol* you find an instruction concerning how to enlighten the dead person that he is really dead.[13] The interesting question here is: How can this be explained? Which primal factors are in existence here to which these statements refer?

3. Now there are not only physical events that cause dreams, but also psychical ones. It happens that certain *psychical occurrences in the environment* are perceived by the unconscious.

In my collection of dreams there is a case in which a child between the ages of three and four dreams that two angels are coming, are picking up something from the ground, and are sending it up to heaven.

Another child dreams that the mother wants to kill herself. Crying, the child runs into the room of the mother, who is already awake; she is just on the point of committing suicide.

---

[11] Tibetan parallel of the icicles, in Arthur Avalon, *Shri-Chakra-Sambhâra Tantra: A Buddhist Tantra*.

[12] In the original: *spricht davon*; probably an error for *spricht dafür* = speaks in favor of it (trans.).

[13] *The Tibetan Book of the Dead: Introduction and Psychological Commentary to the Bardo Thödol* by C. G. Jung. Also in C. G. Jung, *Psychology and Religion: West and East*, CW 11, §§ 831ff (ed.).

In this way, important psychical occurrences in the environment can be perceived. Moods and secrets, too, can actually be "scented" unconsciously. In these instances, one does not know at all how the unconscious comes to perceive this. The strange thing is that these are not always impressive cases at all, as in the dream of the mother's suicide, but sometimes quite insignificant ones. And we can understand even less how one can "scent" completely insignificant things. Let me give you an example of this, too:

> It is the case of a businessman who was, however, interested in telepathic phenomena. He very much wanted to experience something himself. Once he sat in his office; it was three o'clock in the afternoon, and he had dozed off. He saw the postman pull the bell of his house—he lived in the suburbs and his office was in the city—and saw how his maid opened the door and took a package of newspapers and letters from the postman. There was a yellow letter lying on the package. He saw very clearly how big it was, and what it looked like. He came to with the feeling of having slept a bit. Then he suddenly thought: "This was a vision!" He went home at four o'clock and inquired about the letters. The package, as he had seen it, lay on the bureau in the hallway outside, but there was no yellow letter on it. He thought he had drawn a blank. Fourteen days later, the servant came with a yellow letter. It had fallen behind the bureau. He then opened the letter, thinking it contained heaven knows what. But it was a business pamphlet, something completely insignificant!

In my experience I have often come across such cases. The silliest things can enter into dreams and be foreseen, and the identity cannot be disputed at all. This happens far too often to be ignored. There are certainly "illegitimate" sources of dreams. There are things one should not know or is not supposed to know, and yet one does know them, as if one had a nose going through walls. It seeps into one through the atmosphere.

> I had a colleague who was somehow peculiar, but had interesting ideas. He lived in a house in the countryside, with his wife, two children, and a maidservant. He wrote down all dreams dreamed in his

14

house, also those of patients he had accommodated there. It was simply astonishing how the patients' problems appeared in the dreams of the servant, the children, and the wife.

Such phenomena are experienced not only in dreams, but also in society: someone enters the room, for example, and suddenly there is a chill everywhere. Something emanated from this person, one does not know what.

4. Until now, we have mentioned somatic sources, and physical and psychical events in the environment as causes of the dream processes. Now *past events* can also come into dreams. Should you come across this you will have to take it seriously. When a historical name of possible significance appears in dreams, I am in the habit of looking up what the name stands for in reality. I check what person is meant by it, and what his environment was, for in this way the dream can be explained.

Strangely enough, I had such a case only today. A lady, having settled too much in the upper stories, living too much in the head, and on a poor footing with the underworld, recounts the following dream:

There was a very dangerous-looking circle of lions. In the middle there was a pit that was filled with something hot. She knew that she had to go down into the pit and dive into it. So she went in and was somehow burned in the fire. Just one shoulder of her jutted out. I pressed her down and said: "Not out, but through it!"

This dream illustrates very clearly the problem that she had always evaded. Together with the dream, she mentioned a fragment in which St. Eustache was said be her patron saint. The legend of St. Eustache indeed fits nicely: Eustache and his family had converted to Christianity. He died the martyr's death around A.D. 118, together with his family. He was thrown to the *lions*. The lions, however, did not want to devour the holy family. So they heated a brazen bull until it was red hot, and *roasted* them to death in it. This is something the patient did not know.

The occurrence of these past events in dreams is extremely hard to explain. It is just as if this patient had hunted out the calendar of saints in my library. It is also possible, however, that this is a case of cryptomnesia,[14] that the patient had in fact read the legend and does not know it any longer. There are famous instances of such cryptomnesias. We will come back to this later. For the moment we are interested only in occurrences in which it can be proven that one had not read something specific, because one never came near these matters. These cases exist, and it is always worth checking in the books to become oriented about its objective content. A particularly impressive case, which I proved, was that of a mentally ill person who produced a symbolic connection *before* the text of a Greek papyrus had been deciphered.[15] This sounds miraculous indeed, but we have to get used to the idea that such things exist, that elements which in some strange way or other correspond to historical facts can be reproduced from the unconscious. The explanation is to be found in the fact that these are *archetypal* contents. It belongs to the nature of the archetype that it is capable of reproducing again exactly the same images in an identical way. This is often denied, but mostly by people who are not familiar with the matter at all and are in no way able to give an explanation. Ignorance makes it easy to deny these things, as you can see from the following two examples:

> When an agent of Edison first presented the latter's phonograph in the Académie in Paris, a professor of physics is said to have taken him by the throat and called him a "ventriloquist."
>
> Galileo challenged his adversaries to look through the telescope and to convince themselves of the existence of Jupiter's satellites. But they didn't want to look!

At a Later Session [8 November 1938]

Professor Jung: Last time we left off at a discussion of the various *causes of the dream processes*. A further group of causes can be found in dreams that, although having originally had a connection with

---

[14] The unconscious remembering of a fact that, for instance, one had once read, but then forgotten again (cf. below). See also Jung's paper "Cryptomnesia" (CW 1) (ed.).

[15] See Jung, *Symbols of Transformation* (CW 5, § 151), and *The Structure and Dynamics of the Psyche* (CW 8, §§ 317–18) (ed.).

16

consciousness, have long lost it, so that it seems as if this connection never existed.

Let us turn to these *contents* that have *lost the connection to consciousness*. Therefore, the contents of these dreams cannot be reproduced. Persons, faces, situations, buildings, parts of buildings, furniture, or fixtures can appear that were once conscious in childhood, but have fallen into complete oblivion over the decades.

> I remember such a dream that I had years ago. I saw the face of a
> man. After I reflected for a long time, there came a memory from my
> earliest youth, when I was about ten years old. It was of our neighbor,
> a little peasant, long since under the grass. I had completely forgot-
> ten his face. In this dream, it emerged again in its original freshness.
> Consciously, I would not have been able to reproduce it. And when,
> two days later, I recounted that dream, I was again completely unable
> to reproduce that face. It had vanished again. The remembered
> image had been too weak.

In dreams, therefore, *cryptomnesias* may appear, that is, impressions, elements, thoughts, a piece of knowledge that the dreamer once had, which then vanishes completely and cannot be reproduced, until it suddenly reemerges in its original form on some particular occasion.

> I found such a cryptomnesia in Nietzsche.[16] The passage in *Zarathus-*
> *tra* on the descent into the underworld, in which the captain goes
> ashore to shoot rabbits, caught my attention.[17]
>
> I asked Mrs. Förster-Nietzsche, the only person able to supply in-
> formation on the childhood of her brother, if Nietzsche had not
> taken over this motif from the *Blätter aus Prevorst* by Justinus Kerner,
> where it is actually found. She told me that he definitely had read
> this book with her before his eleventh year in the library of their
> grandfather.

Théodore Flournoy, the well-known psychologist and philosopher from Geneva, provided evidence of similar cases in his work, *From*

---

[16] A detailed description of this example is in Jung, *Psychiatric Studies* (CW 1, §§ 180ff), and in *The Symbolic Life* (CW 8, §§ 454ff) (ed.).

[17] Friedrich Nietzsche, *Thus Spake Zarathustra*, part 2, "Of Great Events."

India to the Planet Mars. The title may be fantastic, but it is a scientific book. Flournoy describes Hélène Smith, who had created a sensation in Geneva with her somnambulism. It is about a great animus love story. The glossolalia[18] in this case—Hélène Smith spoke several unknown languages—was also due to cryptomnesia. She frequented a society that owned a small dictionary of Sanskrit. We do not know whether she actually used it, but it can hardly have been otherwise.

> 6. A final group of causes can be found in dreams that anticipate future psychical aspects of the personality, which are not perceived as such in the present. So these are *future events* that are *not yet recognizable* in the present.

These aspects point to future activities or situations of the dreamer that have no basis at all in the dreamer's present psychology. In children's dreams in particular, crucial future events are anticipated in a surprising way. Doubtful are those cases in which, for example, someone dreams beforehand that he will die in a railroad catastrophe, and then is actually killed. It could be a miraculous telepathic anticipation.

Sometimes future formations of the personality, which appear to be quite alien in the present and cannot be explained by it, are anticipated in developmental processes. If those dreams are impressive, they will indelibly remain in memory, sometimes for one's whole life.

A middle-aged woman, between forty-five and fifty years old, told me the following childhood dream that she had had in her fourth year:

She is being pursued by a drunk old woman wearing a red corset.

Nothing like this had actually happened in that lady's environment. She came from a distinguished family, in which this was quite out of the question. Nor did she live in London, where one could have seen something like this in plays, but in the country, in a highly protected

---

[18] The utterance of what appears (to the casual listener) either as an unknown foreign language or as simply nonsense syllables (trans.).

18

environment. At the age of seven she had the second impressive dream:

She has to wash white linen, in a tub filled with blood.

Here you have the red color again. From the age of seven there was a stereotypically recurring anxiety dream:

She is in a kind of hall in a private house. There is a small door on the side that has to be passed quickly. This door has to be avoided. She knows, however, that she actually has to enter there and descend a staircase into a dark basement.

Then, in a dream, it really happens: *She is on the stairs and wants to go down. Anxiety seizes her. Vaguely, she sees a ghost and wakes up with a scream of anxiety.*

She was a person leading a spiritual existence; she also never married. Only at the age of forty-five did she become aware of the fact that she had something called sexuality. It did not exist before; she was completely unconscious of it. She only became aware of it when she had to be treated for having been afflicted with a severe neurosis.

A persecutory dream always means: this wants to come to me. When you dream of a savage bull, or a lion, or a wolf pursuing you, this means: it wants to come to you. You would like to split it off, you experience it as something alien—but it just becomes all the more dangerous. The urge of what had been split off to unite with you becomes all the stronger. The best stance would be: "Please, come and devour me!" Working with such a dream in analysis means to familiarize people with the thought that they should by no means resist when this element faces them. The Other within us becomes a bear, a lion, because we made it into that. Once we accept this, it becomes something else. That's why Faust says: "So this, then, was the kernel of the brute!"[19] It is his devil, Mephistopheles. Until that moment, Faust was split off from it, unconscious of it. When the situation becomes unbearable, he is driven toward suicide. He has to descend in order to find his shadow. He has to turn around once to look at himself from the other side.

[19] Goethe, *Faust 1*, "Faust's Study 1," verse 1323 (trans.).

19

This patient also had the task of realizing that she was split off from her underworld. For one thing, she had to face the factuality of blood, for "Blood is a quite peculiar juice."[20] It is the instinctual substance, what is alive in man. It expresses fire and passion. The anxiety dream clearly pointed to this; it was like an admonition: "Go down the stairs now and take a look at what's there!" Had she listened to this, she would have encountered the other side. She would have had to say to the ghost: "Oh here you are, come and show yourself!" And with this she would have gained a chance to approach her totality.

Now we have difficulty in assuming that a four-year-old child is already familiar with such a problem. This is hardly possible. After all, we cannot credit a child with the psychology of an adult. Strangely enough, however, unconsciously the child already has all the psychology of an adult. As it is, from birth onward—one could even say already from before birth—the individual is what it will be. In the disposition, the basic blueprint is already there very early. Such early dreams come out of the totality of the personality, and that is why they allow us to see a great deal of what we later miss in it. Later, life forces us to make one-sided differentiations. But that is why we get lost to ourselves and have to learn, again, to find ourselves. When you are whole, you have discovered yourself once again, and you know what you have been all the time. I would like to tell you another dream of a child:

> It is the dream of a girl between the ages of three and four, recurring three times during that year and staying burned into her memory ever since:

> *A long tail of a comet swishes over the Earth; the Earth catches fire, and people perish in that fire. The child then hears the terrible cries of the people and awakens from them.*

This is one of those dreams called *cosmic* childhood dreams. Such dreams are like alien phenomena, leaving one perplexed for the moment. From where does the child have the idea of the end of mankind in a firebrand? It is a completely *archaic* image: the terminal fire of the

[20] Goethe, *Faust 1*, "Faust's Study 2," verse 1740 (trans.).

world that destroys the world. What does it mean that the little child produces such an image? Actually this can't be interpreted at all. An ancient dream reader would have said: "This child has a special destiny, one day these cosmic ties will make themselves felt." When adult persons had such dreams in antiquity, in Athens they gave notice of them to the Aeropagus, and in Rome to the Senate. Primitive men, too, sat together to listen to those dreams, because everybody felt that they were of general significance.

We, too, have to try to grasp such a dream, in the first instance, with regard to its *general* significance. It is as if the dreamer should be prepared for a collective part. These persons find their destiny in the collective. Such a collective role bodes ill for a happy family life. One is torn apart by the collective destiny.

The six points mentioned earlier are the most essential causes and conditions of dream processes.

❦ ❦ ❦

The dream is *never* a mere repetition of previous experiences, with only *one* specific exception: shock or shell shock dreams, which sometimes are completely identical repetitions of reality. That, in fact, is a proof of the traumatic effect. The shock can no longer be *psychified*. This can be seen especially clearly in healing processes in which the psyche tries to translate the shock into a psychical anxiety situation, as in the following example:

> Somebody dreams that it is evening. He is sitting in his room and feels that something is going on outside. He does not know what. Yet it seems that wild beasts are nearby. He looks out the window and sees that in fact there are lions outside. He shuts all the doors and windows. But the lions come into the house and burst the doors open with a bang. But that's when the grenades exploded again!

The attempt of the unconscious to integrate this shock psychically has failed, and the original shock breaks through. The reaction of shell-shocked patients is such that a knock, or anything reminiscent of a shot or an explosion, suffices to trigger nervous attacks. The attempt to transform a shock into a psychical situation that may grad-

21

ually be mastered can also succeed toward the end of a treatment, however, as I have observed myself in a series of dreams of an English officer. In this man's dreams, the explosion of the grenade changed into lions and other dangers that he was then able to tackle. The shock was, so to speak, absorbed. In this way, the dreamer was able to master the effect of the shock as a psychical experience. Any time we are confronted with a shock in its "raw," not yet psychical, form, our psychical means are not sufficient to overcome it. We are not able, for example, to cope with a physical injury or a physical infection [directly] by psychical means. We can only psychically influence matters that are themselves of a psychical nature. It also seems that a shell shock is so hard to cure because in most cases it is accompanied by heavy, bodily shocks that probably cause very fine disturbances of a nonpsychical nature in the nervous system.

All other dreams are never exact repetitions of events of the previous day. It is true that there are dreams that repeat nearly identically one or another event of the previous day; if the dream is precisely recorded and compared with reality, however, differences will show.

> I had a patient who always denied that dreams were of psychological significance. She held that they were only a copy of the events of the previous day. One day she triumphantly announced that she had dreamed an exact repetition of an event the day before: that day she had been at the dentist's offices. He had inserted a mirror into her mouth and had made a remark that I do not want to repeat. The dream would have brought an exact repetition of that situation. When I questioned her closely, however, it became clear that she went upstairs to the dentist's, as in reality, but the doorplate was in another place. I went on asking: "Well, what did the door look like?" She answered: "Like yours."
>
> It has to be remarked that I lived at the Burghölzli at that time![21] It continued in that vein until, regarding the dentist, the detail surfaced that in the dream he was dressed in a nightshirt! Well, you can picture yourselves the continuation of the dream!

[21] Between 1900 and 1909, C. G. Jung worked as an assistant, doctor, and head physician under Eugen Bleuler at the Burghölzli, the psychiatric clinic of the University of Zurich (ed.).

She had the dream because the dentist's remark had been highly suggestive, although neither he nor she had noticed it. Her unconscious did notice it, however, and linked it with the erotic transference onto me in the dream. The dream wanted to rub this transference in.

In my experience, this example comes nearest to a verbally repeated event of the previous day. I have never seen a dream that really repeated an event of the day before. There are only *approximate* repetitions. Here is another example:

A patient happened to see a car run over a child. At night he dreamed of it. Here, too, the dream was not completely identical: the child lay on the other side, wore different clothes, and different people were there. The dreamer himself also played a different role.

In this case, too, the dream simply used a situation of the previous day to give expression to an important situation of the dreamer: he runs over his own child. He does not want to see where he himself is infantile. The dream then tells him: "See, that's how the child is run over."

You remember that I remarked at the beginning that we should have a look at dreams from the *causal* point of view. True, we do not know if causality exists, but if we want to work scientifically it is advisable to make the hypothesis that natural processes are not singular events randomly following each other, but that there are causal connections between them. We further proceeded from the hypothesis that the psyche is of a *purposive* nature, shown in its unconscious orientation toward a goal. This hypothesis, too, proved to be important. For working with the dream process there follows the presupposition that we conceive of dreams as purposive and *meaningful causal connections*. This is crucial for an understanding of dreams.

Freud was the first to approach dreams with the conviction that their contents represent meaningful causal connections. He did away with the scientific superstition that the dream is a random series of nonsense and, therefore, could not be explained. But, as always happens when a hypothesis can be applied successfully, a need instantly arises to turn it into a *theory*. This is what Freud was carried away into, insofar as he elevated a point of view, which can in fact be applied to dreams, into a theory.

Freud saw dreams above all as wish fulfillments. The most transparent cases are these: you have been fasting, are hungry, and dream of an opulent, fabulous meal; or you are thirsty and dream of wonderful water or a glass of beer. These dreams stem from somatic sources, and can suitably be explained as wish fulfillments. Now Freud soon came across dreams that could not readily be explained as wish fulfillments. Freud then assumed that these were concealed wish fulfillments, meaning that for one reason or another wish fulfillment must not take place. It follows that there must be a censor. Who is that censor? It can't possibly be consciousness itself! Freud says: it is the existing *rest of consciousness* that is exercising the censorship. So one develops a game with oneself by presenting a wish to oneself, but in disguising it in such a way as not to recognize it. One tells oneself a fabricated story in order to disguise to oneself what one really wants. Thus the unconscious is credited with quite some achievement, for what creates the dream would have to proceed with utmost deceitfulness. First, it knows the wish to which I do not own up, second, it would be able, if it wanted, to represent it directly— but it wants to keep it a secret from me and distorts it. That would actually have to be a little goblin, an evil spirit, saying: "I know perfectly well what you have in mind, but I won't tell you; instead I somehow distort it so that you don't find out." Why, then, does the dream disguise the wish? Freud says: so that sleep is not disturbed. As dreams would wake us up, being so incompatible with our consciousness, the censor benevolently disguises them. This assumption, however, runs counter to the experience that nothing disturbs sleep more than dreams, like, for instance, anxiety dreams, which interrupt sleep and make sleep impossible for hours. You see into what difficulties you run when you explain exclusively on the basis of the *conscious* side. Freud assumes a wish of which I am not conscious. Here the question cannot be evaded: *Who* has this wish? And then our conclusion has to be: the unconscious. But, if these are wishes of the unconscious, where are they?

24

It was these difficulties that induced me to leave aside, for the time being, all theory and approach dreams without preconceptions, in order to see how they really function. To this end I began by using Freud's technique, *free association*, and made the following observation: When you set a person the task of associating freely, you will uncover his *complexes*, but you will not know if these complexes were also contained in the point of departure, the dream. For example, you dream of a lion and associate about it. In this process it turns out that the lion is a greedy animal. It comes to your mind that you yourself are greedy and desirous and—already you are right within the complex. Freud concludes that the complex must therefore be contained in the dream, too. For him, dreams are an improper expression of the complex, of some desirous fantasy, power, or sexuality. In logic, this reductive explanation is called *"reductio in primam figuram."*[22]

But assume you are traveling on a Russian or Indian railway, seeing inscriptions you cannot read. When you start to associate freely, you will eventually arrive at your complexes. So you can arrive at your complexes *in whatever way*, because they are what is attractive and attracts everything. The following happens: in free association, the chain of associations leads to some complex. This happens quite naturally and, so to speak, without inhibition; you just "fall into" the complex. So, if you discover a complex by free association, this does not necessarily mean that this complex is also contained in your dream image. I concluded that this method is not applicable because, although the person's complexes are invariably arrived at, this does not say that exactly these complexes are contained in the dream. It could even be the case that the unconscious had to free itself of precisely these complexes to be able to deal with them! Maybe just this is the achievement of the unconscious! The complexes are, after all, the true troublemakers, and it is quite possible that the unconscious itself stresses the *natural* functioning, and tries to lead us out of that mousetrap of complexes. Because the complex is a mousetrap. For instance, you can talk quite sensibly with a person. The moment you touch upon his complex—it's all over! He is victim to his "silly" ideas

[22] Latin, "reduction to the original image or schema" (ed.).

and turns around in circles. The complexes inhibit and sterilize man and make him a monomaniac. The assumption suggests itself that Nature itself tries to lead one out of this circle.

Thus, to get to the real meaning of the dream, I tried to dissolve the dream, to concentrate on the original image, and to collect associations to it from all sides. I thus proceed *concentrically*, instead of by free association that sort of zigzags away from the dream image and lands in some place or another. So the question to the dreamer is: "What comes to mind about X, what do you think of it? And what else comes to mind about X?" Whereas the question in free association is: "What comes to mind about X? And then? And then?" And so on. In this way, the associations are about *other associations*, instead of about X. In contrast to this method, I stay with the original image of X. I call this method, in opposition to the *"reductio in primam figuram," amplificatio*, that is, amplification. In doing this, I proceed from the very simple principle that I understand nothing of the dream, do not know what it means, and do not conceive an idea of how the dream image is embedded in each person's mind. I amplify an existing image until it becomes visible.

Amplification must be carried through with all the elements, because the dream consists of a number of them. Let us assume the first dream element to be "lion." I start by noting the associations to it, and then I insert the found expression in place of the dream element. When, for instance, the "lion" amounts to "greed for power" in the dreamer or another person, I put "power" instead of "lion" in parentheses. In the same way I deal with the other elements. In the end, we see what the whole sentence means [as shown in the diagram].

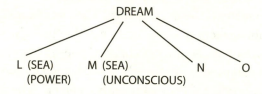

Thus, we grasp the real meaning of the phenomenon. We can see through the dream by way of questioning, by *personal amplification*. We have to have the context of an image to understand what the dream image stands for. In this way, we grasp the full range of meaning of the dream image. Only after many experiences are we perhaps able to advance a theory on the coming into being, and the fundamental meaning, of dreams.

In applying this technique of personal amplification, we are in the first place able to find the subjective meaning of a dream. Now we have experienced that a great number of dream images are not of an individual, but of a *collective* nature.[23] We do not have to look far to find such universal images. They are already found in language, not to mention those that probably rest at the bottom of our souls. So when a woman says about another that she is a snake, everybody knows what that means; or when a man is said to be a sly fox, the picture is equally clear. Thus, we may perhaps interpret the "lion" also according to common usage: the "lion" is the king of the animals, it is "power," and we do not go astray in assuming that this is what is meant when someone dreams of a lion, even if the dream has a personal point. This enables us to translate dreams also without associations, for we possess, in our figures of speech, a whole arsenal of symbols. You can also dream those figures of speech directly, for example, that someone climbs up your back ("You can step on my back!").[24] So if we have such general images in our language, it is quite possible that we are able to understand dreams at least in a *general* way, even without associations.

This is essential in the case of dreams of an impersonal nature, where collective images come to the foreground, and for which we have few associations or none at all. This includes, as mentioned in my introduction, children's dreams, for which it is very hard to get associations. Adults, too, often have dreams to which there are no associations, so that we cannot see what the context of the dream image is. In most cases these are of such a strange nature that their meaning can be brought to light only with the greatest difficulty.

[23] C. G. Jung developed the notion of the collective unconscious in his book *Transformations and Symbols of the Libido*; see also *CW* 5, preface to the 2nd and 4th editions (ed.).

[24] Original: *Sie können mir auf den Buckel steigen!*, roughly: "No way, go to blazes!" An analogous figure of speech in both German and English would be, *einen breiten Buckel haben* = to have a broad back (trans.).

Dreams of that kind always contain a piece of mythology that cannot be interpreted by mere questioning and personal amplification. Neither does it suffice to limit oneself to the general images of language. Positive knowledge is necessary for understanding; we have to know the *symbols* and the mythological motives. We have to know what is in the storeroom of the human mind, we have to know the documents of the people. The more we know, the better we will succeed in understanding certain symbols. In this seminar, we are forced to apply this *ethno-psychological method*, as we are dealing with children's dreams, to which the personal association material is missing in many cases. We will have to see how far we will get with it. We will not always come to a satisfactory solution. The purpose of this seminar is to practice on the basis of the material. The point is not to worm out brilliant interpretations through speculation. We have to content ourselves with recognizing the symbols in their wider psychological context, and thus find our way into the psychology of the dreamer. Let me give you a short example:

> *The dreamer is in a plain house with a peasant woman. He tells this*
> *woman of a long trip to Leipzig. On the horizon there appears a monstrous*
> *crayfish, at the same time a dinosaur, that catches him by taking him into*
> *its claws. Miraculously, the dreamer has a little divining-rod in his hand,*
> *with which he touches the monster's head. It collapses dead.*

What is typical in this situation? There is a peasant woman—therefore something primitive.[25] In any case, it is meaningful that the man in this case has to dream of a peasant woman. It is an older peasant woman—so maybe his mother? Let us put a question mark behind this! Now, it is this woman whom the dreamer tells of his plan to go to Leipzig. There must be a causal connection between these two dream elements. The meeting of the dreamer with the peasant woman brings up the plan. Where is the connection between an alleged mother, a very simple mother, and a great plan? There are examples of this in literature.

---

[25] Jung uses the term *primitive* throughout in the sense of "basic, archaic"; cf. C. G. Jung, *Psychological Types*, CW 6, § 770 (ed).

28

Participant: Peer Gynt.

Professor Jung: Yes, and who else? The writer died only recently.

Participant: Barlach.[26]

Professor Jung: Yes, Barlach, in his book *Der tote Tag* [*The Dead Day*]. There the blind father tells his son of the wonderful images he had seen at night. And the son says: "All these have to enter into reality!" But to this the mother replies: "Such a man has to bury his mother first." And she kills the son's horse with which he had wanted to ride into the world.

Here you have the connection between the mother and the son's plans: *the mother does not want to let the child go*. The boy has great plans that he can only realize, however, if his mother sets him free; and the plans that he makes are all the greater the more he is bound to his mother. The images have to be extremely fascinating indeed to have such an enticing effect as to get free from the mother. For staying with the mother means to remain in an unconscious state, without responsibility; therefore, never get away from the mother! Leaving one's parents is "a temple-desecrating motion backwards" (Nietzsche); it is a sacrilege to sever oneself from one's mother. We can conclude, therefore, that the great plans of the son are connected with being bound to his mother.

To the two symbols "woman" and "plan" comes the third, "monster." The dreamer has hardly told his story when a huge monster with claws appears, a lizard-crayfish, an arthropod, a monster, which takes him into its claws. This is *also the mother*, but the other mother, the one who brings *death*. The mother, as it is, has both aspects: on the one hand she gives life to the child, cares for him, brings him up; but as soon as he wants to leave, she cannot let him go, her heart would break. That is why the mother says in Barlach: "Such a man has to bury his mother first." For this, however, the son has not got the heart; he cannot murder his mother, and therefore she devours him. The mother is also a *sarcophagus* ("carnivore"). She is like Mother Earth, from whom we come and into whom we will go again; she is life, but also death; she is the Ancestress in the West, as she is

---

[26] Ernst Barlach (1870–1938), German sculptor, graphic designer, and writer (trans.).

called in a Polynesian myth.[27] That is why the Etruscans buried the ashes of their dead in the insides of the statue of the goddess Matuta, meaning: in the womb of the goddess.[28] In this way, the dead again entered the womb of the mother. In the present dream the devouring mother appears as a monster. This lets us conclude that there was one thing the dreamer had not reckoned with: he will not get past the mother. For the time being, he does progress with a divining-rod, that is to say with a charm, but with a charm that does not really rescue him.

So we can satisfactorily explain this dream without personal material. It is about an eternal drama, here repeating itself in a particular case: this man had too great plans, he wanted to fly too high; in reality, he could not let go of the backward yearning, and this is how he perished. It really was a drama. At the climax of his life, the unconscious drove him into a neurosis. He got the mountain sickness, vertigo. He wanted to conjure it away, to force the realization of the plan, and that was his ruin.

This example shows you that dreams can be sufficiently explained by an exclusively objective method, without personal associations.

With the help of this example, I would also like to illustrate something else. In the case of complicated dreams, it is advisable to group the dreams. I want to give you a schema that can be generally applied.

1. Locale: Place, time, "dramatis personae."
2. Exposition: Illustration of the problem.
3. Peripateia: Illustration of the transformation—which can also leave room for a catastrophe.
4. Lysis: Result of the dream. Meaningful closure. Compensating illustration of the action of the dream.

Let us go through the elements of the dream we have just discussed:

1. Locale: Place: a plain house. Dramatis personae: the peasant woman, the dreamer.

[27] The name of the Ancestress in the West is Hine-nui-te-po. In Paul Hambruch, ed., *Südseemärchen*.

[28] On the goddess Matuta, see C. G. Jung, *Symbols of Transformation*, CW 5, § 536, and figure 100 (ed.).

2. Exposition: The ambitious plans for the future of the dreamer, his rise.
3. Peripateia: The crawfish that catches him by taking him into its claws.
4. Lysis: The monster that collapses dead.

This is the typical dream structure. Try to look at dreams under this aspect! Most dreams show this *dramatic structure*. The dramatic tendency of the unconscious also shows in the primitives: here, possibly everything undergoes a dramatic illustration. Here lies the basis from which the mystery dramas developed. The whole complicated ritual of later religions goes back to these origins.

2

Seminar on Children's Dreams
(Winter Term 1936/37)[1]

Papers and Commentaries on Dreams of Two Children

A. DREAMS OF A BOY ABOUT NINE YEARS OLD
1. Dream of the Three Young Women
PRESENTED BY DR. MARKUS FIERZ

Text: *I had a dream: From the street one could go down into a strange store. Richard and I went down. Three young women sat at a small table behind the counter. They gave us red sticks that we didn't have to pay for: like sealing-wax that one could smoke. So we put them into our mouths and started to smoke. Then I staggered out of the store; I'd gotten all dizzy and sick.*

Dr. Fierz: I structured the dream as follows:

    1. Beginning and locale: This is the part of the dream until the mentioning of the three young women.
    2. Development: The handing over of the red sticks.
    3. Peripateia: The smoking.
    4. Lysis: Staggering out, dizziness, nausea.

The locale: The *street* is the world of collective consciousness. What happens there is common and normal. Now, from the street it goes

---

[1] First session on 27 October 1936. The dates for the further sessions of this term are not known (ed.).

down into a strange *store*. This store is called strange, and so deserves our attention. A store is a place for exchanging goods: for money, one gets some goods that one doesn't have. Usually, these goods are not manufactured at the store itself, but the store acts as an intermediary between customer and manufacturer. As this store is below street level, underground, it can be conceived as the location where goods, that is, contents of the unconscious, are traded. Therefore, I wouldn't like to simply identify this store with the unconscious. The store table is called a counter; the young women sit at a small table. A counter is reminiscent of a place where people eat and drink, a tavern or a bar. There adults enjoy inebriating beverages—with effects similar to those in our boy. The analogous place for a child would be a candy shop, where one can eat sweets in excess.

Persons: Richard, the friend, can be conceived as a double, as a shadow of the dreamer. I also find it essential, however, that such company in this adventure indicates the common, harmless nature, the collectivity of this experience. It also relieves the dreamer of his responsibility, following the principle: "Not me, he too" (I wasn't the only one, the other was there too!).

Three young women sit in the store. Putting them in analogy with the *three Fates* (Moirae), they are a new manifestation of the "iron woman" of a previous dream.[2] To understand it, the parallel with *Hekate* seems particularly important. This goddess appears in three forms; she is *triformis*.

Professor Jung: That the "iron woman" signifies fate allows us to assume that the three women—exactly because of the trinity—could have a similar meaning. The number three is also "numinous," a synonymous attribute. The motif of the scissors in the previous dream, together with "Fate," points toward the three *Fates*. In this connection the figure of Hekate triformis also seems to be of importance.

Dr. Fierz: She opens and closes the underworld, for which she has the key. So this fits with the store, because in our view it represents an access to the unconscious. Her animal is the *dog*; let me remind

---

[2] See dream series of a boy, dream number 4 (reprinted in the appendix) (ed. and trans.).

33

you of the dream of the dog.[3] The sacrifices offered to her were fishes; in the preceding dream, the fishing giants played the main role.[4]

Now, there are three shrines from antiquity that were dedicated to Hekate, at the same time being temples of Priapus—who is an ithy-phallic river god.

Professor Jung: Even today, in Egypt, Priapus figures are put up as scarecrows in the fields. Such a symbol was embedded in the St. Alban *Schwibbogen*[5] in Basle. In Nuremberg, too, there is such a curb-stone, on the Dürer house near the city gate.

Dr. Fierz: *Diana* = Luna = Hekate: this is the old equation. So let us have a look at Diana (Artemis) too. Although virginal, she was a goddess who helped to give birth. Horace says: "Montium custos nemorumque, virgo! Quae laborantes utero paellas ter vocata adi-misque leto, *diva triformis!*"[6] In Sparta, the most infamous phallic cults of antiquity were dedicated to her. With these materials, one may also interpret the sticks of sealing wax as phallic symbols. Putting those into the mouth and smoking them can then be con-ceived as coitus.

Professor Jung: Even if the sealing wax sticks didn't have a sexual meaning from the start, one could be led to the same assumption from the mythological context.

Dr. Fierz: Something similar is true for the *number three*.[7] Here one would also have to mention the Graeae, the three of whom have only one eye and one tooth (female and male genitalia).[8] Worthy of con-sideration as a further parallel are also the three ladies in the *Magic Flute* (Mozart) who, as we know, hand over the magic flute and the enchantingly beautiful picture to the young man:

---

[3] See dream series of a boy, dream number 5 (reprinted in the appendix) (ed. and trans.).

[4] See dream series of a boy, dream number 6 (reprinted in the appendix) (ed. and trans.).

[5] A suspended arch supported by two walls (trans.).

[6] "Guardian of the mountains and woods, virgin, you who, called upon thrice, answer the maidens in labor, and ward off death, goddess of three forms!" (*Des Quintus Horatius Flaccus' Oden und Epoden*, 3rd book, chapter 22). The mythological references are from Wilhelm H. Roscher, *Ausführliches Lexikon der Griechischen und Römischen Mythologie*.

[7] Cf. C. G. Jung, *Symbols of Transformation*, CW 5, part 1 (e.g., § 182) (ed.).

[8] J. W. Goethe, *Faust 2*, act 3, "Classical Walpurgis Night." Cf. Roscher, *Lexikon der Griechischen und Römischen Mythologie*.

> The Magic Flute will protect you,
> Will support you during greatest bad fortune,
> Through it you will deal all-powerfully,
> To transform the *suffering* of humankind.
> The sad will become joyous,
> *The old bachelor is captured by love;*
> Oh, such a flute is
> Worth more than gold and crowns,
> For through it human happiness
> And contentment will be increased.

The three ladies of the *Magic Flute* are servants of the Queen of the Night; they appear as huntresses and can justly be equated, therefore, with Diana. The *Magic Flute* also shows further curious parallels to our dream series: persecution by the snake; the bird-catcher; the three ladies; and fire and baptism with water—these are the images of the libretto. In the dream series, this corresponds to the persecution by the dog; the fisherman; the three ladies; the fire in the hospital; and water.[9]

As to the *smoking*: "Be a man, smoke cheroots and cigars!" is a well-known advertising line. Smoking is, or has at least been considered for a long time, as specifically male: "The German woman does *not* smoke!"[10] The fact that what is smoked here are sticks of sealing wax, or better, sticks that look like these, shows that this is no normal smoking after all, rather we would interpret it as a specifically male activity, as procreation. This is linked with strong emotions, as strong unconscious instincts are unleashed. The bout of dizziness, the staggering, and the nausea are consequences of being overpowered by the unconscious.

Summary: In this dream the boy is being acquainted with the strange power of sexuality by a significant goddess (Anima).

Professor Jung: The boy is here being initiated, for the first time,

---

[9] Dog, fisherman, water: see volume 2 of the English edition; dream series of a boy: see dream numbers 5 and 6 (reprinted in the appendix); three ladies, fire in the hospital: see this and the following dream of the burning clinic (ed.).

[10] Slogan in Nazi Germany (ed.).

into sexuality, through women of a mythological nature who replace the mother. Procreation, however, is here still in the stage of nibbling sweets. It corresponds to the *nutritive* stage of the libido. Sexuality is still unconscious and makes itself felt only indirectly, in a way that is typical of the unconscious, through nausea, dizziness, and staggering.

The parallel with Hekate is quite valid. But why are there exactly *three* young women?—When a trinity appears, this means that a fateful point has been reached, that something unavoidable will therefore happen.

The three Nornes, the Fates, or the Graeae appear. The *triads of Gods* play a great role everywhere, for example: Brahma, Vishnu, Shiva. Osiris, too, is in the womb together with his two sisters Isis and Nephtys; so are the two brothers Jagannat and Balaram with their sister Subhadra. The triad goes back so far in antiquity that it is difficult to make out something definite about it. One of the most probable structures is "father, mother, son." The *Christian trinity* is in all likelihood originally based on such symbolism. The Holy Spirit was originally female. The symbol of the Spiritus Sanctus is the *dove*, the animal of the goddess of love. Another probable origin is the very basic and quite graphic anatomical triad of the organ of procreation. The transformation into a divine triad is affirmed, for example, by the lingam cult.

That we are indeed dealing with these things is also shown by the fact that the Graeae have *one* tooth and *one* eye. This motif is also found in German fairy tales, as for instance in the tale of the three spinners: one has a big thumb, the second a big lower lip, and the third a big toe.[11] The Graeae are goddesses of the underworld out of the darkest reaches of mythology. It is possible that such archaic images are here involved, for we have to view this one tooth as an exquisitely phallic symbol and the eye as the corresponding female symbol.[12]

In the dream text it says that the boys put those sticks into the mouth. Undoubtedly, this is a sexual allusion, with the mouth rep-

---

[11] Grimm fairy tale (ed.).

[12] Cf. C. G. Jung, CW 5, §§ 306–7: the Indian lingam as a motive for constant cohabitation between the phallus and the female organ (ed.).

resenting the female organ. The simultaneous appearance of the male and the female organ is an archetype, that of *constant cohabitation*. Another aspect of this same type is the *hermaphrodite*, ⚥, or, according to Winthuis, the bisexual being [*Zweigeschlechterwesen*].

Regarding the book by Winthuis, *Das Zweigeschlechterwesen*, I'd like to remark that I don't completely agree with it. Winthuis makes too much out of that motif, but he is right in his main idea that there is a certain *basic idea* present in very many archaic images, namely, the idea of a being that fertilizes itself, that is male-female, that carries within itself the guarantee of its ongoing existence, of its own eternity; and that each human being originally feels identical with this archaic being, or hopes to become *one* again with this being by initiation. Many ornaments and art symbols of primitive nature likely go back to this.

It is a curious fact that these images also appear in a place where I wouldn't have suspected them, that is, in *alchemy*. The basic symbol is the dragon biting into its own tail, the *ouroboros*.

The alchemists knew that the "tail eater" is a sexual symbol: ouroboros fertilizes itself. Similarly, *Ptah*[13] is the creator of his own egg that he also hatches. He is the one who creates himself. The *phoenix*[14] rises again from his own, or from his father's, ashes. All these are images of a being that recreates itself again and again. It is the dragon that impregnates itself, with the phallic tail that he takes into the mouth, "se ipsum impregnat." *Ra*, the sun god, fertilized himself through the mouth with his own semen, and then vomited the world. The inside of his body would thus have been the uterus that he fertilized. He reproduced the world as a creature.

As a consequence, most of the cosmogonic archaic beings are hermaphrodite. This is connected with the fact that man, from the dawn of history, has had a notion of his double gender. As a matter of fact and truth, we are of double gender, because only the greater part of the male genes decides whether the embryo becomes a male.[15] The female genes do not die away in the male, but are there in his struc-

---

[13] Egyptian God from Memphis: besides Amun and Horus the main deity in Egypt (ed.).

[14] Holy Egyptian bird: a symbol of resurrection, transformation, and immortality (ed.).

[15] This concept would have to be put differently today (ed.).

ture, and function according to their femaleness. This accounts for the peculiar fact that in certain men we can perceive certain female traits that correspond to the feminine ideal (and vice versa, male traits in women). There are persons who boast of their bisexuality because it is an archetype: "I carry Eve in me, so I am a god." God has His wife in him. In India, goddesses are only the feminine form of a masculine god: *Shiva* is a *point* or a phallus, and it is enveloped by *Shakti*:

The active existence of these and similar archetypes in the unconscious of the child can, under special circumstances, give rise to "perversities." The children then do strange, disgusting things that, however, carry a symbolic meaning. For they display a too orderly behavior on the one hand, and a too dirty one on the other. A nine-year-old boy, for example, eats a toad, because it disgusts him; a four-year-old child from the city eats excrement on a meadow. A child from the countryside would never do that. Only very well brought up city kids do such things. The motive for such activities is the unconscious search for the original unity. One should rather not call them perversities, but educational mistakes that often balance out later. This archaic image, therefore, leads not only to the most strange, painful, disgusting forms of satisfaction, but also acts as protection, for instance in persons who pick their noses, or who "copulate" with a fountain pen in the mouth. These things are only used as protection: one makes a ring with oneself. In fertilizing oneself one proves that one is absolutely round, the perfect *round archaic being* (the *sphairos* of Empedocles).[16] Nothing can touch it any longer. The archaic being was once cut in two by the Demiurge. The two parts are, however, one and the same being (Plato, *Timaeus*).

[16] Or: "The excellently equipped and completely round archaic being" (Plato, *Symposium*) (ed.).

At the end of the dream there comes that strange drunkenness. It refers to the fact that the unconscious gets out of hand and emerges. It corresponds to the phenomenon of seasickness. Getting sick is the feeling of disgust that is connected with this bout of nausea. In pathological cases, precisely those disgusting things have to be done to reachieve balance. What is disgusting is the unacceptable "other." When children are able to incorporate it, they will become inaccessible by this, meaning that they have attained "divine" independence. The mentally ill, too, act in a way similar to the children. This gives them a feeling of independence and of being cut off emotionally. They make themselves inaccessible by incorporating the disgusting object. The most unappetizing stuff is in the balms and magic potions of the medicine man. When one takes them, one has incorporated the disgusting object and is then immune.

The first infantile autoerotism should not be viewed as immoral, but should be tolerated. It shows itself in attempts at self-fertilization in order to transform oneself; these then give way to attempts to fertilize others. Under the guise of caring concern, children are pushed toward masturbation and the like by educators. For it is completely wrong when children get marked with conscious sexuality by adults touching these things.

The dream just discussed is a case of an anticipation of puberty. The number three belongs to the juvenile age and to the early days of humanity. Being an odd number, it has been male since primeval times (for instance in China or Greece, but also see the Middle Ages in our region), and it points toward the male attribute and its function. The speculations about the symbolism of numbers in the Middle Ages were concerned with the number three, the *Ternarium*, as a divine trinity. Nonetheless, the connections with the primitive sexual image are clearly discernible. Like any archetype, the triad or the Ternarium can be represented either primitively by sexual images, or philosophically by abstract notions. An archetype is neither abstract nor concrete. It can express itself in primitive "instinctual language" (for instance, sexually) or "spiritually." One can replace the other, just as sexual terminology can be replaced by a nutritional one. The Song of Songs, for example, drastically bears witness to this. This *ar-*

39

chetype in itself is plain "three-ness," which can be filled with *any content*.

2. Dream of the Burning Clinic
PRESENTED BY PROFESSOR JUNG

Text: *This night I dreamed that there suddenly was a fire at the clinic Hirslanden,[17] in the basement, coming from the heating. We wanted to go down the stairs near the elevator for goods, but the staircase unexpectedly broke off. We took the elevator to go up, but could no longer fetch the beds from the first floor, where the little kids are. They must have got them out through the windows.*

Professor Jung: The location of the plot is the clinic Hirslanden. The child had been there as a patient. The place where one is cared for often takes on a motherly meaning, in a figurative sense. One gets a personal relationship with it, more or less as to a mother. It then contains some directly personal quality. A house where one is psychically and physically cared for, where one is caressed, becomes an extension of the family web. So the clinic Hirslanden can become a dream figure for the boy and his psychology, which is situated in it.

In the case of neurotic children, the new environment is brought into relation to the mother. The school, the church, and the like, become the mother in a too personal sense. Through this, she grows out of proportion within the child. The relationship to the real mother becomes impossible, because the child makes outrageous demands on her. This is, as such, already a neurotic situation, namely, the well-known neurotic demand placed on a person that he or she should be *everything* to one. Once such a demand is made, relationships no longer work. This happens quite often; as soon as one makes the acquaintance of a person, all hell breaks loose. One has made that person a part of one's psychological sphere, and he becomes a pawn on one's psychological chess board, until he complains or a misunderstanding arises. That is why one often keeps people at arm's length, because otherwise one would simply become a psychological object in their psyches. Something unconscious settles down on one; one is

---

[17] A (still existing) private hospital in Zurich (trans.).

included in a family matter, meaning one has to embody a father, a grandfather, or whoever. This can be very bothersome.

As to our dream: a fire starts in the *basement*, originating from the heating. The basement is the underworld, the abdomen of the boy. In there is the heating, the stomach, the digestive system. This produces heat. From this area of heating the fire starts, threatening to destroy the whole system, to burn down the clinic Hirslanden. The breaking out of a fire—as, for instance, in the phrase *Feuer im Dach*[18]—stands for an emotional outbreak that threatens to mess up the whole psychical system. Here there is an emotion coming up from down below. Here we could possibly also consider a preoccupation with sexual questions. *Es überläuft einen siedend heiß,*[19] when one is seized by a thought as by fire. One blushes when one becomes aware of certain things. Often one is caught in an embarrassing situation, or one notices, for example, that an idea leads further than one had thought.

The boy goes down. The staircase breaks off. He can't go into the basement. The elevator only goes up. He can't save the little children on the first floor. The little children are in danger. At the time of the dream, the boy was still at the clinic. If one is restrained in a place in a too infantile state, the unconscious will have a tendency to destroy that place. On the one hand, the hospital should burn down, as one doesn't want to be so infantile any longer. On the other hand, one has sympathy for the little kid, that is to say with one's own childlike quality, and one hopes that this quality will be saved.

3. A School Dream
PRESENTED BY DR. PITSCH

Text: *I've had a "school dream." One morning I spilled Indian ink in school—no, it was ink—the sleeves of my pullover and the shirt were all full of it. I had to take off the pullover; a band-aid[20] was stuck all over the shirt. I then went home with Ehrhard—we made a detour and came to a*

---

[18] Literally, "fire in the attic," "the roof's afire"; a problem that needs immediate attention (trans.).

[19] Literally: "something scalding hot runs over me" (trans.).

[20] Original: "Leukoplast," a European brand of band-aid (trans.).

41

stable; it was pitch dark. Stairs led up at the side, but it was so dark that I didn't find the first step. Ehrhard knew this stable well.

Now a man entered with a dog, and the wall changed into a glass wall, there were vegetables and flowers behind it, and a lot of people shopping.

Ehrhard went home, and so did I. When I ran past, upward, near the locksmith S., I saw a father with two boys in a garden; they wanted to make a well. They drove a post into the ground. Suddenly I realized that I didn't have a coat; I was cold and ran back to get it.

All of a sudden there appears the image of Gl. [the former place of residence], the upper part near the Strenger Bach.[21] Regula Z. comes. I ask her how late it is. Regula doesn't know, she doesn't have a watch. Then Ellen comes, and she's got a wristwatch; in the beginning it's very small, but then it suddenly gets so big that it has to be carried. Ellen says the time is half three.[22] Then I quickly ran home.

When I sat at the table—suddenly it was again the table in Z. [the present place of residence]—I wanted to start telling something, and said two strange names, like in the "Thousand and One Nights"; I wanted to say I'm one of them, and—finished—I woke up!

Dr. Pitsch: The dream can be divided into the following sequences: 1. the scene in the school; 2. the scene with Ehrhard in the stable; 3. the man with the dog and the transformation; 4. the father with the boys who make a well; 5. the scene in Gl. with the two girls; 6. the scene in Z. at the table at home.

The dream begins with: "I've had a school dream." Actually this dream taken as a whole is a dream of school or apprenticeship. The actual content is: the dreamer spilled *ink*; originally he says *Indian ink*, and then corrects this to ink. The difference between Indian and ordinary ink is that the former, the writing material of the Far East, is blacker than ordinary ink, which is not as black and can, with some effort, be removed again. This is a kind of moderation, a subtle nuance. The sleeves of the pullover and the shirt are full of it. A dark

---

[21] Roughly: "Raging Brook" (trans.).

[22] Original: "halb drei" = German for "half past two"; here translated as "half three," even if this actually means "half past three" in English, because of the symbolism of the number three referred to later (trans.).

42

spot developed that certainly has to be connected with a certain guilt feeling, owing to the fact that sexual processes and sin are only too often mentioned in one breath.

The dreamer has to take off the *pullover*. In Swiss German one says: *Es hett eim d'r Ärmel ine gno*,[23] that is, that one has had bad luck, which is partly one's own fault. A band-aid is stuck all over the shirt. Perhaps this is about sexual events of later puberty. Think of night emissions of sperm.

There is certainly a relation between the ink, the sticky shirt, and sexual processes in the present dream.

The dreamer is burdened with a certain guilt feeling. The above-mentioned topic is taboo. It is not stated explicitly if he goes on walking without the pullover, but this seems to be confirmed when he is suddenly cold and looks for his coat. In any case, taking off the pullover means giving up a part of oneself, specifically, of a particularly warm cover. Such a cover can perhaps be seen as a mother symbol. The boy entering the years of puberty will have more and more to live his own, increasingly manly, life.

Now he wants to go home with Ehrhard. Ehrhard, presumably a friend of his, is all one with the dreamer, his alter ego. But they do not go home directly, as one should, but make a detour. Boys often make detours, much to the chagrin of their upset parents. Their fantasy and investigative spirit let them often forget that there is a table set and waiting for them at home. I know the dreamer and I know that coming home on time is not really his forte. He is not one of the so-called well-behaved boys, he's a real boy.

As it is, the school of life is always a detour. How much is there that we strive for, and that we reach only by detours!

They come to a *stable*, in which it is pitch dark. This dark stable is the same as the dark forest, the caves, the "john," very attractive places for boys, and places that stimulate fantasy to the highest degree. There are stairs leading up at the side, presumably inside the stable. The dreamer does not find the first step, however, but Ehrhard

---

[23] Roughly: "My sleeve has been caught in it," evoking the image of a maelstrom, a monster, or machine, which threatens to devour the whole person (trans.).

easily does. This stands for the instinctual aspect that finds the right way even in the darkness of the stable, that is, the unconscious. In reality, too, they are completely different types. In my view, Ehrhard seems to be the more balanced one.

The motif of the *first step* still has to be considered. It presumably represents the first step from childhood to the growing personality. This step has to be made in darkness. It is best made unguided, naturally. In the healthy child one should let this develop more or less without interference. If one introduces something artificial, the first step will not be found.

Then comes *the man with the dog*. "Through the mind of the dog the world exists," it says in the Vendidad, the oldest part of the *Zendavesta*.[24] Since primeval times, man has been unthinkable without the dog, and this all over the world. Brehm[25] says: "Man and dog complement each other a hundred and thousand times over, man and dog are the most faithful of comrades. No single other animal in the whole world is more worthy of man's friendship and love than the dog. He is part of man himself, and indispensable for his thriving and well-being." "The dog," says Friedrich Cuvier, "is the most remarkable, perfect, and useful conquest that man has ever made."

Descending from the jackals or wolves, the dog has truly become "brother animal" to us; he just lacks language to become a fully adequate replacement for many a human comrade. I have spent much time with animals. Often the clever, questioning eyes of a dog have made me retract a stupidity or an idea, or to get off my self-made little throne. My dog is always part of my own personality. He knows his master's language, he observes the master's finest movements, he knows when his master is sad or glad or when he is in a bad mood. He rejoices and mourns with his master. I have observed that old dogs assume the posture and the facial features of their masters, and vice versa. As a lover of dogs, I may say that the dog is a part of man, a kind of shadow. Many famous persons are entities only with their dogs, for instance, Frederick the Great with his Bichée, Prince Bülow with his poodle, Bismarck with his mastiff. There are less famous ex-

[24] The holy scripts of the Parses; Old Iranian (ed.).
[25] Alfred E. Brehm, *Brehm's Tierleben* (ed).

44

amples: the retired neighbor with his pinscher, or the drunkard whose equally shabby mutt accompanies his master from one pub to another.

So, in the present dream man and dog belong to each other. In mythology, the dog has outstanding responsibilities. I refer to the work of Professor Jung, *Transformations and Symbols of the Libido*.[26] The dog is the gravedigger who disposes of the bodies, as happened in ancient times in Persia. There it was also customary to lead a dog to the bed of a dying person who then had to grant the dog a bite, presumably to appease him so that he spared his body. Cerberus, too, is calmed by the honey cake of Heracles. In the Mithras reliefs, a dog jumps up on the killed bull. Cerberus is the guardian between life and death. Anubis with the jackal head helps Isis to gather the dismembered and scattered body of Osiris, so that he can be incorporated by Osiris and reborn. The dog helps with dying, and consequently also helps with rebirth. In the present case, a man comes with a dog, and their appearance causes a transformation.

Unity, agreement, and evenness can work wonders. Man and dog stand for a harmonious unit between man and animal, that is, between consciousness and less consciousness, to put it cautiously. Strangely enough, by the way, one often speaks about human characteristics while meaning animal ones. In this man-dog pair the unconscious (the consciously domesticated dog) is, so to speak, bound, and so the miracle can happen.

What was dark and opaque is suddenly seen through; a *glass wall* appears, and with it brightness, light. The boy looks through the window like a yearning child pressing his nose to a shop window. Already once, the dreamer was in a *store* in a dream, in a shop below street level, where he then got sick because of smoking the wax sticks. Here he is separated from the store by the glass; he looks in, but quite reasonably he himself is not yet in there, presumably he needn't buy anything yet. He sees many people buying vegetables and flowers. The transformation took place before his eyes. It was the dog, the helper in dying and being reborn, who caused this—from the unconscious

---

[26] Now renamed *Symbols of Transformation*. See especially *CW* 5, §§ 354ff (ed.).

to consciousness. Out of the eternal cycle of nature, products of the earth emerged before the dreamer—once he saw in a dream a transparent mouse, a microcosm within the macrocosm; now he sees creation, a synthesis. Our body, decomposing after death, serves again to create beauty, usefulness, and the products of the earth and so, again, life. Darkness, the first step, has been overcome.

It further says: "Ehrhard goes home, and so do I." That means they separate. The dreamer is in a hurry, because he runs past the house of the *locksmith* S. Locksmith and smithy represent archetypal symbols that, for adults, could stand for a regression but, for the boy, are rather the "black man" or the bogeyman.

Then higher regions are reached. But very soon there is again something to be seen. Three persons—a *father and two boys*, so to speak a Laocoön group without snakes—want to bore a well. We have already talked about the number three. Notice the ambiguity of the expression in the dream text: "They wanted to make a well."[27]

"They drove a post into the ground." Here we are dealing with a phallic symbol, as in the sealing-wax sticks. The "male" is incorporated into Mother Earth. This creates a source, a well. Similar ideas are frequent in mythology. Wotan, Baldur, and Charles the Great let sources flow in this way. A blow with a rod—or a horse's hoof—makes the ground yield water. A saint puts a branch into the ground, Pegasus made the Heliconian hippukrene[28] with a hoofbeat. Rhea created a source in Arcadia with a staff, as did Moses for the thirsty Israelites. In Old High German, source is called *Unsparing*, which means something jumping or bubbling out. The staff makes something bubble out. So the dreamer is seeing the act of procreation in symbolic language.

But now he has eaten from the tree of knowledge and knows that he is "naked." He gets a fright, and he is cold. He shudders at reality. He has to go get his *coat*. Again he puts a warming maternal cover around himself, and promptly goes through an *abaissement du niveau mental*:[29] all of a sudden he is at *the place where he lived in earlier child-*

---

[27] In Swiss German this can also mean: "to urinate" (trans.).

[28] Literally: "horse well" (trans.).

[29] A term coined by Pierre Janet (see *Les obsessions et la psychasthénie I*), designating a psy-

hood, in Gl. at the "Raging Brook," where untamed water, still uninhibited, not yet having become a more or less large river, bubbles over
stones. There Regula and Ellen, who would actually have to be at the
present home, come toward him.

Thoma would not have been able to depict "yearning," in his beautiful picture of the same name, by the body of a woman. Woman is
more related to Mother Earth than man is. She floats much less in
higher spheres. So these girls are the animas that have to bring back
the boy as a consequence of his outing. He also asks them for the time.

I know Regula and Ellen, two sisters, rather well. Regula is corpu-
lent, phlegmatic, slow, sleepy, also always comes late; Ellen is the opposite: sharp, always ready, quick, and perhaps less likeable than Regula. Two completely different temperaments.

Asked for the time by the dreamer, Regula has no *watch*. Ellen does
have one, however, a special one that gets bigger and bigger, so that
one "has to carry" it, meaning, presumably, that one has to hold it in
one's hands. If in a dream something gets bigger to the point of un-
naturalness, one should pay particular attention to this symbol. The
clock is man's memento of the flow of all time. It transmits the structure of the day and, with that, our tasks.

One says: "You will know it when the bell tolls for you." The so
impressively swollen watch in the dream says: it is half three. To his
fright, one of the animas makes him realize that the time is half three.
Both girls show him, however, that he should actually be in Z.

The number *half three* is not easy to interpret, if we do not simply
see it in a concrete way, as the actual hour it stands for. The symbolism of numbers is something special. I refer to the article by Professor Jung, *Beitrag zur Zahlensymbolik*.[30] One often does not succeed in

---

chic state that can be caused by psychic shocks (strong affects), fatigue, intoxication, or pathological brain processes. A narrowing of consciousness and a lowering of the levels of attention
and orientation are observed. In this, mostly only temporary, disintegration of consciousness,
it is infiltrated by unconscious contents that cannot be sufficiently inhibited, so that consciousness no longer, or not yet, controls unconscious "ideas." At the same time, so much energy is withdrawn from certain conscious contents that they are blacked out or become unconscious (ed.).

[30] This seems to refer to "On the Significance of Number Dreams," in C. G. Jung, CW 4,
§§ 129ff (ed.).

getting to the bottom of the numbers appearing in a dream. Frequently, one sees the most obvious thing only at the very end, and needs the most detailed knowledge about the dreamer's environment for a more exact interpretation.

An example: In a dream in which traveling and a train station played a role, the numbers 2.10 and 2.30 appeared. An attempt to break down these numbers in all possible ways failed. Only later was it found out that 2.10 was the phone number of the local train station, and 2.30 the phone number of the inn The Three Kings. The connection could be established. The dreamer did not consciously know these numbers.

It fits in with the previous dream, however, that the dreamer had failed—as often before—to appear for lunch. So he runs *home* quickly, that is to say, guiltily. Everything experienced so far pathetically collapses, for he has to take his place at home at the table, which is the *father's* table, meaningful insofar as one cannot move away from it[31] as long as one is young, not yet grown up, and dependent.

So now he would like to give an account of his experiences at that table, to his probably not all too pleased parents, presumably to distract them—something that's just like him. He can't quite utter something intelligible, however, but just a kind of a slip of the tongue. Only two names out of A *Thousand and One Nights* come to his mind, names so strange as to fascinate him. But he finds it preferable to keep them to himself; otherwise, he could make a fool of himself.

Perhaps he identifies with Aladdin, perhaps as a consolation that a little good-for-nothing can still become a king. In most of the stories in A *Thousand and One Nights* there is eventually a happy end. Partly the dreamer is ashamed, partly he consoles himself.

I want to try to bring some structured coherence into this dream by means of a curve. [See the illustration.]

---

[31] Original: "als man seine Füße unter ihn halten muß", literally: "as one has to keep one's feet under it" (trans.).

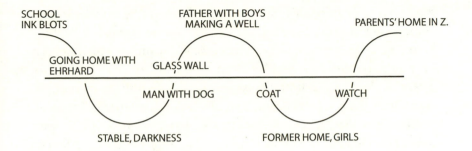

After the school and the ink blot, there is a lowering of the *niveau mental*. The man and the dog have to help to raise it again so that everything becomes "transparent" again. Then again there is a lowering, through the father with the two boys. The dreamer needs a coat und seeks shelter in a previous place of his childhood. There the animas tell him how late it is, and where he really belongs.

Professor Jung: *Indian ink blots* happen inadvertently. This is about something dark, opaque, for which one might also get punished. It is about the secret of puberty that was already then announcing itself. That is normal, but naturally it is an anticipation.

Band-aid: This dream can no longer be explained quite as well with the help of archaic material. This material is replaced by personal relations with the environment. These are normal phenomena that are to be expected, and that occur regularly. The boy is of an age in which the archaic world of mythical conditions gradually subsides, and the figures begin to get contaminated with those figures whom we meet in everyday life. Those three young women are now replaced by less archaic figures, namely, by these two girls. The "three-ness" of the young woman now blended into something male, the father plus two boys. The two-ness as a "female," even number is more appropriate for the girls. And after the dream of the clinic Hirslanden, in which the little children, childhood, could no longer be saved, there now follows a dream about the personal relationship to the environment. And that is why we would actually need the personal associations of the dreamer. One could really ask him about them, and for a thorough analysis of the dream we would actually be forced to let the boy himself speak. In the case of the dream of an adult, we actually

49

ought not to proceed this way, that is, to bring it in parallel with archaic material only; with the one exception when we are dealing with a so-called great, that is mythological, dream, to which people very often have no associations at all. The band-aid, for instance, is a very modern image. It probably means *that which sticks*, it could be that which sticks something on something. The dreamer still has too few personal experiences, he is still too little; but he knows about using a band-aid on a wound. The sticking, something that adheres to one, and that one cannot easily get off again, would also refer to the blots. These refer, as mentioned by the speaker, to the sexual sphere.

As to young Ehrhard, with whom he experiences the adventures: here again one would have to know which kind of boy this is. The role in the dream seems to point to a perhaps somehow more balanced, more grown-up personality. In any case, we can presume that the dreamer projects a *leader*, an ideal, onto his friend. In every school class there is usually one leader. He is the one for fights, and so on. It's always someone who shows off; he's always one for the show. These leader figures regularly appear in dreams and fantasies, similarly in the case of girls. You wouldn't put anything past those figures, anything you yourself would never presume, or have presumed, to do; this is the soil from which rumor epidemics arise, in which everything imaginable is attributed to these heroes. I assume that the boy Ehrhard plays such a role. He is the figure within the dreamer who is already a bit more grown-up and mature, who is already "in the know." This Ehrhard is about one to two years older than the dreamer (information from the mother).

We always have to be aware of the fact that children[32] also contain a future personality within themselves, the being that they *will be* in the following years. The experiences of the coming years are, so to speak, there already, but only unconsciously, as they have not yet been made. The children already live in a tomorrow, only they are not aware of it. This figure exists *in potentia*, naturally in a projected form.

[32] The original transcript of the seminar reads "adults," obviously a mistake for "children" (ed.).

50

This is quite distinctly so in pathological cases, linked to the fact that these persons remain below their level, below the line. They are living a couple of years behind themselves: a twenty-year-old behaves, in consciousness, like a fifteen-year-old. In this case, the second personality is nevertheless already present, has even been lived, but unconsciously. Such people then cling to a more mature personality in their environment, attach themselves, so as not to be forced to live their own maturity. This is a neurotic condition. In the case of children, the imitation of a role model is normal and quite all right. Children cannot yet be truly original; they are not yet mature personalities, they still have to search tentatively for the ways of life. They do it by taking hold of the hand of the leading person. So it is all right for children until the age of twenty to have their ideal figures. Later, it becomes more difficult. In certain cases pathological inadequacies may develop. But given that most people are immature and lack independence, it is good for them to have leaders.

As to the interpretation of the *stable*: A relation to Christ, born in the stable, seems to be a bit far-fetched. This motif, the birth amidst ox and donkey, means: being born in the world of animals, low as animals. Nativity has taken place in a cave, and this cave in Bethlehem is still being visited. Even today people partly live in caves together with their animals. This is an extraordinarily archaic place, reaching far back into human history. The cave is the most original of all places to live. The savior is born amidst the animals. This symbolism recurs at the end of the life of Christ: the thieves, here again the lowest of all men, among whom he dies. It is also the lowest of all births: an illegitimate birth. This, however, is the most meaningful: the low, sad human life, beginning in lowness and ending in lowness, as the highest possible symbol. It means: remember that you came from the stable, from the world of animals. There is a (possibly Gnostic) bust called *sotér kosmú*, the *savior of the world*; it exists in a double form, sotér, the savior, and the phallus.

Our development begins in the unconscious. If we do not realize this, we forget that we are descended from the animal world. Then we will imagine that we live in a two-dimensional world without depth, the newspaper world for instance, or the paper world. The

51

body is an animal, our body soul an animal soul. One must not forget this. This is the great difficulty: that we have to reach, from the completely unconscious animal soul, the stairs on which we can ascend to the heights. The Pueblo Indians[33] have a mythical image for this: in the development of mankind, one cave on top of the other has to be reached. We are descendants of cave dwellers. There is within us an immortal memory of the time in the cave world. The dark blots of Indian ink are those dark memories of the cave world, in which one was unconscious. The inevitable inner growth of the animal soul creates the big, dark spots in human life: "To earth, this weary earth, ye bring us, To guilt ye let us heedless go."[34]

It is quite necessary to ascend from this unconsciousness. The boy/ leader Ehrhard shows the way up; then things become transparent. The glass wall appears.

The *glass wall* is a typical symbol, one often comes across it. One needs this image when one is emotionally separated from the object. You can look through it, but nothing else passes through it. One is cut off from contact. This means that the dreamer is now separated from that underworld store, where he got the sealing-wax sticks from the Fates. It is the idea that now there exists a wall between him and the mythological archaic world. He sees flowers and vegetables. Flowers usually stand for emotions, while vegetables play with erotic innuendo.

In the stable an adult has to enter as the leader: the man and the dog. He is the master of the dog, which obeys him. The unconscious is correctly integrated. The man, accompanied by the dog, is a unity, just like horse and rider. The man is consciousness, the dog obeys him, or the horse carries him. This is the ideal solution in the relationship toward the animal unconscious.

In Persia, the dog is the companion of the dead. To give it bread is a ceremony: one gives it bread instead of the body, meaning, don't tear me apart, don't tear my soul apart, but guide it to the destination through the desert of *Hades*. Anubis, the Egyptian jackal god, helped

[33] In 1924/25 Jung made a research trip to this Native American tribe in the American Southwest. Cf. C. G. Jung, Memories, Dreams, Reflections, ed. A. Jaffé (ed.).

[34] J. W. Goethe, *Wilhelm Meister's Apprenticeship*, book 2, chapter 13 (ed.).

Isis to gather the pieces of Osiris. This jackal is a son of Osiris and Nephtys. Isis and Nephtys are characterologically separated. Isis is the beneficial goddess of vegetation. Nephtys is identical to Hathor; her later form is Venus/Aphrodite. She has one doubtful aspect; therefore, she is not the wife of Osiris, but the wife of Osiris's evil brother, Set or Typhon, who also represents the shadow of Osiris. Due to a little misunderstanding, Nephtys became pregnant from Osiris. The jackal god was the son: brother dog is thus a descendant from the gods. Symbolically speaking, he came from the liaison of consciousness with the unconscious—even with the unfavorable side of the unconscious. Nobody, therefore, has a good relation to his unconscious if he cannot impregnate the dark. This is actually possible only through a misunderstanding. Something to meditate on!

The *locksmith*: he really stands for the smith. He is a magic figure; the black man dealing with the fire, the evil one who knows how to do it; the sorcerer, the medicine man, the enigmatic man working in the underworld, practising secret arts. He often stands for the devil.

The *father with the two boys*: here it is quite useful to think of Laocoön and his two sons. Laocoön dared to come too close to the sea— the unconscious—and was gripped by it, in the form of a snake. In sexual, primitive terms: the male is captivated by the female (coitus); abstractly speaking: the unconscious overpowers consciousness.

The essential point is the *number three*, here as in the further course of the dream, the time "half three." This could mean: it is not yet quite three o'clock, there is still a half hour left until then. All over the world the number three has a male meaning; this is in connection with male anatomy. The number three is not yet complete; there is no ripe fruit yet, no sexual maturity.

The post bringing forth a well: this is the motif of *boring a well*, conceived of as an act of impregnation. This is a parallel to the numerous traditions of fertilizing a field, of the phallic plow, the fertility gods who should fertilize the fields.[35] Priapus too was simply a post of fig wood. He is the ithyphallic Hermes, simply represented by a

---

[35] See C. G. Jung, *Symbols of Transformation*, CW 5, §§ 214ff, with notes 21 and 22 (ed).

wooden post. He also exists already in megalithic form, because the menhir too has a phallic meaning.

It makes us shiver to sense connections that point far into the future. These insights are "shivery," they cause a feeling of coldness. A cold wind is said to always blow before the appearance of ghosts: "Sharp spirit-fangs press from the north."[36] A cold, ghostly draft is always a concomitant of a being that essentially has no body. When we are mentally taken by somebody into a region where we no longer feel at home, we speak of "ice-cold heights of the intellect," or about him, "a cold person." Whenever something is taken too far, we at once have the idea of coldness. When we can no longer humanly empathize with something, we get cold and sad at heart. So when we have an idea we cannot yet grasp, we sense a shivery draft; we are instinctively afraid of new ideas that somehow go too far, because instantly there is the fear of being driven insane by them. And with the fear there also comes the coldness. A cold shiver runs down our spine, and our hands and feet are cold.

This feeling makes our dreamer put his *coat* on. What makes him shiver is the realization or the view of a future in which he himself is not yet present. The coat is a protective cover giving him warmth. Wrapping himself into the coat corresponds to going back to a warm, safe place where one still is surrounded by the feminine and the motherly. The motherly is represented by the two sisters, Regula and Ellen. Here again we have the Osiris situation!

In the dream, the two girls are different, that is, opposites (information from the parents), with compensatory differences, as is often the case in sisters. We have already talked about the contrast between Isis and Nephtys, the two sisters of Osiris. The two girls have a watch, and this watch is getting big and heavy. Heavy is *gravis*,[37] meaning that something is serious, a difficult matter. "This is a weighty issue":[38] such figures of speech convey important relation-

---

[36] Goethe, *Faust 1*, "Before the City Gate," verse 1130 (trans.).

[37] Latin: "heavy, significant, pregnant, serious" (trans.).

[38] Original: "Nun kommt es dick!" Literally: "now something heavy is coming," that is, something that is much more important and threatening than anything that happened before (trans.).

ships. The watch swells. Reducing this to its sexual meaning, one may interpret this as early sensations of intumescence. However, this is also an image describing how an unimportant matter becomes "weighty" (similarly Faust: "It's growing in my hand! It shines and glows!").[39] In the Christophorus legend the little child gradually becomes too heavy for the giant, because he is carrying the king of the universe. Similarly, in a legend of the *Mahabharata*[40] the (unrecognized) Hanuman makes himself so heavy that not even a god can lift him.

What makes the watch so heavy? It is the problem of time; it is a problem that becomes important in the course of time. The two girls are the two anima figures (Osiris myth). It is the anima, split into a positive, active side, and a more negative, passive side. The watch is in possession of the anima. This watch is something that looks very far ahead: it is the watch we carry within ourselves, the Self. It is the iron wheel, the machine of fate. Just a tiny wristwatch! But it tells the time that the whole fate carries in its womb. It is a mandala and represents the dynamism of fate, it is heaven's watch, the zodiac, the twelve signs standing for the houses in the sky. Therein fate is inscribed. Men have been convinced of this since time immemorial.

These two anima figures carry fate. They are impersonations of the unconscious that holds our own peculiar fate. Woman is man's fate. Otherwise he is suspended in the air and has no roots. Woman is always the bearer of fate; the woman to whom a man is bound is his fate, she makes him take root in the earth.

It is from this world, then, that a foreboding of his fate approaches the boy. The girl will be fate for him; something unforeseeable, improbable, ungraspable. He wants to tell about that, he happens onto *A Thousand and One Nights*, "Contes des Fées," age-old stories. This points back to the impression he received from the watch and from the girl as anima. These are mythological themes, a faint impression of something long gone.[41] In Goethe's poem *Erlking*, the king tries to

[39] Goethe, *Faust 2*, "A Gloomy Gallery," verse 6261 (trans.).

[40] The great religious, philosophical, and mythological epic of India, a keystone text of Hinduism (trans.).

[41] Cf. the first dream of the three young women (ed.).

lure the soul of a boy away from his real father, to become a playmate for his own daughters! In the end, he takes it with force.

Those mythological themes also pull the dreamer back from reality. He therefore has to tell "fairy tales" to get away from this. That's quite similar to the glass wall! He even no longer knows the names of those people. Presumably, the two names only refer to the two girls. The real name, however, is the real innermost nature as it is given in the unconscious in its totality already at birth. But it is also the watch, because the human character is determined by the point of time of birth. This is a wonderful thing, just as a wine specialist knows when and where a wine is "born."

This tiny watch is his fate, developing out of the course of time; it seems to be light at first, only to become unbearably heavy in the end. We ourselves are our fate, as Seni says to Wallenstein: "In your bosom are the stars of your fate." The Self revealing itself in time is represented by the instrument that determines time and fate, the watch.[42] As a mandala, the circle also expresses the deity unfolding in space. Hence the circle metaphor of St. Augustine for the deity: "God is a circle whose center is everywhere, and whose periphery nowhere." The archetype of the circle, the mandala, means concentration on a midpoint, meaning either the Self, the deity, or both simultaneously, for example, "Atman."[43]

B. DREAMS OF AN EIGHT- TO NINE-YEAR-OLD GIRL
4. Dream of the Lion, the Bread, and the Magic Mirror
Presented by Margret Sachs

Text: *I went into the forest, then a lion came. I wasn't afraid of the lion, I wanted to stroke him and ride on him. But I fell off. Then he ate me up, and I was dead. Now my mommy came and took me on her arm. She went home with me and laid me on the bed. Then I discovered a magic mirror in the pocket of my apron, which I turned toward myself, and then I woke up again; I had enchanted myself.*

I had also put a spell on the whole house, and there was a store down-

---

[42] Cf. Jung, "Individual Dream Symbolism in Relation to Alchemy," CW 12, §§ 44ff (ed.).

[43] Sanskrit, originally meaning "breath," later: "vitality, personality, the Self." Atman is finally one with Brahman, the godly Self of the world (ed.).

stairs, and everything was completely different now. The people walked all slanting, me too, and I kept thinking I'd fall over, but I didn't.

I went and got a loaf of bread in the store, and the woman said: "You have to hold on to the bread." But I let the bread fall, and then many worms came out of it. Now she had to give me another loaf of bread, and then I walked up the narrow staircase and fell over myself. There was a hole in the stairs; I stuck the bread into the hole (I don't know why), threw the money away, and brought Mommy a couple of stones. She was angry with me and beat me with a switch. Then I woke up.

Additions, context, and fantasies associated with the dream:

In the mirror, I saw, for instance, a burning house and people running out of the house; but they were very small people: little men, women, and kids.

On the other side of the mirror there stands[44] a tree, and a kind of string and a head are tied to it; a head like a skull, with four things like horns or legs protruding from it, no eyes, just holes, no nose, everything decayed, just teeth, and that scared me. Then the magic mirror turned its light toward me, and I had to throw up. Then I climbed up the tree and I clung to the skull; then my legs and arms fell down, and also the body, but then the legs and arms came up again, only the body stayed down. (In the Wesem-lin church[45] such arms and legs hang in the chapel, what is that?)

Mrs. Sachs: The dream is of a girl eight-and-a-half years old. In the year she had the dream she had to repeat the second grade. The teacher complains about insufficient results, absent-mindedness, and superficiality. Her intelligence is—according to tests—quite adequate for her age. The girl comes from a lower-middle-class background, and has three brothers. The mother claims that she has not been able to get the girl to help in the household at all for a half year or so.

The dream is long and seems very complicated. In a work of Professor Jung we read: When there are a couple of scenes in one dream, each

---

[44] The change of tenses is significant for the content; the girl thus expresses distance from or closeness to the dream (ed.).

[45] A small church in Lucerne.

of the scenes usually shows a specific variant of dealing with a complex. This seems to be the case here too. As to the individual motives:

The *forest*: it is the unknown, the dark, the place of danger where the mysterious happens, as in fairy tales. Forest also means a place of transition and passage into another life: in the *Divine Comedy*, for instance, the *Selva del Tevere* stands before the gate to the *Inferno*, and the *Divina Foresta* at the end of the *Purgatorio* and as a passage to the *Paradiso*. For the girl this might possibly mean the transition into the age of puberty, or rather prepuberty.

The *lion*: it is the mightiest and most powerful animal; as a symbol for power, it is often used as a heraldic animal (the British lion,[46] the Lion of Judah[47]). The constellation of Leo[48] is the constellation of the greatest summer heat and symbol of the most powerful desire. According to Steinthal,[49] Simson kills the sun god, the zodiacal image of the August heat, the lion that devastates the herd. According to a Rosicrucian fable (in the article by Silberer),[50] the *Myste*[51] has to tame the lion. In the Mithras cult, the lion symbolizes the fire; the fourth grade in initiation is the lion grade. The officiants, says a Church Father, roared like lions. As the libido appears here theriomorphically,[52] it represents animal sexuality. The zodiac of Leo is thought of as *domicilium solis*,[53] and "the libido is justly called sun," as we read in *Symbols and Transformations of the Libido*.

Alone in the dark forest, the child encounters a tremendous force,

---

[46] Throughout most of its history, England has employed the crowned lion as the official heraldic symbol of the royal families. The lion appears on almost every coat of arms in the British royal line going back at least seven hundred years (trans.).

[47] From ancient times to the present, the Lion of Judah (going back to Revelation 5:5) has been one of the most popular symbols of the Jewish people. Both the tribes of Dan and Judah are compared to lions, although it is Judah whose name ultimately became inextricably linked with this symbol (David, a descendant of Judah, is identified with the lion, as is the Davidic monarchy and the Messiah who will spring from this royal house) (trans.).

[48] Cf. C. G. Jung, *Transformations and Symbols of the Libido*, on lion and sun, for example, CW 5, § 425 (ed.).

[49] Hajim Steinthal, "Die Sage von Simson" (ed.).

[50] Herbert Silberer, "Phantasie und Mythus" (ed.).

[51] Somebody initiated into the secrets of the ancient mysteries (trans.).

[52] In the form of an animal (in ecclesiastical history, a term used for deities in animal form) (trans.).

[53] Latin, "domicile, house of the sun" (trans.).

the lion, the fire, the libido. After the fact she says she was not scared by it, she wanted to stroke it and ride on it, but then fell off after all and it devoured her. She wanted to tame, to direct, the powerful force. But she is defeated and devoured.

Her *mother* comes, takes her into her arms, and at home gently tucks her into bed. This could be a sign of regression; she is absolutely helpless. The mother's arms—after all, the greatest comfort and security for the child—do not have the desired effect. The child has to bring herself to life with the help of a magic mirror. Doesn't this show that the child's soul has already made the step away from the security and comfort in the mother and her home, and that she is no longer in that *participation mystique*,[54] as one might assume? It is this point that lets us also assume that the child does not dream the conscious or unconscious problems of the parent.[55] So the question remains: Are we dealing with the child's own problem, or with a general human difficulty?

The *magic mirror*: In a mirror you do not see your true image, but a deceptive one. With the mirror, the girl charms herself into an unreal world, a fantasy world. She herself and the whole environment are transformed by this charm. One goes slanting, not straight, moves on an inclined plane, is uncertain, has lost orientation. This seems to illustrate her situation at the moment, in which she is superficial, unreliable, and inefficient, at school as well as at home. As the people around her are charmed too, this could be about a conflict concerning all human beings.

Bread means, in the language of symbols, the nurturing substance, the body that is sacrificed. Think of the shewbreads[56] in the Temple of David, of the Holy Communion in the Christian Church. We read in *Symbols and Transformations of the Libido* that, once the libido has regressed to a presexual stage, one might expect the nutritional func-

[54] Jung took over the term *participation*, or *participation mystique*, from Lévy-Bruhl. It means that a subject is not able to distinguish itself clearly from an object, but is connected to it by a partially unconscious ("mystical") identification (cf. C. G. Jung, *Psychological Types*, CW 6, §§ 741, 781) (ed.).

[55] Cf. C. G. Jung, *The Development of Personality*, CW 17, §§ 80ff, for the strong unconscious influence of the parents' situation on the still-small child (ed.).

[56] Consecrated unleavened bread ritually placed by the Jewish priests of ancient Israel on a table in the sanctuary of the Tabernacle on the Sabbath (trans.).

tion and its symbols—such as the bread—to replace the sexual function. According to Freud, this would be a regression to the *oral* phase. Sexuality would thus be moved to the stage of presexuality, where nutrition plays a great role.

She fetches the bread down in the store and lets it fall despite the woman's warnings; then many *worms* crawl out of it. Worms live on something rotten; they are lower life forms, they do not possess a cerebrospinal nerve system.

With the second loaf of bread, she tries to climb the stairs, to bring it to her mother. Climbing up the stairs may mean the attempt to come to a higher form of consciousness.

The *hole*: the dreamer throws the bread and the money into a hole in the stairs. With that, she throws the bread—a symbol for life and the "sacred body"—away, into a hole, into darkness. According to Pausanias, there was a sacred room in Athens, in the *Temenos of Gaia*.[57] In the floor there was a foot-wide crack, and it was said that after the flood in the times of Deucalion[58] the water flowed into it. Each year, wheat flour kneaded with honey was thrown into this crack, presumably as a sacrifice to ward off a new flood. At the *Arrhethophoria festivals*,[59] too, little loaves of bread in the form of phalluses and snakes were thrown into a crevice. In Rome, money was sacrificed into a former crevice, the *Lacus Curtius*. This crevice could be closed only through the sacrificial death of Curtius;[60] as a typical hero, he traveled into the underworld and thus saved the city of Rome from destruction. Also at the *Asklepieias*[61] an offering was thrown into a hole in which a snake was said to dwell.

---

[57] Gaia=Greek earth goddess (ed.).

[58] In Greek mythology, son of Prometheus and father of Helen. When Zeus, angered by humanity's irreverence, flooded the Earth, Deucalion, warned by Prometheus, survived by taking refuge with his wife, Pyrrha, in an ark. Later, an oracle told them to cast behind them the bones of their mother (i.e., the stones of the Earth). From these stones sprang men and women who repopulated the world (trans.).

[59] A mystical celebration of the great feeding mother, concerning the blessing of the harvest and of children (ed.).

[60] Marcus Curtius, 362 B.C. (ed.).

[61] Greek temples of worship and healing, named after the legendary Asklepios (Aesculapius), son of the god Apollo and a mortal woman, Greek god of medical art. His symbol—the snake wound around a staff—is used to this day by the medical profession (trans.).

To throw the bread into a hole could thus represent a soothing charm, a sacrifice. Heracles, too, placated Cerberus with a honey cake.

The disappointments the girl brings to her mother—and probably also the teacher—could not have been depicted more clearly than by her bringing stones instead of bread.

Now follow fantasies about the reverse side of the mirror, in part additions to the dream. As it is not possible to question a child of this age for many exact details, it is not so easy to distinguish the one from the other. The girl should neither be upset nor feel important and interesting.

The *burning house* and the little people saving themselves again indicate a state of panic, of dissolution and need.

The *reverse side of the mirror* bears the symbol of death. Sarah Bernhard had a skeleton standing in her boudoir, in whose chest a mirror was set. This may be due to the whims of a theatrical actress; in a child, however, this juxtaposition of death and life has an extremely disconcerting effect and can be understood only if the layer of her consciousness and her personal unconscious is penetrated until the collective unconscious is reached.[62] A similar juxtaposition of death and life can be found in the following part, in which a skull hangs from a green, living tree.

The girl gets sick from the light of the magic mirror and has to vomit. Realizing that a spell was put on her makes her lose her sense of security; she clings to the skull despite her fear of it, and she wishes death would come as a salvation and a way out. Since arms and legs come up again, and only the body stays down, it could be thought that she wants to be relieved from the body in particular. What is meant here is the abdomen, where the unconscious and the uncontrollable emotions reside. Here, too, it becomes clear once again that the symbol of death—like any other symbol—allows for two interpretations. In the analytical sense, the skull means dying; in the hermeneutic one, salvation.

[62] Jung developed the notion of the collective unconscious in his work *Symbols and Transformations of the Libido*; cf. *CW* 5, introduction to the 2nd and 4th editions. Definitions, etc., also in *CW* 9, vol. 1, §§ 88–90, and *CW* 13, § 11; or in the glossary of *Memories, Dreams, Reflections*: definition of *Unconscious* (ed.).

We feel it may be justified to assume that this problem is not a conscious problem of the infantile soul, but rather a general one that finds expression in this dream: the fight of the spirit against physical matter, the longing of the creature to be saved from the bonds of the flesh, the fight of the higher against the lower powers. In the arts, the most striking expression of this motif is Rodin's female Centaur. She stretches her upper body forward, she reaches forward with her arms with an immense longing, and one senses her ardent wish to be completely freed of her animal body. The artist's intuition and the dream of the $8\frac{1}{2}$-year-old child speak the same language, as both of them take their images from the collective unconscious.

An *association experiment*[63] made with the dreamer—with an average mean reaction time of 2.6 seconds—registers rather strong reactions that could point to the beginning of a neurosis. To the stimulus word *to sin* she reacts with *death*, and explains that she thought of mortal sin in this context. Four weeks after the dream, the child has no recollections of it whatsoever; it was completely eradicated from her consciousness, which in itself could point to the fact that it emanated from the deepest unconscious.

Professor Jung: The dream begins as follows: "I went into the forest," meaning, I went into my *darkness*, where anything that cannot be explained comes from. It could also have been still water—running water has a different meaning—or a labyrinth, a cave or the basement, the dark space of the house, the dark attic, the toilet. For this is the place of fantasy; there creative work is done. There are children who cannot defecate without fantasizing. In the case of adults suffering from constipation, it is sometimes necessary to stir up again the fantasies that alone make them able to defecate.

In Kundalini yoga,[64] *Muladhara* (Sanskrit, literally: root support) is the lowest chakra. The *Perineal* chakra is situated in the *hypogas-*

---

[63] A psychological test method for determining complexes; cf. C. G. Jung, *Experimental Researches*, CW 2; or the glossary of *Memories, Dreams, Reflections*: definition of *association experiment* (ed.).

[64] Cf. *The Serpent Power, Being the Shat-Chakra-Nirupana and Paduka-Panchaka*, trans. and ed. Arthur Avalon. This book give the first detailed information on Kundalini yoga. See C. G. Jung, *The Psychology of Kundalini Yoga* (trans.).

trium (lower abdomen), the so-called cloacal zone. There the kundalini lives in her lotus. She is the creative fantasy par excellence.

So going into the forest, to the dark place, means concentration on those regions of the body that belong precisely there, in this darkness. A gloomy, evil darkness, filled with fantasies. And now there comes a lion, the devouring monster. This is the instinctual life. The child is $8\frac{1}{2}$ years old, already in prepuberty. If a cathexis with libido happens here, a phenomenon of prepuberty may appear in the form of an immature sexual instinct, or this may happen in the form of a flooding with fantasies that only later in puberty will become actual sexual fantasies. The lion is a kind of fantasy that grasps and completely devours the child. All the images in this dream go back to primal situations. In former times, the woods were really full of danger zones. Robbers were in it. In dreams, the forest is the uncanny place, which is filled with the projections of fantasy: Pan, witches, wild hunters, *Rübezahl*,[65] or any other delusion spreading panic-stricken fright.

The dreamer is $8\frac{1}{2}$ years old. Between eight and nine years of age, the transition toward ego consciousness takes place. The child frees herself from the closest ties to the familial milieu. She already has experienced a part of reality. The libido that had been tied to the parents is decathected, often introverted, goes into the unconscious, and arranges something there.

As to the *lion*: it is the king, the mighty instinctual energy, the fiery principle, the heat of the sun, desire.[66] In royal coats of arms it stands for great courage, strength, and power. The *deus leontocephalus*[67] is the *god of time*. He appears at the climax of the zodiacal circle, at the end of July and the beginning of August. He stands for fire.[68] The lion is also the symbol of Mark the Evangelist and of St. Hieronymus. Most often it is depicted as the animal supporting the pillars of portals, the pulpit, or the font. This lion, as a Christian symbol, is the

---

[65] Mountain gnome in German fairy tales, lord of the underworld (trans.).

[66] Concerning the lion as a symbol of wild desire, cf. Marie-Louise von Franz, *Alchemy*, pp. 104–5. (ed.).

[67] Latin, the "god with a lion's head" (ed.).

[68] Cf. Franz Cumont, *Textes et monuments figurés relatifs aux mystères de Mithra*, vol. 1, pp. 76–77.

sign for domesticated paganism and is meant to stand for the power of heathen Rome. That is why the lion is the bearer of the pillar of the church. The constellation of the Lion is the *domicilium solis*. In the Mithras cult[69] there were underground grottos, for example, at the Saalburg near Frankfurt-on-Main. In these mythraeums, most often there stood a strange statue near the altar, a man's figure with a lion's head, with a snake coiled around it that laid its head on that of the lion. This is the *deus leontocephalus*, that is, *Aion*, meaning infinitely long time, the god of time who combines the opposites. This is an old Persian image.[70]

In the north, the bear appears instead of the lion. Originally these probably were animal masks. In antiquity, in the Mithras cult one even went so far as to imitate the voices of animals. It was believed that the god would hear better something roared in the voice of an animal; or one whistled and clacked one's tongue to attract him. His animal attribute was thought to listen more to that. This goes back to the fact that the gods were originally conceived as animals. Another conception, that of god as a bird, is still found in Christendom: the dove of the Holy Spirit, corresponding to the feminine aspect of the Holy Spirit in early Christendom. In the so-called *Acts* of St. Thomas, the Holy Spirit is simply the feminine side of the deity, the Woman God.

The lion is always goal oriented, a directed fire. When a lion attacks, it always runs toward its target in a direct line. It is, by the way, always interesting to know about the natural character of animals. Whenever animals appear in dreams, read Brehm![71] Our forebears knew even more about the life of animals.

The Rosicrucian conception of overcoming the lion is that of overcoming the instincts. In alchemical tracts there are descriptions of how the lion's paws are chopped off.[72] In the Mithras cult, as well as in *The Epic of Gilgamesh*, it is the bull that is overcome.

[69] Mithras, a sun god worshipped since ca. 1000 B.C. in Iran. His cult was spread in the first century A.D. by Roman soldiers, and was serious competition for early Christianity (ed.).

[70] Cf. the picture of Aion in C. G. Jung, *Symbols of Transformation*, CW 5, fig. 84 (ed.).

[71] Brehm, *Tierleben*; at the time, the most popular authoritative source on zoology (trans.).

[72] See the illustrations in C. G. Jung, CW 12, fig. 4; or in H. Baumann, "Tier und Pflanze als Symbole."

In our dream the lion embodies an instinctual force that the girl does not have under control. We know only that she is overwhelmed by something instinctual, stronger than she is, by an instinctual force that is represented by a feared beast of prey. She is the victim of an animal instinct. The child then acquires a psychology that would no longer be appropriate for her age, but for an animal. She regresses to an animal-like being.

The lion means all-consuming fire; that is why it is the symbol for the heat in August that burns all the vegetation. So the child comes into a state of inexorable desire. The desire will also play a role later on. Examples of such states are when the Malaysians go berserk or run amok. The Maenads,[73] those raving women, tear up young goats and eat them raw in Dionysian orgies. The Indian goddess *Kali* has got teeth like a wild animal; she has drunk wine and blood and is dripping with blood and grease. She is a raving lioness. In most pictorial images, she is riding on a lion, or goes over the bodies of her male victims. When she went into a fury, her husband Shiva was called. He lay down among the bodies of her victims; she then came to him and recognized him, thus coming to her senses.

The consequence of the regression in this child was that she could not concentrate. Regressing adults, too, can't concentrate, but revert to a primitive state. Similarly, primitives, or civilized persons who stay primitive, cannot concentrate.

We also understand why the child wants to ride on the lion: this is the *backside*.[74] But then she fell off, that is, she falls down into those regions where one is completely being driven, loses consciousness, and is devoured by fantasies. In primitives, this phenomenon leads to various measures of precaution out of fear of such emotional states. The same may happen in the case of adults when they have all too

---

[73] In Greek mythology, Maenads were female worshippers of Dionysus, the Greek god of mystery, wine, and intoxication. The word literally translates as "raving ones." They were known as wild, insane women who could not be reasoned with. The mysteries of Dionysus inspired the women to ecstatic frenzy; they indulged in copious amounts of violence, bloodletting, sex, intoxication, and self-mutilation. They were usually pictured as crowned with vine leaves, clothed in fawn skins, and carrying the thyrsus, dancing with the wild abandon of complete union with primeval nature (trans.).

[74] Which is also an instinctual area (ed.).

lively fantasies or embarrassing ideas. They fear those fantasies because they easily fall victim to them. That is why one avoids speaking about certain things or thinking of something particular—because then one can be robbed of one's soul or devoured by the
fantasies. When this happens to the child, it becomes clear that she
can no longer follow in school or is superficial; her interest is occu-
pied by an overpowering fantasy production. Her interest vanishes
and her achievements become unsatisfactory.

So here comes a well-known solution: when you are in this passive and vulnerable situation, you have to call in sick. You are paralyzed; someone has to take care of you. If an adult happens to be devoured, he eventually has to call the doctor, so that the latter may
carry him on his back, or accompany him and play the roles of mother
and father, until he has found himself again. In our dream, this happens when the mother brings the girl home and lays her down in her
bed. The bed is the place of shelter and care. Now this is precisely
the opposite of the situation at the beginning of the dream: originally
the child wants to stroke the lion, just in the way little kids do.

She has started to play with her own force. It is possible to lose
consciousness to a certain extent during play, and then to become
identical to this play. So this is also dangerous. We can, for instance,
see that when primitives perform dances: eventually they become
identical to their roles. In play, the child becomes unconscious with
the lion, and identical to it. This means that she wants to assimilate
the instinctual forces. The center of the ego has to be equipped
with the instinctual forces. This, however, entails the dangers of the
rapacious animal, namely, being devoured by it. The same happens
in the dream: what the mother takes home is precisely the child devoured by the lion. The child has turned into a little lion, she has become an invisible lion child. We find such ideas also in primitives: in
some South American tribes, the humans turn into parrots. Although they don't look like parrots, they feel like parrots.

A new situation arises out of this transmutation: in some way or
another the child is bewitched. But now she discovers that she has
got a *little magic mirror*, and it is in the pocket of her apron. This is a
very suspicious place; we must not overlook this. This is the place

where children keep all sorts of things. Boys have pockets in their trousers, girls in their aprons. In our case this means: this is the pocket that the girl has within her own body, again that region of the Muladhara, that region from where certain fantasies come forward. She can change reality with that strange little magic mirror, and she can change it at will. She can use witchcraft, she can cast a spell. This is a favorite idea of children, to change the world according to their own wishes.

In this case, there is no magic wand, but rather a magic mirror. She holds it in front of herself; seeing herself in it, she herself is also immediately bewitched and so, at the same time, is the whole world. It is a knowing mirror, as in the fairy tale of Snow White.

The ancient Greeks, too, found the mirror, when it appeared in a dream, uncanny. It meant the death of a person; this is so because the image one sees in the mirror is one's own double. It is the Ka^{75} of the Egyptians. It is an image of the soul. That is why the primitives do not want to be photographed, out of fear that their *double*, their soul image, be taken away from them, thus causing a loss of soul.

Seeing one's own double means death. Narcissus sees his image and drowns in it. The student from Prague,[76] who sells his own reflection to the devil, no longer has any image, that is, the soul has left the body, and this means disaster. We find the same problem in Chamisso's *Peter Schlemihl*,[77] about a man who does not cast a shadow, and in Oscar Wilde's *The Picture of Dorian Gray*.

The mirror has a murderous effect. A magic used by the Aztecs consisted in filling a bowl with water, and then putting a knife into it. Then they had the person whom they wanted to harm look into his mirror image in this water. He would be killed by this, because there is a knife in his mirror image.

So we see that the mirror in this dream is a highly charged sym-

---

[75] Equivalent to "shadow" soul; body soul (ed.).

[76] The protagonist of *Der Student von Prag* (1926), a motion picture starring Conrad Veidt; directed by Henrik Galeen. The film is strongly inspired by Chamisso, and shows how the shadow of the conscious man is split off from him, so that the shadow begins to act independently. C. G. Jung called this student "a kind of second Faust" (cf. C. G. Jung, *Dream Analysis*, pp. 49, 49n, 259) (ed.).

[77] Adalbert von Chamisso, *Peter Schlemihls wundersame Geschichte*.

bol, seized on by the child in a natural way in order to perform the magic of awakening on herself. Originally, the child was kind of ill, overwhelmed by the fantasy, and had lost her identity with herself. The mirror brings one's *own* image in which one can recognize oneself. Here, therefore, a mirror is needed to reestablish her own identity.

I had a patient who once asked me for a mirror. She had forgotten hers. At first I thought that she wanted to check her hairdo. But she said: "I am all confused, and cannot start speaking unless I know again how I look."

The mirror in the dream stems from Muladhara, the dark instinctual region. Now if I am able to contemplate that region I regain a feeling of myself, I again know who I am. As it is, the loss of one's own self consists in turning a bodily factual reality into a fantasy system. Then one reverts to bodily reality to prove to oneself who one is. People often fool themselves, thinking they are this or that, in any case someone different from who they really are, because they forget about their bodies. Like isolated ghosts, they live in their fantasy and forgot that they are real, bodily persons.

But then the uncomfortable consequences show. Although the dreamer had considered her bodily sphere—to reestablish her self— her self-knowledge shows her how slantingly she is standing. But all the other people are also slanting, meaning she is *seeing* everything lopsided. The house is different, everything has become different. There is a store down in the house, there's coming and going, all the people rush in. It is like on the street, one has a chat; a store has been opened, and *anything* can go into it. This is an inundation from below. Down there everything is now coming in, the whole environment; and it's just so for all the other people. In spreading herself over the whole world, the whole word is also entering into her. Introjection *and* projection: I am all of them, I have them all in me. Driven by instinct, one has become universal. If someone is blinded by instinct, he naively supposes that all the others will view things the same way he does. This also plays a role in the psychology of love. The man supposes that the woman would like the same things that he does. The disaster of the whole world stems from the fact that people think

68

that others have the same psychology they do. When we are within an emotion, in an instinctual state, we are no longer able to account for other people's condition. We are radiating our state onto the others. This affects them. Nothing is as contagious as emotion. Every emotion is an *outward motion*. One leaves one's house and blends with the others outside. This brings about a psychology that is characterized by instinct, and causes a projection that makes it appear as if the whole world were in this state, too. This is a very uncomfortable situation, it is the thickening of the plot. A peripateia[78] has to take place.

The peripateia comes in the second part of the dream: she buys a *loaf of bread* in the store, and worms come out of it; she falls on the staircase with the second loaf of bread, and it falls into a hole; she throws the money away. She brings stones instead of bread to her mother, and is beaten for it. Presumably, this dream has to give insight into the child's actual situation. There is something malicious in it. She deceives her mother and gets a beating for it: so this is the solution.

Where does she get the bread from? Down in the store, in the underworld, in the instinctual world, in which she is identical with the whole world. What is this bread? A loaf of bread is a body.[79] Body consciousness is being gotten from the instinctual sphere. This is understandable: she gets a consciousness of the body from there. Nature has intended that many animals initially limit themselves to eating, and only then develop sexual organs, for example, the butterflies: before, as caterpillars, they only eat; as butterflies they are nearly completely a function of sexuality. So here we are dealing with a displacement from the instinctual sphere to the presexual stage of the feeding instinct. This is a step backward, a typical occurrence in the transformation of natural instinctual energy into the so-called mental processes. The natural instinct would flow only into sexuality. But if it is to become spiritual, it has to transform itself backward, so to speak, to the presexual level, that is, to the original nutritional form.

[78] See the seminar "On the Method of Dream Interpretation," in this volume.
[79] In German *Laib* (loaf) and *Leib* (body) are homonyms (trans.).

69

That is why we find the symbolism of nutrition in the mysteries of transformation [*Wandlungsmysterien*].

The dreamer is still a child. Given this dream, it can be supposed that her fantasy world is sending out feelers to sexuality, and because the sexuality is still completely unconscious, a corresponding unconsciousness in the head ensues. The stage of nutrition, however, was experienced consciously. So when the instinctual state is deflected into nutrition, it is actually reshaped into something conscious, something known. She does not yet know the sexual instinct and its gratification, but she does know hunger and eating. A creative person, who is plagued by completely new and, therefore, difficult states, goes back to a time when he was helpless, back to his mother who nurses him. Or, he will talk about things he has already experienced before. He will remember that things are like they used to be, when he painted this or that, or wrote poems. That is not true, however, as now something new is happening, but he is looking for an analogy, and through this analogy he can save himself into consciousness. The caterpillar, which has become a larva in the pupa, is in a state of which it is not aware. It does not know that it will become a butterfly, it can only make use of the memories of the caterpillar stage. We always have to dock onto something conscious to reach a new state of consciousness. You need stairs. There is no *direct* way from the unconscious to consciousness. So this is why the whole problem, in the dream, is transformed into eating. The new instinctual state wants to say: remember eating! It is a different, but known form of instinctual gratification. Hunger, too, and what should feed us, can be brought into connection with the instinctual core.

But now something unpleasant happens. The hunger instinct should keep her on that level. The bread, however, falls down and dissolves into worms. This bread, which she buys in the store, is hollow within and rotten. It cannot be used as it already contains, and covers up, live contents—fantasies—that belong to the sympathetic nervous system. The presexual state is already hollowed out within. There is an early awakening of a *new* stage. Now she has to go and get a new load of bread. She has to go up the stairs with it, that is, with her original body consciousness. This time she falls down. Also, there is a hole in the stairs. This simply means: just as her ascent had previously been made impossible by the fact that the bread contained worms, she is now again hindered by something, and is pulled downward to that unconscious instinctual state. The money, too, is thrown away. Money is libido, the possibility to buy bread, also sweets; it is disposable libido. This possibility too is abandoned. This attempt to gain consciousness only leads to her giving away the possibility of getting another loaf of bread, and also giving away the fetched one, thus relinquishing a bit of consciousness, coming home in a new state that just earns her a beating.

At a Later Meeting of the Seminar

Professor Jung: Let us go through the dream once again, step by step, as there is much more contained in it. Let's remember: Why does the girl have a little magic mirror? By using a magic mirror one is removed into a mythological situation. One comes into an *inflation*.[80] The situation in an inflation is like riding in a balloon. It ascends, and we feel the ground fall from beneath our feet. We feel unreal, dizzy, too light, gaseous. We lose touch with reality, are governed by the unconscious, no longer feel our weight, and lose orientation in space. In our dream it says: the people walk around slanting in the room. Whenever the unconscious reaches a certain level of intensity, there are feelings of dizziness or outright symptoms of seasickness, a feeling of the ground surging. The moving surface of the water represents the unconscious. In such situations, people feel as if they stood on ship planks on rough seas, or were lifted into the air by the wind. Even vertigo, nausea, palpitations, and vomiting occur.

It is, in those cases, as if we had lost the physical, lost the body. Then we have to cling to the physical and descend into the body.

Now in this dream the girl has to go down into the store and get the loaf of bread there. The physical is expressed by this nutritional motif. She has to descend to that nutritional level because of the inflation. She goes down, so to speak, into her own belly.

As to the woman in the store: She tells the dreamer to take care and not let the bread fall. She is the older, more experienced one, the

---

[80] On the notion of being psychically "inflated," see C. G. Jung, CW 7, §§ 226ff (ed.).

mother; not the real mother, but rather the *archetype of the mother* (she is the counterpart to the "wise old man," the imago of the father). She is a witch, the "old woman," the earth, Erda,[81] *earth goddess*. She is the old one who gives good advice. In the course of development, the archetype first stays with the real mother, or with the father. The unconscious, however, seeks to sever the parental figure from the archetype to make one understand that the idea—the archetype—and the natural mother are *not identical*. This leads to the reconstruction of an archetypal world, in which I am not the son of my natural mother, but of the archetype "mother." This is a kind of magic world, of a world of gods or a spiritual world, and as this does exist, and as this has always been so, men have always talked about two kinds of reality: one that we see with our eyes and touch with our hands, and one that cannot be experienced with our senses. Here two different principles show. The Aristotelian will say: the archetypes are ideas derived from the experience with *real* fathers and mothers. The Platonist will say: fathers and mothers have only come into existence out of the archetypes, as those are the *primal images*, the pre-images of the manifestations, stored in a heavenly place, and it is from them that all forms come from. That is the origin of the term *archetypos*. Where truth lies, we cannot decide. We are forever encapsulated in our psychological experience. We are in the world of images. Whatever we say about the psychical, we always are talking out of an archetype. When Freud says that sexuality is the base and the beginning of all that happens, this too is an archetypal idea. It is the primitive idea par excellence, as in Adler's aspiration to power. We find these two ideas in the ancient philosophers, in the Gnostic-alchemical concepts: nature delights in nature, nature rules nature. This is also expressed in the symbol of the snake biting its own tale, the Ouroboros. So when we imagine we have said an absolute truth, we are mistaken; we have just expressed an archetype. What it boils down to in the end is that the archetype lives. It lives in Freud, Adler, and also in myself.[82]

[81] Ancient German earth goddess (trans.).

[82] In the original edition of these seminars there was a reference here to the principle of "tetrasomia," the state of having four bodies [not to be confused with the genetical disorder of

When one is seized by such an archetypal idea, one thinks one has surpassed everyone; it is an inflation. If an idea comes to your mind and you think you "possess" it, it is actually the other way around: you are possessed by it. You can do nothing but speak it out loud. These ideas have to be spoken and elaborated. It is through the living of these ideas that we live. These are the *flores cerebrariae*,[83] this is the "brain stone" of the ancient alchemists; the plant that grows through us and out of us, and that is about to open—which is perfectly all right. It's just not right for our devil of knowledge, he wants to have the *definitive* truth. Absolute truth, however, cannot be established anywhere, and least of all in psychology.

In the dream, the wise old woman now tells the girl to cling to the loaf of bread and not to let it fall. But now it happens that she does let it fall. Then nothing but worms come out of it. Worms feed on decomposing things. Worms are an indefinite number of small, living entities. That is to say: the body has disintegrated into many living entities. The body is composed of hereditary entities, of Mendelian[84] entities. Let's take the face of a child: the nose is from the father, the beautiful eyes from the mother, the ears that stick out from the grandfather. When you have pictures from your ancestors, you can single out parts of your face and detect them in the various pictures of the ancestors. The same is true for the whole body, and likewise with the soul. Certain of its peculiarities stem from certain forebears, and these bits are, in general, naturally merged in the single person, though not without some sutures. It can be seen where the parts have grown together. If the sutures do not close, a schizoid personality will develop, a compartmental psychology, which, if everything goes wrong, may turn into schizophrenia. The personality will then disintegrate into islands that no longer have any relation with one another. An atrophy of affect will develop, an insufficient con-

---

the same name; trans.], an important principle in Jung's psychology. Cf. C. G. Jung, *Psychological Types*, CW 6, and, regarding the term, CW 13, §§ 358ff (ed.).

[83] Latin, "brain flowers" (trans.).

[84] Gregor Johann Mendel (1822–1884), an Austrian monk, often called the "father of genetics" for his study of the inheritance of traits in pea plants. His findings later became known as Mendel's Laws of Inheritance (trans.).

trol of evaluating emotions, and the impression of a personality that has fallen apart. The single clods are no longer a whole, because they were never quite properly grown together in the first place. The years of *Sturm und Drang* are, so to speak, the time of bringing things to a boil, when the scattered pieces should melt together. If a part is not integrated, an "inclusion" will result, which will be encapsulated. If an entire part is left out, this will make itself felt very unpleasantly. Our psyche is parceled out, just like the body and its organs. Under neurotic or psychotic conditions, organ representatives can separate from one another and begin to march on their own. That's when those strange attacks occur, tachycardia for instance. The heart behaves like a lunatic no longer under control; digestive problems or some paralyses may occur as well. The functions become independent of one another. Something similar to schizophrenia is taking place. In metabolic factors, too, the same dissociative phenomena occur, just as in the psychical sphere. In the case of the child whose dreams we dealt with last winter semester (the child died soon thereafter), there were dreams of disintegration into many small insects, ants, and midgets. These are the smallest living entities, like the single cells of the body. Each cell is actually a living system with some autarchy, and when the whole organism is dissolving, the single groups of cells start out on their own.

When the girl drops the loaf, this means: she is no longer the living entity of her body, but leaves the system to its own devices; then it falls apart. When the government dodges and leaves the country, everybody does as he pleases, just as in today's Europe,[85] which is no longer held together by an idea. Instinctively, a higher brain will then be sought. The League of Nations, for instance, is such an attempt, and it is the same in the psychology of the individual. We always seek to discover a holistic idea, allowing us to live as a whole, and to create an optimum of possibilities in life. If our ego consciousness is removed from its bodily basis by inflation, however, dissociation will set in.

The dream continues: the girl again goes up, and falls; a hole is in

---

[85] 1936 (ed.).

74

the stairs. Stairs mean gaining consciousness step by step; they correspond to the segmented structure of the sympathic and spinal nervous system, the single vertebrae. The ganglia are arranged in different levels, like a ladder. The stairs are the steps, the system of the rope ladder, that makes itself felt. That's the reason why we encounter these steps in all those cults dealing with developing consciousness out of unconsciousness.

In America, a fusion of the lower part with the virginal earth—where primitive man lives—takes place. As a consequence, consciousness stays above, removed from the primitive functions: ideals on the one hand, primitiveness[86] on the other. This explains much of what is absurd in America. The ground of the basement has sunk a few meters. There is no access: the door to the basement is walled up, the stairs leading down are missing, and so the American is living in a world of reasonableness and idealism. It was an American who invented the League of Nations! If an American wants to go into his lower regions, he will have to make a leap into the dark. That is why often those "perverse" stories can happen, such as the young girl who runs away with a negro or a Chinese, or other things that are rather uncommon in this part of the world. An American businessman, for example, wanted to get a divorce from his wife, with whom he had four children, after twenty-two years of happy marriage, because he had fallen in love with a young woman. He had married according to the law, he argued, and he could also get divorced according to the law. When I pointed out to him that it's a bit rich to walk out on the mother of his children just like that, it dawned him that, in the end, this might indeed be about a matter of feeling. A person with warmth and blood is below, unconscious; above everything happens "correctly," respectably. The person above does not see the person below.

The dream goes on: There is a *hole* in the stairs. When a step is missing, this stands for a state of unconsciousness. A "hole" is something unconscious. We do not notice it. The scotoma, the blind spot

---

[86] Jung consistently uses the term *primitive* in the sense of "original, archaic." Cf. C. G. Jung, *CW* 6, § 754 (ed.).

75

in the retina, also exists in psychology. When patients fall into the dark "hole" of the doctor, they are the victims. At the same time, however, they have power over the doctor. They are always standing where he does not see them, and can then exercise their magic—but not as they want, but as it happens to them. This is how relationships develop that the analyst would rather not have. We ourselves create effects we do not like, because we do not see ourselves there. Such a hole is missing consciousness.

The child throws the bread down into the hole. With that, she throws away her body, and thus remains in the inflation. The money, too, she throws away. Money is libido, so it would enable her to reestablish the connection with the body. If she is now throwing the money away, this means: to cap it all, she also throws away the awareness of her body, down into the hole. She brings her mother a few stones instead of the bread. "Stones instead of bread." Stones are something hard and dead. Why the mother? She no longer has the natural affective relationship to her mother. The most probable reason is: the libido for the mother is in the magic mirror, in the inflation. It causes a buoyancy and is necessary for hauling consciousness upward. For women, the mother also stands for the relation with their own instinctual sphere (uterus), that is, precisely the relation to the unconscious. The latter *is* also the mother. The unconscious is the mother of consciousness. Empirically speaking, the physical and psychical world are not the same, even if we would like to always see them together; so, mother means: my mother as a person, but also the mother of my consciousness as the origin of my ego, simply—the unconscious.

As the mother is a very essential person for this child in the real situation, we have to say: the dream refers to the real mother. The child's relation to the mother is vitally important. When she says "mommy" in the dream, this does mean the mommy. When vitally important persons are dreamed *exactly*, then this means them.[87] The dreamer utterly disappoints her mother. She does not give her love; if she does not pay the necessary attention to her own body, she also

---

[87] On the objective plane (ed.).

76

will not give her love. For adults this means: when a woman does not pay the necessary attention to her body, she does not love her mother. When she has difficulties with her, she also has difficulties with her instinctual sphere, this without exception. It can clearly be inferred from this dream that the relation to the mother is disturbed.

❀ ❀ ❀

After the actual dream, now come the fantasies and supplements to the magic mirror. On its backside, the child sees horrible things: a tree with a skull. The body has rotted away, the head is still attached. The face described by the child seems to be a mask. She says: The eyes are like holes. Then, the *horns*: they somehow have to do with the uncanny, devil's horns. What are those four things, such as the horns and the legs? These are the crossed bones shown with a skull, or four arms and legs. The body is missing. The libido has fallen down into the underworld. Then you are dead. The image initially conveys: if you let your body fall, you will be dead; a skull, a floating head with crossed bones.

The image also reminds us of the *sun wheel*. It is through inflation that the girl turns into this object. This is a *solificatio*. The sun is thought of as being born out of the tree—as in many myths and cults such as the Mithras and the Ra cults—because it rises into the air like a bird. For the Druids, the mistletoe that grows on the tree is also a symbol of the sun. The unborn sun is the skull. When you are in the tree and are not born, you hang. Christ is hanging suspended on the cross; so does Odin on the tree:

> "For nine nights I have been hanging on the wind-moved tree,
> Been wounded by the spear, ordained to Odin,
> Myself, and to myself."[88]

Wotan's victims, prisoners of war, were hung on trees and used as targets, pierced by spears. In the Attis cult, the picture of Attis is hung on the fir tree. Moreover, the fir tree is also Attis himself.

Only the *skull* is hanging above. When you give up your body, you

[88] From the *Edda*.

77

are hung, you do not fly like a bird, but hang like a hanged man. But there are four extremities.

Then the magic mirror in the dream turns a light toward the girl; it casts its light on her, enlightens her, she can see herself. Then she gets sick and has to throw up. The mirror that turns onto her, enchants her. This is inflation. This makes one unreal. Just as she saw people askew, under a spell, she herself is now askew in space. She notices that she herself is askew. This is when she gets attacks of seasickness. She climbs up the tree and holds on to the skull. This is an identification with the skull. *She* is the dead one. It is a voluntary sacrifice made by her. "Then my legs and arms fell down." What previously happened to the dead person is now happening to her.

At a Later Meeting of the Seminar

Professor Jung: Given the contents of the dream, it would not be surprising that one remembered it vividly. Such dreams, however, are often forgotten. It would have been much more common that the child had forgotten this dream.

Such a dream is also interesting in an objective sense. The personal side is a *quantité négligeable* [negligible quantity]. Peculiar relations to mythological ideas in the Wotan religion, and also in the Dionysus cult, can be detected in this dream. In a way, Wotan resembles Dionysus. The two are similar gods of emotionality, ecstasy, prophecy, the mystical, the peculiar and the wonderful, the mysteries, the dervishlike states of intoxication. With Dionysus we find the Maenads, with Wotan the Berserkers.

When such a relation presents itself so clearly in a dream, deeper layers of the unconscious have been set in motion. This happens only when important, fundamental matters occur that disrupt the quiet flow of life. I cannot tell from the dream what the motive of this situation was. We have to leave open the question of the causality of this dream.

What happens first to the dreamer is that she is overpowered by the lion. The latter, too, refers to a myth. Dionysus also has something to do with the lion: about to cross the sea, he is captured by sailors, whereupon he transforms himself into a lion and tears them apart. The lion is the animal that overpowers the dreamer. So Dionysus is that enigmatic instinctual being that causes the agitation. In the Dionysus cult, ecstasy and invasions of the unconscious are also specially cultivated. One could say: the dreamer was overwhelmed by the unconscious.

In the language of the dream, this lion is the sun animal. The sun has attacked her and wants to devour her. This is the god. Wotan seizes her. Unfortunately, this very much corresponds to our present situation. Now those things occur that happen to somebody who has been eaten by the god. The dreamer has to perform magic to escape the clutches of the god. She has magic means, the magic mirror. Her psychology contains it: this mirror must refer to a psychological capacity, with which transformations can be achieved—fantasy. This child is able to imagine something; now she simply imagines something different, and thus magically removes the unpleasant situation at the same time.

A parallel case to this dream is that of a five- to six-year-old little boy with a vivid fantasy life. He told the mother that he saw an enormous horse such as doesn't exist in reality, or an enormous house. The mother says: "But that's impossible."—The boy: "So I've got yellow glasses, and when I look through them things just are that big."— The mother: "Where have you got the yellow glasses?"—The boy: "I've got them in here!" He points to himself: the little magic mirror!—The boy often dreams of mounting a high tower, but on rotten wooden stairs, off which one might easily fall. In the dream the boy fears something could happen to him. And indeed, the stairs cave in. He falls down, is dead; the mother picks him up, and he comes alive again. Here we have the same process: climbing down from the height of this fantasy. Or he dreams of big animals, a big camel. It comes from the street and then wants to push in the window of the bedroom to eat him. Father and mother stand before the inner side of the window, but the camel gets through nevertheless and wants to eat him. This is the parallel to the lion!—At the time of the dream some deaths occurred in the boy's environment: a canary, a dog, and a man in the neighborhood. Moreover, the boy was nearly run over by a truck and was slightly injured. He is endangered by the impression of death. The boy is in a situation similar to that of the girl, only he is younger and his character is not yet as individually shaped. Such endangerings occur at certain moments of psychological development; then one has to be careful.

※ ※ ※

Children's dreams are often extraordinarily important because the infantile consciousness is still weak, so that such dreams can surface uninhibited from the collective unconscious. Consciousness is: *this* time, *this* here and now. Consciousness wants to let everything appear as a *here and now*. The unconscious, on the other hand, is an eternity, a timelessness, and has no intentions regarding the here and now. Accordingly, the values are also on a quite different level. When a part of the collective unconscious reaches consciousness, and is perceived as alien by it, a shattering of consciousness, a splitting—that is, dissociation—may ensue. So if an important part of the collective unconscious, which stands in starkest contrast to consciousness, forces its way through, there is always a certain danger of being overwhelmed. If consciousness is weak, it can get into the wake of that content from the collective unconscious and be towed away by it. This is possession, "the peril of the soul."[89]

The starting point in the present dream is the forest. We have already discussed that. The forest, as an aspect of the unconscious, is the dark place where we go, or let ourselves go, on forbidden paths. The child has given herself into the hands of a something, and immediately is in the tow of the unconscious. We sense danger. "You can't just do what comes into your mind," we say in primitive fear of something we do not do of our own will. It *is* indeed dangerous; we cannot just leave ourselves to our own resources, particularly when consciousness is weak. For then it is possible that something will emerge, and that it will carry us away. What emerges are instincts, instinctual forces. The instinct, the desire, appears as a lion in the dream. This is so because the lion is a devouring, overwhelming animal; precisely because there is the danger of being overwhelmed.

[89] This expression is in English in the original (trans.).

80

At first, the child strokes the lion; this is letting herself get lost tenderly in the fantasy. That is why we say that fantasizing is unhealthy. This is right, it is indeed unhealthy.[90] What is unhealthy is the *moral* aspect, for we lose our capacity to decide. The lion devours the girl, meaning that the instinct, the instinctual force of the unconscious, has now gained the upper hand, and what follows is an involuntary, unstoppable process. The spirit goes down in the instinctual commotion. This is the typical onset of a descent into the unconscious; as in Dante: at first he encounters wild animals. Poliphilo[91] goes into the Dark Forest. For the Romans, the Dark Forest was a mythical place. For Europeans, Tibet, among others, is the place of their unconscious. For the ancients it was Ethiopia or *Ultima Thule*, the unknown region of the Earth.

The mother is the rescuing figure in the child's helplessness at the beginning of the dream. She brings her to bed. This may be a rescue, but only by regression. It is somehow as if somebody sees a great adventure lying before him, but realizes that he may really be destroyed in it. The reaction in such cases: immediately home to mother, into bed! The same for little children: they just become even smaller. Our child, however, has learned something. She has seen that you can leave yourself to the fantasy, and that very interesting things will happen. The *magic mirror* means: I see things in the reflection of my spirit. The mirror changes everything in a magical way, and the girl becomes enslaved by it immediately. There follows the phenomenon of seasickness, the people's lopsidedness. Then comes rescue again: the *loaf of bread*. This is hard to interpret, forcing us to go so carefully into the details. It is bread, food, but also a body. This is an allusion to the middle of the body, the stomach region, from where one is fed. At the same time this is the seat of the vegetative bodily functions, the largest concentration of sympathetic ganglia. This region also always plays a role as the center of the body, in the solar plexus.

[90] As is evident from other comments of Jung, this is not his final view on the role of fantasizing. He finds it harmful only if it leads to losing oneself and to a loss of reality (ed.).

[91] Francisco Colonna, *Hypnerotomachia Poliphili*; or in Linda Fierz-David, *Der Liebestraum des Poliphilo: Ein Beitrag zur Psychologie der Renaissance und der Moderne* (ed.); *The Dream of Poliphilo, Related and Interpreted by Linda Fierz-David* (trans.).

The body always makes itself felt whenever there is an intuition that transcends the body. We are reminded of it when the fantasy threatens to get lost in the unreal, to rise into the stratosphere. The loaf of bread replaces the mother. The mother is much less a sexual object for the child than a nurturing object. She is the breast, the nurturer. So a loaf of bread can take the place of the mother. In short, the mother reappears, but as a feeding function, as body-unconscious. She had to get this loaf of bread on the mother's instructions; this becomes clear from the end of the dream. Again the protecting hand of the mother comes up, which wants to save her from the danger that threatens the child of getting lost in the unconscious fantasies.

Having the bread, she can go up the stairs. She can climb to the world of light, the world of consciousness. But she sees the hole. There is a disruption in that ascent. She falls over. There is a figure of speech, *umfallen*,[92] meaning that although somebody made a decision, he cannot stick to it. This means: she cannot hold her body, which is nurturing her, she cannot integrate it into the world of her consciousness. In throwing the loaf of bread and the money down there, she has thrown out and rejected the body. She no longer receives tenderness for this, but a beating. With this beating, the disruption of the conscious state should be reversed again. This is a kind of *talion*, an "atonement,"[93] to make her become one again with the body. Consciousness is reestablished, but the after-dream shows that she cannot let go of fantasizing: again she has to come back to the magic mirror. Although she has been punished and could now repent, she does return again and imagines what kind of things could be seen in the magic mirror.

Here the real danger appears: the girl sees the house on fire. The house is the real world of consciousness, the psychical space in which she is. This world of consciousness is destroyed by fire. Before that it was latent, invisible. The *dynamis* of the unconscious is invisible. It feeds the intensity of our consciousness. When consciousness diminishes, the fire breaks out; that's why it is often used as a symbol

---

[92] *Umfallen*: "to fall over; to retract one's statement, not to do what one promised" (trans.).
[93] This word in English in the original (trans.).

for this situation. When the world of consciousness is invalidated, the world fire breaks out, according to Germanic mythology. Hell consists of fire, because fire that has erupted destroys everything.

Consistently the dream continues: on its reverse side, the mirror depicts death. More precisely, death in the guise of an already decayed, hanged man. That, of all things, it is a hanged man and a tree, is extremely peculiar.

The *tree* is the world tree. Odin was hanged on a tree. Also, the wood for the Christian cross comes from the tree of paradise. Christ is crucified on the tree of life. Strangely enough, the cross has a feminine meaning. It symbolizes the *woman*, the *cruel woman*, in whose arms Christ died. There is a legend that Mary talks to the cross, which she addresses as "mother cross," how cruelly she would treat her son. Here, too, the tree as a cross takes the place of the mother who, however, was completely depersonalized. She is the mother of death. The mother gives birth, and at the end of life, as earth, she again receives the dead in herself. In a Maori myth, death is the old ancestress Hine-nui-te-po. She sleeps with her mouth open. Maui, the hero, wants to overpower her in order to defeat death. He has arranged with all creatures that none of them make a sound when he creeps into her mouth. But a little bird cannot stifle a laugh. Hine-nui-te-po wakes up and snaps her mouth shut. So that's how Maui finds his fate. The ancestress is in the past, but also in the future. She is the beginning and the end.

The Madonna too, the heavenly mother, has her hellish counterpart in the *devil's grandmother*; likewise, Kwannon, the goddess of mercy, has a hellish manifestation. In the East it is not believed that deities can be good only. Also the mother has got a reverse side, like the mirror; there she becomes the tree of the dead, in which the dead are buried. A Germanic legend recounts: the last men on earth vanish again in the tree from which they originally came out. There has to be a consciousness that mirrors the world; otherwise, the world would not exist at all. The primitive man still had a premonition that the world will cease to exist when consciousness ceases to exist. This will be when the forest reappears; Earth will belong to the forest. The tree is the vegetative, unconscious life, which will emerge again when human consciousness has been extinguished.

83

Death, as he appears in the magic mirror, is a "hanging" [*Aufhän-gung*]. Hanging is a ritual in sacrifice. Christ too was called the "hanged" by the pagans. On the other hand, death is also character-ized by the motif of dismembering. This connection is also evidenced historically: the relation to Wotan and Dionysus. Dionysus is the dis-membered one.

In this dream it is a dismembering into four pieces. So I ask my-self: Why exactly four? Whenever *four* things appear in a dream, I "see my chance."[94] I have always found that we are doing a dream in-justice if we overlook the fact that the motif of the Four appears in it. This Four is four entities, just as the extremities are differentiated entities, like parts on the body fulfilling specific functions. They are symmetrical: the left hand is like the right one in the mirror. So ac-tually they are two pairs, which fall apart. As it is, only the head is still hanging in the dream. Arms and legs have severed themselves from life; these are the organs, differentiated members, that can sep-arate themselves. What psychological meaning do they have? There are four functions of consciousness.[95] They make up the essence of consciousness. They can separate from one another and fall apart. This dismemberment is simply a dissolution of the psychic body, of the body of consciousness.

Now the mirror turns against the dreamer. The climax has been reached. The magic now turns *against herself*. So she has to throw up. It is as if she had taken poison, as if she were seized by vertigo. It is not there in the dream, but absolutely conceivable, that it is the re-vulsion against that carrion, that gruesome image of destruction. She feels revulsion or fear, a primitive reaction. When certain animals are being chased, they too vomit their stomach contents, possibly out of fear of death. These are cramps of the stomach muscles, like a seizure. The stomach tells you: "Spit out what you have eaten. It's poison!"

Then there comes a peculiar, analogous offer of a sacrifice: she hangs *herself* on the tree. Arms and legs fall off. She decomposes, then composes herself in a new form; so it is a regenerative sacrifice,

[94] See note 82 on tetrasomia (ed.).
[95] See C. G. Jung, *Psychological Types*, CW 6 (ed.).

and identification with the one hanged on the tree. This is exactly what is done in the *Exercises* of Ignatius of Loyola:[96] you contemplate the crucifixion and suffer the same death, thus being regenerated. Through identification with Christ we also go through hell with him, only to rise again with him. Our dreamer says that her arms and legs have fallen off of her, but then they come up again. She is put to-gether again, but the body remains down there and turns into earth. What remains are the four functions of consciousness, hanging with a head on the world tree. This is a very dark image and, characteris-tically, it is on the reverse side of the mirror.

When we have a look at that dream, the following thought strikes us: a collective idea—an archetype—came to light in the child. Ei-ther consciousness is almost pathologically weak, or the archetype extraordinarily strong. Question: what is the reason for that? What weakened consciousness to the extent that a content could become visible? This I don't know. It could be something physiological. That the background becomes so prominent is also found in connection with deaths in the family or neighborhood, or when threatened by illness or other things. It could also be the problem of the mother. There may be no external reason, the reason lying rather in the child's constitution. In this case, we would have to take into account that this psychic constitution is perhaps not quite unproblematic. The threshold to the unconscious is very low. For the prognosis we would have to make a little question mark.

[96] Ignatius of Loyola (1491–1556) was the founder, in 1534, of the Society of Jesus, com-monly known as the Jesuits. He was canonized in 1622. See his *Exercitia spiritualia* (ed.).

85

In adults, such important dreams are always linked to something special. There is always something going on here. In an adult we could find out what happened; in a child this is extraordinarily difficult. In such a case we should put forward all possible hypotheses. We could ask, for instance, if there was an illness in the child's family or in the neighborhood. A doctor, for example, once examined the dreams of a patient, then his own dreams, those of his wife, of his children, of visitors and maids, and found a considerable correspondence.[97] Spouses, too, often dream in a parallel way, often in opposites which, however, are connected with each other. It is uncanny how we dream out of our environment and take up problems. Themes from all around flow in, although no word is spoken. The air is full of all that. We always think that only dreams of important persons are important, but this is wrong.

In any case, this dream contains a perfect series of symbols, which represent the way of solution and at the same time the way of initiation, but with a minus sign. If a person in the second half of life had had this dream, we could say: this is the descent into the underworld, the experience of the *Myste* in hell. And the end would be the sunrise. One would have become a "child of the golden head." We find this expression in the third century, in the *Tracts* of Zosimos.[98] The image of the dead body on the tree is also reminiscent of the wonderful "Story of the Indian King with the Corpse."[99]

In the case of this child, however, this is not about individuation; her dream produces abhorrent images in order to prevent her from going astray in fantasy. For the child lets herself go in her fantasy; the dream scolds her for that. It says: if you do this and disobey the mother, that is, the life instinct, something will happen to you—

[97] In moments of great tension or of special importance, the constellation of the situation is conveyed to a great number of people in very similar images from the collective unconscious (ed.).

[98] Zosimos of Panopolis, an important Greek alchemist und Gnostic in the third century; in Marcellin Berthelot, *Collections des anciens alchémistes grecs*; cf. C. G. Jung, "The Visions of Zosimos," CW 13 (ed.).

[99] Translated and edited by Heinrich Zimmer in *Weisheit Indiens* (*The Wisdom of India*).

death! Then you will be badly off, then you will turn, *nolens volens*, into a hanged god. And this is extremely uncomfortable!

※ ※ ※

You asked me how we should deal with such children in a practical way. We have to pay attention to the child and try to stabilize his or her consciousness. The child should draw to make the fantasies concrete; the freely floating danger will thus be made concrete. Writing and drawing cause a certain cooling off, a devaluation of the fantasies.

Another question was: "You describe the woman in the store as the archetype of the mother. Why then does it say in *Faust*: 'the mothers'?"

In the scene of the mothers in *Faust*, Mephistopheles says to Faust, before he goes to the mothers:

> Sight of a glowing tripod will tell you, finally,
> You're in the last deep, deepest there might be.
> By its light you'll see the Mothers,   6285
> Some sit about, as they wish, the others,
> Stand and move. Formation, Transformation,
> Eternal minds in eternal recreation.
> Images of all creatures float, portrayed:
> They'll not see you: they only see a shade.   6290
> Be of good heart, the danger there is great,
> Go to the tripod: don't hesitate,
> And touch it with the key! (Part 2, Act 1)

Why *mothers* and not *one* mother? It's like in that dream of the child of the heavenly virgins,[100] who are the many mothers. This is connected with the Fates, Norns, Muses, and similar figures. These are actually all mother figures. The plural means that this is not about one mother with a specific personality. The *pluralis diminutivus*[101] is

---

[100] See dream series of a boy, dream number 1, reprinted in the appendix (ed.).
[101] Latin, "diminutive plural" (trans.).

to be interpreted apotropaically.[102] That's why we address each other in the plural:[103] *Wie geht es Ihnen* [How do you do]? This actually means: *Wie geht es Dir?* This has an effect, this is magical. That is a protective formula, a polite phrase. The *pluralis diminutivus* takes away the importance. It is a euphemism with which we actually want to create a counter effect. "Pontus Euxinus," for instance, was called the "hospitable" sea; this was the name for the Black Sea, because it was notorious for its storms. Similarly, the Eumenides[104] were called the "well-meaning." In English there is no [informal] *Du*, so you can always remain the well-protected gentleman.

If you can say "to the mothers," it can be a thousand figures. But if you say "to the mother," it is specific, personal, it immediately becomes problematic.

When you say: "the ancient wise men tell us," this means nothing at all. "*That* old man told *me*," however, is something concrete, then you are committed.

5. Dream of the Mountain and the Murder of the Mother
Presented by Ilse Berg

Text: *I dreamed that I was on a high mountain and went for a walk with mommy. Then mommy slapped me, because I went too far out (toward the precipice). But I got very angry at her and beat her to death with an ax that was lying around there, and the flesh was all hanging down. But I was standing on a wooden board, like on a bridge, and suddenly the board breaks and I'm falling down. Many dead persons and skulls were there, they filled up a whole barn; there was also a man (alive), he had 120 cows. My brothers were allowed to milk the cows, and we could all drink milk. There was also a bell. I rang it for a long time, whereupon an elevator came. The man in the elevator took us up, but suddenly the suspension cable of the elevator broke, and I fell down into a big, wide tube (of glass, and at the top like what I saw in the Glacier Garden;[105] glacial mills). I*

---

[102] I.e., "to ward off danger" (trans.).

[103] A peculiarity of some languages, including German, differentiating between a formal address (*Sie*) in the plural, and an informal one (*Du*) in the singular. There is no equivalent in English (trans.).

[104] The Erinyes (Latin: the Furies), the Greek goddesses of vengeance (trans.).

[105] A natural monument and tourist attraction in Lucerne, showing glacial potholes of impressive proportions, glacial mills, etc. (ed.).

kept falling and falling down, until all of a sudden I landed on a burning ground. There was a stick that looked like an iron staff with a hook on top (crosier). This staff was unbreakable. I stuck the staff into the fire, which had started to burn more and more, and suddenly I was sitting on the stick (on a board). And now I had to remain sitting on the stick for ever and ever and ever. But then water gushed down, and the fire went out at once.

Then there was a little road going uphill. I had grown long (as long as fingers) finger nails. So I clung to the path and went up. There was a hole in the tube, and there I slipped in, just into a house and there were also many cakes in it. I had gotten hungry and ate them all up. The dream would have been longer, but then daddy came to wake me up.

Mrs. Berg: We have divided the whole dream into three parts, because it seemed to us that these parts represent three different phases of one and the same process.

First Part

We have structured the first part, which we have conceived of as going until the collapse of the board, as follows:

1. Locale: The child with the mother on the mountain.
2. Exposition: The child goes to the precipice, is warned by the mother and gets beaten.
3. Peripateia: The slaying of the mother.
4. Lysis: Collapse of the bridge.

We have already seen in the previous dream that the child is hostile toward the mother. She brings her stones instead of bread, and is being beaten for it. There it seemed as if the libido—the bread and the money—would sink into the hole, that is, into the collective unconscious: Now she has arrived there. And in the present dream, the unconscious itself seems to want to pull the child down. The mother again steps in to prevent that.

As the personal mother, and not a collective image of her, is appearing here, we have at first to pay some attention to the significance of the *real* mother for the child. The mother figure symbolizes a part of the child's libido, the part that is rooted in the world and is integrated into it. The mother is the first image for the feminine at-

89

titude toward the environment, she also is the link with it. However, she also represents, in her deeper, impersonal aspect, the life instinct itself. She is the home, the earth, the ground on which we stand. If that hold is given up, on the one hand, the loss shows in a dissolution of the persona: in our case, for example, by her inattentiveness in school and probably also by other things. On the other hand, this being at the mercy of the world of fantasy is a consequence of such a dissolution of the persona. The violent murder of the mother lets us conclude that the unconscious has gained a devastating force of attraction, clearing away any obstacle through the loss of libido, that is, its sinking into the unconscious, as already hinted at in the previous dream. As all this is happening on a *high mountain*, we might infer an *overly heightened* level of consciousness, maybe even an inflation. This would result in a precocious attitude and a certain arrogance in daily life.

The girl then walks on a *bridge*, on a board, which—as the dreamer depicted it in a drawing—is above an abyss. The bridge over the abyss is a very frequent mythological motif. It is said that in the Koran a bridge over hell is mentioned, thin as a string and sharp as a sword, that only the righteous can cross. A Muslim legend tells of a bridge between the Temple of Jerusalem in the East and the Mount of Olives in the West. Below is hell, into which those who are not righteous must fall. A Celtic legend tells of a *bridge of horrors*, not broader than a string. Moreover, in a Persian collection of legends there appears the so-called Chinvat bridge, on which angels and demons fight over the souls of the people crossing it.

The mythological importance of the bridge is further based on the idea that a spirit or a god is at the bottom of the abyss. By building the bridge, man has evaded the influence of his direct power. So as not to provoke him, various sacrifices were offered to him; human beings at the beginning, later puppets in human form and other things. The chapels built on bridges remind us of the last remnants of this idea. Over the course of time, the original meaning of the sacrifice offered to the god or demon down in the depth faded; the old places of sacrifice were used for profane purposes. As an example, let us mention the chapels on the big bridge in Paris, which were used for public money transactions. Or, a clothes market was held in a chapel on a bridge in Leeds (England). An interpretation of this change could be that the potential dangers in crossing a bridge have been pushed into the background by the rise of civilization. To the degree that bridges became safer, the fear of the spirit down in the depths diminished, as did, however, also the knowledge of their existence as such. Yet the bridge remains the place of danger, the precarious hold above the abyss. Psychologically, it represents the weak spot of consciousness, the place where it might cave in. Seen from this point of view, the slaying of the mother—that is, the destruction of the persona and of the relations to the environment—seems to be a preliminary stage of this collapse.

Second Part

1. Locale: In the barn; dead persons and skulls; a shepherd with 120 cows.
2. Exposition: Milking the cows by the brothers; drinking milk.
3. Peripateia: Ringing the bell; going up in the elevator.
4. Lysis: Breaking of the elevator cable; falling down again.

The libido, which had been forcefully withdrawn from the mother, is now introverted, and in this way resuscitates figures of the collective unconscious.

Let us now concern ourselves with the deeper mythological meaning of the *cows*. There is a lot of evidence that cows are mother symbols. In Indian religion, cows are extremely highly revered. Not only they themselves, but also their five products: milk, quark, cheese, urine, and manure are holy, and have a cleansing effect on man. Earth itself was conceived as a cow by the Indians, from which the creator *Prtu* milked everything edible. Then came, according to their conception, all the other living creatures, including the mountains, to milk this primal cow for the milk they need. In Egyptian mythology, heaven is often thought of as a cow, the so-called sky-goddess Hathor, bearing the sun disk between her horns. She is the heavenly mother of the sun god, who recreates himself in the evening by entering into her mouth, to rise again in the morning as his own son.

91

In her motherly aspect she is often identified with, or portrayed at the side of, the life tree, administering heavenly food and heavenly drink to the dead souls. Let me mention in advance, already at this point, that this conception of Hathor later became unified with the figures of both Isis and Ishtar. These two goddesses display still further aspects of the cow symbol, that is, the godly mother, of which I will speak later on.

The *multitude* of the cows probably corresponds to the splitting of a figure so frequently found in myths and fairy tales, so as to make this figure appear more depersonalized and abstract.

We do not want to give further details on the number *hundred and twenty*. Let us just mention that the Picts in Ireland protected themselves against the poisoned arrows of their enemies by taking a bath, prepared from the milk of 120 white, hornless cows.

If it can be concluded from all this that cows have a motherly meaning, then it is the motif of the two mothers—found in many heroic myths—that appears. In drinking the cows' milk the dreamer gains immortality, that is, a life from the godly mother. There are numerous parallels in mythology, as in Heracles or the legend of Romulus and Remus.

The whole process from the collapse of the bridge to the drinking of the milk has to be understood as a rebirth fantasy, of which so many examples are described in *Transformations and Symbols of the Libido*. As is set out there, these images serve to resuscitate the incestuously bound sexual libido and to raise it, by the way of fantasy, to the level of consciousness.

The *brothers* that milk the cow are animus figures, whose function as such is to establish contact with the collective unconscious.

The *man* standing there seems to be a kind of peasant or shepherd, a guardian of nature's life-giving forces. On the other hand, the dead and the skulls in the barn point to his connection with the underworld. A figure combining both characteristics in himself is the sun god Osiris. In the most original meaning, Osiris, the brother-husband of Isis, is the god of change in nature in the broadest sense of the word. As such he can, on the one hand, be portrayed by the daily and yearly path of the sun, causing the greatest change in nature; on the other hand, he is also the god of death. Perhaps it should be mentioned here that in almost all portrayals, his attributes are either a staff ending in a hook, or also very often the symbol of the Tau cross, which will become important for the following part of the dream.

Tammuz, too, whose cult was widespread in the Semitic countries since prehistoric times, was a dying and resurrecting god. His cult was founded on the belief in a tortured saint, Dumuzid,[106] which means "faithful son," who died and rose again, thus becoming a god. In a song he is addressed as follows: "Oh Dumuzid, Lord, Shepherd of the glorious Anu," or "Lord of the herds, which art the highest and most glorious." So, as a shepherd, he gains a specific significance in our dream. In the same sense as Osiris, he represents nature that is dying and resurrecting again in spring. Here Hermes also has to be mentioned, the thief of the sun cattle of Helios, also the escort of the souls in the underworld. So the man mentioned in the dream can probably be interpreted as a *fatherly* archetype,[107] in any case as a *positive* animus figure. In a general way, he would represent the function of holding together and guiding the forces of the unconscious.

We now arrive at that point in the dream where the girl calls for the elevator by ringing the bell. All of a sudden a modern mechanism appears in this mythological world. We have tried to explain this in the following way: the regaining of the libido, symbolized by drinking the milk, is now put to use in a mechanical way that does not correspond to the meaning of the rest of the dream picture. It is an attempt to move upward again, comfortably and as fast as possible with the help of a mechanical device. This elevator is being operated by a man, definitely a *negative* animus figure, who helps her to

---

[106] Also called Dumuzi. Misspelled in the original as "Dunuzi" (trans.).

[107] Probably rather the archetype of the shepherd and escort of souls than the fatherly quality (ed.).

93

set the whole thing in motion. It seems, however, that she does not succeed in reaching the level of consciousness in such a way, as the elevator breaks and takes her to a new depth.

Third Part

1. Locale: Glass tube; burning ground.
2. Exposition: Sticking the staff into the ground; sitting for ever and ever.
3. Peripateia: Gush of water and the fire goes out.
4. Lysis: Ascent to a higher level.

Falling down in the glass tube, reminiscent of the first fall from the bridge, would mean a new introversion of the libido, and simultaneously a renewed entry into the maternal womb, as we can interpret the penetrating of, pulling through, or slipping into narrow holes.

She now comes to a *burning ground*, actually a fire that burns higher and higher. Here an analogy with the fire in the interior of the Earth seems to suggest itself. This concept is still more general than what we found in connection with the cows. No longer one of her creatures, but Earth herself becomes the procreating maternal womb. We can also attribute, therefore, a feminine meaning to the fire. In a Maya mandala, which represents a cosmic idea, there is the fire goddess *Xiuhteti* at the center, the center of the Earth. She is "the Mother," but also the "Father of the gods in the middle of the Earth." Primitives often address the fire as "mother fire." As a symbol of the terrifying mother, it also appears as a fire-breathing dragon or a child-eating Moloch. The cleansing and purifying effect of the fire is a very old concept, which also found its way into the Christian world in the form of purgatory.

In our dream there is now an *iron staff*, a crozier, that the girl sticks into the fire. In this connection, we would like to call to mind the Hopi myth that Professor Jung read to us in the last winter semester. This is a myth describing the evolution of mankind by a slow ascent through three underground caves, lying on top of one another. The fourth and last step would be the surface of the Earth. When man was still in the lowest cave, a plant, a bamboo plant, was brought to him, enabling him by its growth to climb up. We may probably interpret this little plant brought from above, the germinating seed sunk into the lowest cave, as an act of fertilization. In this case it would again signify one of the numerous attempts of the restricted libido to reach ever higher levels of consciousness by way of fantasy.

In this connection, we might refer to a Greek concept that is found in Plato's *Timaeus*. According to it, the *Moira*, the personification of inevitable fate—the mother—is in the center of Earth. The iron axis of the world, around which the whole cosmos is revolving, goes through her womb. In this dream, sticking the staff into the fire also means an act of procreation. It is interesting that the iron staff as *crozier* is also the symbol of Osiris, as it is the attribute of the shepherd or of the male deity in general. So here the image of an animus figure is reduced to a simple symbol of the creative and procreative force, similar to what happened with the mother image.

The dreamer now has to sit *for ever*, for ever on the staff, on a board, that is. When we look at the drawing made by the girl, we are struck by the similarity with the above-mentioned mandala figure. Here the tree of life is rendered in the form of a Tau cross. Although the bird on it is certainly a fertility symbol of phallic meaning, we think we can find a connection in the two drawings, which would point to the hanging on the tree of life, a motif which had already appeared in the previous dream.

Another important symbol is found in a very old Egyptian sign, the "key of life." It has the general meaning of stirring up the dead to eternal life, and later becomes the overall sign of the Babylonian goddess Astarte, whose name is translated as "She Who Gives Life." Astarte stands in close connection with, and is often identified with, the divine goddess Ishtar, an Asian goddess of love and war. Her animal is the lion, and she is often depicted as standing or riding on him. In the previous dream, the lion was interpreted as an unbridled, desirous, and instinctual force. Ishtar too represents a wild, unbridled instinctual force, uninhibited desire. She transforms the men she desires into animals; in the Gilgamesh Epic, for example, she unleashes the heavenly bull against whom Gilgamesh has to fight. The only one she really loves is the young man Tammuz, mentioned earlier. His death induces her to go on a journey through the underworld. In doing so, she falls into the hands of Ereshkigal, goddess of the underworld, who wants to keep Tammuz for herself and takes Ishtar prisoner. Only after she is soothed by a gift from the Earth goddess does she set both of them free by pouring the water of life over them, thus reawakening them.

This myth ends in the same way as that part of the dream just discussed. A gush of water pours down on the dreamer, too, the fire goes out, and she can again reach a higher level. This myth confirms anew that this is about a rebirthing process. That the fire ceases immediately probably symbolizes regaining the libido, which has, so to speak, entered into the girl herself, and can be compared to the drinking of the milk in the previous dream passage. The deep level on which this rebirth fantasy is taking place can be explained by the strong splitting off of the unconscious instinctual force, as depicted by the slaying of the mother at the beginning of the dream. Through this, the libido regresses deeper and deeper, and can resuscitate ever more archaic images of the collective unconscious.

With the help of this regained libido, she now succeeds in reaching a higher level. As the dream says, she clings to the path leading uphill and comes to a house, where she can eat many cakes. Here the ascent is achieved by quite different means than previously with the help of the elevator. It seems to be a piece of instinctual, animal libido that can be lifted only with difficulty. In this way she does not yet reach the level of consciousness, however, but—to come back to the Hopi myth—only the second or third cave, where this animal maybe has to be reborn in a new way and in a new maternal womb, until it can finally reach again the level of consciousness in human form.

In concluding, we just want to say that we have mentioned the Ishtar myth not only because it, too, confirms the rebirthing process in the third part of the dream, but also because it seems to us that the archetype of Ishtar is of special significance for this girl, and because this dream contains hints at how such a descent can become somebody's fate.

※ ※ ※

Professor Jung: The *mother* at the beginning of the dream is reality. When the relationship with the mother becomes bad, then a piece of reality is shattered. The girl goes for a walk with the mother. This is a common situation, but for the girl in the dream this feels like being on a high mountain. Now this is very conscious. Because there is an inclination toward the underworld, she feels as if being in the normal world were like being on a high mountain. So the child has difficulty remaining conscious. There is always the danger that she sinks down into a mythological prehistoric world. A part of the collective, primal world has burst open: she *slays* the mother. Children are cruel; they find legends of murder and slaughter quite natural. The child is herself actually still stuck to a great extent in that legendary world, within the collective unconscious. In comparison, she experiences the normal level of consciousness as a high mountain. She approaches the *abyss*, because to do so is actually within her; she is always being attracted by this depth. The mother is the counter-tendency. Her example, indeed, shows how one should be conscious. Because the child goes too close to the abyss, she is beaten. This resuscitates in her precisely that affect, and subsequently she goes down into the depths.

As to the *bridge*: it hints at the continuity of consciousness; the child lacks the wholeness of consciousness, the latter consisting of irregular contents that alternately establish relations with ego consciousness.

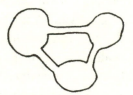

One part is the nice child of the mother, the other is the devil. The child can unscrupulously be the evil, or nothing but the nice child. The child can say: now I am this or that. We find the same constellation in the mentally insane, who alternately identify with varying figures. This is the discontinuity of consciousness. Only over the course of time do land bridges emerge in the child, connections remain, whereupon a coherent consciousness develops. The ideal case would be a wholeness of the personality at *every* moment. As a rule, we do not have this wholeness. Sometimes we play this role, sometimes that role. The land bridges and islands never become a perfect continent. Remnants of the primitive and infantile condition remain.

We are living on various single islands of consciousness. In the view of the primitives there are demons on the islands of consciousness by whom we are possessed. Psychologically speaking, we are possessed by an affect there because we completely identify with it. For in the affect we can *totally* be what we feel. That is why it has something fascinating about it; there are many people who worship the affect they have at that moment. This is childlike. Such a person forgets that he is also the other. The noble forgets that he also has a mean side, and the ignoble—if he is still able at all to muster a feeling of inferiority—that in some place he is also a decent guy. The great prejudice against psychology is caused by the fear of becoming conscious. The greater the fixation to affects, the greater the aversion to becoming conscious.

The images of the *skull* and the *barn* appear side by side. This is a peculiar constellation: skulls characterize the vault of the dead, but here it is a barn at the same time. The motif of the skull was already present in the first dream, in a highly significant connection. Seen in this light, the unconscious is a kind of charnel house. These are the remains of lived lives, remnants of various generations. The unconscious represents a kind of graveyard of the past. This simply means: the breakthrough from the past into the future goes through death.

The charnel house usually belongs to a church, however, and is not a barn. Here enters the strange idea that the place of death, where the skulls lie, is not a church or a chapel, which always seem cold and unfriendly. A barn, on the contrary, is mighty comfortable and warm, and has a friendly, vegetative, animal atmosphere; it has a fecund feeling. The barn means the second mother. We find the same story in India, where there is an ancient cow culture, in which the cow symbolizes protective, feeding, rebirthing qualities. In the classrooms in school we have a calf to clear the atmosphere. The Indians hold their hands underneath to catch the cleansing matter, the cow dung. Somewhere in India there is a leather cow through which the people crawl in a rebirth ritual. So the cow stands for the Earth cow, the cow of heaven, the world cow. This cold place of death, this uncanny grave, is thus, at the same time, also warm and fecund and nourishing like a barn.

The fact that there are *many* cows is a multiplication of the *one* idea, of the one cow that simply stands here for the fertile, feeding mother goddess. Cow barn for cow—that's like Downing Street for the prime minister, or the Vatican for the pope.

The *number one hundred and twenty*: symbols of rebirth often refer to time, for example, the Mithraic "seven steps." Then the god of these mysteries corresponds to the number 365, that is, he represents the year, Abraxas[108] or Abrasax. We find the same thing in the mythology of Christ: Christ is the ecclesiastical year. Of Prajapati, the Indian creator of the world, it is said: he is the great Self. He became absorbed in the year, that is, he represents the year and the yearly cycle, because creative power is identical with time. Proclus[109] says: "Where creation is, there also is time." That is why the god of creation, for instance, in *Stoicism* or in the Neo-Pythagoreans, is called *Chronos*, a god of fire, light, and time. This dream cannot be about a male matter. Wherever a female rebirthing symbol appears, we have to consider female connections, for instance, the moon, or the month. With the cows there comes the number one hundred and twenty. We can link this number with the astrological calendar. One hundred and twenty days are four months. Our Western astrology comes from Mesopotamia and Babylonia. There we find only three seasons: winter, summer, and fall. This corresponds exactly to a duration of four months each, that is, one hundred and twenty days.

Dr. Frey: One hundred and twenty days correspond to 120 degrees on the zodiac. This forms the astrological aspect of the *trigon*. The exact aspects of the trigon always combine signs of the same material quality, that is, three fire, earth, water, or air signs each. It was nat-

---

[108] A Gnostic image of God (ed.).

[109] Greek Neoplatonist philosopher (A.D. 412–487), headmaster of the School of Philosophy at Athens (ed., trans.).

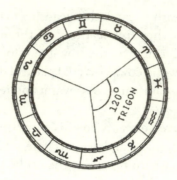

ural for astrological speculation to bring the various elements into a certain sequence of stages.

Professor Jung: This idea also suggested itself to the classical Pythagorean and the Neoplatonist philosophers. The Gnostics,[110] too, had a sequence of stages of earth, water, air, and fire.

Dr. Frey: In *modern* astrology, other points are more important for the classification into stages. In connection with the trigon, the following applies: in the fire trigon, for example, Aries represents the deepest, Leo the middle, and Sagittarius the highest stage. In psychological terms, we could say that the first stage is the unconscious, the second what is colored by the ego, and the third one the superego. The order in each trigon group results from the fact that in each respective case, the first signs—Sagittarius, Taurus, and so on—are more collective, more primitive, than the later ones.

Professor Jung: The idea of a sequence of stages is the image of a creative process: an emergence from the earth through water, through air, and through fire. We find this image in those philosophers of Neo-Pythagorean and Neoplatonist orientation.

The four stages correspond psychologically to the four stages of individuation. Earthly man—a Gnostic concept—is *hylikos*;[111] then a higher development is *psychikos*, water and air in one. The word "psy-

---

[110] Gnosticism, from the Greek *gnosis* (knowledge); a belief system that flourished in Hellenistic culture, with a profound influence on Christianity. Gnostics held that the physical world of matter was corrupt and evil, a deterioration of spirit, and that salvation could be attained only through the embracing of the eternal goodness of the spiritual. Gnosticism was declared a heresy in the fourth century by the Christian Church (trans.).

[111] Greek, "material, bodily" (trans.).

100

che" (soul) is connected to "physein" (Greek, to blow); *psychos* corresponds with *psychros* (Greek, cold, damp). "The soul of a drunkard is moist," says Heraclitus. The soul oscillates between air and water. It is always the go-between for the two principles marking the extremes: below there is earth, the material matter; above there is *pneumatikos* (spirit), air, and fire. Dry, hot air—this is the spirit. The psyche is originally moist vapor: brooding mist, a creature of the mist. The air settles on the water, fertilizing. "The spirit of God moved upon the face of the waters"[112]—like the hen on the egg—He impregnated it. The *germ of fire* enters man as his soul, as his life, and makes man warm; this is a kind of *descensus*[113] of the spirit into matter. The mysteries are about setting these germs of fire free again. This is an idea that goes way back to megalithic times. All initiations have had the goal of creating an immortal human being, surviving death. This is always about peeling the immortal germ out of mortal nature, and giving this germ a form, that is, there is an effort, so to speak, to replace consciousness, identical with the ego, with the new, the *spiritual* man. The dogmatic life of Christ demonstrated all of this: the transfiguration, when the fire man, the light man appears; the death, the rising again, the ascension into heaven. This idea is also prominent in the teachings of Mani.[114]

This process is always linked to time, and in the case of complicated numbers, these *numbers* have always to be viewed with reference to coming into being and dying. For there is no coming into being and dying but in time. This is where the meaning of numbers enters the picture. The number in a dream always has a meaning. If we cannot find this meaning, *we* are the idiots, not the dream. There are *particular numbers* in many initiation rituals. We would need much material, however, to get to the bottom of them.

Our unconscious has a quite fabulous relation to time. People have been hypnotized with the posthypnotic suggestion to count seconds. When they were hypnotized again, they could tell the exact number

---

[112] Genesis 1:2 (ed.).

[113] Latin, "descent, journey through the underworld" (ed.).

[114] Mani, born in western Persia (ca. A.D. 210–275), religious preacher and founder of Manichaeism, an ancient Gnostic religion (trans.).

of elapsed seconds. We are unconsciously oriented about time. You can wake up at a certain minute if you intended to do so. This is possible only because of the perfect time function of the unconscious.

Astrology presupposes that we are *identical* with time. It expresses the quality of the moment at which we were born. Insofar as the reconstructions of character in astrology are correct, we evidently have to be identical with the moment of birth, or with time. My view on this is that time is a psychological function, identical with living as such. Such a view cannot be proved but is extremely valuable heuristically.

When numbers of no distinct mythological meaning appear, we can ask if they might stand for years. For example, when someone dreams of the number seven, we can ask: what happened seven years ago? When someone dreams of birth, or a completely new factor appears under the sign of birth, and when we count back nine months to the time of conception, we sometimes can uncover a very important event that happened at that time. Years or periods of time are also often represented by animals.

The regression in our dream is actually a sin: it is a falling down into hell, hence the motif of *suspension*. The girl remains attached to the staff. She falls into the ground of the world, which is male and female at the same time, and simultaneously neither male nor female. The primal being exists before any differentiation has taken place. The dreamer falls down into her innermost being. There, in a way, life starts again and again.

The staff represents guidance; it will become a guide as an *inner law* when someone came into the inner ring of fire and remains suspended in the soul fire. In humility we stay on hanging in the fire, until we are burned up. That's how the transformation of the ego into spiritual, immortal man goes.

There are many mythological images of this: Isis holds the little son of the king of Phoenicia over the fire at night to make him immortal. But once the mother happens on this, she cries out loud; Isis quickly has to draw the child out of the fire, and immortality is lost.

Mr. *Baumann*: The same happens to Demeter with Demophon, the son of the queen Metaneira, whom she nurses.

102

Professor Jung: In our dream, too, the fire appears, but it does not lead to rebirth. The dreamer remains sitting on the staff "for ever and ever." Then comes the gush of water, extinguishing the fire.

Dreams like the present one otherwise only appear in persons who are somehow *in danger*, for instance, in critical moments of their lives. If we are able to give them the meaning of such a dream, something may happen, a healing, for instance. I have never been successful, however, except when it was possible for the dreamer to consciously register the meaning and the intention of such a dream.

In the case of this dream, however, we have to take into account that we are talking not about an adult, but about a *child*. A child is always nearer the collective unconscious. So no quasi-fatal regression at all is needed to create such a dream. We must not attach too much significance, therefore, to the disturbing quality of this dream.

3

Psychological Interpretation of Children's Dreams
(Winter Term, 1938/39)

1. Dream of a Five-Year-Old Boy of the Man
   Covered with Hair
   PRESENTED BY MRS. MARGRET SACHS

Text: *In the dream, there appears a man covered with hair, who suddenly comes up from the dark basement. He wants to seize the little boy and pull him down into the basement. The boy wakes up crying loudly in fear.*

Mrs. Sachs: The boy is five years old, at an age when first impressions are still very important, when fast developmental steps are made, but the personal world of consciousness is still very small and strongly under the influence of the collective unconscious, which is still close to consciousness.

A *man covered with hair* appears in the dream. Now, what could this mean to the child? Being an adult, this man is superior to the child. In addition, he is covered with hair. This man is something that induces fear and terror, of which one is afraid, reminiscent of a giant; we may think of *Rübezahl*, the bogeyman in the *Erzgebirge* [Ore Mountains] who carried children away in a sack. Here in Switzerland, this figure is known under the name of Böölima; in Flanders, he is called Biete Bouw; in Scandinavia, the kids are afraid of the troll, and in the United States of the "man in the woodpile."[1] In children's imaginations, he is always covered with hair and has a long beard.

In the imaginative world of primitives, too, hair and beard play an important role. In *The Golden Bough*, by James George Frazer, we read, among other references, about the significance of hair: the chiefs and magicians of the Masai, the African tribe, were afraid to lose their supernatural powers if they let their beards be cut; in many primitive cultures, hair and beard are considered "taboo." In order to become immune to danger, they are not cut at all. The Frankonian kings were not allowed, from childhood on, to cut their hair. Cutting the hair would have meant relinquishing the throne and the power. Hair is regarded as a sign of extraordinary power and magical strength. The young warriors of the Teutons cut their hair and beards only after having slain the enemy. Samson, too, was deprived of his power after Delilah had cut off his curls. Cut hairs are kept in sacred places such as temples, graveyards, or trees. In Swabia, cut hairs are hidden in a place where neither sun nor moon may shine. Frazer gives a multitude of examples, from the Tyrd in Scotland and Ireland, from Siam, North Germany, Melanesia, and Patagonia, from Tahiti, or from the Solomon Islands. Everywhere the guiding idea is that there is a sympathetic connection between the cut hair, symbolizing power, and its former bearer, and so it has to be hidden from hostile influence.

This dream is a parallel to another dream discussed earlier. There it said: "something gruesome came in through the window, no bear, a man, he had those feet and stood on the quilt . . . " At the time we put this figure in analogy to a bear. In our dream, too, we can put the man covered with hair in analogy to a *bear*, which plays a great role in children's imaginations. For thousands of years, our ancestors saw the bear as something threatening and dangerous, and it was one of the worst enemies. These impressions have been kept as such, and have an effect in the collective unconscious. There is a report about a belief in Scandinavian literature that very old bears had something

---

[1] This expression in English in the original (trans.).

105

devilish within them, and that they could not be killed with a normal shot, but only with a silver bullet. In this connection we have also to draw attention to the connection between the bear and the Berserker. The Bear Skinner[2] is a vague allusion to it. The notion of the soul is connected to the fur, the skin, the shirt, the outer form, for shirt (e.g., the swan shirt)[3] and fur stand for a great potential of transformation in the Teutonic tradition. Still today we use expressions such as *aus der Haut fahren*,[4] an allusion to the bear, the skin of the Berserker. The bearskin was taken off in the evening, when other people slept; it gave an enormous increase in strength, the respective person got beside himself with rage, a raging demon took possession of him. The heroic song of King Rolf Krake, from the Danish house of Skyoldung, tells of such a *berserkergang*.[5] In the werewolf legend, too, the pelt of the wolf gives enormous strength. Summarizing the amplification of the "man covered with hair," we get the following result: something children are afraid of, an uncanny and colossal power that can overwhelm you and make you so enraged as to lose consciousness; a magic force that overcomes you all of a sudden.

For every child, the dark *basement* is an uncanny place. If consciousness is mostly symbolized by a house, then the basement is the unconscious, the place where one loses consciousness, the dark where all those things happen of which we are afraid, and which we do not know yet. In the child's imagination all the gloomy, all the undreamed of and mysterious things happen there.

The dark is the place where we feel lonely, where bad dreams come from, and where danger lurks. We speak about the dark powers, the dark abyss. The Chthonic Forces rise out of the dark; the Chinese Ying is dark, it is the shadowy principle. Dark is the night, which devours and eats up the day; at night all things are made anew and are changed while we sleep.

---

[2] A fairy tale by the brothers Grimm, the title of Richard Wagner's first opera, and also the literal translation of *Berserker* (trans.).

[3] A shirt worn by the Valkyries, the servants of Odin. With its help they are able to turn into swans. They take it off only for bathing, and whoever can grab such a shirt will also possess the virgin (trans.).

[4] Literally, to leap out of one's skin = to hit the roof (trans.).

[5] Term for the Berserker's "going berserk" (trans.).

The man covered with hair seizes the little boy and wants to pull him down into the dark basement. He took possession of him, he let him feel his power. Here the dream breaks off with the cries of fear of the awakening boy. The dreamer is not yet overwhelmed completely, not yet deep down in the basement, but there is the danger of an inundation from below, the danger that he will be overwhelmed by a still unconscious instinctual state, by greed, passion, or desire. He is threatened by an uncontrollable instinctual force, stronger than he, which tears him into the dark and threatens to devour his small world of consciousness.

As we do not know more about the child, we can make only some vague assumptions. His being overwhelmed and pulled down into the dark womb of the house can be a danger for his psychical development. Without insinuating conscious sexual feelings in the five-year-old child, we may still perhaps assume that the dream anticipates a later emotional outbreak. The dream would then anticipate the future.

Professor Jung: I thank you for your paper. You have taken into account all the important aspects in your discussion of the dream. I have chosen this case because with its help we can discuss the various possibilities of working with a dream in the simplest form.

As we saw in the last session,[6] in most of the cases the dream is an unconscious reaction—albeit always in a different way—to a conscious situation. So we always have to take into account the symbolic context of the unconscious as well as the individual psychological situation of the dreamer.

Children still have a vivid memory of that archaic world; it was born with them. For this reason alone we cannot but notice the collective background of the dream. The ubiquitous archaic images, the archetypes, play a very important role in the infantile fantasy. That is why fairy tales in particular make such a strong impression, because they touch on a world related to them.

You have seen in the paper how we approach collective symbols. This method of treating a dream is not sufficient, however, if a prac-

---

[6] Cf. the introduction, and the session of 8 November 1938 (ed.).

tical decision becomes important. For practical treatment, it is useless to talk of archetypes and bearskins. We have to ask more specific
questions about the events of the previous day, and in general about
the whole *individual* situation the child is in. In this case, I do not
know the psychological situation of the child. We can try nevertheless to discuss the possibilities.

Suppose you know only the child's mother, who presents you with
the dream and tells you that the child is difficult. What would you
say? How much could you possibly see in the dream?

Participant: I would ask what the child had experienced the day before, and also, if he is fearful during the day, too.

Professor Jung: Yes, but this is not sufficient when it comes to the
practicalities.

Participant: Couldn't we interpret the man covered with hair as a
compensatory figure to the dreamer's conscious situation? In the paper
he was portrayed only as a danger. But perhaps he also points to something positive, which the child still lacks and which would have to
be accepted by him.

Professor Jung: This is a correct point of view. Is he a real danger
or, on the contrary, something to be accepted? If the latter is true—
what could we then say with regard to the child's consciousness?

Participant: It would be too "light," having too little relation to the
unconscious.

Participant: It would be too rational.

Professor Jung: Oh no, no, even with the "best" education, a four-
year-old child can't be rational!

Participant: It is educated too well.

Professor Jung: Yes, that's a possibility. It could actually be the case
that the child is too well educated. As a consequence, there comes
the Böölima, who is bad like an animal. He can do anything the boy
cannot in the house. In families where the children are too strictly
educated, it is as if they were some little devils. They then create the
nicest anxiety dreams. So the wild, hairy, black man may threateningly appear in an anxiety dream; but it's only the nasty tricks of the
child that he can't play in reality. A too-virtuous education causes
rebellion, and the children then play the wildest tricks.

Participant: Wouldn't the fact that the man covered with hair is an adult point into the *future* of the child?

Professor Jung: Yes, that's also a possibility. What would it then mean?

Participant: That the child is *too infantile*.

Professor Jung: Right. Children have to be infantile, because otherwise they wouldn't be children. But it may happen that a child is too infantile, for instance, when children were bedridden for a long time because of illness, and are weakened. Then they talk like little babies, cling to the mother—things they had already forgotten how to do. They fall into a regression, and then such an anxiety dream can occur. The dream is the natural reaction of their organism, which defends itself against the ridiculous infantilism. It is not a moral reaction, but a reaction of nature. When a seventy-year-old man thinks he could still accomplish the same as in younger years, nature will tell him, too, that he cannot—quite physiologically. When children regress under a certain level of infantilism, such figures as the threatening, wild man may appear, but this is already an indication of a serious regression. Here I would much rather assume that this is a well-mannered child who is too much under the influence of the mother. Some mothers always try to turn their sons into paragons of virtue, who are terribly nice and decent . . . , and then it happens to them of all people that their boys are complete rascals. That's how it has to be! It can also be the case, however, that the boy loves the mother, is very much attached to her, and does not want to cause her distress. Then what is in him cannot come out; if he waits too long, then it will "happen."

Participant: The Gilgamesh Epic is a good example of an education that is too good.

Professor Jung: Yes, there you have the animal man Enkidu or Eabani, who is supposed to pull Gilgamesh down, because he is the all-too-perfect son of the mother.

Participant: Don't we have to take into account both sides of the figure of the man covered with hair, the helpful and the dangerous sides?

Professor Jung: This double aspect is always there. Not only as a motive of the dream, but also regarding its effect. Such a dream can have a very destructive effect, because it contains the evil. When such a dream ends badly, we have an "anxiety child," who cries every night out of the fear that the dream might recur. On the other hand, a natural reaction is also possible. Something in the child can understand: this is "he"! It very much depends on whether the child has the right instinct or not. Equally in the adult: the instinct decides whether we understand the dream correctly or not. We then sense that something is about "so." When such a boy gets a bit older, he develops a certain pleasure in this hairy man and imagines all kinds of things he himself could do if he were like him. Half consciously, half unconsciously, he draws the right conclusions after all. Here we must trust nature. If the anxiety in the boy is reinforced, however, he is drawn into the wrong attitude, and only the destructive effect is intensified.

Participant: Couldn't the hairy, wild man also have something to do with the parents?

Professor Jung: A dream need not always be mysteriously related, by unconscious infections, with the parents. But this, too, is a possibility. It could be about an ongoing conflict in the parents' marriage, because the man covered with hair actually is the apeman, the primitive instinctual man. There could be a connection with the father, or also the mother, most often with only one of the two parents. As a rule, the situation in a marriage is such that the one sits in the warm nest and thinks that everything is all right. The one is completely protected and warm, just like in the womb or on the lap of the father. The other—outside—thinks, however: "This is quite nice, really ideal, if only there would be something that held me also!" It can be the father who sits on the sill and looks out of the window. In this case, it is there that the apeman is constellated, of whom he is afraid himself. Or it is the mother who dances around on the edge of the nest, while the father is sitting inside, smoking his pipe. So she dreams of a dreadful man of whom she is terribly afraid, while at the same time hoping he would break in sometime! In both cases, the apeman can enter into the little child. The more vital this is, the greater its effect. It is extremely important in education, therefore, for the parents to know what they are doing, to know their problems

110

and not to ignore them; otherwise, the children have to lead a life that is simply impossible. They are forced to do dreadful things, which are not in their nature at all, but have been taken over from the parents. Here we find really interesting phenomena. When we study the history of a family, and investigate the relations between parents and children, we can often see the red thread of fate. Sometimes there is more than *one* curse on the house of Atreus[7] in a family.

Participant: Before you rejected the experiences of the previous day. But perhaps such an experience did indeed trigger the dream situation? For example, I know of the case of a little girl who saw her father naked and then dreamed of it.

Professor Jung: In general, being naked does not make an impression on little children. But if a certain kind of education is at work, it can indeed make an impression on the children. I want to give you an example:

> When I was a little boy, between five and six years old, an old aunt took me to the museum to show me the stuffed animals. This interested me very much, and I took a long time. Then the bell rang; we had to leave. The aunt could no longer find the exit and came into the hall with the sculptures, with the statues of gods! She pulled me after her and said: "You naughty boy, close your eyes!" I didn't even think of it, because for the first time I saw pictures of gods, and I found them wonderful. That they were naked I only discovered because of the affect of my aunt.

I myself have seen my father naked more than once, and I was not traumatized by it. It all depends on what soil such an observation falls. When there is an overly satiated atmosphere, when the children are provoked and fed by unnatural blind affection, when the daughters slip around on their knees before the father, when the mother licks her son, but, on the other hand, everything is suppressed

---

[7] Atreus, the king of Mycenae, had a brother Thyestes who bitterly resented Atreus's kingship. Thyestes seduced his brother's wife, and in revenge, Atreus invited Thyestes to a "reconciliation dinner," during which Atreus served a stew whose main ingredient was the flesh of Thyestes' own sons. After Thyestes found out what Atreus had done, he pronounced a terrible curse on the house of Atreus—that generation after generation of family members would destroy one another (trans.).

by "education"—then we have the right breeding ground for neuroses. When the child *then* sees the father or mother naked, a trauma ensues. These natural things are never traumatic; otherwise, the whole of Africa would have a hell of a neurosis, but, of course, it wouldn't even dream of it.

2. Dream of a Six-Year-Old Girl of the Doll and the Monster[8]
PRESENTED BY DR. LILIANE FREY

Text: *When I first dreamed this dream, I was definitely not older than six. It recurred a couple of times when I was a young girl.*

I undressed the doll of my eldest sister and put it into the doll bed. On coming up again, the doll is sitting fully dressed in its chair. I undress it again and go downstairs. A moment later I go up again, curious what might have happened now. The doll is dressed again. Once again, I undress her and go down the stairs. But in turning around I'm seeing a monster that did that, and which is now following me on the stairs. The monster has a very big body, which completely fills up the staircase. It moves sluggishly and clumsily, with short, nearly invisible paws—meaty. I am terribly afraid.

Dr. Frey: We can divide the dream into the following four parts:

1. Locale: Place: playroom, stairs. Dramatis personae: child, monster.
2. Exposition: The child is playing with the doll of the eldest sister.
3. Peripateia: The game is thwarted three times.
4. Lysis: The child meets the monster.

The dream begins with the following sentence: "I undressed the doll of my eldest sister and put it into the doll bed."

What does the *doll* mean to the child? In the form of the *butterfly pupa*[9] it embodies the transitional stage between a crawling animal, closely nestling against the earth, and a winged one. In myths and in poetry the butterfly is often *the* symbol for the *psyche*. The soul soars up from the cocoon in the form of a butterfly. So we might say that the pupa/doll represents a transition between a primitive, earth-

---

[8] Session of 22 November 1938.
[9] The German *Puppe* is both "doll" and "pupa" (trans.).

bound stage and a freer, disembodied, winged, and elated one. We also speak, for instance, of "shedding the pupal skin of our heart"[10] to gain inner freedom. Dolls have also played a great role in the history of superstition: until the late Middle Ages, they were used to ward off evil spirits or as carriers of certain magical powers, and still today we find the mascot, a lucky magical doll. There are many examples in the most varied countries, how dolls are brought to life, and how spirits are laid by being forced to stay in them. In connection with the motif of bringing a doll to life, I would like to refer to the figure of the homunculus in Goethe's *Faust*. With the help of Mephistopheles, Wagner artificially creates the homunculus in a vial, an artificial little man without soul. The problem is how to fill him with soul and thus make him into a real human being. But the vial of the homunculus is smashed to pieces on Galatea's chariot and pours out into the sea waves, whereupon the homunculus rises again as a living man out of the waters of the unconscious.

But what does the doll in the girl's playroom mean? What does the doll mean to the child? It seems that the external form of the doll is not decisive in children's games. Aniela Jaffé has observed that children take a bottle of medicine or a piece of wood into bed and play with them as if these were the most beautiful dolls. Just like a primitive man, the child brings the doll to life with the images of her unconscious, and so animates, "en-souls," it. In the hands of the child, the doll is just a receptacle into which the internal potentialities are laid, and through which the child's world becomes alive. Quite generally, the doll/pupa is the receptacle, the cover, containing the child's psyche—the butterfly—as a present and future potentiality. In addition, for the little girl the game with the doll is also quite specifically a preliminary exercise of later biological functions.

The child plays with the doll of the *eldest sister*. The eldest sister or the eldest brother is a theme that appears again and again in fairy tales. The elder siblings are most often the much-admired, beautiful, proud, seemingly virtuous children, favored by father or mother. But they often fail precisely when the most difficult task has to be re-

---

[10] Original: daß man "die Puppenhaut seines Innern abstreift" (trans.).

solved, the treasure that is so difficult to attain has to be obtained, or the prince or princess has to be set free. Most of the time this is done by the youngest sibling.[11] In all these cases, the elder siblings stand for the more developed capabilities. They are mostly *examples* for the younger siblings. In our dream, too, there is probably this same relation between the dreamer and the eldest sister: she is the role model for the younger child.

In this part of the dream it further says that the dreamer is playing with the doll. What does that mean? It probably indicates that the dreamer tries to live her life, her future potentialities, the way her sister does—which will perforce drive her into one-sidedness and into a crippling of instinct. Moreover, it is a rule in the children's room to play with one's own doll, not with the sister's doll. Each child has her own doll, belonging to her and containing her own potential *in nuce*. The dreamer, however, plays with the sister's doll. This shows us that she does not stand by herself and her own potentialities, but rather she is trying to cope with reality in her elder sister's way. She copies her way of adaptation, behaves as she does toward the external world. The child probably feels that something is not right, because later on in the dream it says that she puts the doll into the bed. What does that mean? The dreamer is in danger of an identification with the sister. She sees her as her role model. That is why the sister's soul—the doll/pupa—has to be put to sleep. The sister's effect should be rendered ineffective. In this way the dreamer tries to get out of the state of adaptation to the sister. We will see if the attempt succeeds.

After undressing the doll the child goes downstairs. During her absence something inexplicable has happened, for the doll is dressed again and sits in its chair. This process is repeated three times. Each time her playing activity is reversed, made ineffective, during her absence. The child is shown that something about her attempts is wrong.

Let us go through the individual motifs: the *number three*, the motif of *above* and *below*, and the *thwarted game*. Thrice the game is interrupted, thus underlining the gravity of the motif. The appearance of

---

[11] Cf. the Grimm fairy tales "The Golden Bird" and "The Golden Goose" (ed.).

the three always has a fateful meaning. In the dream seminar of 1936/ 37, Professor Jung says: "When trinity appears"—the three Fates, or triads of gods—"this means that a fateful point has been reached, that something unavoidable will therefore happen." Here there is no simultaneous appearance of three figures, however, not the motif of the triad, but the *triple repetition* of the same process. We find this theme, for instance, in the triple repetition of the conjuration or in-vocation. Conjuring up the evil three times over is found in many legends. Goethe's *Faust* has to call out "Come in!" three times before Mephistopheles enters. We also find this motif in St. Peter's thrice-repeated denial of knowledge of Christ. "I tell thee, Peter, the cock shall not crow this day, before that thou shalt thrice deny that thou knowest me" (Luke 22, 34). Or a trial is repeated three times, as in the temptation of Christ by the devil. Doing the same thing three times is, so to speak, a magic to make something *effective*, and in many fairy tales it leads to the solution. Or it establishes the connection with the demonic. What is most important happens *afterward*: a des-tiny is set in motion, the connection with something transpersonal is established. We can also formulate the idea this way: *the number three triggers the number four*, causes something that should establish the wholeness of the person.

. . .[12]

In the present dream we can clearly see how the process being re-peated three times—the undressing of the doll and its being myste-riously dressed again—forcibly brings about the fourth process, set-ting in with all its might: the confrontation with the monster.

Besides the theme of the thrice-repeated process, another motif is important in that part of the dream, namely, the alternation of *above* and *below*. Each time after having undressed the doll, the child leaves the children's room to go downstairs. It is as if she cannot find rest anywhere. If she is above, she is forced downward, and the other way around: if she is below, she has to go up once again. Perhaps we may deduce that the child is insecure about the Above and the Below. This alternation of above and below shows the continued sinking of

---

[12] Ellipses in original edition (trans.).

the child into the collective mythical prehistoric world, into connectedness with the family, or into the mysterious depth of fantasy, into the world of emotions and of the body. At the same time, the dream shows the thrice-repeated attempt to free herself from this, to go upstairs and to gain a conscious attitude. The further dream text will show us whether the Above or the Below is "right."

The third motif is that of the *thwarted game*. Again and again the doll is sitting dressed in its chair. A foreign power forces its way into her game, intrudes, thwarts the goal of her attempts in the game. The child happens upon an unknown, powerful factor in her life, which prepares for a different direction of her play: the doll is to remain sitting dressed on its chair.

What does this mean for the child, this intrusion of a foreign, superior force into a personal sphere? The personal activity is made ineffective and included in a transpersonal process. Whenever this happens, the personal activity is too strongly directed against the original, natural inner destiny of the person, and his nature is oppressed. We have already assumed earlier that the dreamer is too dependent on others, and imitates too much the mode of her sister's adaptation. She tried to free herself by putting her sister's doll to sleep and thus reduce her sister's influence on her. In this context, the thwarting of the game means that this attempt is being stopped, and not accepted, by the unconscious. Her way will have to be a different one.

In the next part of the dream there are the following motifs: that of turning around and that of the monster. So when the child looks back, she sees a monster following her. In fairy tales and popular belief, *looking back* is always a dangerous thing to do, and strictly forbidden, therefore, in most cases. According to the Bible, Lot's wife becomes a pillar of salt because she cannot bear the terrible sight of what is behind her—Sodom and Gomorrha under a rain of fire and brimstone. On the other hand, *back* is also the fertile womb; the rocks that Deukalion and Pyrrha throw behind their shoulders turn into the first humans after the deluge. Probably, however, a very special inner situation of desperation and pressure is necessary to be able to

116

bear the sight. The child *has to* turn around. She has to see what follows her, she has to encounter her *shadow*.

It is also not without importance that the shadow blocks the way upward. The girl can no longer go up. She has to go down, into the dark womb of the unconscious. She will have to confront the foreign and the dangerous, precisely because anything that is split off from the girl, anything that is a "complex," and which is now threateningly personified in this monster and persecuting her—because all this, as Professor Jung explained in our next to last meeting, basically *wants to come to her* in order to become one with her, so that she can become whole.

Before we enter into the interpretation, I would like to quote some more parallels in mythology and literature. The first example coming to mind is the monster *behemoth* in the Book of Job. Job, who boasts of his virtuous life, who can say: "My foot hath held his steps, his way have I kept, and not declined" (Job 23:11), Job is humiliated by God and visited by the devil in the form of two monsters, the behemoth and the leviathan. The form of the monster [in the dream] is described as follows: it has a very big body, it moves sluggishly and clumsily, with short, nearly invisible paws. When we try to find an animal roughly fitting this description, the hippopotamus would come closest. As we shall see later, it often appears in connection with evil. Faust's poodle also takes on the form of a hippopotamus; it says:

> "It's no doglike shape I see!
> What a spectre I brought home!
> Like a hippo in the room"
> —*Faust* I, verses 1252ff

In view of the monster's form, particularly the heavy, meaty body, it is suggestive to think of those myths in which the "voracious maw of a fish" appears, for example, the myth of the whale described by Frobenius, or the myths of the dragon that the hero must kill to attain the treasure. The *Lamia*,[13] the terrible female ghost who fright-

---

[13] Lamia, daughter of Belos and Libye. When Zeus fell in love with her, she was driven into

117

ens children at night, steals them, and eats them, was originally also a voracious sea fish. Here we encounter the theme of the monster as the *terrible mother*, a symbol of *death*, which has to be overcome.

Now to the interpretation of the monster. As shown by the analogy with the behemoth, such monsters represent the wild, dreadful side of nature's abysses, the raw bestial nature of instinct. As the child is in danger of alienating herself from her nature, as she has lost her body, she has to descend again into these depths, has to encounter this monster in order to attain bodily consciousness. This bodily consciousness is attained from the instinctual sphere—after all, the monster is an animal. The child has to regress to a state that she has already experienced earlier. For we can only progress from a basis we know already. She should remember that she has a body that is hungry and that she should feed. This is the meaning of the meaty monster with the fat, rotund body, which grunts and gargles and roots through the mud. This disgusting animal has nevertheless a beneficial aspect insofar as it wants to unite the child with the split-off parts of her personality.

After all these explanations the meaning of the dream becomes clearer. This may not only be a dream that prepares the child for the erotic storms of puberty. In addition, the dream seems to indicate a problem of individuation, that is, it "is a process of *differentiation*, having for its goal the development of the individual personality."[14]

Professor Jung: Let us once again take a closer look at the basic motifs of this dream! First, the *eldest sister*. Simply because she is older, she is a model or an anticipation for the younger sister. The object of the game—the doll—is the playful preliminary exercise for the future. The little girl identifies with the doll that belongs to her sister, as if this image of the future, the creative anticipating fantasy of the sister, were her own. She sheds her own skin, so to speak, and projects herself into the eldest sister with all her vague wishes for the future.

---

a rage by Hera, in which she first devoured her own children, then all the children she could get hold of. In historical times, Greek mothers used to threaten their children with her story (ed.).

[14] C. G. Jung, *Psychological Types*, CW 6, § 773.

The dream begins with the dreamer undressing the doll and *putting it to bed*. What does this mean? Let us be totally naive, as we have to be in such cases. It is analogous to a mother putting her child to bed. Why does she do this?

Participant: To make the child sleep.

Professor Jung: Yes, that is also the intention of the little girl in the dream. The doll should sleep. Now what does that mean?

Participant: The anticipating activity of the sister should be put to sleep. It is thus rendered ineffective; it is a secret, somewhat malicious act against the sister.

Professor Jung: Exactly. How children play with dolls appears, so to speak, magical. It has an effect on the persons who stand in relation to these dolls. When the child puts to bed the doll of her eldest sister, she insults her. It is as if she sabotaged a favorite activity. She sort of tells the doll: "No more anticipating now. Just don't do anything. You sleep!" When the doll sleeps, the game between her and the sister stops! The eldest sister is paralyzed, so that she can take over her functions herself. We often see such acts of sabotage in children. For instance, they put on their father's hat and ruin it on occasion, or they smoke the father's pipe and let it fall!

What happens in the dream is that the little girl—after a short absence—finds the doll sitting dressed in the chair! An invisible monster has probably come, a cunning, crafty thing, which has taken possession of the doll and quickly dressed it again. Whatever it is, the child's prank is ineffective—the doll is being restored to the "status quo ante."[15] The little girl sinks again back into the unconscious state. She has gone up, has reached the level of her sister—and now everything is as it used to be. She had not only wanted to take something away from her sister, but also to achieve something for herself in this way, that is, to make the sister's anticipating fantasy her own.

She repeats the dressing and undressing three times. This motif of the *number three* has been quite correctly interpreted [by Mrs. Frey] as a fateful process with a magical effect.

As a matter of fact, the "three" is always dynamics, rhythm. The

[15] Latin, "the previous state" (trans.).

119

dynamism of the world in Hegel's philosophy is partly based on the *three phases* or the *three stages*. We also find this triad in the development of Goethe's *Faust*: the boy charioteer, the homunculus, and Euphorion. The *boy charioteer* is the *soul-guiding function*. Here we find the motif of "puer aeternus."[16] In his book *Reich ohne Raum*, Bruno Goetz gives an excellent description of this figure.[17] In it, he has anticipated a process in contemporary history in an interesting way. The figure of the "puer aeternus" is born, so to speak, directly out of the unconscious. The second figure in Goethe's triad is the homunculus. He, too, is an inner being, seen in a vision. This figure also appears in Hermetic philosophy. As you know, there is an idea in alchemy that one could create a wonderful being with godlike qualities in the phial through various procedures. One alchemist even calls this being "deus terrestris."[18] This is a metaphor for the inner experiences of the alchemist, who in his work experiences his own contents in the unknown matter. The main figure in Hermetic wisdom is Mercurius, the well-known Re-bis (who consists of two things).[19] He is also called hermaphrodite because of his male-female double nature, or "lapis philosophorum,"[20] or "lux moderna," that is, the modern light. In this latter sense he is viewed as "light of the lights," a well-known term in alchemy. The third figure in Goethe is Euphorion. He also is a son figure. He is the fiery spark created by the unification of the opposites of the male and female, an alchemical figure as well—volatile Mercurius. The fate of these "pueri aeterni" is remarkable. All three attempts to keep the fire-boy alive fail: the boy charioteer vanishes in the fireworks, the homunculus is smashed to pieces on Galatea's chariot, and Euphorion runs after the beautiful nymphs and goes up in flames. Precisely because of their doom, these figures are of importance to us as the devilish ambushes, into

[16] Latin, "the eternal boy"; a boyish or adolescent deity in antiquity, e.g., Attis, Adonis, Tammuz, the young Dionysus, Eros, and Mithras (ed.).

[17] Bruno Goetz, *Das Reich ohne Raum*. Cf. the edition of 1962 with a psychological commentary by Marie-Louise von Franz (ed.).

[18] Latin, "earth god, earthly god" (trans.).

[19] Representing sulphur and mercury after their conjunction, something double in characteristics (trans.).

[20] Latin, "philosopher's stone" (trans.).

which we run in such inner processes, become evident. This is particularly impressive in the case of the homunculus: he meets Galatea—and the process is already disturbed. "It" has burnt out in him, the lid did not stay on the pot, he is out of steam. In this respect, women are very dangerous for male intentions. A beautiful woman comes along—and he's gone in a second! There is a similar danger in women when they have to give birth to their inner child. But in their case this is less transparent than in men. How does the "puer aeternus" go to hell in her? Well, the danger is that she meets the "spirit"! By chance she reads a textbook or a newspaper article, written by a complete nonentity, but "it was written there," and the steam is gone. It says in alchemy: "Vas sit bene clausum, ut qui est intus, non evolet."[21] Well, three leads to *four*! It leads to a result. This is a process. This has already been said in the paper, and it is very important. What is the fourth form of the "puer aeternus"?

Participant: Faust himself in the "choir of the young boys."

Professor Jung: So this form is already beyond death. Faust has arrived in the timeless sphere. This is the fourth form resulting from the three attempts. Here, however, we won't go into that.

In our dream, the three leads to a, so to speak, catastrophic solution. Being a solution, however, it also has its positive side. How do you interpret the *monster*?

Participant: As a figure of the collective unconscious.

Professor Jung: In Egypt there exists such a monster, a goddess of the underworld, a devouring mother goddess—Tefnut. She is known for always being present in the scene of "weighing the heart"[22] in the Books of the Dead. She is always standing there. Should the heart of the dead person be found unworthy, she will eat it. As a consequence, the dead person is then given over to the chthonic underworld, the cooking pot of creation, to be dissolved. So the interpretation of the monster is quite correct. It is a *devouring mother*, a negative mother, who does not give birth, but devours the creatures herself. There is,

[21] Latin, "the container should be well closed, so that what is in it does not evaporate" (trans.).

[22] This expression in English in the original (trans.).

however, also a positive aspect to this devouring: maybe it is the preparation for a new birth.

How do you interpret the monster's appearance on the top of the stairs, and not below? Only when the dreamer goes down the stairs for the third time does she *turn back* and see the monster. This is fateful. The three has been fulfilled. Through the three stages comes the solution: there's an impact, and something new begins. Otherwise it would be incomprehensible why she could not see the monster already the first time. For the monster is actually the soul of the doll/ pupa in herself, the *primal being*, the dark abyss in man, which playfully creates life and creation. The whole creation is this great primal being's toy, playing with the doll of the elder as well as that of the younger sister. It is the unconscious that undresses and dresses the doll, and that is in the way when the child turns back, that is, when she does not look ahead, but back. Because at the back the sphere of the unconscious begins. The magical effect comes from behind; that is why the primitives have neck amulets, often hewn out of stone or wood, as a deterrence against the evil eye. These amulets have strangely rolled eyes: this is the evil eye with which the other's evil eye is fought, on the principle of "similia similibus."[23] So the danger zone is in one's back. In looking back the child gains a certain insight into the unconscious, and suddenly becomes aware of what is really at work here. She gets a terrible fright.

Participant: How would we have had to interpret it if the monster had come from below?

Professor Jung: If the monster had been below, the child in the dream would have fled upstairs. Then the family uterus would have been in danger. But in our dream she is invariably driven downstairs: "Don't go to the upper floor ever again, don't play there ever again!"

Participant: The child has made a mistake, and the unconscious reacts to this. Because she made the mistake at the top, the unconscious, too, appears there.

Professor Jung: Yes, wherever something happened that was not right, the hostile effect of the unconscious makes itself felt. If the

---

[23] Latin, "(to pay) like with like" (trans.).

child had played the "baby," had always been within the family, or had identified with the little dog, the monster would probably have come from below. But it comes from above, because the mistake was made there.

Participant: I notice that the monster is giving orders as if it were a *mother*.

Professor Jung: Yes, you could well say that. But what would be the matter with the real mother then, if we linked the monster with the mother? How would she have behaved in reality?

Participant: She would have held the child too tight and bound her to her.

Professor Jung: No, that wouldn't have been the case.

Participant: The mother would have looked after the child too little, and so the monster has to behave as the mother should have.

Professor Jung: Yes, the monster has to intervene to keep the child from such tricks.

The dream shows a typical process in the infantile soul that is so subtle, however, that the usual education does not notice it at all. The child lives the life of the elder sister. So she herself comes to a standstill in her development, and after some time becomes infantile. The "nicest" neuroses develop out of such habitual *identifications*. This can reach the point that people do not come to themselves at all; they cling to the ground to make sure to evade themselves.

Participant: Doesn't this repeated pull to the top point to a yearning, an attempt in the child to come to this upper level? But this attempt fails. Does this mean that it is the child's fate not to belong in that sphere at all, despite her efforts?

Professor Jung: That is a very good question. This situation is decisive for the child's soul. An identification is developing here that has to be stopped immediately. The unconscious, the independent, autonomous functioning of the psyche, stops this identification because it could become dangerous. It is stopped at the very beginning.

We can see no reason why this undertaking of the child would be harmful. We can only understand the whole scenario of the dream, if we draw the most extreme consequences out of the tendencies that are present here. If the child goes on identifying with the elder sis-

123

ter, she will soon find herself in the situation that she no longer lives her own life, but instead replaces it with the model of "elder sister." Her life will then become unoriginal. We can indeed slip into the skin of somebody else.[24] There are individuals who do not live their lives at all. They slip into the father or the mother, and then at the age of forty-five or fifty go to a doctor who is supposed to help them. Such cases are tragic and can end in catastrophe.

There is the most subtle, nearly inaudible allusion to that in this dream. Such early warning dreams appear because those identifications are so extremely dangerous. Consciousness knows nothing about such identifications, but nature does. Just as it reacts to a bodily infection, although consciousness is not aware of it, the unconscious reacts to such identifications. If you consider this point for a long time, you can draw highly interesting conclusions: Why, for instance, should it be dangerous at all not to live oneself? Why is nature interested in living itself?

It is an extremely typical infantile dream: the child identifies with the elder sister. She tries to free herself from this identification in putting the doll of the sister to bed. She believes she can paralyze her sister in this way, and regain her own creative activity. But this trick fails. We cannot solve psychic conflicts by acts of sabotage. The warning to get off the high horse and come down again is repeated three times. Here you see a mechanism at work that is driven as by clockwork: the triad is fulfilled, and then it happens. The child turns back and sees the monster. She has to take a look back and register the danger zone. What will result from this encounter with the devouring monster we do not know. The child awakens in fear.

3. Dream of a Six-Year-Old Girl of the Rainbow[25]
Presented by Dr. Emma Steiner

Text: *The dreamer says: "There was a beautiful rainbow, rising just in front of me. I climbed up on it until I came into heaven. From there I called down to my friend Marietta that she should also come up. But she hesitated so long until the rainbow disintegrated and I fell down."*

---

[24] Referring to the German expression "*in der Haut von jemandem stecken*" = to be in somebody's shoes (trans.).

[25] Session of 29 November 1938.

124

Dr. Steiner: First, let us structure the dream:

The locale shows a natural event: there was a beautiful rainbow, rising just in front of the girl.

The exposition indicates the event: the girl climbs up on the rainbow until she comes into heaven.

The peripateia, or the change, happens through her calling to her friend Marietta to come up too. But she hesitates to come, and the lysis comes: the rainbow disintegrates, and the girl falls down to the ground.

Let us move on to a broadening of the context, the amplification: the girl dreams of a beautiful *rainbow*. Our personal associations to "rainbow" are the following: the rainbow is a wonderful, oscillating bridge; it leads to a castle in the air and from there to the ground. So the rainbow is a symbol *linking heaven and earth*. This unification of heaven and earth suggests a link between above and below, between spirit and matter. Although the rainbow owes its existence to a pair of opposites, the coming together of rain and sunshine, it is at the same time also a symbol of harmony; for in its magnificent play of colors and its structure according to natural law it is a perfect reference to harmony.

Let us consult the interpretations that popular belief has made of the rainbow since ancient times. The rainbow as a colorful spectacle has always stimulated the fantasy of all peoples. The Old Testament sees in the rainbow a symbol of peace. God sealed his covenant with Noah after the Flood with a rainbow. Here we see again the connection between heaven and earth, between God and man.

According to the Christian view, the righteous and the chosen ones go on a rainbow to the Last Judgement, while the unrighteous fail in this attempt because the rainbow breaks down under them. The faithful see in the rainbow the *bridge* on which the Christ child and the angels float to earth.

According to an old gypsy belief, the man who finds the end of the rainbow at Whitsun can climb up on it and find eternal health up there.

In many instances, powers hostile to man are also ascribed to the rainbow. It pulls anything that comes near one of its ends. So it pulls

125

ashore the fishes, but also pulls little children into the air. An old legend from Transylvania says: A shepherd boy was very nosy. He would
have liked only too much to see how the rainbow attracts water. He
was punished by being pulled into the air himself, and now has to
tend the sheep in heaven for all eternity. Here the old wisdom is
brought to life that man should not tempt the natural powers, for
they are a matter of the gods.

Let us also consult those passages in *Traumsymbole des Individua-
tionsprozesses* [*Dream Symbols of the Individuation Process*][26] that describe the following visual impression: "A rainbow should be used as
a bridge. One should not cross it, however, but walk under it; for he
who walks on it will fall to death." Professor Jung comments: "Only
the gods can walk rainbow bridges in safety; mere mortals fall and
meet their deaths, for the rainbow bridge is only a lovely semblance
that spans the sky, and not a highway for human beings with bodies.
These must pass 'under it.' But water flows under bridges too, following its own gradient and seeking the lowest place." Popular belief
also ascribes magical powers to the rainbow. It is said that a hat
thrown over the rainbow will fall to earth filled with gold. Iron and
lead, thrown over the rainbow, will turn to gold. A girl younger than
seven who walks under the rainbow will turn into a boy.

In our dream, the rainbow is the connecting symbol of the bridge.
The girl climbs on it up to heaven. Heaven is not described in more
detail. For the child it is the epitome of the beautiful, a *castle in the
air*, something magnificent, something inexpressible. It is probably
also the fairy-tale fantasy world of this child. It is so beautiful up there
that the child is completely spellbound and cannot describe it because of its sheer magnificence. But she would like her friend Marietta to share in this magnificence. So she calls to her to come up, too.

The *friend* Marietta is probably not the physical friend of the child,
but the other side of the girl, a side she is even more unconscious of,
the *earthy reality*. Up until now we have learned quite enough about
the one side of the girl, that which longs to be in heaven, which
builds castles in the air, and paints fantasy forms, the side that she

[26] Also in C. G. Jung, *Psychology and Alchemy*, CW 12, §§ 44ff, 69, 70 (ed.).

126

symbolically relives in her walk over the rainbow. In this call to Marietta, her earth-bound friend, the girl's ego tries to pull the friend upward to an unreal world. For a moment, the updraft, the current of this unreal tendency, is stronger than the real world personified by Marietta, because it was precisely this updraft that has carried the girl up into heaven.

Let us return for a moment to the actual life situation of the girl, the situation before she had the dream. On the basis of the dream and the symbolical updraft of its unreal tendency we may assume that in the everyday life of the child, too, there is a (albeit unconscious) tension between her *fantasy world* and *reality*, which she calls Marietta in the dream. Such a tension at that age—the girl is six years old—may well be seen as a typical infantile situation. There are very many children who are exposed to these tensions between fantasy world and reality every day. The dream makes this tension acute, that is, a splitting occurs, a distancing from below, a walk over the rainbow, a distancing from Marietta, the reality. Here we could ask whether it would have been dangerous if the child had succeeded in pulling up Marietta, the reality. In any case, the child tries to undo the splitting by calling Marietta.

In the dream, however, a different solution occurs. The splitting is undone by the unconscious, the upward tendency of the unreal sphere diminishes, and earth and reality gain force. The rainbow vanishes through Marietta's steadfastness—she hesitates to follow suit into the illusory world—and the child falls to the ground, back to reality.

We do not know about the circumstances in the girl's life in more detail. The dream could be a *compensation* for an all too sober, uncomprehending environment. But it could also be a compensation for inner troubles of the child. I would like to view the rainbow dream as an illustration of a typical situation of a child. There are many children, probably those with a more intuitive disposition, who are, for this reason, very often exposed to such tensions between reality and the fantasy world, and who are looking for a discharge by way of dreams, such as happened in this rainbow dream.

Professor Jung: In the case of this dream, we are in the same situa-

127

tion as in the case of most dreams we are dealing with in this seminar: unfortunately, we know nothing about the personal causes of the
dream, for instance, about the events of the previous day. So we cannot say anything specific about the *motivation* of the dream. We
rather have to try to put ourselves in the typical situation of a six-
year-old child to find out the various possibilities of such motivations;
for we can notice that similar situations regularly produce similar motifs in dreams. This motif of an *ascent* to a *magic world* in particular
can be found in numerous children's dreams. So we may probably assume that here we are dealing with a particularly typical problem of
the infantile soul, as quite correctly indicated by Dr. Steiner. It is
really a typical children's dream, coming from a typical children's
situation.

Participant: It reminds me of a dream that we discussed in the
penultimate seminar, the dream of the boy flying to the virgins in an
airship.[27]

Professor Jung: Yes, it is the same theme. But we must not overlook
the fact that there is a rainbow in this dream, not an airship. The
rainbow connects heaven and earth; it is the place where heaven
touches the earth. In folklore we find that rainbow cups are found
where the rainbow touches the earth. The Gallic gold bracteates[28]
have been explained in this way. Here the rainbow is just the *bridge*
to an Above, set in opposition to a Below. Which psychological figure would correspond to this Below?

Participant: The *shadow*.

Professor Jung: Yes, it is the shadow. In psychology we call the
shadow the inferior figure, bound to the earth. It is just like the actual shadow that is always lying on the earth, too. The term *shadow*
should be taken literally, so to speak. The notion of the shadow was
taken directly from the psychology of the primitives. Earth and
shadow are identical for the primitives. It is the epitome of being
bound to earth, that which can never leave the earth. The shadow is

---

[27] See dream series of a boy, dream number 1, reprinted in the appendix (ed.).

[28] The gold bracteates (Latin, "bractea, a thin piece of metal") are flat, thin gold medallions or coins from the time of the migration of peoples; they show runes similar to the Roman
emperor medallions (trans.).

one of the most primitive definitions of the soul. When you hurt the shadow, you hurt the person; when, for instance, you step on the shadow, it is as if you gave the person in question a kick. The chief loses his mana when someone walks over his shadow. It is as if somebody had thrown himself at him and overcome him. The primitives have another peculiar notion of the shadow: in southern countries, noon is the witching hour. At noon the shadow is shortest, giving rise to the fear that it might disappear altogether. This would be uncanny, for then one would have lost the shadow, the connection to the earth; one has suffered a loss of soul.

The shadow is the second person. It is a personification of what follows behind us, what lies in the shadow of consciousness, and as a rule it also has—except for pathological cases—the meaning of earth. In our dream, Marietta is the actual, real friend of this little girl. For reasons unknown to us, she has to represent the earth shadow of the dreamer. It is actually not uncommon that friendships are formed in which one partner is the shadow of the other. A psychological structure is expressed in this. The language also refers to this, with expressions such as: he follows him like a shadow, he always runs after him. In the case of children, we can often observe that one is taller than the other. Or one is more stupid, the other more intelligent, one comes from a "special" family, and the like. And yet these are friendships! One of the two has, as it were, accepted the role of the follower, of the shadow.

In the dream the child tries to climb up from below, she climbs the rainbow bridge. How do we interpret this *ascent*? The speaker has quite correctly stated that the motive for walking over the rainbow bridge into a magnificent other world could be a certain deficiency in the environment, an all too rationalistic attitude in it. This path is not without danger. When the child gets lost in fantasy, she is in danger. In fact, children can really go too far into fantasy, and so be exposed to psychical dangers. It is possible, therefore, that the dream is based on such a thing. But I wouldn't like to attach too much importance to this, as this is certainly not the only possible motivation. There is a much more general reason for such an ascent.

Participant: The desire to go back, to the collective security.

Participant: So would this dream indicate a regression then? I know children who still at the age of ten have that attitude, who are happy when they are in caves and who build little houses.

Professor Jung: So do you mean that these are regressive fantasies? Are they really regressive fantasies? Is this dream a regressive dream? With this question we arrive at a very important but difficult problem. To begin with, in the "climbing of the rainbow bridge" a collective image finds expression. She repeats something that she could not yet have experienced in her own life. Because of such archetypal images, children can produce dreams the contents of which they can in no way have experienced. We can say that the child goes back to archaic ideas, to archetypal forms. In this respect the dream appears like a regression, but it is a "reculer pour mieux sauter."[29] True, she goes back, but only to climb up. The building of, and living in, caves by children have just been mentioned: if we interpret this phenomenon purely reductively, we will have to understand it as slipping into the maternal womb. But this slipping is also an isolation, effectively severing the child from his or her environment. It is an isolation of consciousness. In building a hut the child, so to speak, says: here we live. There are also games in which children draw borderlines on the ground: this is my land, this is your land! All these are personality boundaries; the participation with the environment is ended.

So the walk on the rainbow bridge does not indicate a regression, but a personality *development*, which happens only partially, however, as one part remains on the ground. Here we are touching a normal phenomenon, characteristic of this age. This is the age at which children go to school, and the first contact with the world takes place. The child is expected to adjust. How does the child achieve this adjustment?

Participant: With *consciousness*.

Professor Jung: Yes, the child has to learn to become conscious. For example, children have to know their names and addresses. That's what is expected in school. The children gradually learn that they are not in one big family, but that they are *this* child of *this* family.

---

[29] French, roughly "to go back to be able to jump higher" (trans.).

The child begins to differentiate the world in a different way than before, when there were only parents and servants and children, and perhaps also dogs and cats and cows. This becoming conscious is an elevation from below to above, an elevation from the dark into the light. But at the same time this also brings about a danger: whenever a decisive progress in consciousness occurs—not only in children, but also in adults—the danger of a *splitting* appears. When someone has a new thought, he simply gets carried away with it. He is hypnotized and loses consciousness of everything else. Everything else disappears from memory. This danger is greater in children because they are extraordinarily impressionable. Children can easily get into something to make an ascent upward. We can detect this danger of splitting in our dream. The ascent happens only partially, because another part of the personality remains in the shade. The shadow stays down below. The ascent is a kind of illusion that cannot be maintained for a long time. There appears a splitting between something too childlike, too primitive, on the one hand, and something already too adult, on the other. The children then often fall under the control of the fantasy and no longer achieve what they really should. As such phenomena of splitting can become very dangerous, the unconscious seeks to put a stop to this process by such dreams.

Dr. Steiner has quite rightly referred to that passage in the Eranos yearbook where a dreamer also wants to go over the rainbow bridge. This dreamer, in the work mentioned earlier, wanted to solve his problems beyond reality, in the heavenly "skull"—for that's what heaven really is—and in doing so has left his reality to its own devices. The dream shows him that the way does not go above, but down below! He has to stay on the earth with his shadow. This is the typical case of an intellectual, who believed he could somehow "think," or even un-think, his life. He seems to have thought he could switch it off, and then it would cease to exist. In our dream, too, there is a similar situation: the original splitting is done away with by the little dreamer's falling to the ground. The dream very clearly says: This does not exist! You have come back to earth again! This case wants to stop a *progress in consciousness* going too far, which would lead to a *loss of reality*.

131

The dream portrays the typical situation of a child. The child goes to school and has to learn to adjust to the world, and to free herself from participation with the environment. This happens through the development of consciousness—expressed in the dream through the ascent into the magical world. This brings about the danger of a splitting between presumption, on the one hand, and primitiveness, on the other. In the dream her friend Marietta, the inferior figure of the shadow, stays down below. The dangerous walk on the rainbow bridge is stopped—the dreamer falls down to the ground. Reality is brought back to the child in this way, and what had been separated is united again. In concluding, we can say that the dream aims at keeping consciousness and shadow together.

At a Later Meeting of the Seminar [6 December 1938]
Professor Jung: Last time we discussed the dream of a child who climbs on a rainbow to heaven, and then falls down again. As a supplement, Mr. Kadinsky will tell you about an analogous case.

Mr. Kadinsky: This is a dream of a feeble-minded fourteen-year-old boy:

> He dreams that he comes into heaven. St. Peter tells him he should go back to the earth. But he does not want to. So St. Peter turns him into a rabbit. Up until his eleventh year this boy could keep up well with the others in school. Then he was no longer able to follow; he was not promoted after the sixth grade. Later he no longer dreamed of going to heaven, but of climbing up to the North Pole. Recently his performance has become better again.

Professor Jung: Here, too, the performance at school gets poorer because the child distances himself too much from the earth. In both dreams the unconscious tries to stop this process. First the boy is turned into a rabbit—so his wings are clipped—and then the change occurs at the North Pole. What does the North Pole mean?

Participant: The North Pole is the point around which the earth revolves.

Professor Jung: Where does the North Pole, or the polestar, appear in mythology?

132

Participant: In Egypt, the polestar played a role in the construction of the pyramids. In the Cheops pyramid, for example, there was an exit on the northern side that, when its line was extended, pointed exactly to the polestar.

Professor Jung: Yes, and what does it say in the Mithraic liturgy?

Participant: Mithras appears as a fiery god, as an adolescent deity. In his right hand he swings a cow's shoulder.[30] This is the Great Bear, rotating around the North Pole.

Professor Jung: The cow's shoulder thus represents the connection with the Pole. With it, the god holds the whole sky and from there rotates the world. The Pole is therefore a very important symbol, something transcendent. It is the place where the world axis goes through, it is the *center of the world*. The boy's consciousness evidently knows nothing of this importance. When a boy dreams of being at the North Pole, he thinks of a mysterious place where nobody except a few adventurers or explorers go. In the unconscious, however, this is different: if someone dreams of going to the North Pole, then this is right. It is in accordance with the situation to dream of the North Pole.

As it is, the unconscious functions according to the archetypes. When it functions correctly, it could lead to the discovery of the world or to the reinvention of world history. It is not we who have those images, but they are within us, and we are shaped by them. These are preordained modes of functioning. The way it happens in us is how it happens in nature in general. An insect does by itself what it has to do after hatching. It is not welcomed by benevolent parents or midwives, and all the same it spins its threads correctly. It flies to the plant where it finds its food, and so on. It just does the right thing. Similarly, the mental functioning of human beings is not something that each individual has to learn anew for him- or herself. We do what our ancestors have always done. It is not the school that brings this about. On the contrary, we have to be careful that the school does not destroy the natural functioning of the psyche.

[30] Albrecht Dieterich, *Eine Mithraslithurgie*. Cf. Franz Cumont, *The Mysteries of Mithra* (ed.).

As we saw last time, the first school years bring about a couple of adjustment difficulties for the child. The process of the development of consciousness includes the danger that sometimes splitting phenomena between consciousness and the fantasy world occur. This manifests itself in children's being "in the air," unable to pay attention. They are really devoured by their intuitions. It is as if they had a leak through which everything leaks out. These two dreams of the boy also confirm what was explained in the last session: that flying upward, and floating in the air, are a danger. That is why the unconscious intervenes and tries to stop the process. It is incredible how fine the nose of the unconscious is! It produces dreams like that of the ascent on the rainbow, or it gives the child a clue in threatening to turn him into a rabbit. Or it compensates the child's attitude by the ascent to the North Pole. We could ask ourselves why the unconscious did not let this be followed by a warning in the form of falling down. This is because the archetype of the North Pole has a centering meaning. For it is, as we have seen, the center of the world, that is, of the unconscious, around which everything revolves. Our consciousness revolves around the unconscious, not the other way around. The center of a human being lies in the unconscious. It was an error of the nineteenth century to say: The center of the world is the ego. The ego is, so to speak, a clown acting as if it were the leading actor. At best it wants what happens anyway. And we are always talking about how we'd want this or were able to do that. But the conviction "The will can achieve anything" is merely a superstition of the ego. We want to see ourselves as having supernatural powers. We think we got unlimited freedom. But there's no question of that. Because we forget that again and again, and underestimate the unconscious, such dreams as that of going to the North Pole come up.

Participant: In the Talmud and in the Kabbalah there is a ban on looking at the rainbow, because it would lead to God. It would be an insult to God.

Professor Jung: The rainbow is a numinosum. It has a divine meaning, as it is an unusual vision. It is a bridge leading into the hereafter. It can also appear as a circle, as a halo around the sun or the moon. It contains all colors, which is a special motif. It means: all qualities.[31] Since prehistoric times, colors, as well as numbers, have had a sacred meaning. This has even been preserved in the Church colors. A certain dark yellow is the sacred color in Buddhism. In China yellow is the correct color, the color of heaven, of the emperor. Remnants of the original meaning of colors are also found in the paint of the primitives. Each color that is used for ritual paint also has a magical meaning. So it is little wonder that the rainbow has a magical meaning also in the Jewish religion.

Participant: In an African myth, the rainbow is a devouring animal. Where it touches the ground, its jaws devour many people.

Professor Jung: This corresponds to the primitive's fear of the mana. The mana is believed to have not only positive, but also deadly effects. As it is, the gods have effects for better and for worse.

4. Dream of a Four- to Five-Year-Old Boy of the Robbers' Den[32]
PRESENTED BY DR. HANS WESPI[33]

Text: *All of a sudden I was in a dark robbers' den that was lit only by a fire in a corner. A couple of figures sat around that fire. I especially noticed two robbers; one of them was very tall and strong, the other was a hop pole, thin as a rake, that laughed mischievously. I was hungry and asked for a piece of bread. The big one came toward me and scared me with curt words. Meanwhile the hop pole was slicing little pieces of clay off a big lump of clay that were given to me with a lazy smile. Both were standing beside me, until I had eaten the pieces of clay. I was really disgusted by it and woke up from it.*

Professor Jung: This dream was dreamed by a boy between four and five years old. This dream, too, was not told by the child, but remembered by the adult. As I mentioned in the first session, we are

---

[31] In alchemy, we often find the symbol of the *cauda pavonis*, the peacock's tail, instead of the rainbow. The colors, arranged in circles around the golden center of the tip of the peacock feather, are an image for the totality of all colors, as well as of all qualities, that is, totality. Cf. C. G. Jung, *Researches into the Phenomenology of the Self*, in CW 9, § 580, and CW 12, *Psychology and Alchemy*, fig. 111 (ed.).

[32] Cf. the session of 29 November 1938.

[33] Session of 6 December 1938. Dr. Wespi's paper is lost, except for the few passages worked into the seminar text (ed.).

dealing only with such dreams here. Childhood dreams still remembered by adults are not just any dreams, but have been preserved by memory because they completely contain human life in either longer or shorter periods. When we have a cursory glance at such a dream, at first we do not understand why it has been remembered. If we are able to trace it back, however, we can in most cases find clues as to why it has gained such importance. If things have made a deep impression on us in childhood, we may assume that something highly important lies within what impressed us as such, or that a very important event happened in the neighborhood of what we kept in our memory, something which is meaningful for the whole later course of life. There are such childhood memories: suddenly there is a smell of bread in the air, or of bread or milk, or the memory of a scene when the mother let a plate fall on the ground—all of them seemingly completely unimportant in themselves, but in whose proximity there are events or conditions that are very important for the later development of the child. If we cannot reconstruct these events with the help of the parents themselves, it is not always possible to verify them. Even then it is extremely difficult, because these are often things the parents do not want to remember. Also, often the parents cannot contribute anything because such dreams originate in a sphere of which they themselves are not aware. In the case of such material we have to realize right at the beginning that we are not able to tackle the dream with the usual means. As we have seen in one of the previous sessions, we have to use the ethno-psychological method with dreams that cannot be solved by personal questioning or personal amplification. Nature itself speaks in such dreams. The wisdom of the child is the wisdom of nature, and it needs the utmost cunning to follow nature. You know the saying: "Children and fools tell the truth." The truth is hard to understand, for the simple is difficult, and the simplest of all is the most difficult of all. You'll have to have studied all there is to study to reduce such a dream to a simple formula.

Let us now have a closer look at the basic motifs of the dream. There is a robbers' den into which the boy comes. A couple of figures sit around a fire. Two robbers in particular stand out, one of them very strong, the other thin as a rake. How would you comment on this?

Participant: This dream reminds me of another one, which we discussed in the seminar of 1935/36, the dream of the two giants who fished from a roof and fell into the water.[34]

Professor Jung: Yes, the analogy is suggestive. Where do you see the similarity?

Participant: We interpreted the dream of the two giants as an anticipation of being adult. The boy dreamed himself into being an adult. It was shown to him that one can fish something out of the unconscious—the value of being an adult—only if one falls into it oneself. Couldn't this also be the meaning of the eating of the clay? Perhaps the boy has to understand that he has to eat clay to become an adult.

Professor Jung: Yes, this is a substantial contribution. You have heard the suggestion to make an analogy between this dream and the dream of the two giants. It was assumed that the two giants could be *anticipations of being an adult*. This assumption is supported by the size of the two figures. Things have completely different dimensions for a child than for an adult. When you later come to a place where you were in your childhood, you will be surprised at the proportions of the whole environment which, as a child, seemed so much bigger. Buildings and streets, too, stretched into infinity for you as a child, but later you see that it's only a couple of steps. The same happens to the impression that adults make on children. They seem like giants to them. When a little boy dreams of a giant, one may therefore assume that he dreams of being an adult. Children generally look out into the future. This is quite regular. The grownup, too, thinks of the future much more often than of the past. Too much thinking back is neurotic. We don't like to swim against the tide, and if we do it, there are specific reasons for it. For a child, looking backward would be unnatural. On the contrary, children want to grow up as fast as possible. Boys want to have long trousers, and girls want to be young

[34] See dream series of a boy, dream number 6, reprinted in the appendix (ed.).

ladies. The boys play soldiers and think they are grown up. When you watch children play you can observe the strangest things, for instance, how enthusiastically they identify with adults. So we may safely interpret this dream as an anticipation.

Participant: Can we just explain these "giants" by the child's psychology alone? Maybe we should rather equate them with the giants of the Germanic god sagas?

Professor Jung: We cannot single out a *time period* in which these forms took shape. *They have always been there a priori!* We find them simply everywhere. In primitive tribes, in their typically childlike mental state, there are already differentiated concepts and images. So we would have to go back to a mythical prehistoric world in order to see how such forms came into being.

When we find these same ideas in a child, we cannot assume that this child invented them for the first time; they are already there. Sometimes they are there because the child has been told fairy tales. Fairy tales are easily absorbed by children. Perhaps this boy has been told fairy tales about giants. He gladly takes this in, because it gives him an expression for something that is already active in him. Children don't take in anything that does not exactly fit them. A great deal of ideas are simply rejected, because they do not fit, they do not mean anything to the child. This is why fairy tales are so important, to give the children concepts for contents that are in them. The witch, for instance, gives expression to specific psychical facts. The story of the stork is also much more in accordance with the infantile imaginary world than rationalistic enlightenment about where babies come from. The latter is often rejected and the story of the stork taken up again. Children do not believe in a birth by coincidence, happening on earth, but they believe that we are born in a magical way. These ideas are expressed in myths: the hero, for example, is a particularly fine specimen, and is never born in the usual way.[35] If this happens anyway, a second birth is assumed. The so-called birth chambers in Egyptian temples bear witness to this. Their walls dis-

---

[35] See C. G. Jung, *Symbols of Transformation*, CW 5, § 493, and Otto Rank, *The Myth of the Birth of the Hero* (ed.).

play events showing how the pharaoh, after being regularly conceived and born by Mr. X and Mrs. Y, is produced once again by the gods: divine coitus, divine pregnancy and birth are presented as evidence that the pharaoh was born twice, as a son of the gods. In primitive tribes, too, the young men have to know that they are spirits, or sons of the sun. Only then are they human beings. Before, as they say themselves, they are only animals. They absolutely need to give expression to these facts. It is just our rationalism that no longer understands these things, because we think we can live with rational ideas only. Well, you see how far things have come in the world when we want to live with sheer rationalism. Then people become crazy, because they have no expression for the things that move them. Just take a look once at how much ill persons suffer if they do not find expression for their inner contents, and how much it means to them when they find a mythical expression for them. This is a tremendous relief. We have to familiarize ourselves with the fact that there is a being within us that is not content with rationalism.

The boy in our dream, therefore, experiences the fantastic story that he falls into the hands of the giants—as if giants still existed! In the psychical world, however, giants do still exist. It is completely beside the point whether they really exist. Primitives are convinced of their existence, because they are within them!

We now have to ask how we should interpret the giants. Most obviously and most probably the giant is the adult, as we have seen.

Participant: Isn't it important that the two giants are a pair of *opposites*? In the other dream of the giants, if I remember correctly, they are completely alike.

Participant: But we have seen that this equation of two figures has a meaning; the meaning being to bring out this figure of the unconscious and to *perceive* it.

Professor Jung: You will often notice that certain motifs appear in *duality*, as two identical figures. This duality indicates that in fact we are dealing with *one*, which is still unconscious, however, for you cannot perceive something positive, if at the same time you do not distinguish it from something negative. These are coordinated apperceptions, comparable to a coordinated innervation. If you want to

139

stretch your arm, you will have to innervate the flexor, and when you perceive something, you will also always have to somehow negate what is perceived positively, that is, you will have to *distinguish*, to make distinctions: this or that; this is this, and that is his shadow. It is impossible to clearly perceive without making a certain criticism of the perceptions, otherwise you will immediately fuse once again with the whole environment. This is indicated in our language by certain terms for the process of realization, such as "to divide up," "to crystallize."[36] These terms contain a negation. In the process of realization, we try to separate what we actually want to make conscious from the knot; so, for instance, we say "No" to the knot as a whole, but take something specific out of it—and this will then become knowledge. Conscious perception is discrimination. Figures in the unconscious are distinguished from each other, therefore, when they reach the threshold of perceptibility, and then such a figure presents itself as two, but two completely identical figures, the one and the other, but this before it is clear which is the one and which the other.

Now the reason for this duality can—as in our dream—lie in the fact that the two figures are *different*; for example, Castor and Pollux: the one is mortal, the other immortal. Do you know other examples?

Participant: David and Goliath.

Participant: Jacob and Esau.

Professor Jung: In our dream there is a clear distinction between the two robbers; one is an athletically built giant, the other a thin, long hop pole equipped with a malicious mind. What do these two represent?

Participant: Raw strength on the one hand, and mischievous intellect on the other.

Professor Jung: And what is your opinion on that? What does this mean for the boy?

Participant: These are both qualities that he does not yet possess and that he experiences as something superior to him.

Professor Jung: Yes, these are both the world powers he has already

---

[36] In the original: *Abtrennen, Herausschälen*; literally: "to cut off, to scrape out." There are no exact equivalents in English for their figurative use in German (trans.).

experienced. The force he experiences through the father, and he can trick his mother out of something with a ruse. The two figures represent ruse and power. The thin one is something like the devil, but a very intelligent devil who knows *how* it has to be done, who understands life. The thin one gives him the clay to eat!

At a Later Meeting of the Seminar (13 December 1938)
Professor Jung: Last time we saw that the two robbers represent the two world powers of ruse and power. In mythology there are many examples of this pair of opposites.

Participant: In Greek mythology there are many such pairs. I am thinking above all of the various relations of Odysseus with violent persons. He always represents the cunning one. Ajax and Odysseus, Agamemnon and Odysseus, Diomedes and Odysseus are such pairs. The strong one always commits a heinous crime, and the cunning one is always the one to find out. Odysseus is the typical cunning one. In all cases he meets a violent comrade. After they had been in the underworld and had achieved what they wanted, they fell out with each other again. The same happens with Theseus and Pirithous. The strong one is the victim, and stays in the underworld. The crafty one comes up.

Professor Jung: The strong one remains attached to the rock. With all his strength, he is eventually taken in after all. This short overview shows you that the idea of power, on the one hand, and ruse, on the other, are archetypal ideas that are already found everywhere. These pairs of opposites are also found in primitive tribes. What is remarkable in that respect?

Participant: The contrast between the *chief* and the *medicine man*. The chief is the executive power, and the medicine man is the shrewd one.

Professor Jung: In the life of a primitive tribe, these two personalities are really the decisive authorities. The chief is violent; he is the strongest man of the tribe. The moment he is no longer strong, he is killed on the spot. In the New Testament there is also an example of the slaying of the former king: Christ is sacrificed, and Barabbas is set free. This referred to an old custom, namely, that a criminal was al-

141

lowed, on a certain day of the year, to freely walk around the town. He could rob everything—provided that he was not caught after sunset, in which case he was killed. He was a king, and had royal power. This custom stemmed from the fact that the king has absolute authority as long as he is in power. The moment he shows a slight weakness, he is finished. Another example is the Nordic kings. They were allowed to rule as long as the harvests were good. If the harvest was bad, however, they were killed, because in that case they had not fertilized the country well. It was uncomfortable to have been king of the primitives. The counterpart of the powerful man is the medicine man; most often he is the intelligent one of the tribe. I myself was able to notice that either he is the crazy one of the tribe, or a man of superior shrewdness, simply more intelligent than the others, or dangerous because of his cunning. He has contact with the spirits and receives their revelations. He can even rule the tribe, over the chief's head, through divine revelation.

> There is a wonderful example in the book of Rasmussen[37] on the Polar Eskimos: There is a story told about a medicine man who, when his tribe suffered great hardship because of a lack of food, had a vision of a land offering food. He persuaded his tribe to go with him over the ice of Baffin Bay. They came to the shores of North America, where they found plenty of food. One half of the tribe turned back before that, and perished. The other half went with him, and was able to be saved by him. He had the inner certainty of a sleepwalker, with the help of which he led his people to the right place.

This is what the medicine man can do. It need not always be cunning; the idea that will save the situation can also come from the heart, as in this case. The prophets in the Old Testament also were such medicine men. There often is a conflict between the chief and the medicine man. The chief is often afraid of the medicine man. I have experienced such a situation myself. A chief wanted to tell me something about the medicine man. Out of fear he took me into the bush with him and posted sentinels. He only whispered—when I

---

[37] Knut Rasmussen, *Neue Menschen: Ein Jahr bei den Nachbarn des Nordpols.*

asked him why he talked in such a low voice, he answered: "If the medicine man knew, he would poison me at once."

In our dream this archetypal contrast, which shows its effect in the life of the adult, is anticipated. The little boy is able to dream the contrast because he too has these two possibilities within himself, as archetypal images. This even dawns on him already, because the contrast has come within the scope of his perception. Let us look further at the dream. What do you have to say?

Participant: I would start with the fact that the robbers are in a cave. Could this perhaps be interpreted by way of the boy's still being in the uterus, in the bosom of the family?

Professor Jung: The cave is not the uterus. In addition, it is quite normal that a boy of five years is still feeling secure in the bosom of the family. In the dream, the boy is *coming* into the cave, he is not already there. He came there on his nightly travels, and now he suddenly finds himself in this dark place with the robbers. He unexpectedly falls into the hands of *evil*, just like in the fairy tales, for example, in "Little Red Riding Hood," who is eaten up by the wolf, or in the tale of "Hansel and Gretel," who both are captured by the witch.

This evil, however, has got a fire in its center! What is your opinion of the fact that a *fire* is burning in the middle of the cave?

Participant: I would say that these two robbers hold the Promethean fire for the boy.

Professor Jung: I would not immediately rule out this possibility. The fire is always a *center of life*, a place where it is warm and light, a place where people gather. In this sense it has a positive meaning. Going back to the original importance of the fire, we can see that the fire is a benevolent power, of greatest importance to primitive man. You'll have to experience that yourselves, what it means to come to a wretched place in the dark, wet and cold, not knowing where you are, feeling that anything could happen now—and then a fire is made! At once people gather round the fire. You can warm yourselves up, cook something—then you will feel at home even in the wildest wilderness, and feel safe and secure. So the fire is something positive: it is what gives shelter, provides a home for the stranger, it is the sacred home.[38] The fire also has an incredibly high capacity to ward off disaster, not only with regard to evil spirits, but also regarding wild animals. When you stay overnight in a place where lions roam, it is very disagreeable to go to bed; but when you light a lamp, you will feel secure at once. When you are in the bush and sit by the fire, a leopard can come very close—but it is alright, for you are in the *fire circle*.

I would lean toward the assumption that in this dream, too, the fire has a positive meaning and stands for a center of life. The cave is the closed-off place to which the boy came by coincidence. There the secret fire is found, by which the giants sit. This is the representation of a thought that could be put into words as follows: in the dark depths of my unconscious I am finding those figures of the *future*, the great conditioning powers, in the light of the *fire*, around which people gather, and where they find *shelter* and *food*.

In the dream, the two robbers sitting round the fire try to make the boy accept *clay* instead of bread, which he had originally demanded. Admittedly, this is a highly strange idea. Eating clay, as such, is not unheard of. When still very little, the boy had perhaps also put dirt into his mouth, or eaten earth. Under which circumstances is clay also eaten?

Participant: During famines.

Professor Jung: Yes, very rich, fine clay was eaten during famines. During the Thirty Years' War, peasants were known to eat clay, to get a feeling of satiety in their stomachs and to suppress the agonizing feeling of hunger. So it does happen that clay is eaten in extreme distress. But how can it happen to such a boy to eat clay? This must have a special meaning.

Well, you have heard from Dr. Wespi that clay and earth are the *food of the underworld*.

> Excerpt from the paper: What is of special importance to us is the tradition that clay was the food of the inhabitants of the Babylonian-Sumerian underworld. In the Epic of Gilgamesh, too, it is said of the dead: "Dust of the earth is their food, and clay their meal."

[38] Original: *der heilige Herd*, literally: "the sacred stove." Here in the sense of *heimischer Herd* = by one's own hearth (trans.).

In Babylonian texts we find the idea that the dead eat their own excrement; the dead have to eat the heavy, indigestible clay. You will find the corresponding notion in the Epic of Gilgamesh: just as the earth eats up the dead, the dead now have to eat earth, too. The dead eat earth like a sarcophagus. They have to get the earth into themselves, for earth they will become. The corpses will become earth, the flesh will become earth. What comes from the earth will become earth again. This is the familiar idea from the Holy Scripture: "for dust thou art, and unto dust shalt thou return."[39] There is another passage in the Bible where there is an analogy to eating clay.

Participant: In Genesis, where God curses the serpent: it will have to crawl on its belly and eat dust.[40]

Professor Jung: Do you know yet another parallel to the eating of clay?

Participant: In *Faust* it says:

> "He'll eat the dust, and with an art,
> Like the snake my mother, known for sinning."[41]

Professor Jung: Yes, who says this?

Participant: The devil in the Prologue in Heaven. He also mentions it in the talk with the student who waits for Faust:

> "Just follow the ancient text, and my mother the snake, too:
> And then your likeness to God will surely frighten you!"[42]

Professor Jung: Yes, these are crucial passages. The dust that has to be eaten undoubtedly refers to the earth. In a figurative sense, the dust means: the worldly food, which has to be eaten by man who was born a spirit. So at which conclusion would we arrive as far as our dream is concerned?

Participant: The wish for a piece of bread is expressed by the little boy; he wants to have his food as he is accustomed, as he received it

---

[39] Genesis 3:19 (trans.).

[40] "Upon thy belly shalt thou go, and dust shalt thou eat all the days of thy life" (Genesis 3:14) (trans.).

[41] J. W. Goethe, *Faust 1*, "Prologue in Heaven" (ed.).

[42] Ibid., "The Study II" (ed.).

145

as a child from the mother. But this is a wish that is not granted as such. It is an infantile wish.

Professor Jung: Which is the infantile wish?

Participant: The wish to be comfortably cared for.

Professor Jung: So you would see it as a regressive factor. As we have just seen, however, the fire indicates a nourishing situation, building up one's strength. Seeing the fire, the thought of eating strikes the boy: now there's food. One gets hungry just smelling the smoke. The boy wants bread, which is normal, but it's clay he gets. This is what is new, this is why he has the dream in the first place.

Participant: We have seen that clay is also the food of the dead. Couldn't we conclude from this fact that the dream has a regressive meaning? The clay would then be the food that corresponds to a state before birth.

Professor Jung: You have to be aware of the mental state of the child. The giants are the adults. They force him, his anticipations force him, to grow up into this world. This is done through eating clay. He is forced to eat earth. If he does not do that, he will not grow up. This is no regression.

Participant: Any regression aside, doesn't eating clay in reality come before eating bread?

Professor Jung: Think of certain sayings, such as: "He can do more than just eat bread,"[43] or "Here you've gotta do more than eat bread." This implies the thought that eating bread is a very simple matter, and that there is still another way of eating that is considerably more difficult. How is this expressed in history? Where does eating bread symbolically stand for that other way of eating?

Participant: The host is such a symbol.

Professor Jung: Yes, for many it does not mean anything today, it has become worn out and trite, but originally it was a symbol full of life. In former times such meals were dark mysteries. The totem meals of the primitives also belong here; they often are cannibalistic. An enemy is slain and eaten up.

---

[43] "Der kann mehr als Brot essen," German saying (trans.).

The cousins Sarasin,[44] who explored Celebes, report: A captive is tied to a column in the house of the spirits, then all the men of the tribe come, stab him in the skin, and lick the blood from the knife or the spear.

This is a mysterious, ritual sharing of blood. Eating bread is human. The other way of eating is no longer human, it is a mystery. That is why these meals are taboo. The same is true in the Catholic Church: you must not touch the host. When it is dropped to the ground, a sacrilege has occurred.

A Spanish Jesuit in the seventeenth century reports the following case: A *donna* came to church with a little lapdog. When the priest offered her the host, the dog snatched the host away from her. The church was closed; the case was brought before the Holy Inquisition. The women got off with a fine of two hundred Dubloons. The dog was confiscated and consigned to death by fire because of its obscene, blasphemous behavior.

Here you see the taboo surrounding the holy meal. This is the other, the very dangerous meal, which is more than just eating bread.

So this is the way I would view the eating of the clay. I think it has become clear to you why I do not consider this dream a regressive one, but a simple anticipation of what is to come. We have to take an even closer look, however, at the *symbol of eating clay*. We have seen that the symbolic meal is more than the everyday one. This is about absorbing something strange and different, about incorporating the other being. What does this mean for this five-year-old boy? What does he have to take in, when he is forced to eat clay?

Participant: Up until then he got bread to eat. Now something else is offered to him—heavy clay. Apparently, this is the *hardly digestible reality* as such, an allegory of reality, which has to be eaten by him.

Professor Jung: That's it. He who eats the heavy clay will become heavy himself. This pulls one down to earth. Because earth food is

---

[44] The Swiss researchers Fritz (1859–1942) and Paul Sarasin (1856–1929; founder of nature conservation in Switzerland), who explored Ceylon, Celebes, New Caledonia, and Thailand (ed.).

the food of the underworld, we become mortal. The idea of *eating the world* is also found in the Yoga Sutras of Patanjali.[45] The world is eaten, one has to swallow the world as it is.

Viewed from this broad horizon, it is no longer surprising that the boy dreams of this. He is between four and five years old; he will soon go to school, at least to nursery school. This world is earthly, heavy, and will pull him down. And this world he has to eat. He does not want to. Why not? Shouldn't one expect a child to desire the world? Why does he have a resistance? And why of all things should it be shown to him by the dream that it is disgusting to eat earth? Here we are confronted with the strange fact that this dream can be reduced to and summarized by the nearly edifying formula: It is hard to accept this earth. You really have to eat dust, it is disgusting. Where does this idea come from? This is not just a concept like any other, but an *archetypal* concept. It is the idea that gives expression to all the revulsion the child feels toward matter.

Participant: Perhaps because of a certain intellectual milieu, an ascetic-Christian milieu, for instance?

Professor Jung: But couldn't others, too, have this dream? Christianity no longer has such influence, otherwise the theologians wouldn't have to make such an effort.

Participant: Adam and Eve already shied away from worldly reality.

Professor Jung: Yes, they nearly stayed in heavenly paradise. But Eve gave the apple to Adam, the world, that is, and seduced him into eating it. Imagine the world of this little boy. He comes into the world of the adults. This is a mystery for the child. It is a robbers' den. You do not know what happens there. There is something fishy about it. Then these devilish powers force you to eat earth. But what is the resistance of the child based on? Let us assume that this is not merely something subjective, but a worldwide affair.

Participant: Everybody resists accepting something negative.

Professor Jung: That's it exactly. We are fooled: "Life is beautiful. When you are married, everything is just fine. You have a job that of

---

[45] *Patanjali-Yoga-Sutra.* Yoganga-Text, chap. 3, p. 35; in Jakob Wilhelm Hauer, *Der Yoga als Heilsweg*, p. 108.

course is fulfilling, and those lovely little kiddies . . . " But why, why have people been fooled that marriage is the happiest of all states? Precisely because life is extremely difficult. The boy, too, was offered a lopsided image, but he realized what bullshit he was told. It says in the dream, therefore: "You'll have to swallow that dirt!" Why can't we just accept it as natural that there is pleasure and pain, dark and light, day and night? Where does such a little boy come from?

Participant: From an environment in which up to now he could take the liberty of doing as he pleased.

Professor Jung: First of all, he comes from a milieu of lavish care and attention, surrounded by caring and concerned parents, nurses, aunts, doctors, and grandmothers. And now the world is coming onto him, and this is revolting. You can observe this disgust everywhere. Everything smells right in one's own family, but other people smell wrong, they are unappetizing and you cannot trust them. The idea here is: "We are right, but those over there, they are terrible and disgusting, we can't have anything to do with them." We have revolting images of everything foreign in general. What is foreign is either fascinating or disgusting. Children feel a distinct revulsion against anything foreign—the world, that is. But now they are entering into it, getting in touch with all those strange children. Just have a look at the children, at how shy and frightened they are of strangers! And why? Because the strange is uncanny, it is repulsive. They do not accept anything from a stranger, exactly because of this feeling. Only after they have seen through the trick will this change. At first everything is disgusting, and so the child, from his sheltered and cared-for position, in which he experiences nothing but pleasure, has a resistance against the strange life now appearing.

This is where the archetypal symbols appear. These are helpful images that may orient us about the further development. A dream may, for instance, announce a difficult situation in the following way: "There are rocks over there, you have to be careful there, they are just closing in behind you, but luckily you are through!"[46] The fire

---

[46] Jung is referring here to the motif of the clashing rocks in the legend of Jason and the Argonauts (ed.).

can also be such a helpful archetype. Then we maybe dream: "You come into a desolate situation, into despair and loneliness. With the help of the fire, however, you are able to ward off any danger, you can fight the great danger. You are consumed by desolation; but then you are making a fire in the dragon's body, the dragon's body croaks, there is a hole in its side. You walk out again and take with you all it has eaten up!"[47] Such motifs always appear when we are facing a difficult transition. These images help us to achieve deeds of courage, which otherwise we would never have been able to accomplish.

> A clear example of such an archetypal influence is the murder of King Albrecht.[48] Parricida could already have killed him before. But only when they were riding into the ford did he summon his courage: "Why should we let ride this *Chaib* in front of us any longer" (a *Chaib* is horse carrion), and he drew his sword and killed King Albrecht.

"In the ford" is the archetypal situation in which the murder can be done, in which great danger is threatening and can be overcome. The archetypal is a powerful emotion brought into its original form. When someone is able to perform the art of touching on the archetypal, he can play on the souls of people like on the strings of a piano.

In this dream too, then, helpful images appear: the whole dream unfolds in the light of the warming fire. In it the boy sees the two gigantic figures, the two governing forces of his future, ruse and power. These devilish powers approach him, the foreign, repulsive world wants to pull him down. He is forced to eat clay. He does this with great disgust, but he does do it: he swallows the barely digestible reality, into which he is growing. He masters the dangers, the evil can't harm him, for he is in the fire circle!

In concluding, we can say that the dream is an *adhortatio*,[49] that is, a preview of the world now unfolding, which approaches the boy and which he has to swallow in God's name.

---

[47] Allusion to the theme of the night sea journey, e.g., Jonah's journey in the belly of the huge fish (ed.).

[48] The murder in 1308 of King Albrecht I, when crossing the river Reuß, by his nephew Johann Parricida (1290–1313) (trans.).

[49] Latin, "warning, encouragement" (trans.).

150

5. Dream of a Five-Year-Old Girl of the Death Masks
of Her Parents[50]
PRESENTED BY DR. NOTHMANN[51]

Text: *In the first dream I heard my father call. When I got up and went into the sleeping room of my parents, I saw a pyramid made of ash above each bed, and above each of those the death masks of father and mother.*

In the second dream I was standing in a desolate place full of craters. Far away, too far to reach, my father was standing in one of these craters and called for help.

Dr. Nothmann: To begin with, we will treat these dreams—on which I worked with the assistance of Mrs. Adler and Mr. Kadinsky—according to Professor Jung's schema, to be able to enter into their special characteristics afterward. The characters in the first dream are the father and the dreamer; the locale is the parental sleeping room. The plot (exposition) consists in the call from the father, its thickening occurs when the dreamer enters the parental sleeping room and visually perceives the situation in it (climax). No lysis follows after this visual apperception. The symbols are the sleeping room, the beds of father and mother, two pyramids of ashes, and four death masks of father and mother.

Because of the symbols used alone, the atmosphere in the dream is impressive and gloomy. But the way they are positioned in the room, too, exerts a strong influence. When we try to schematically draw the dream image, we see a threefold structure in the vertical line: bed, pyramid, and death mask. The effect of the powerful symbolic language is increased by the lack of an actual lysis. Something very gloomy has happened to the dreamer, but she remains untouched and inactive, although some reaction to the father's call would be appropriate, a stirring of emotion, and an effort to do something.

Father and dreamer are also the "actors" in the second dream. The mother, portrayed in the first dream by the bed and the death mask, is here symbolized by the crater. Again the father calls, but the in-

---

[50] Session of 17 January 1939.

[51] The paper by Dr. Nothmann is reproduced in a slightly condensed version. Cuts have been marked by suspension points in square brackets (ed.).

tensity of the call is heightened to a call for help. The closeness between father and dreamer of the first dream is gone; there is an infinite distance between them. The dreamer has stepped out of her home into the world, into a desolate world full of scattered craters, in which almost nothing living remains. Indifferently she is standing in it; and what the dream compels the dreamer to do—to come to the help of the father—she does not do, for the deed seems impossible, the distance too insurmountable, to her.

After this short sketch let us go into a discussion of the dream symbols in the first dream.

The *father* symbolizes the procreative, form-giving figure. He is the spiritual principle that gives meaning. He is the one who leads the child [. . .] into life. It is the father who, as *pater familias*, rules and leads the house, as pope the community of the faithful, as *pater patriae* the country and his people, and, finally, as God the Father the world. But there is also a destructive and misleading counterpart corresponding to this procreative and guiding father principle. This is the case when the child does not succeed in cutting, at the right time, the spiritual ties linking her to the father and overcoming him. Then it may happen that someone does not live her or his own life, but that of the father. Negative qualities, in addition to procreative and guiding ones, are often ascribed to God the Father. The daily Jewish prayer portrays Jehovah as the one who gives life and who kills. [. . .]

Following the call of the father, the dreamer enters the *sleeping room* of the parents, the place where the child is born and spends, still in complete identity with the parents, the first years of life. The child is called into this room; here is the nightly resting-place of the parents. The dreamer sees the beds of her parents. These are the symbol for sleep, that is, unconsciousness. The bed is not only the place where the child was conceived, however, but also the place where the parents will die; it is thus the allegory of the eternal cycle as such.

Then the dreamer sees the *pyramids*. The symbol of the pyramid we are most familiar with is that in the Egyptian cultural environment and in China. In Egypt, the pyramids even give a great historical epoch its name, the Age of the Pyramids. The pyramids are burial sites, tombs of the kings. For the ancient Egyptians, however, the king was much more than merely a real figure of social life, more than a representative of foreign and domestic politics; he stands in a special relation with the gods. He is of divine origin, successor to the god Re, who, having grown old and tired, had retired to heaven and given over the reign to the kings on earth. Frequently the name of the god Atum or Horus was added to his own, and he is often directly referred to as the sun. After death he becomes a god again, namely, Osiris. There is a spatial connection between his tomb, the pyramid, and the temple in which the god is worshipped; the former is even sometimes directly addressed as Osiris. The pyramid [. . .] is entirely based on the Egyptians' ideas on life after death: man is composed of at least three parts, the body, the soul (Ba), and the Ka, a being of its own, for whom it is hard to find a translation.[52] After death follows the resurrection. It can take place only if the form of the deceased's body has been preserved by embalming. Ba, the soul, often rendered as a bird, has to be able to visit the embalmed body; its way goes through the tomb shaft, situated in the pyramid. After death, the pyramid itself serves as a home for Ka. Obviously, Ka is the most important element, an independent spiritual being who has his home in the living individual, guides him through the entire course of life, and after death continues the life, which the deceased began here on earth, in the grave. Ka is supplied in the pyramid tombs, therefore, with all the household things that are necessary for his housekeeping after death: food and drink, personal objects, weapons, rouge-pots, mirrors, and so on, even the domestic servants who do the housekeeping for him.

For the resurrection it is also necessary that there is a portraitlike mask of the deceased in the grave. It is either laid over the face of the corpse or is displayed, in the form of a sculpture or picture, in a special place in the burial chamber. [. . .] In the Cheops Pyramid, as well as in the grave of Osiris in Abydos, another characteristic of the resurrection is stressed as important: the burial chamber is subterraneously connected to the Nile by special channels, through which

---

[52] See Adolf Erman, A Handbook of Egyptian Religion, or Die Religion der Ägypter, ihr Werden und Vergehen in Jahrtausenden, or Ägypten und ägyptisches Leben im Altertum (ed.).

the fertilizing water of the Nile can find its way into the burial chamber in times of inundation. [. . .]

In China, the second cultural environment in which pyramid tombs were erected, the idea of resurrection is symbolically expressed by the choice of the grave site. It is situated between the mountain and the valley, between heaven and earth, in the Fengshui—that is, in the most favorable geomantic position, where the sun and the south wind can reach it—and among trees, at the roots of which water pours out of the ground. In all ethnicities building pyramids as burial sites, there exists, according to Baumann, the idea that the process of physical centering is preceded by destruction, only after which can the new emerge in durable forms.

So we are able to deduce death and resurrection, the destruction of the one personality and the building of a new one, from the symbol of the old pyramids.

The pyramids in the dream are made of *ash*: ash, the residue of combustion, can take on different meanings. Some primitives, for example, use it as a means of protection again demons, by spreading it on the forehead of the newborn as a protection against the evil eye. In particular, ash is used as a protection against the spirits of the dead. [. . .] We still have to deal especially with ashes as the product of cremation. All cults of cremation have an idea in common, to assist the dead person on his way to the hereafter, that is, to assist in resurrection by freeing the soul through destruction of the mortal remains: the soul can thus float into the next world, into heaven. The custom of simultaneously cremating his possessions, even his wife, with the dead person, is connected with this idea. This concept is very clearly expressed in an Indian prayer, which the man conducting the funeral addresses to the dead person during cremation:

"[. . .] move on, on the old paths on which our forebears passed away. [. . .] Join the fathers there in the highest heaven [. . .] leaving behind all that is imperfect, assume a new body, aglow in beauty."

The phoenix's ashes have become the epitome of the symbol of the resurrection of the dead; that miraculous bird which, coming from

Arabia, flies to Egypt after having lived for five hundred years, where it sets itself on fire after self-laceration, to give birth to itself out of its own ashes. But the flight to Egypt is the flight to Heliopolis, where the old phoenix is buried as a god. So the ashes and the pyramid are both symbols of the resurrection of the dead, although they belong to different cultural environments. [. . .]

Above the pyramid there are the death masks: in order to understand them, let us start from the notion of the mask. [. . .] A special, and the most frequent, form of the mask is the death mask. We have already talked about the Egyptian death mask. It can be effective in resurrection only if it is portraitlike. Death masks are still in use today: on tombstones, often in an artistic form—let me remind you of Italian cemeteries—they show a portrait of the deceased as true to life as possible, and so keep his memory alive for the bereaved. Death masks are frequently used by primitive peoples in puberty rites, those dramatized representations of the process of puberty, of the death of the infantile personality, and the rising of the adult personality. [. . .]

Now let us try to discuss the second dream according to Jung's schema. In it, too, the father and the dreamer are the actors. As in the first dream, the father calls, but he calls for help. The dreamer is called on to help the father, but the help does not come. Instead of an action, there only remains a resigned "It-doesn't-work," "It-is-impossible." [. . .] Compared with the first dream, the atmosphere is even gloomier, the cosmos of the outer world has been torn apart, and there is a discrepancy between the distress in which the father is caught up and the complete passivity of the child who is called on to help. [. . .]

The location of the dream process is a place full of craters. The motif of the crater appears in multiplicity; the Earth's crust is full of holes. Regarding this multiplicity, I would like to bring some examples of dreams from psychopathology. Jung tells of dreams in which the "room is full of mice or cats." In dreams for which I have to thank Dr. Meier, the dreamer dreams of "a pool, in which many corked bottles float, each of them containing a message." In another dream there is "nothing but broken window panes." The most far-reaching analogy, however, can be found in the following dream, for I which I also have to thank Dr. Meier:

> I am on a street which, however, consists of nothing but deep holes. They are open manholes. There are no drain covers anywhere. I have the impression that the holes communicate down below, and in a way form an underground street. Perhaps, to make progress, I will have to go down after all.

The motif of multiplicity indicates a splitting of the soul. We find this motif particularly often in the dreams of schizophrenics. So we find the dreamer in a desolate, split world, in which there is only *one* being, but that is split off, far away in the distance, too far to reach, standing helpless in a situation of introversion, unable to move forward or backward. This part, split off from the rest of the personality, is the father, the spiritual principle. [. . .]

Our dreams are characterized by a progressive development from the first to the second dream. In the first dream there is still the trace of an action, missing completely in the second dream. Something has happened to the dreamer, which she can only counter with a resigned, "Nothing-can-be-done-about-it." In the first dream there is still the sleeping room of the parents, even if it is darkened by collective symbolism. In the second dream, however, the world has been cosmically destroyed (by an explosion from within). In the first dream there is still the attempt of the dreamer to respond to her father's calls, but in the second dream there is an infinite distance between the split-off spirit, captured in introversion (the father), and the rest of the personality. And this second dream ends without even the trace of a turning back, of a return to life, to the living. The world remains bleak and torn apart. [. . .]

Professor Jung: The present dreams come from a woman who consulted me at about thirty years of age, in a very difficult situation, shortly before the outbreak of schizophrenia. She writes that these two childhood dreams have haunted her throughout her whole life. They are the first dreams she can remember. We must assume that they have made a special impression on her. When you hear such

156

dreams, you naturally have to be ready to use your intellect. But sometimes it is much more important to consult your feeling function. You cannot do psychology with an excellent intellect alone. You also have to identify the feeling values, not only the meanings. In the case of a dream such as the present one we can, without any special gift for fantasy, put ourselves into its atmosphere. The fact alone that the father calls, at night, is something exciting and frightening. The father doesn't call at night! It is the child, at most, who calls at night. If the father calls at night, there is something wrong! Imagine lying in your bed at night as a child, hearing the call of the father—something terrible has happened. So, consequently, the child gets up in the dream; she breaks into the room of the parents, and in this place, where otherwise the parents are, the warmth of parental love, open arms ready for her—in this place she sees two heaps of ashes and death masks above them! This really is a catastrophic impression. The frightening call of the father is also repeated in the second dream. Out of the depths of the crater he is calling for help. When you hear such dreams, and feel what they mean, you can approach them intellectually and ask, for heaven's sake, what do these horrible-looking dreams mean.

To begin with, let us apply our schema to these dreams! In the first dream, the child and the father are the dramatis personae, the location is the sleeping room of the parents, it is night. The exposition is the call from the father. This call contains the problem. The climax of the dream, the peripateia, consists in the child's getting up, going to the sleeping room, and making the horrible discovery, which mounts until the sight of the parents' death masks. And there follows *no lysis*.

In the second dream, the locale is the earth, a desolate landscape, full of craters. We are overcome by a feeling of being lost and lonely. There is little development in this dream, still it comes to that climax (peripateia), when the father calls. It is a call for help from far away. Again the lysis is missing!

Now I know from experience that dreams of such a horrible nature, if they don't have an outright catastrophic meaning, usually end with a lysis. In such a case, it could have said at the end of the second dream: "I went to his help as best I could, and did all I could to reach him." If the dream had ended this way, we could say: "Well, there is something the dreamer can deal with. She can at least try to do something." As examples, let me tell you two similar dreams of a child, who died shortly thereafter from spinal muscular atrophy. When the child had the dreams, the diagnosis was still doubtful. I let the dream be told to me because I wanted to see what the unconscious had to say about the illness:

> The first dream: The child comes home. He[53] is living on the fifth floor. It is dark already. There is a cold draft. The doors and the windows are open; the child enters, the door to the living room is slightly ajar. He opens it and sees the mother swinging to and fro on the chandelier.

Here you have again the growing suspense, until the feeling of horror, and no lysis. There is nothing that would indicate a salvation.

> The second dream goes as follows: The child is at home; there is some horrible pounding noise. He sees that a wild horse is shooting around in the hallway. All of a sudden, in one leap the horse jumps out of the window. The child hurries to the window sill. The horse lies shattered on the ground.

Here, too, the ending is nameless horror.

These are dreams without lysis; they are simply catastrophic. From the fact of the missing lysis I deduced an unfavorable prognosis. It is dangerous when nothing like a solution is presented. The solution could, for instance, also consist in waking up from the anxiety dream with the feeling: "It's only an anxiety dream." A typical solution is also when the danger cannot reach you at all, because you wake up before that happens. Usually we can still see something conciliatory somewhere. In times of old, therefore, the doctors observed dreams and made their diagnoses accordingly. Let me remind you of Artemidorus.[54] He mentions the dream of a man in which he sees his father

---

[53] It is not clear from the German text if the child was male or female. I have used the male form to avoid the tedious repetition of "he or she" (trans.).

[54] Artemidorus of Daldis, *Symbolik der Träume*. For a detailed discussion of his dream book, see vol. 2 of the English edition (ed.).

in a burning house. A few days later, the dreamer himself died from a feverish illness.

Participant: What sense does it make to dream dreams of a purely catastrophic nature?

Professor Jung: This is the secret of dreams—that we do not dream, but rather we *are dreamt*. We are the object of the dream, not its maker. The French say: "Faire un rêve."[55] This is wrong. The dream is dreamed to us. We are the objects. We simply find ourselves put into a situation. If a fatal destiny is awaiting us, we are already seized by what will lead us to this destiny in the dream, in the same way it will overcome us in reality.

One of my friends, who was attacked by a mamba (cobra) in Africa, dreamed of this event two months in advance in Zurich. The snake attacked him in the dream exactly in the way it later did in reality. Such a dream is anticipated fate.

Participant: So we cannot always assume that the dream wants to make something conscious?

Professor Jung: No, not at all. This is anthropomorphic thinking. We can only try to understand what the dream offers. If we are wise, we can put it to use. We must not think that dreams necessarily have a benevolent intention. Nature is kind and generous, but also absolutely cruel. That is its characteristic. Think of children. There is nothing more cruel than children, and yet they are so lovely.

If I had such a dream, I would naturally react differently from the woman in question. But as I am a different person, I also have a different dream. So that's not how we should think. We can only compare. The hopeless case has the hopeless dream, the hopeful one has the hopeful dream.

Participant: Is it possible to understand all dreams? Isn't it already in the nature of such a dream that it cannot be understood?

Professor Jung: If the dreamer had had it in her to understand this dream at some point later on, there probably would have been a suffix of hope added to it. There would be a ray of light at the end, which

---

[55] "To make a dream" (trans.).

159

would give the doctor a hint. He could then say: "You have had a very alarming dream." And the patient would perhaps understand him. If she understands the dream, she will be on her way to integrate the pathological part.

With this patient, I had talked about dreams. Interestingly, she did not mention these dreams. But when she was gone, they came to her as an *esprit d'escalier*.[56] She then told me about them in a letter. If the dreamer had actually told them, I would have been even more scared. I had seen her a couple of times, but had not come far enough to identify the content of her peculiar disturbance. She did not come into a mental institution, but hovers above the ground as a shadow. Right before she came to me, she had undergone a psychotic phase. She came to me during the downhill phase of a psychotic interval.

You can see which fate the two dreams from childhood have anticipated.

Participant: Couldn't there come positive dreams again later on, which would lessen the uncanny aspect?

Professor Jung: Positive dreams may well follow, but none of them have the importance of the childhood dreams, because the child is much nearer the collective unconscious than the adults. Children still live directly in the great images. There are high points in life— puberty, midlife—when the great dreams appear again, those dreamed out of the depth of the personality. In the life of the adult, dreams mostly refer to personal life. Then the persona is in the foreground, what is essential in their personality has long emigrated, is long gone, perhaps never to be reached again.

Participant: Does the dream not always have a compensatory meaning?

Professor Jung: Here this connection is destroyed, as it is; it functions only to a limited extent. So the lysis is missing. It is actually a dream that stops with the peripateia, we could say: the catastrophe is anticipated, and no lysis occurs.

A couple of years ago, a participant in our seminar developed a schema of the dream process, based on a discussion of symbolic

---

[56] French, roughly "afterthought" (trans.).

processes in the English seminar. I would like to ask Mr. Baumann to give you a short exposé of the rhythm of the symbolic process.

Mr. Baumann: In studying the dream process, I was led to differentiate between phases, which can best be visualized [in the illustration].

The various phases show certain situations, named A, B, C, D by me. This sequence is repeated again and again (A^1, B^1, C^1, D^1).

A   stands for the unconscious or approaching the unconscious.
B   stands for the archetypal situation, caused by the sinking into the unconscious, that is, a regression, the experience of the past, archaic situations.
C   stands for consciousness, the generalization or broadening of a psychological situation, an overview of the latter.
D   stands for progression, hints, directions, ideas, and so on, resulting from the overview given in C.[57]

I have tried to define the various situations in our two dreams. They run analogous to each other, as follows:

Dream 1	Dream 2
A^1 State of sleeping	A^2 Desolate place
B^1 Call of the father	B^2 Crater
C^1 Pyramid of ashes, death masks	C^2 Call of the father
D^1 Progression missing	D^2 Progression missing

Professor Jung: I am convinced to a large extent that symbolical processes run like this. This is in accordance with their inner nature. These are no logical thought processes, but irrational processes, the unfolding of actions. Symbolic thinking is thinking by doing, and,

[57] Details in Hans Baumann, *Zentralblatt für Psychotherapie und ihre Grenzgebiete,* 1936, pp. 213ff, and fig. 4.

therefore, always follows a regular sequence that somehow has to do with the sequence of life. You can also find this regularity in both our dreams.

Mr. Baumann talked about the archetypal situation caused by sinking into the unconscious. You can clearly see this descent into the unconscious. The first dreams starts with the child sleeping in a room. This is an absolutely clear situation. Suddenly the father calls. Now this is the descent into the unconscious, because in reality the father did not call at all. The child follows the call: as you can see, the descent into the unconscious immediately draws after it the remains of consciousness. The dream leads us into an action, into an experience, that no longer corresponds to conscious experience. When we submerge into the unconscious, we again live in that kind of instinctual experience that is characteristic of the nature of unconscious activity. We experience archetypal situations, that is, situations that humankind has experienced from time immemorial. These are situations that always repeat themselves, in various forms. We experience them as we have experienced them at all times. The descent into the unconscious is always dangerous. It can be visualized as being devoured by the whale-dragon, as going down into a dark cave or into the castle of the evil magician. We go there to get something. As a rule, it is a valuable treasure or a marvelous precious stone. Or it is a virgin who must be saved. In each case, this is about bringing up an archetypal value. At first, this is done in a certain degree of unconsciousness. We do not know exactly what we caught fishing in the depths. Subsequently, however, we again come up into the world of light, and there the brought-up content mixes with the conscious contents. It is compared with them, or it can be realized— undoubtedly an *acme*,[58] a climax. Or there follows a frightening insight into a certain situation, or also a positive insight. And then there follows the lysis, leading us back to the point from which we started. At the beginning there is the conscious problem with which somebody is burdened. He then slips into the unconscious background, comes into the instinctual life, and brings up an archetypal

---

[58] Here in a medical sense, i.e., the culmination point of an illness or fever (ed.).

form that enriches him. This is also the reason, for example, why we like to sleep on a problem that is still unclear to us. Even if we do not have a dream, something can become clear during sleep, and the answer may come to mind in the morning. During sleep, we enter the natural previous life, where we find the helpful archetype, always there, in every dangerous situation. We find a way out, because the archetype is that form of the process that makes the eternal melody of all life possible; it blends melodically into a solution, into another form, with no consideration for the life or death of the individual. When somebody reaches the archetype in a dream, he has, so to speak, found the treasure, the key with which the closed door can then be opened, or a magic with which the dangerous situation can be exorcized. This fact was already known to the ancients in prehistoric times. They gathered for incubation sleeping states in underground caves or in temples. In Hal Saflieni, in Malta, there is such a neolithic temple, twenty-five meters below ground. Sleeping in the temple was used in order to dream of the right diagnoses or remedies. The people fell asleep with the problem. In diving into the stream of the never-ending activity of life, they were seized by archetypal figures and they found a salutary saying or image.

At a Later Meeting of the Seminar [24 January 1939]
Professor Jung: Let us now enter into a detailed discussion of the symbolism. In the case of such a dream, which, as it is, is quite lacking in events, we have to take a very close look at each detail. First of all, the *sleeping state* of the dreamer is mentioned in the dream. This underlines, "You are in a sleeping state, you are *unconscious*." Then we come into the *sleeping room of the parents*. This room is what is closest to the child, her earliest and most intimate reality. So the dream shows that this is about the most intimate reality of the dreamer. Now comes that image of the *pyramids of ashes with the death masks*. Dr. Nothmann quite correctly interpreted this image as a cremation grave. These are really the ashes of the parents, perhaps also of the bed, the household effects, the pile of wood, on which they were cremated. One single person does not leave so many ashes. This is an image of a death that has already happened, that is, there has already

been a burial, a cremation. The beds of the parents, too, have turned to ashes. We also find this idea among the primitives, the idea that persons should not be buried alone, but together with their household effects. Everything that belongs to them should fall victim to destruction. Do you know for what purpose?

Participant: So that they can find these things again in the next world, in the form of astral or smoke images.

Professor Jung: Yes, that is correct. The smoke rising into the air contains, so to speak, the spiritual substance. The subtle images of the objects are sent after the subtle bodies of the dead into the semi-substantial world of the spirits. The objects are burned or simply broken into pieces. In Africa, I saw how water jugs, axes, cooking pots, and also jewelry were thrown together in a heap and broken into pieces there. It all remained lying there for two months, and then it disappeared. It is touched by nobody for as long as the excitation has not subsided. There is no ban on it, but it simply is not opportune to take away these things earlier. It is unhealthy, the spirit could accompany them, and therefore one does not do it.

Participant: In the *I Ching*, too, the bed stands for the intimate situation.[59] It says in one oracle (number 23, Splitting Apart): "The leg of the bed is split—the bed is split at the edge—the bed is split up to the skin."

Professor Jung: This is a very good parallel: the bed as a symbol of the inner situation. The oracle points to the fact that the dissolution reaches the unconscious. There are signs of a complete dissolution of consciousness. The example was taken from the *I Ching*, a work of Chinese philosophy from the second millennium B.C. The version as it is available today was written around 1190 by King Wen and Prince Chou. They were imprisoned and passed their time by observing how outer events corresponded with psychical situations. This is a highly peculiar problem, which seems strange to a Western man or woman.

We have seen that the pyramid of ashes is a burial ritual. Now we have to ask ourselves, however, what this archetypal burial, this death, means. We have to take the dream text literally, just as it reads.

---

[59] *I Ching, The Book of Changes*. See *The Complete I Ching*.

We have no right to assume that something is incorrect or forged. After all, there is no one there who would manipulate it. The dreamer does not manipulate. She sleeps. The Talmud states quite correctly: "The dream is its own interpretation." We can't do anything but amplify and enrich the dream. So we may ask ourselves, with regard to this elaborate mountain of ashes and the death masks put above them, where similar ideas are found in the mythological experience of peoples. And it may come to mind that the same idea is found in Egypt, the idea of the burial chambers, above which there is the Ka, the semimaterial soul of the Egyptian. This Ka keeps the likeness,[60] not to be lost, so that the dead person, when looking for his body, is reminded of what he actually looked like. The dead person was, for instance, also given little ladders into the grave, so that the Ka could climb up into heaven; or there stood twelve identical portrait statues in front of the Ramses temple, so that the king would not lose his identity. It was assumed that through embalming, the body kept his identity, his Ka, his living image, so that he remembered his appearance. For when he dies and becomes a spirit, he might possibly forget who he was.

The dreamer has made a quite correct burial according to the archetype. She has seen to it that the parents do not lose their identity. If you remember the schema of Mr. Baumann, you will notice that this burial rite is the archetypal situation, brought up from the unconscious. Experience shows that we should now expect something helpful to happen. Usually a helpful image appears at this point. Here this is not so. What could have been that helpful something in this dream? If, for example, someone carrying a different destiny in himself had had this dream, there could be a hint of a possibility to understand the meaning of these identity masks. After all, they are there for the destroyed parents to remember who they actually were. The parents could be restored again, and life would go on. So the masks are there to remember, as a provision for a possible rebirth. The dreamer could be reconceived and reborn. This possibility is not effective here, which is also evidenced by the second dream.

[60] This word in English in the original (trans.).

What is remarkable in the second dream is that a five- to six-year-old child dreams of a *crater landscape*. This is not childlike. Probably the child did not even think of the word *crater*. We must not forget that the dream is a remembered one, and so there are expressions coming from adult language. Obviously, the child must have dreamed of a ground full of holes, constituting a counterpart to the pyramids of the first dream. The crater is a hollow, corresponding to the towering pyramid. Such a correspondence can be found in reality. On the occasion of excavations in the Canton of Aargau from the Neolithic period, the corresponding holes were found in addition to the *cumuli*.[61] So what we see in our dreams is at first what has been piled up, then what has been hollowed out, its negative. These are burial holes, later called craters by the fantasy of the dreamer that did not quite know what to do with this image. We should not go too far, therefore, in the interpretation of the term *crater*. I should be cautious with interpretations such as "explosion" or "eruption," although the idea of danger is always associated with the idea of hollowed-out ground; because when someone digs up the ground, we come into the underworld, into the prehistoric world, into that *aljira*[62] I already talked about.[63] Often *aljira* is even thought of as being in the ground. It is told that the ancients had withdrawn after time had come into being and humankind had been been created, and they had sunk into the earth. It is not always dangerous to dig up the ground, however, and to come into the *aljira*, but it can also be an advantage. For when we find our forebears again, we come to the source of life. This is the reason why we dig for treasure, for the precious object, and bring up water; this is why the primitives make holes in the ground, which are then fertilized. Symbolically, we have to conceive of this as fertility magic, because these holes are the entrance to mother earth. The womb of the earth is opened up.

We still we have to deal, however, with the meaning of these burial holes, which correspond to the piles in the first dream.

---

[61] Latin, "heaps, piles." Jung seems to refer to grave-mounds, tumuli (ed.).

[62] The aboriginal word for "land of no time" (trans.).

[63] In the discussion of Lincoln, *The Dream in Primitive Cultures*, now reprinted in vol. 2 of the English edition (trans.).

Participant: The crater landscape is reminiscent of a lunar landscape, and this makes sense, because the moon is the first place souls come to after death.

Professor Jung: From where does the child know what a lunar landscape looks like? These are all adult terms. It seems much more reasonable to suppose that the child had open graves in mind. Sometimes, however, children also happen to have quite strange dreams with extremely odd features. I will leave the question open. When we think about these phenomena, we arrive at very strange things. Let us leave this *in suspenso*.

Participant: When the dreamer uses the word *crater* when telling the dream, supposedly she has to associate this with a feeling of anxiety—otherwise she could have used the word *funnel*.

Professor Jung: Yes, quite right, but do we know if the child did already have this corresponding feeling? Yet, I don't want to say yes—and I don't want to say no! For the moment, let us pursue the idea that the crater landscape is reminiscent of the lunar landscape. There is such an idea in mythology, namely, that the moon is a landscape of graves. The moon actually is sometimes the place of departed souls, absorbing the souls. If it absorbs many souls, it is said to become humid. The psyche is, after all, the humid breath—"psychros" is cold, and is related to "to blow." In Heraclitus we find the idea that the souls turn into water. In recent years, one Gurdjieff[64] claimed that the moon was so fertilized by the many souls of soldiers killed during the last World War that a green spot appeared on it.

But we are still dealing with the question why a pyramid is piled up in the first dream, while there is a corresponding cavity in the second dream.

Participant: The mother is no longer present in the second dream.

Professor Jung: What importance would you attach to the fact that the *mother* is no longer present? Which of the dreams do you find more uncanny?

Participant: The second dream.

---

[64] George Ivanovich Gurdjieff (1866?–1949), a Greek-Armenian mystic, composer, and "teacher of dancing." According to Gurdjieff, the moon consumes the fine matter of human souls after we die. Like a magnet, it draws our souls into it (trans.).

Professor Jung: Yes, by all means, and we have the proof that the second dream is more dangerous. What proof?

Participant: The cry for help.

Professor Jung: This wouldn't be a positive fact.

Participant: The multiplicity of the craters?

Professor Jung: No.

Participant: The devouring aspect of the earth.

Professor Jung: Yes, the earth is opening up her mouth. She is the great ancestress, opening her mouth.

Participant: In contrast to the first dream, the second one no longer has a ritual aspect, and thus also lacks anything human.

Professor Jung: This is quite crucial. The earth is simply naked cosmos. This is the nothingness, the eternal emptiness. We have such a feeling when we stand in a part of nature untouched by human beings, the feeling of which Nietzsche says: *Crimen laesae maiestatis humanae*. Nature doesn't give a damn about man. This is expressed by the absence of the mother, as just mentioned. What does the mother mean for this child, or for a girl in general?

Participant: The body, the reality.

Professor Jung: Yes, one's own feminine nature, the basis, nature, life. All this is associated with the mother. Hence that known disorder when the relation with the mother becomes negative. Then a disorder within the feminine nature occurs. So the absence of the mother means that human nature has been lost. There is no longer a basis for the child in the human world. Such a being is living "on the moon," to take up again the previous comparison between the lunar and the crater landscape. The notion of the moon brings to mind another terrible aspect. What does the moon mean?

Participant: It can also mean mental illness.

Professor Jung: Yes, of course. Think of the French *lunatique*,[65] or of our *mondsüchtig*.[66] Such a person is in that landscape that corresponds to the moon. Human nature has been lost, the mother is no

[65] "Moody" (trans.).

[66] Literally: "addicted to the moon"; sleep-walking. The English *lunatic*, of course, would be another, even more striking example (trans.).

longer there. There is only the spirit of the father left. Because the real father is dead already. A spirit is calling her. What happens when a spirit calls?

Participant: In fairy tales, the spirit lures us away to lead us into the world of the dead.

Professor Jung: The call of the spirit, being addressed by a spirit, is an uncanny experience. It means an invitation to come into the realm of the dead. The primitives have a very pronounced fear of this. I myself have seen this quite often: most often the paths leading into the village are protected against the spirits that might come back to the village at night, to get their next of kin. For this purpose, and because the spirits exert such a strong influence on the living, spirit traps are set, or medicines are hung up, that should stop them. This goes back to the idea that one falls under the shadow of death when one loses a close relative. Then the level of the will to live is somewhat lowered. We are partly drawn into the grave. This can cause far-reaching damage, neuroses, and outbreaks of illnesses. Or the whole personality may change. These changes are caused by the dead person's entering into the living one, and living on in him. They will be of a positive nature if the dead person has had a positive influence. But even then there is something alarming and uncanny. [. . .] It is always uncanny if someone dead still goes on having an effect.

You may now be better able to empathize with the situation of our dreamer, and feel her horror when she is addressed by the spirit of the dead father. The *father spirit* is present at the beginning of the first dream, and is still there at the end of the second dream—as the only living being! What conclusion would you draw from this? What does this mean for the dreamer?

Participant: The father stands for spirituality; maybe this spirit could guide the child through the dangerous situation.

Professor Jung: But he is helpless in these dreams; it is as if he were captured; obviously, he can't do anything. But still, what might this mean for the future?

Participant: It could bring about an insight into the situation.

Professor Jung: So does she have a view of it?

Participant: No, the father does.

169

Professor Jung: Yes, the father knows it. Suppose you were in that situation. Nothing would be left but the voice of the father, the spirit of the father. What effect would this have?

Participant: This would indicate that one would function with paternal thinking only.

Professor Jung: Yes, one would live only in the spirit of the father, of the symbolic father, that is. What is that called?

Participant: God.

Professor Jung: Not necessarily. We needn't go that deep into the metaphysical. This is called *animus*, the male spirit! So we might assume that this woman, if she can somehow keep herself, will to a large extent get under the influence of the father, of the personal father perhaps or, more likely, of a general, symbolical father. This might take the following forms: intense religious possession, religious delusions, or a ruthless intellectuality, as seen in the reading of various textbooks of philosophy. It could also be a mental illness—which one?

Participant: A paranoid form of schizophrenia.

Participant: But the crater is completely burnt out already.

Professor Jung: But that's it exactly. There are people who are burnt out completely, and for this reason are completely intellectualistic.

Participant: Could it not be the case that this animus could again establish contact with the unconscious, as an intermediary?

Participant: But then he wouldn't call for help.

Participant: Couldn't it also have the effect that such a woman would live completely in the spirit of the parental home?

Professor Jung: You mean that such an individual could live at home, possessed by the spirit of this house—in a word, crazy. There are such cases of schizophrenia, which are inconspicuous. Also, in many offices there are crazy people who calmly carry out their duties, and nobody knows that they are absolutely crazy.

We cannot tell how this animus, who alone has stayed alive, will function. We know only that the animus will remain in the end. There will, therefore, be spirits in the air. How this will show itself in life cannot be inferred from the dreams.

I will tell you what happened later on: this woman married a completely bizarre man. Nobody would have expected her to choose such an impossible man. The marriage was not good, steadily declining in the following years. Then a man came into her life "who had fabulous ideas." He was a man of inferior thinking, who built castles in the air and examined and twisted words down to the last detail. She thought he was the savior and was taken in by him. All this led to great complications, resulting in a depression. She had to be hospitalized in a sanitarium, where I was consulted. She slowly recovered, and was discharged as fairly socially adjusted. Essentially nothing had changed. What happened from there? She has withdrawn from all friends and acquaintances, living in a romantic house in the country. Together with her husband, who is a complete nonentity, she leads a life full of appearances and deception, full of the most absurd philosophical ideas, in a ghostly and unreal world. This is anticipated in these dreams. There is no hope left; there is nobody who could help. For a moment, this animus slipped into me, and then I was the savior, but soon enough I was it no more—and then nothing happened any longer. Are there any more questions?

Participant: Does a dream in which such a cosmic emptiness appears always have such a catastrophic meaning?

Professor Jung: It depends on the dream as a whole! If, for instance, a favorable afterthought is added to such a situation, it might not be so catastrophic. In this dream this would almost have been possible, because there still is a living spirit present. If only the mother were still alive, there would be a receptacle to contain the father spirit. But there is no receptacle. Anyhow, you should not get stuck on single dangerous symbols and conclude from them that things look completely bad. It depends on what context these symbols stand in. It is always best to get fully into the spirit of the dream situation. When you touch a dream with feeling and carefully measure the feeling values, you will see at once if the dream is favorable or unfavorable. In this dream we realize at once: there is a hole! Put a bit of your heart into the dream, and you will already have done half the work. There is an "intelligence du coeur,"[67] of which the brain knows nothing.

[67] French, "intelligence of the heart"; a reference to an expression used by Pascal in his *Pensées* (trans.).

6. Dreams of a Four-Year-Old Girl of the Wedding Carriage and the Little Angel[68]
Presented by Cornelia Brunner

Text: 1. "The shutter of the one window very gently rises, and I see a wedding carriage on the gravel path in the garden, turning round the corner of the house. A wedding couple is sitting in the carriage, with the devil on the box as coachman. All of a sudden the carriage is ablaze, and disappears in the rising flames. I am very scared."

2. The dreamer stands in the bathroom of her parents' house and looks at herself in the mirror. In the mirror image she sees that, very slowly, wings grow out of her shoulders, so that she looks like a little angel.

Mrs. Brunner: It seems that the two dreams belong together in a double sense: in a way, the second dream of the little angel shows the lysis of the first one, but at the same time it could also be the first dream's starting point and cause—opposite motifs are radiating from their shared center, and there is the possibility of a sudden change from one pole to the other.

The question arises whether the disappearance of the carriage may be interpreted as lysis, or whether—because of the anxiety interrupting the dream process—this is a dream without lysis.

We can structure the dream as follows:

Locale: Situation of the dream: in the sleeping room.
                  Situation of the action: in the garden of the parental house.
                  Dramatis personae: wedding couple, devil.
Exposition: Entry of the carriage.
Peripateia: Burning of the carriage.
Lysis: Disappearance of the carriage in the rising flames.

Let us now have a look at the individual symbols. The *wedding carriage*: a carriage is a man-made means to move things or persons from one place to another. Its wheels go back to the sun wheel, thus to a mandala. We use a carriage when we have to cover long distances, or

---

[68] Session of 31 January 1939.

172

when an important *transition*, as for instance a marriage or a burial, is approaching. We find remnants of a ritual carriage procession in the *Sechseläuten*,[69] or in the carnival parade.

The *wedding couple*: Tacitus relates the journey of Nerthus: each year in winter a priest leads the goddess Nerthus—Mother Earth— to the humans in a carriage drawn by cows. Then come peaceful times and happy days. Nerthus is the *Ur*-mother of humankind. In Sweden, the god Frey takes her place, called the "light one" in the *Edda*. In winter he drives through the country in a wagon with his priestess. People believed that he was being married to her. The wagon journey and the marriage of the divine couple anticipate, in the form of a ritual, future events. In Nerthus's case, the *fertility* of the approaching spring should be furthered; in Frey's case, the *return of the light*. The high-spirited frenzy, reigning in winter and spring festivals up to this day, is meant to call on life, frozen in ice, to new procreation. One of these festivals is the Walpurgis night, in which (according to De Coster) King Lenz (King Lucifer), together with his sweet and fair wife, frees life from the bonds of the winter giant.

This leads us to the *devil*: our concept of the devil has developed out of the Old Testament, the New Testament, and, above all, the later Christian dogma. In the Old Testament, the devil pales beside the almighty Yahweh. In the Book of Job he is still listed among the "sons of God."[70] By his association with the Persian Ahriman he acquires Persian traits. Ahriman is the *antagonist of light*; he means *darkness and death*; he comes from heaven in the form of a serpent. Philo was the first, following the Persian view, to make the serpent of the Hebrew Fall of Man the Satan and the image of evil lust. In the New Testament, the devil fights, as the lord of this world, against the kingdom of God. Consequently, he not only becomes the master of all evil, but also of what could have endangered the spread of the Church's power: the Church saw Gnosis and Reformation as temptations by the devil.

[69] Literally, "ringing the bells at six o'clock"; a Zurich spring festival of the traditional trade guilds, a parade in historical costumes (ed.).

[70] Job 1:6, *King James Bible*. In the *New International Version*: "angels" (trans.).

In the Gnosis,[71] several pairs of gods, none of whom assume a material form, stem from the highest god. From Sophia, the divine wisdom, a relatively ignorant being is born, the Demiurge, who creates the world. Later, the Church Father Irenæus[72] replaces the Demiurge with Satan, the fallen angel of pride. The notion of the fallen Lucifer means that a being of the light has fallen under the law of gravity, that it has assumed a *material body*. In Dante's *Divine Comedy*, Lucifer, with his three heads in the earth's deepest abyss, is the counterpart to the Holy Trinity.

In the New Testament, the devil is still rather shapeless. He became the devil *incarnate* only through ideas introduced by non-Jewish converted and subjugated peoples, whose gods had been degraded to devils by Christianity. To the saints, the devil appears in his incarnate form, so, for example, to St. Simeon in the form of the man on the cherub carriage telling him: "Come, get on the carriage, so that you may receive your crown." To St. Paternian the devil appears in the form of a girl. When his voluptuousness is aroused by this, he recognizes the Tempter and remembers that all who soil themselves with wantonness will be punished in the fire.

In the thirteenth and fourteenth centuries, the belief in the devil reached its climax. Misfortune, illness, blasphemy, passion—all these were attributed to the devil and his sorcery. Pagan magic and rituals were revived in the belief in witches, particularly in its feminine and natural aspects.

In the seventeenth and eighteenth centuries, belief in the devil decreased. The devil was rationalized and depersonalized. He was no longer the evil power at whose mercy mortals lived, but he became the evil instinct within man's heart—egotism. The vital symbol was reduced to a pale allegory.

Let us summarize the most important characteristics of the devil concept: the devil is the black one, the opposite of light. When he appears red, he is of a fiery, that is, passionate nature, and causes wantonness, hate, or unruly love. As the "green one" he is related to veg-

[71] On Gnosticism, see the notes to seminar 2 (ed.).

[72] Greek Church Father, ca. A.D. 202. He is considered the father of Catholic dogmatism, and was instrumental in the fight against Gnosticism (ed.).

etation and nature. He appears as a goat, snake, cat, or poodle; he is seen with a cloven hoof, filthy and with a tail. He is living in the earth, and represents the earth power of the Titans and man's being bound to the earth. He stands for our *animal nature*. As a wild hunter and heir to Wotan, he is the spirit of eternal unrest, who storms through the skies on his horse. His wings point to his relation to the thinking function. As Mephistopheles, he is arrogant, egomaniacal, cunning, and eager to draw man into dust and matter. Finally, as Lucifer, true to his name, he is the *bearer of the spark of light*, who descended through the planetary spheres from the highest light down into matter, seeking to liberate it as a work of salvation. Filthy and rough like a tomcat below, but more brilliant than the sun above— that's how a judge of the witch trials described him.

He who becomes slave to the devil has to burn in the *fire*. For those who have not been redeemed by Christ on the cross, the fire of hell will be eternal agony. As Purgatory, it has the effect of *purification* by which man attains sight of the face of God. Frazer offers a great deal of evidence for fire's power to purify and to promote light and fertility. In all cultures, fires were, and still are, lit on the eve of great feasts and great changes, as in the Walpurgis night, at midsummer celebrations, at Easter, and so on. The old god, or his earthly representative, is burned in the new fires. Cremation should enable *rebirth* in the next world. The prophet Elijah went into heaven on a fiery wagon.

According to Heraclitus, the world was created in fire, and will perish in fire. His fire is the power of God. Similarly, Simon Magus[73] sees the *dynamis* of the fire at the origin of the cosmos. It is logos; it is the primeval unity and it is the root of the cosmos. Fire has a double nature, a hidden and a visible side. In the hidden fire above heaven, all things are preserved. Through fire, which consumes the material form, the soul becomes the pure image, godlike and immortal.

In alchemy it says: In this fire, which God created in the earth, just as he created the Purgatory in hell, God Himself is glowing in divine

---

[73] Simon Magus was a Samaritan magician. Although he was considered an archheretic by the Church Fathers (cf. Acts 8:9ff), he played a central role in Gnosticism. The Gnostic sect of the Simonians saw in him the incarnation of God. Regarding his teachings on the fire, see C. G. Jung, CW 11, § 359, and CW 13, § 408 (ed.).

love. And Jesus Christ says, according to an apocryphal word of the Lord: "He who is near me, is near the fire." So the *savior* is of a fiery nature. In the Krishna legend, however, the savior is born to a parental couple, at whose wedding the carriage is steered by evil demons.

Now let us have a look at the second dream of the little angel, which can be structured as follows:

Locale:	Location: bathroom in the parental house.
	Dramatis persona: the dreamer.
Exposition:	She sees herself in the mirror.
Peripateia:	The growing of wings.
Lysis:	She looks like a little angel.

In the *mirror* we see our *true nature*, the image of our soul; reflection brings about insight and knowledge. The *bathroom* is the place of *cleaning*. A wing carries the bird into the skies. Homer compares the wing to a thought. The *angels* are the light counterpart to the devil. The *mediating function* of the angels is most beautifully expressed in Jacob's [dream of the] Ladder.[74]

I have tried to interpret the dreams, first as a collective time problem, then as a transition in infantile development, and finally as a midlife problem. The symbolic connection indicates, in all its details, a *transition*.

"The shutter . . . very gently rises, and I see a wedding carriage on the gravel path . . . turning round the corner of the house": still unconscious and sheltered herself, the little girl sees something that comes from the outside, from the collective world, into her garden. In the carriage there sits a wedding couple: this is the god and his Shakti, his female power, from which couple a world is created; or these are the *opposites*, pertaining to all materialization of matter, and which have to be melted, so to speak, to make room for a new order. The carriage as a symbol of going from one place to another indicates

---

[74] "And [Jacob] dreamed, and behold a ladder set up on the earth, and the top of it reached to heaven: and behold the angels of God ascending and descending on it" (Genesis 28:12) (trans.).

176

the transition to something new. Just like the Ark of the Covenant,[75] it is a receptacle created by human beings to contain the divine forces. It might perhaps be seen as the ritual in which humans call the gods. The lead, however, was not taken by the gods themselves, but by their negative side, the devil. Beelzebub drives the horses, the instincts, across the earth, so full of arrogance as not to acknowledge any master, any law, above him. He uses the wagon of the prevailing views to pursue his own goals: he wants man to eat dust; he evokes unbridled hate, unbridled love. The passions erupt in a hell fire, a primeval element, unruly and destructive as ever. In the rising flame vanish carriage and gods, the traditional laws, rituals, and sacraments. The flames consume the mortal remnants, thus separating the matter from the idea, and carrying the purified spark of light into the skies.

In the flame Agni ascends to the gods. So the fire joins, as a fourth element, the trinity that the devil formed with the wedding couple. Nebuchadnezzar threw three men into the oven, and in the fire he saw a fourth man, "looking like a son of the gods."

The prevailing *Weltanschauung* is melted in the fire of the emotions, and its quintessence is to be brought out of the embers of illumination. This interpretation leads far beyond the infantile world. Regarding the little dreamer, the dream wants to tell her that she will have to take part in this collective process of transition, instigated by "Part of the power that would always wish evil [and always works the good]"[76]—"I am very scared," it says at the end of the dream. The encounter with the arch enemy and the flaring up of archaic emotions are reasons enough to frighten the dreamer.

The four-year-old girl should free herself from the realm of collective images. She is still identical with the little angel, she grows wings herself, while the devil is the evil coming from the outside. The dream has to remind her of the devil, because her consciousness identifies with a little angel. In the unconscious, the devil takes the lead.

---

[75] The sacred chest where the ancient Israelites kept the two tablets containing the Ten Commandments (trans.).

[76] Mephistopheles in Goethe's *Faust 1*, verses 1336–37 (trans.).

To begin with, he will bring the "little angel" down to earth, ensnare her in guilt and agony, and burn her up in the fire of passions.

In addition, the fire dream prepares for a change in the child's development. The announced emotional eruption should liberate the strength for some spiritual development. With this, her view of evil should also undergo a change.

The devil is the seducer. For the dreamer, however, sin is linked to the wedding couple, that is, to the problem of instincts and relations. When this problem approaches her in later life, the fire, the uncontrollable power of god, will erupt from the unconscious. And if she lets herself be seized, and suffers the fire's heat, the soul will be formed out of the unconscious body and spirit, the soul that is able to float, as the body's essence of light, between heaven and earth with the wings of the spirit.

The carriage, too, the thing made by the hand of man, is dematerialized by the fire. Its archaic image, the four wheels and the square, is "preserved in the hidden fire, in the eternal place." Dante sees the three wheels of Trinity in the light of the beyond. With the carriage, the fourness is completed, with it the divine mother, the light, who had been with the devil, came back to the father. And so the same that happened to Dante can happen to the dreamer in her midlife. Dante's *Divine Comedy* ends with the words: "Tanto ch'i' vidi de le cose belle che porta 'l ciel, per un pertugio tondo. E quindi uscimmo a riveder le stelle" [Till I beheld through a round aperture / Some of the beauteous things that Heaven doth bear; / Thence we came forth to rebehold the stars].

Professor Jung: After this splendid paper, let us come back once again to the starting point: the dreamer is in her sleeping room. This is the location of the action. The shutter gently rises—the shutters represent the eyelids, as it were. When they open, we discover a part of the world. So here, too, something is being prepared, a vision, so to speak. This is the exposition. The dreamer sees a wedding carriage with a wedding couple—the plot thickens already, and immediately we come to the acme of the story: the devil appears; this is the peripateia. There follows the catastrophe of the burning, and the lysis is the dissolution in the fire. The whole goes up in smoke. We might

178

ask ourselves if this is actually a lysis. The speaker doubted it. It would not be a lysis if the child herself sat in the wedding carriage. Then she would end up in the catastrophe herself. But as she is not sitting in it, and as the whole image is only a *seen image*, we have to deal with the image itself, which, as a matter of fact, really represents a lysis. The whole beautiful image is destroyed by the fire. There is an emotional tension that goes up in the fire. You will find that relieving and freeing effect of the fire in religious cults and also in poetry. Think of Goethe's beautiful poem "The God and the Bayadere."[77] When the Bayadere wants to follow the god into death, he lifts her up into heaven with fiery arms. There, the rising of the smoke and the fire are definitely felt as a lysis. This is in accordance with an ancient tradition. Consigning the sacrifice to the fire is a religious lysis for all present. The same idea is also found in the Indians of the southern states in Mexico: a down feather is held above the abyss, and is carried upward at the rocks by the breeze. The event in the dream can be compared to a ritual action in which God is killed and eaten. These are rites leading to a lysis. In the Christian mystery, the painful death of the Lord as well as the redemption his sacrifice signifies are described.

In our dream we are, so to speak, right in the middle of this kind of experience. The image, of course, is appropriately childlike. A child takes delight in a beautiful wedding carriage and a wedding couple, for children enjoy splendor. Here in these parts, they also get sweets that the wedding couple throws them. This, after all, is a child from this country. She is four to five years old, and since she is obviously a bright child, such impressions are already definitive experiences. She knows, of course, what a wedding is. She also knows about the devil. He is mentioned in many sayings, and also in fairy tales. It makes a big impression on the child to hear, for the first time, about a being that she can't simply encounter on the street. She tries to incorporate this figure, but also other motifs from fairy tales, into a game. If the devil takes down with him the whole thing in the dream,

---

[77] English translation at www.everypoet.com/archive/poetry/Goethe (14 March 2007) (trans.).

however, this far exceeds the child's consciousness. The smell of a catastrophe suddenly intrudes into the thoughts of the wedding party. It is a frightening experience, and in the dream the child also does not know that this is only a vision, so to speak. Naturally, she is seized and experiences the whole action, happening before her eyes, as a real experience.

She is separated from this action, however, by the window. This is often the case. We are safe, the dangerous situation happens somewhere out there, and we have just seen it. Whenever this occurs in a dream, this means: not that I am in that situation, but *it is* such a situation. Now this can refer to events of contemporary history, or to a collective event in general, of no personal concern, but a shared destiny. At that moment, in any case, it does not refer to the dreamer. So we may call it a kind of *vision of the future*. The child anticipates her future life, which naturally appears kind of absurd in light of her young age. We don't understand that children can have such visions—as a matter of fact, they really shouldn't happen to them! The proverbial innocence of the children is in our way. But we have to get used to the idea that, especially in early childhood, we have dreams or visionary experiences that are simply not childlike, whereas they would be quite appropriate in adults. A girl of sixteen who, in the first blossoming expectancy of the upcoming feast of life, is seized by a gloomy premonition of the hellish fire into which she will draw her husband—this we can understand. Sure, she is cute, with innocent eyes, full of expectations, and she is walking on cloud nine—but it is entirely possible that she will get a premonition of who she is, who she is as a shadow, and that she will know: "Once I'll have a man, I will show him what I'm capable of." The moment she does have him, all hell breaks loose. Unfortunately, this is no uncommon experience; it is as if a woman would only wait until she has her man—and then she shows him what she's capable of! We have to be particularly wary of altruistic personalities! We are no gods, after all; we have a shadow, and we have some dark premonition that something is somehow not right behind our back. Sometimes it takes fifty years to realize this.

Let me tell you an example: I knew an American man; he was a very respectable person. From his fortieth year onward he became gloomier and gloomier. Before that, he spent much time in clubs and societies and got along well with other people. Then he became a moralizer, however, sticking his nose into other people's affairs, which became increasingly unbearable to his wife. He chastised everybody in his overblown moralistic attitude. He looked after all kinds of things, was churchwarden, and read the lesson in church on Sundays. Gradually, this developed into a very dark situation; everybody feared and hated him. All of a sudden, at the age of fifty-five, he sat up in his bed at night, and said to his wife: "Basically, I'm a scoundrel!" No sooner said than done. From that moment, until his death, he squandered all his assets. He no longer gave a damn about anything. It was only in that moment that he discovered he had a shadow.

Not everybody takes that long to discover his or her shadow. A child nearing the age of puberty can already have a dark premonition of something evil, something fiery, as can even a little child hardly out of her cradle, as evidenced by our dream. Even if we can hardly understand it, the child did have this dream, and the whole twaddle about the innocence of children is completely useless. This child dreamed that the devil had got hold of the wedding couple and that all went up in flames. Basically, in its crude form this tells us enough. It tells everything: that the wedding feast, the beautiful feast, stands in relation to a terrible moral catastrophe, obviously connected to the fire—with instinct. When instinct emerges, so does evil! And it is also obvious that the wedding feast has to do with instinct. If a child can have such a dream, we will have to assume that something in her knows about this process. We can hardly suppose that her mother had told her, "When once you marry, the devil will get you"—because in that case she wouldn't have had to dream this. She would have known it already. So we are forced to assume that this knowledge, which is in her *in potentia*,[78] is a *knowledge born with her*,

---

[78] Latin, "as a potentiality, in potential form" (trans.).

a knowledge she brought into the world with her. Where does she have this knowledge from? It is in nature, in the make-up of her brain. She is born with a complete brain, in which there are proto- types of all the processes of human life, and which, therefore, will function in this typically human way. And these processes will occur, as they have always occurred in human life: death will come, or evil, or both. This is a form of human life, a form repeated millions and millions of times over; it is a typical process.

Educational matters can change nothing about this basic fact. On the whole, it does not matter if the child has had this or that educa- tion, or was exposed to this or that influence. In a way, there is *no de- velopment of the personality*. It has always been there, only not in an empirical sense, but invisible, as a potentiality. Education can do lit- tle more than polish the surface, or also change it a little bit, but the basic nature is not touched by it. We cannot add to it or take any- thing away from it. Education is nothing but a differentiation to a specific goal; it can make us wash our hands, brush our teeth, or put on a certain collar. But "education of the personality"—now what should that be? Has anybody seen that yet? Human life simply takes its course in the way a human life takes its course in general, and it will obey the laws characteristic of human life.

If we may assume, then, that human dispositions are there in pro- totypical form, we are free—indeed it behooves us—to prove that these are *ideas* and *images* that can be found throughout the whole history of mankind. The wedding couple in our dream, the carriage and its ritual use, the devil—these are ideas, images, which have had their clear impact on the history of peoples, and which are present again *in potentia* in every child. They are particularly vivid in chil- dren, because children are still nearer the collective unconscious. *The mental state of the first years of life does not differ from the collective unconscious*; it is a world rich of images. There is nobody to look at them, because no consciousness exists. It is a world ocean full of the strangest figures. The child emerges from this sea. Later in life, peo- ple sometimes still have a faint memory of this golden background. The more memories of what had been exist, the more difficult the adjustment will seem. This can even have the effect that no real interest in questions of the present can be summoned. It can also lead to the fact that such children do not really get into their bodies, that many body zones are not cathected at all. They know the body only from looking at it, they themselves are not in it, so as to feel through it. The breathing teacher then says: the breathing does not go through at all. They are incapable of completely inhabiting the body. This can be seen in the clumsy and stiff posture of such persons. They walk around as if they pulled themselves on strings. These are effects of the past that still projects out [into the present]. It is still too strong. "That life which was before, and which is different from the life we are leading now"—this is a theme you will encounter more than once in the history of peoples. The best example is the *Tibetan Book of the Dead*, the *Bardo Thodol*.[79] The Bardo lifespan is forty-nine days. The souls live, so to speak, in a collective world, and are confronted with spirits and other images of life, "images of all creatures," as Goethe says in *Faust*.[80] There are still other examples of this prehistoric world. Do you know any?

Participant: The concept of a paradise without time and space.

Professor Jung: The whole legend about the Golden Age in general, the idea that in prehistoric times there was golden glory, and that subsequently the world became more and more evil. This world of wonderful things, which once was, is the *aljira* mentioned earlier. In the *aljira* myth it says: In primordial times, when there was no time, there lived the half-animal ancestors, the great creators. Everything was wonderful, everything was done by enchantment. All things were created very wisely. Then these *aljira* gods or heroes sank into the earth and were no longer seen, but they did leave traces. These traces are now objects of ritual worship. During cults we remember what had been before. So when the primitives, for example, perform dances, they make strange patterns in the sand, which are beautiful to look at. This is something the ancestors did in ancient times. When it is repeated, the ancestors are still alive. The ancestors make life beautiful again. They lead a part of the underworld upward again.

[79] See the notes to seminar 1 (ed.).
[80] Goethe, *Faust* 2, 1, "Dark Gallery," verse 6289 (trans.).

If you give that mythical material to the child, you will give her back a part of the glorious life she had before. For some time, she will then continue to live in that world, whose memories she sheds only with difficulty.

Participant: Actually, the beginning of many fairy tales—"once upon a time"—also refers to these primordial times.

Professor Jung: Yes, of course. I also found this attitude among the primitives. When the rice does not want to grow, you have to tell it how it used to grow originally.

Participant: Couldn't it also become harmful to give oneself over too much to these inner images? Couldn't they also become too powerful?

Professor Jung: Yes, this is quite possible. In mental disorder, for instance, you have to start by strengthening the ego. Sometimes it is necessary to say with vigor: "Come on, that's just a fantasy." First of all, the fantasy is devalued by this, the ego and the vision are torn apart, a distance is put between them. Sometimes you have to take very drastic measures to bring about the differentiation. So it can be necessary to shout at somebody to wake him up, when he is drifting into a kind of collective sleep, or to grab hold of people and shake them, so that they know who they are. A slap or a shove can work wonders, so that the person feels: "This is me." There are circumstances when a good smack, morally or physically, is the most effective way to counter the great fascination of the images.

The child has to step out of this primordial world, to be able to really enter into life. There is a Gnostic myth that after God had created the world, he spread a general ignorance, a general forgetting of what had been before. This is a precise description of this primordial state; first there are the "images of all creatures," then comes the great forgetting, and only then does human life begin. This transition of the child, however, from the Bardo time, from the prenatal psyche, into ego consciousness, is a critical transition.

So it sometimes happens—as in this dream from early childhood—that quite unchildlike things are seen, stemming from that collective region in which all of human destiny is present in images. This is what happened to this child. When I deal with such a dream,

I offer as much mythological material as possible, so that this *collective content* can be *incorporated into conscious life*. This is also why religious rituals have a healing effect. One is reminded of what had been long before. In this way memory is transformed into graphic images.

This is also how we want to approach our dream now, trying, to begin with, to understand the symbols of the dream out of the ideas that humankind has created about these processes. Let us first deal with the *symbol of the carriage*: the comparison of the carriage with a mandala is correct. You will better understand the meaning of the carriage and of the wedding couple if you consult some parallels in ethno-psychology. In India, for example, the gods are drawn in big rectangular carriages with eight wheels, built in the form of a mandala. On each of these carriages full of woodcarvings there stands a pagoda, in which the god or the divine couple is sitting under a baldachin. So the deity is at the center of the mandala. The form of the mandala indicates perfection: this is hinted at by the roundness of the wheels as well as by the fact that there are four corners. The fourness stands in relation to the four horizon points and the four seasons. The roundness is complete fulfillment. The divine couple in the carriage is also a symbol of completeness: the feminine and the masculine are together. In Tibetan tradition, the gods are depicted in sexual union, in eternal cohabitation, or even as hermaphrodites. This idea reemerges in the Occident at around the end of the fourteenth century, in Hermetic philosophy, which proceeds from the assumption that the perfect being is hermaphrodite: every Adam would carry his Eve within himself.

The idea of the divine couple, in the form of the divine marriage, the *coniunctio*,[81] represents a climactic point in life, which will, however, soon fade. The revelation of the deity is immediately followed by an enantiodromia,[82] in the former of utter destruction. Life cannot pause on the climactic point, it has to continue to reach the op-

---

[81] Latin, "connection, conjunction"; in alchemy: "union" (ed.).

[82] In Heraclitus's philosophy, the term *enantiodromia* (Greek, running counter) stands for the play of opposites, i.e., the view that all that exists will eventually turn into its opposite (cf. C. G. Jung, *Psychological Types*, CW 6, §§ 713–14) (ed.).

posite to come to a new climactic point again. This is the cycle of existence of the so-called *samsara*,[83] the eternal up and down, ascent and descent of the gods. In this context it becomes understandable that the carriage is a *symbol of transition*. You will find it closely linked to the *transitus* of the gods. This is clearest in Egypt, although there the god does not use a carriage, but a boat. We talk about the *culte de passage*. The god is taken for a trip to the West on a barque. This *transitus* portrays the ecliptic of the sun across the sky. It is the cycle of rising and setting. In other places, these transitions take place in a carriage. Processions in which images of God are drawn on carriages have the same meaning: the gods are walking. On a primitive level, this turns into the roaming of the ancestors, the totemistic ancestors, the half-animals, who walk the earth and create everything. In our regions, it is the devil who represents the remnants of those times of the *aljira*; he is half-animal, with a cloven hoof and other animal attributes. You find the walking up and down of the gods also in Germanic sagas and poetry, for example, in Spitteler's *Olympischer Frühling* [*Olympian Spring*].[84] There, too, a walk in the distant sky is described; one moment the planet gods are visible, the next invisible; the subject of the whole epic is the eternal cyclical motion of the events.

In this cycle of rise and fall, the end of the world is, as we know, depicted also as a *fire ending*. For Heraclitus, life itself is a flow of fire, the "everliving fire."[85] The fire thus becomes a basic symbol of life. The godfather is given a burning candle at christening, therefore, as a symbol of illumination and vitalization, and of spiritual life. Fire is always a *coniunctio*. Something spiritual and male, the oxygen, combines with something visible and female, the wood. In the act of this combination in fire—for example, in the Vedic tradition[86]—the underlying piece of wood is female; the rotating wooden stick is the cor-

---

[83] In Hinduism: transmigration of souls. As the continuous round of birth, death, and rebirth, it is the context for all experience (trans., ed.).

[84] Carl Spitteler (1845–1924), Swiss poet and winner of the Nobel Prize for literature (1919), largely in recognition of this great epic (1900–1906) (trans.).

[85] Diels-Kranz Numbering System, 22B30 (trans.).

[86] The Vedas are religious scriptures that form part of the core of the Brahminical and Vedic traditions within Hinduism (trans.).

responding male part. Together they produce a spark. When the marriage takes place, the fire flares up.[87] The eruption of the fire is the actual union, the union of two opposites.

The union of the Two produces the Three, and out of the Three develops the Four. This is the Witch's Tables [Hexeneinmaleins].[88] This progression is an old axiom of alchemy, the axioma Mariae, a Jewish philosopher of the first century, from whom a text of doubtful authenticity is extant.[89] This axiom is also found in fragments by the Byzantine alchemists, for example in Christianos.[90] So it is as follows: the One is the unconscious; everything is still unseparated. The Two is the appearance of the opposites, of male and female. The Two creates the son, the child, and this is the fiery spark. We mentioned already that the climax of life is a moment that turns into its opposite. Wherever there is the Three, there always is the devil, too. So the divine spark already contains the burning. As we know and have discussed earlier, the figure of the son in Faust also perishes in the fire. This burning leads from the Three to the Four, to the whole. This desired state, however, is at the same time the original one. Why?

Participant: When all is burnt, all is unseparated again.

Professor Jung: But then what is the difference between the original and the final states? What happens when the things are burned? What happens, for example, according to the primitive view?

Participant: The things go up in smoke and rise with the smoke.

Professor Jung: The smoke carries the images, the subtle bodies of the things, up again to the seats of the gods. This means: what was created by the transformation of the Original One is transported back again into eternity in the form of images. All that happened is elevated to an image and returns to the seat of the gods. But the origi-

---

[87] Cf. the detailed discussion of this topic in C. G. Jung, Symbols of Transformation, CW 5, §§ 204ff, 211ff (ed.).

[88] "You shall see, then! / From one make ten! / Let two go again, / Make three even, / You're rich again. / Take away four! / From five and six, / So says the Witch, / Make seven and eight, / So it's full weight: / And nine is one, / And ten is none. / This is the Witch's one-times-one!" (Goethe, Faust 1, verses 2540–53) (trans.).

[89] On the axioma Mariae, cf. C. G. Jung, The Practice of Psychotherapy: Essays on the Psychology of the Transference and Other Subjects, vol. 16, pp. 207, 306, 308 (trans.).

[90] Marcellin Berthelot, Collection des anciens alchémistes grecs, vol. 6, p. 383 (ed.).

nal and the final states are not the same. In the original state we are victims of the events, we are not detached from them, we do not have any vision. In the end, however, the images, the whole richness of our experiences, returns in the smoke to the gods. The view of the Catholic Church on unbaptized children is also based on this idea. What does the Church say about them?

Participant: That they do not have eternal souls.

Professor Jung: No, not that. All men have living souls.

Participant: They are excluded from the redemption through Christ.

Professor Jung: That's clear anyway. But the crucial point is that they are deprived of the *Visio Dei*, of seeing God. A very little child who dies before baptism is not condemned, not stigmatized as some hellish brute, but simply deprived of the *Visio Dei*. It is up to the mercy of God what to do with this unfinished soul. Seen from our context, this is absolutely consistent. It has not experienced the images of life, and the images of life are, as it were, the fiery images that come from the original fire, and contain, so to speak, the core of life. The things have to be purified before they can rise to the gods and be offered as an earthly sacrifice to the spirits. This happens, as we have seen, in the fire, and the fire, therefore, also has the meaning of purification. It enables differentiation, a disintegration into separate figures. The ashes fall down to earth, and the purified subtle body rises into the heights. This purification process, which consists in the separation of heavy and ephemeral bodies, is possible only when things have a body. When something disintegrates, there always is a body. When things do not have a body, they are not separated. Where there is a body, there always is fusion with matter—and consequently a sacrifice of matter is also necessary.

Participant: "Carrying earthly remains / Is hard to endure."[91]

Professor Jung: Those who are not yet completely redeemed are afflicted with earthly remains, which then have to be burned out. This is very beautifully expressed in Dante, in the transition from Purgatory into Heaven. There Virgil has to turn back, because as a heathen he is not allowed to go through the flame of love. Dante goes

[91] Goethe, *Faust 2*, lines 11954–55 (trans.).

through the flame, in which all of his impurity is burned out. This is the only way he can get into heaven. In the mysteries, too, purification plays a role. The mystic is portrayed as somebody in need of purification; he has to cleanse himself of the blackness of his sins to receive, in a purified state, the teachings of the mysteries.

In our dream, all these ideas appear in a very simple form and extremely condensed. What caused the contamination, making a burning necessary?

Participant: The devil.

Professor Jung: The influence of the *devil* has, as it were, caused the contamination. The devil is the blackness; the evil is the blackness. The pure innocence of the joy of marriage is darkened. The divine spark between the opposites has hardly flared up before the evil, the devil, interferes in the form of instinct, of the physical body. This is the *admixtio diabolicae fraudis*, the admixture of diabolical fraud. It becomes evident that there is no such thing as complete purity, that things are mixed with the impure, with matter, and that, therefore, the burning ensues. The purification occurs in the fire, so that the pure being may rise into heaven, while the ashes fall down to earth.

We may assume that in this dream there is an admixture of evil in the dreamer's nature, which she unconsciously experiences as a contamination. The question now is how the dreamer will deal with this evil, in what way she will free herself of the contamination. The whole thing is a vision in which the dreamer herself is not involved. She is standing behind the window and watches, sheltered in the warmth of the parental house. The factor of *purification* is in the foreground of the second dream. The dream begins with the child in the bathroom of the parental house. The *bathroom* is very often mentioned by patients in precisely such a context. The consulting room of the physician is often portrayed as a bathroom, if not an even more intimate place. The ablutions, the *ablutio*, are a famous motif in alchemy. There the *ablutio* regularly follows the so-called blackening, the *nigredo*. The blackening is often identical with the *prima materia*, which is black or lead-colored. This color has to be washed off. So in this room of ablutions the dreamer looks at herself in the *mirror*. The mirror is a frequent allegory of self-reflection. The attention is directed to oneself, one "mirrors oneself." Schopenhauer says we should "hold up a mirror" to the blind (unconscious) will, so that it will recognize its face and then negate itself. So the mirror is an instrument for looking at oneself, for self-reflection.

> You find this same connection between *ablutio* and self-reflection in the beautiful legend of St. Ambrosius. Ambrosius was addressed by a young knight, who asked for instruction. Thereupon Ambrosius told him: "Your face is black; wash it first." Then he ordered him to look at himself.

In our dream, self-reflection is on an appropriately infantile level, and hence has to be interpreted in a completely primitive sense: "Look at yourself in the mirror, and see who you are." This is of special importance. To understand this completely, we have to go back to the preceding dream, because it is connected to it. The preceding dream represents a manifestation of the collective unconscious. Experience shows that in such archetypal situations a danger often arises. What is the danger when an archetype manifests itself?

Participant: One is devoured.

Professor Jung: Possibly. But there is a much more common and typical occurrence.

Participant: Identification.

Professor Jung: This too is being devoured.

Participant: Ego-consciousness is dissolved.

Professor Jung: Yes, but how is it dissolved?

Participant: A splitting occurs.

Professor Jung: Yes, disintegration, dissociation. Then we no longer know who we are. This is a typical phenomenon that occurs when an archetypal situation becomes overwhelming. When an archetype is constellated, there is always the danger of an assimilation into the archetype. One doesn't know this experience before one has had it. If this has never happened to you, you won't realize at all what kind of danger this is. Those who come into such a situation usually don't realize it at all. We see this most clearly in people in panic, or in a great mass of people that is moved by some common idea or emotion.

190

The individual does not know that he is in a state of dissolution, although he has lost his head just like everybody else. This approaches us stealthily. We are dissolved from within, and all of a sudden we are something else and do not even know it, and this is what is so uncanny in this phenomenon. Consciousness is simply depotentiated. At least we still have a certain protection. There is still just one moment left to say: "Hey, stop, so that's what it is!" If you realize this just in time, you are already protected against it. But if you don't know any longer that you have been touched, you are already in a state of dissolution. When a person is in danger of dissolution, it is necessary that he look at himself, in order to reestablish identity with himself.

> I had a patient who was, so to speak, in a state of habitual dissolution. When she came to see me, she did not know what to talk about. Whenever she came, she just babbled along. Once she was late, apologized, and said: "Let me just quickly do something." She took out her pocket mirror, looked at herself in it, and remarked: "I've got to do this to know who I am. Otherwise I wouldn't know what to tell you." This is the identity that has to be established.

In everyday life, too, we are constantly concerned about our identity. When you go to some festive event, for instance, you ask, "Do I look alright?" or "Am I ok?" or something like this. One is perhaps inclined to rationalize this, but on a deeper level it is always a reassurance about our identity that we seek. We would like to have it confirmed that we are really in one piece. It is a rudimentary *rite d'entrée*.[92] Before going out hunting, the primitives put themselves into the mind of the hunter. The identity with the role has to be determined beforehand. In a way, these are rudimentary remnants from a time in which consciousness was not always at our disposal, and when we couldn't simply bring ourselves to do something. Central Australians even have a rite of getting angry; otherwise they could not rouse themselves to get really angry, and would not do anything.

Looking in the mirror in our dream is a direct answer to a preced-

---

[92] French, "rite of entry" (trans.).

ing, dangerous intrusion of the unconscious. When a child has such an anachronistic dream, it is always a reasonable assumption that *the necessary separation from the collective unconscious*—in which she is originally rooted—*is not proceeding quite correctly*. The prenatal state is still very powerful, and the child does not want to enter into reality. Therefore these *rites d'entrée* are necessary to put such a child into her individual reality. In this sense, looking at herself in the mirror happens at the absolutely right time, because this sets something in motion. A process ensues, reaching a climax: she grows *wings*! This is the result of the self-reflection. What does it mean that she grows wings? What could come to her mind with regard to what will happen?

Participant: She could ask herself if she would like to stay on earth at all.

Professor Jung: Yes, if she wouldn't rather depart at once and fly into heaven. But something else could be the case when someone grows wings. Who else has wings?

Participant: The devil.

Professor Jung: Yes, she could also have dreamed of getting bat's wings. She could also have turned into a devil. So it is expressly stated that she turns into a *little angel*. We must not completely leave aside Mrs. Brunner's assumption that she may perhaps fly upward as a little angel.

There is actually a well-known expression in our colloquial language; we call a child a "dear little angel." Perhaps we may suppose her to be an absolutely nice and pure child, no longer with the least stain of an admixture of the black. Still, I would like to put a question mark after that. There is still another possible interpretation of the little angel. It is also possible that she is still a little angel, because she has not yet become a human being. It would be possible that an early manifestation of "evil" was so completely washed off her that she did not have any chance at all to sever herself from the collective unconscious. In this case, she would not have got a human body yet, basically, would not have been completely born yet.

I would like to read to you a report about the dreamer, so that you can judge for yourselves. She is a medical student of very delicate features, very shy and highly sensitive, so that she hardly dares touch the patients, out of fear of hurting them. She has religious and philosophical interests, and takes part in the Oxford movement. You see that the dreamer, now twenty-three or twenty-four years old, still has the attitude of the little angel. She is encapsulated against the world, won't let the world come into her. She is really still in the egg. Well, there are some occasional little outbursts of defiance. She naturally tries to tear herself away from the mother, makes feeble attempts at getting out of her cover, like the little chicken that pecks at the eggshell, very modestly. So in this way she tries to come out of the primeval state. This example gives you a clear picture of how such dreams anticipate the later personality.

7. Dream of a Five-Year-Old Girl of the Fairy and the Snakes[93]
PRESENTED BY WALTER HUBER[94]

Text: *A good fairy protects me. She is all-powerful. She leads me into a big house with endless corridors and many doors. Finally we come into a room, and there are three snakes in the center, coiling around in a circle. The fairy steps into the center, and a fire flares up, into which she disappears. I'm at a loss and I know that I can't find the good fairy again, and I run back through all the rooms, and after a lot of searching I manage to find a way out. Finally I come to the street, where I meet a playmate from nursery school. The fairy is also standing there and takes me under her protection.*

Professor Jung: Don't you notice something?

Participant: As in the last dream, fire plays an important role.

Professor Jung: As a matter of fact, here, too, something that was good burns up in the fire. There it was a wedding carriage, here it is a fairy. I did not have this parallel in mind when I chose the dreams for our discussions, but it is really a similar motif. Mr. Huber gave a quite exhaustive account of the fairy myths. Let us try to find an approach to this fairy in which she is not seen from too great a mythological distance, in which she would be intangible. So what would be a good fairy for a little child?

[93] Session of 14 February 1939.
[94] Mr. Huber's paper is not extant (ed.).

Participant: The mother.

Professor Jung: Yes, this seems the most reasonable assumption. We'd first think of the mother. For a little child, completely in the mother's care, the mother is the figure who appears at the right moment, from whom everything good and loving comes, who wonderfully provides for everything the child wants. So well-meaning people are inclined to suppose that a child, who dreams of a good fairy, is dreaming of the mother. But, for heaven's sake, we have to go a bit further for scientific reasons, and to take into consideration the fact that the child could easily have dreamed of the real mother as well. Why did she have to turn the *mother* into a *fairy*, an illusory being nowhere to be found? The dream gives no indications for that. We can just state that the dream prefers to speak of the mother by presenting her as a fairy, to make the fairy, not the mother, real. It translates the mother into a fairy, so to speak. What are the grounds for the child's need to translate the mother figure, so near, so much more important and powerful, into something as distant as a fairy? Why can't the child just dream: my mommy protects me, she is omnipotent, she leads me into a big house, and so on?

Participant: To deprive her of her actual importance; it sort of reduces her potency.

Professor Jung: With this you are going too far already. You consider the effect of the translation. Before doing that, we want to have a closer look at the phenomenon itself.

Participant: We have to assume that it is not the real mother who is meant.

Professor Jung: Yes, we have to arrive at that conclusion. In such cases we can say: "We don't know why this is so. It is only clear that the unconscious has an urgent, inexorable need to say 'fairy,' not 'mother.'"

Participants: Archetypes are more graphic than reality.

Professor Jung: Yes, we always forget that in a dream archetypes are stronger than outer reality. This means, in this case, the fairy is stronger than the mother. This seems irrational to us. But when you go back in the history of mankind and investigate the psychology of the primitives, you will find similar phenomena. You will see that the

194

primitives talk precisely about those strange figures that run counter to all experience. None of them has ever seen such a creature, half man and half animal, but it takes hold of them much more than anything rational.

Participant: Isn't the mother also a powerful archetype?

Professor Jung: Of course the mother is a powerful archetype. Originally, for the child, who is completely living in the collective, the only archetype at all is that of the mother. This archetype she projects onto the real mother, or to another person who takes her place. For the originally existing unconscious there is nothing but the archetype of the motherly woman, no real mother yet at all. This brings about strange complications. Then the mother often assumes a superhuman, demonic character. She can become a witch or a snake, a wicked wolf, a cat—anything people with a negative mother complex project onto the mother: that she secretly mixes poison, that she is threatening, that she has any other evil influence. The comparisons drawn in these cases of a negative mother complex would be much more appropriate for a mythical being than for the real mother. The original disposition of the child is a *mythological* one. When the dream says "fairy," not "mother," it expresses precisely this mythological quality. If it said mother, it would mean, not the archetypal, but exactly the concrete form. From the view of the child's consciousness, we could well say that it means the mother, as the mother is still of a mythological character. So the dream interprets the mother as a fairy. If we reduce this archetype to the mother, the whole projection will fall onto the real mother. This would have the consequence, for instance, that the child might make the mother responsible for a negative content. She would, from then on, ascribe any demonic effect to the mother's influence. The archetype belongs to the child, and must not be taken away from her. If one pointed out early on to the child, for example, that the fairy were not the mother—I for one wouldn't tell her, but let's just assume it—it would be possible that the child could ascribe the characteristics of the motherly quality to the fairy, and form a relationship with the mother that would be reduced to an infantile level.

When the unconscious says: "It is a fairy," then please stay with it.

Archetypes are extremely powerful; they assimilate reality. When people make an archetypal assumption about somebody, they won't let themselves be persuaded to give that up; they are possessed by it. The archetype hypnotizes, it takes possession of you, and you will be captivated by it.

So when the child tells us such a dream, we had best tell her something about the good fairy, so that this mythical being will come alive in her. If we are asked who this fairy really is, however, we will have to know a bit more about her. We can't just repopulate the world with fairies. Perhaps in Ireland that's still possible, but not in the Canton of Zurich. Here it is out of the question. So we have to bring the fairy home somehow. Now what does the fairy mean in the child's imaginary world?

Participant: She is a powerful and wise figure.

Professor Jung: Yes, she is powerful, wise, has wonderful qualities, which are all things the child has not.

Participant: She is a *guiding figure*, a kind of female guide.

Professor Jung: Yes. In a man's case, this would be a superior man. Just think of Goethe/Faust, Nietzsche/Zarathustra, Dante/Virgil!

Participant: The guiding figure corresponds to the figure of Hermes, the guide in the spiritual world who guides the philosophers.

Professor Jung: Yes, Hermes Trismegistos[95] is the initiator, the *psychopompos*,[96] and the fairy is his female counterpart. She is that wondrous figure of the grown-up woman, the woman the child is not yet, a being naturally surrounded by miracles, magnificence, and power for the child, a superior figure, her own inner superiority. It is the anticipation of what the child will perhaps become herself later on. But what must happen before? The dream tells it.

Participant: The fairy has to go up in flames.

Participant: There is a very similar figure in the visions of Zosimos,[97] a figure of a priestly guide, who goes up in flames.

Professor Jung: The parallel with the visions of Zosimos is quite

---

[95] Thrice Great Hermes (trans.).

[96] Greek, "soul guide" (ed.).

[97] Cf. C. G. Jung, *Psychology and Religion: West and East*, CW 11, §§ 344ff; and C. G. Jung, *Alchemical Studies*, CW 13, "The Visions of Zosimos," §§ 85–144 (ed.).

convincing. We are talking about an image seen by Zosimos, a philosopher and alchemist in the third century. Its main feature is that he encounters a strange figure, the figure of a little old man, an *anthroparion*, a homunculus. The little old man is sacrificed by a priest, or he is himself the priest who transforms himself in the fire, devours, and then spits himself out, being cooked in the bowl-shaped altar. He is the illuminating guiding figure, a *psychopompos*.

The image of the fairy *burning herself* is something we have to pon-der for a long time and look at from many angles, in order to become reasonably clear about it. This is highly remarkable symbolism. The ceremony itself is significant. What does it tell us? To begin with, we have to look at the whole situation from the child's viewpoint. One of these fine days, the good fairy takes the child with her, as if she'd said to her: "Come with me, my little girl, we are going into the big palace; I'll show you something there." She leads her into the big room, and there is a demonstration of a burning. The fairy is not burned completely, because at the end she appears again. It is like a magical trick to frighten the child. Nothing bad happens; in the end everything is as it was in the beginning. The strange ceremony, which happens here, surprises us. There is a complete *restitutio ad integrum*.[98] The fairy reappears as if nothing had happened. This is the central problem of the whole dream. The dream is a kind of sketch of the fu-ture. The fairy demonstrates something, she shows what the child will have to go through herself sometime in the future. In the visions of Zosimos, too, the philosopher is only a bystander, watching. There, too, the figure of the guide burns himself, to show the alchemist the way. The soul guide appears in the dream and shows him: this will have to happen to bring about what you are looking for. What he is looking for is the *hydor theion*, the divine water, the secret, the means to make incomplete bodies complete. It is identical with Christian baptismal water, which is made in a very similar way. In a compli-cated ritual, the baptismal water is composed of exorcized water, ex-orcized salt, *oleum unctionis* (the consecration oil), and Chrisam, the oil of anointment. This ritual is one of the ceremonies performed at

---

[98] Latin, "reestablishment of the previous situation, full recovery" (trans.)

Easter. The instructions for the preparation of baptismal water can be found in the *Missale Romanum*, the Roman Missal.[99] The consecration of the water is performed on the eve of Holy Saturday. The *hydor theion*, which had been prepared in advance, is fertilized by the immersion of a candle, so that it may give birth again to man in the uterus of the Church. It is an extremely meaningful rite, a kind of *hierosgamos*.[100] Modern priests are quite unfamiliar with these things; the average priest usually does not know about it. It is one of those secrets that constitute the power of the Catholic Church over the unconscious.

This dream is about something similar, only it is expressed in a simpler form. Without doubt, the fairy is the superior, enigmatic, magical being, a kind of helpful spirit. Fairies, like elves, are beings of nature; they do not have Christian souls, but are beings of nature who come from nature and live in nature. This means: in our own nature, in the unconscious, in the natural soul, there is such a figure, and it is clearly expressed in our dream. But why does the fairy disappear in the fire?

Participant: This is a revival of the fairy.

Professor Jung: There is nothing in the dream to indicate that the fairy had been revived. There are some parallels to the process of burning that may be of help here, for example, in a story of Plutarch, *De Iside et Osiride*.[101]

> Isis got herself employed as a nanny by the king of Phoenicia. The child's mother catches her holding the child right above the fire until it burns. The queen shrieks with fright. Isis takes the child out of the fire and says: "Now everything is in vain. If you had not shrieked, I could have given the child immortality."

Participant: The symbol of the phoenix also belongs here.

Professor Jung: Certainly; the phoenix achieves a new existence by

---

[99] The book containing all the fixed and changeable prayers and readings for the conduct of Roman Catholic masses (trans.).

[100] Greek, "divine marriage" (trans.).

[101] Latin, *On Isis and Osiris* (trans.).

198

burning itself. Every five hundred years it burns itself with incense and other fragrant wood.[102] Do you know other examples?

Participant: Heracles also burns himself, and then rises to the gods.

Participant: Achilles, too, is held right above the fire by Thetis to immortalize him in this way. But then the father happens upon the scene and prevents the completion of the task. That is where Achilles' vulnerable heel stems from.

Professor Jung: So burning oneself means *immortalization*. The fairy in our dream goes through this process of change. She transforms herself in the fire and thus assumes a fiery nature of an eternal quality, just like gold, which no longer changes in fire. This is also the meaning of the visions of Zosimos—that fire bestows immortality. Here, too, as in the previous dream, fire stands for a purification from all corruptible substances, a disintegration of the body. We have to go through the fire, therefore, to be freed from this imperfect matter, to rise to heaven, so to speak, as a *spiritus*, a spirit, a subtle being. Because the pure form has been established forever, we assume immortal nature. But fairies are not subject to the law of mortality, they no longer have a carnal body, they are spiritual beings removed from the corruptibility of matter. So what the fairy does can have no meaning for herself, but the ceremony must have a meaning for the child. The fairy is the omnipotent, all-protecting, powerful being who has taken the child by the hand and reveals a secret to her. This is an obvious anticipation, a symbolical preparation for what is to follow. The guiding element, the adult element within the child, experienced by her as something extremely powerful and omnipotent, tells her: "Look, this is how it happens, this is how it is done, how you can change." And what should the child learn from it?

Participant: It could mean: "If you encounter a situation such as this circle of snakes, do not stay away. Go into the center, just like the fairy, and then you will go up in the flames and escape from the danger."

Professor Jung: You see, we have to bear in mind that the situation

---

[102] See the discussion by Dr. Nothmann earlier in this seminar of the dream of the five-year-old girl of the death masks of her parents (trans.).

is absolutely frightening for the child. A place where snakes are coiling in a circle is a place you'd better avoid. So the child does not go into the center herself, but the guide does, meaning: "Do not stay outside, step into it, whatever will happen; you will be consumed by the fire. You will turn into smoke, and then you will be here again." What does that mean? We can relate this to other things already discussed. Do you remember what we previously said about fire?

Participant: That it is related to the affects.

Professor Jung: Yes, in the dream of the wedding couple and the devil, too, the couple is consumed by fire. Fire is an emotional outbreak, an outbreak of the libido. That is why the libido is always compared to fire. So this means: "The libido will come to you, and you will be burned by it." But what does the *magic* circle, which is described here, mean?

Participant: Aren't these snakes chthonic figures? And isn't this circle the unconscious itself into which the child has to go?

Professor Jung: Well, I wouldn't just say "the unconscious." I don't believe that children have the task of getting closer to the unconscious, because they are not far removed from it anyway. The dream would express such a thought differently. We have to pay very close attention to the form, the *Gestalt*, we encounter here. There is talk about a circle; this is circularity, a sign of wholeness. So this is a situation referring to wholeness. Circularity is a very primary vision. It is the oldest symbol of mankind, already found in paleolithic rock drawings in Rhodesia. This most ancient symbol of circularity can be found from the Stone Age to the Bronze Age, and up until the present. It has always been interpreted as a sun wheel [see illustration].

This is one of the most archaic forms, however, found before wheels existed at all. It is completely out of the question that this is just a wheel. More likely it could be a portrayal of the sun, but then the drawing is not realistic enough for that, because paleolithic drawings are incredibly true to nature. Animals, for example, are drawn without feet, because the feet, standing in the grass, are invisible. These very early paleolithic artists saw nature in absolutely clear perfection and with unsurpassed realism. They did not make symbolic drawings, except when they depicted visions. And this drawing of a circle is a vision rather than reality. It can be found in the most inconspicuous places, for instance, in Ignatius of Loyola, who describes this in his autobiography. He had frequent visions of a golden circularity or a big golden ball. It hovered in front of him and filled him with a wonderful feeling. I do not know what it meant to him. You also find the symbol of circularity in the *Ecstatic Confessions*, in the confession of the theologian Symeon.[103] He describes how he searched for God, traveling everywhere without finding Him anywhere, until He rose in his heart as a little round sun disk. Circularity is a primeval vision.

Participant: Hildegard von Bingen[104] also describes such a vision.

Professor Jung: Yes, you will find this vision everywhere. In Buddhist meditations it also says: "Be round and round." The roundness has to be reestablished; this symbol has appeared again and again since primeval times, and has always had this same meaning of wholeness, of rotundity, of rounding off, and of completion.

So the circle of snakes in our dream means: "If we encounter a situation that requires our wholeness, and fail in this situation, we will have forfeited the wholeness." For we have to put ourselves completely in it, at the risk of being consumed by the fire. The further course of the dream shows that the burning did no harm, because the fairy is there afterward as she was before. The transformation did not adversely affect the fairy. The core problem of the dream is this demonstrated transformation, which occurs in a person who moves into the roundness, despite the potential danger represented by the snakes. After all, the snake is first and foremost an anxiety symbol. Monkeys and horses are also instinctively afraid of snakes. When you

---

[103] Martin Buber, *Ecstatic Confessions* (trans.).

[104] Hildegard von Bingen (1098–1179), abbess of a Benedictine monastery, German mystic, famous for her visions; cf. her book *Scivias* [Know the Way] (ed.).

see a circle of three snakes you will take good care not to step into it. You will experience anxiety. Should you step into it nevertheless, the transformation, meant to create the immortal being, will follow. The fulfillment of the meaning of life is linked to the idea of immortality. This does not tell us anything about immortality, as such. We only state that human beings have this emotion, and therefore talk about such problems. It is simply a psychological fact. In all of life's highest points in which we face life *completely*, we also have the feeling of the meaningfulness of life, and this feeling is always linked to the feeling of eternity. In alchemy, for example, the roundness that is manufactured is the *lapis philosophorum*, the philosophers' stone. It is the incorruptible object, the *corpus glorificationis*, the body of completion and perfection, or also the body of the Resurrection with which we are clothed, so to speak, on the Day of Judgment. The roundness in our dream, however, is a circle of *three snakes*. From the psychological point of view, we'd find four snakes much more appropriate, don't you think?

Participant: No, the Three is exactly right. Cerberus and Hekate also have three heads. The Three symbolizes male sexuality, the demonic sexuality.

Professor Jung: This is about *emotionality*, not only about sex. The other seven devils are implied too: wrath, *concupiscentia*,[105] avarice, envy, hate, in short, all the devilish things. That's what the Three is! We have to form a very concrete picture of this in the case of our child! It is a child, after all, whose body is still growing. The whole libido and the vital spirit are actually absorbed by this development; the body has to be built, and therefore plays a very great role. The instincts, which have built the body, will get ever stronger in the course of future development, and will burst to the surface in the form of emotions such as sexuality, envy, hate, anger, ambition, avarice, and so on. It is like a hellish fire.

> The child had another dream: She opens a door and sees the glow of a fire in the room. She knows: "This is hell." Then she leaves.

[105] Latin, "lust" (trans.).

She looked for the way to heaven, and saw hell! She was absorbed by it. This hell is the hell of instincts. The child had a premonition of the instinctual hell into which she will enter. In alchemy, this state of instinctual hell is represented as a snake with three heads, the so-called *serpens mercurii*. It leads the soul into the afterworld, and is identical with the Gnostic *Nous*,[106] which had originally come down from above and combined with matter. In other words, the divine Nous is also present in this instinctual phenomenon, this instinctual hell. Through the agony of the fire it then turns into the *corpus glorificationis*, into gold, into that which is eternal and unchanging. So, in a way, these three snakes symbolically represent the hell of instincts, and that is also why the child is afraid of it. In this fire one has to stand in order to be changed. Who never has been changed by the fire of passion is only on the run from himself, is merely a deserter from life. The three snakes, or the snake with three heads, can also simply stand for Satan. Where is he described as having three heads?

Participant: In Dante.

Professor Jung: Yes, Satan has three heads in the Inferno.

Participant: He is the counterpart of the upper Trinity.

Professor Jung: Yes, he is simply the countergod in the depths. Now what can be said about this trinity, be it of hellish or divine authority?

Participant: The Three is permanent unrest, the flame that flares up, the dynamic force.

Professor Jung: In our regions and in the Near East, the Three is a sacred number. This is not so everywhere; for the Indians, for instance, it is the Four. For them, the Four stands for everything beautiful. A prayer has to be said four times, for example.

Participant: When the call has been repeated three times, something will happen.

Participant: It is the ever-renewed synthesis of the opposites, which never stagnates.

Participant: The three Fates represent the coming into being and the fading away of what happens.

Professor Jung: In Mahayana Buddhism, you will find the Three as

---

[106] Greek, "mind, reason." In Greek philosophy, the spirit that forms the world (trans.).

the center of the carnal world: a cock, a snake, and a pig. The cock is lust,[107] the snake envy, and the pig ignorance. These three are the roots of the world, these are the three causes of what happens in the world. This can be found in the so-called Kilkor Mandala, which has these three figures at its center.

At Friday's lecture you heard about the visions of Mahasukha, and that he had three eyes to see the past, the present, and the future.[108] This shows that the Three stands in connection with time. The Three is time, and time is always identical with the *flow of energy*. We can conceive time only on the basis of movement. There must be change to make time possible. Proclus[109] says: "Wherever there is creation, there is also time." The Neoplatonic god of creation is Chronos, that is, time. This is the original form of Bergson's idea of the *durée créatrice*. Time has these two aspects: that which lies behind us, and that which lies ahead. Certain [American] Indians have only one word for time: day. Pointing forward means tomorrow, pointing backward yesterday, and a movement downward today. Threeness designates the course things take. Time is identical with the course things take. Time, as such, does not exist at all. There is only the course things take, which we measure with the notion of time. For primitive man, who is close to nature, the course of time is no abstraction. For him there is only a then, a now, and a before. He doesn't have a watch, does he, on whose numbers he could read the time. He completely exists in that stream of events, which is permanently flowing into a dark hole, which comes to us from a dark future, which flows through us, and sinks into eternal darkness behind us. Primitive man has no history; there is no history before the grandfather, prehistory lies only about three generations back. The primitive is most deeply impressed by this strange stream of events, however,

[107] In the original: *Wohllust* (a neologism; roughly "the pleasure of feeling well"), probably a typographical error for *Wollust* (lust) (trans.).

[108] In Buddhist Tantra, *Mahasuka* is the name for a state in which subject and object, sense and sense field, are nondual, imbued with unconditional bliss. Vajrayogini, a red, seminaked dancing goddess related to the Prajnaparamita and known as the "Mother of all the Buddhas," has three bloodshot eyes symbolizing her ability to know the past, present, and future (trans.).

[109] Proclus Lycaeus (412–487), called "The Successor," Greek Neoplatonist philosopher (trans.).

coming from the tomorrow, flowing through the today, and sinking into the yesterday. For him this is a directly experienced fact of life.

This continuity of events is also at the basis of the Chinese concept of nature, according to which everything happening at a given moment is happening exactly as it has to. You will find this idea in the Book of Changes, the I Ching. When I throw a handful of peas, they will roll in all directions. Try to interpret this, and you will understand the importance of the *moment*. If you practice such a method to some extent, you will see how remarkably well the meaning of the I Ching matches the psychological situation. It is more than a *façon de parler*.[110] It is a highly remarkable fact that can also be proven by data from astrology—which is not just superstition, provided you have the necessary experience. Astrology has to do with stars only insofar as the course of events is measured with the help of them. Telepathic experiences also belong here. Some smart alecks say it's all nonsense, but most often they have never heard of such experiences, simply because this does not fit into their worldview.

All these phenomena of *synchronicity*—which are really striking once we pay attention to them—only mean that *corresponding things are happening at the same moment*. This points to the substantiality of events in time. It is an archaic experience such as that of expanded space.[111] We have seen that time has three aspects: past, present, and future. The *three snakes* in our dream are probably a reference to *time*. Originally time itself was depicted as a snake, as in the Zodiacal snake. Religious heroes were often portrayed in connection with time. In the Upanishads, too, Prajapati is the year, is Chronos, the creator of the world. Christ is also the ecclesiastical year; in certain early Christian drawings he was depicted as a snake carrying the stars on its back—twelve stars representing the twelve disciples. It is the time, the year with its twelve months. Time symbolism also played a great role in the Mithras cult. The figure of Aion usually stood at the main altar of the Mithras cult—he is a man with a lion's head, enveloped by the Zodiacal snake, *Zrvan akarana*, meaning "boundless

---

[110] French, "manner of speaking" (trans.).

[111] Cf. C. G. Jung, *The Structure and Dynamics of the Psyche*, CW 8, "Synchronicity: An Acausal Connecting Principle," §§ 836–958 (ed.).

time." As you can see, there is ample evidence for the snake as a symbol of the passing of time. In our dream, the child is told to go into this circle of snakes to transform herself. The transformation is inevitable because she is stepping into the fire with the corruptible body. In our rational thinking this would equal self-destruction, but the irrational meaning is: transformation to immortality.

Participant: How should we interpret the *playmate* in this so very archetypal process?

Professor Jung: The playmate is very important. Why?

Participant: Because she belongs to her *reality as a child*.

Professor Jung: This is correct. She reestablishes the connection to her age. When the child goes with the fairy, it is as if she were drawn into the beyond. The typical threat a constellated archetype poses is to temporarily draw the person into unreality, into prenatal psychology. The dream counters this threat with the figure of the playmate. Her importance lies in reconnecting the child to her childlike reality.

8. *Three Dreams from Adolescence (Fifteen-Year-Old Boy):*
   Of the Tiger, the Snakes, and the Magic Herb[112]
   PRESENTED BY PROFESSOR JUNG

Texts: *1. I'm lost in the desert, wandering around and thirsty. The sun burns down mercilessly, and I'm about to die of thirst. The moment I'm starting to collapse I see an oasis. As I crouch to quench my terrible thirst, I see to my great horror a giant tiger, preparing to leap to kill me. Its eyes have a reddish glow, and I feel paralyzed. It crouches, ready to jump; I'm covered in cold sweat from every pore, and I wake up.*

2. Again I'm in the desert. The sun is not shining, but still it's unbearably hot. I'm wearing high boots so the snakes can't harm me. The sand is teeming with snakes, and I just don't understand where all those wild animals come from. Suddenly, a terribly big boa appears; it is white as snow and her back is full of black crosses. At first the snake doesn't seem to pay attention to me, but then it turns around, spots me, and already I'm under its spell. Very slowly she curls around my legs, then winds around my neck and starts to strangle me. I can already hear my bones cracking, then I wake up with a sick feeling in my stomach.

[112] Session of 21 February 1939.

3. I'm looking for a certain herb on the prairie. It's supposed to grow under a nearly transparent stone. The moment I think I've found that stone—I see it right in front of me—a mighty lion appears before me that also eagerly heads for that stone and the magic herb. I feel I have to retreat, but still manage to shout a spell-word to the lion, which can either destroy or rescue me. The lion is so puzzled that it calmly lets me reach for the stone, but then it seems to come to its senses, my magic call fades, and the blood-thirsty lion comes nearer. In ultimate desperation, I call out for my mother; she comes with the bicycle, takes me with her, and we are rescued.

Professor Jung: These dreams are from a fifteen-year-old boy; they are typical adolescent dreams. I would like to use them for comparative reasons, because we can note some interesting differences from childhood dreams.

To begin with, it will be useful to make some general introductory remarks on *puberty*, because the psychological situation at this age is completely different from that in childhood. During puberty, the ego is already more or less independent; it has already freed itself of the phenomena of the collective unconscious. The child has grown into a specific human world, into the world of the family and the world of the school. There already exists a certain personality that, however, is now suddenly exposed to the shock of sexuality. It goes without saying that this destabilizes the standpoint gained so far, sometimes in an outright catastrophic way. A remarkable change of the personality, therefore, takes place at this age. It is also possible that mental disorders become manifest at this age, under the influence of that fateful power which is sexuality. Something completely new is befalling the person here, and it hits an ego that is not yet prepared for this at all, because it has only known the infantile instincts, which, thanks to education and the training the child has had in school, have been more or less integrated. All this is now suddenly knocked over by the invasion of sexuality. This is what the dreams talk about. These are the only dreams the dreamer wrote down during his adolescence. Obviously, that was a phase in which he himself noticed that something of very special importance happened. Let us now try to understand the dreams in detail.

In the first dream the situation is very clear. The dreamer wanders around in the *desert*. How do you interpret the desert?

Participant: As an isolation.

Participant: It is a dangerous place.

Professor Jung: Yes, it is the place of fear and danger. We must not start out from the locals' view of the desert. This is not an Arab child but a European. The desert is a place of horror, the loneliness in the desert is always filled with ghosts. Those wonderful wadis in the desert are populated by devils called *djinns*. For the dreamer, who presumably lived with his family here in Zurich, the desert is something new and adventurous, which naturally also suggests the idea of loneliness and abandonment. So the dreamer is in, and completely at the mercy of, a peculiar psychological situation. What does it mean that he is thirsty, but not hungry?

Participant: The fire, his own instinctuality, is burning in him.

Professor Jung: Yes, it is very hot, that is, the situation is very hot, and so naturally this makes you thirsty rather than hungry. The boy is about to die of thirst; he is now seized by a desire, a need, that is alien to him. This is precisely what he is helplessly at the mercy of. Now comes the complication, the drama: the moment he starts to collapse, he discovers an *oasis*. So something helpful is occurring at this moment. It is the old story that someone, lost in the desert, dreams of an oasis: he sees a Fata Morgana, the well-known pool of water in the desert, always around noon, valleys with wonderful blue lakes, where before there had been nothing but desert. These are well-known phenomena. So the oasis is a helpful place, where there are palm trees and other plants, and naturally also water. What does this oasis indicate—if we don't directly interpret it as a wish fulfillment? This would be way too cheap anyway. The oasis has to mean something, because otherwise it would be equally possible that someone came with a jug of beer or water.

Participant: There is *ground water* in the oasis; therefore, there is a contact with the unconscious.

Professor Jung: Exactly; wonderful, clear water is flowing there. In psychological terms: salvation is coming to the surface, which could quench his thirst and solve his whole complicated situation all at

208

once. This has to be a revelation of the unconscious. What it means still lies in darkness, so let's leave it open for the moment. First, there comes the *tiger* ready to jump. What does the tiger mean?

Participant: Because the unconscious comes closer, it is its instinctual aspect that first comes to the surface.

Professor Jung: Yes, the tiger, just like the bull, is always a personification of the *instinct* that is directed *against* us. So, for example, when you dream of an evil animal chasing you, of an evil dog or a wild bull, you can always be absolutely sure that you are somehow separated from instinct and have reached a contradictory situation. You are not at one with the view taken by nature, and hence nature turns against you. Then nature approaches you in the form of an animal image. You meet your animal. Being chased by an animal does not necessarily have an unfavorable meaning. It just says that you are hostile toward it, and so it assumes a hostile attitude toward you. Then you ought to make the gesture of politely taking your hat off and asking: "So what do you want of me?" And you will see: the animal has something to tell you.

Of course, the boy is against instinct, because it is that alien and uncanny thing that put him into a completely new environment. It now confronts him and becomes a danger for him. This is a typical motif found in many myths: the dragon or the snake that guards the hotly desired magic well. Sometimes, also, an evil spirit or a witch guards the well. The well is always guarded by the evil that wants to come to us. This being would like to seize us, it is what we have abandoned, what is in us and from what we have run away. That's why it is against us. If we want to reach the fountain of life again, the place, that is, where we no longer have to die of thirst, we will have to face the danger of meeting the evil being there, the evil because of which we went into the desert in the first place, in order to escape from it. We search to escape from it, and, therefore, it comes after us.

So, the dreamer must get into this danger here, because, if he wants to find the fountain of life within himself, he has to be reached by instinct. Basically, this double aspect of the source—oasis and tiger—is one and the same.

Participant: We find similar ideas in astrology, too. Under the constellation of Virgo there is the water serpent. This is the same image as above: the virgin as the fountain of life, and the dragon who guards her by her side. And above the source there are the heroes who make the descent: Heracles brandishes his club, and Ophiuchos brings the snakes under control.

Professor Jung: Yes, this parallel is very interesting. Here, too, the way to the fountain of life leads through the evil animal, through instinct. Now let us see how this development continues.

In the second dream the dreamer is in the desert again, and it is unbearably hot; but there is a difference from the first dream—the sun does not shine. What does it mean that the *sun* no longer shines?

Participant: That one no longer sees the reason for the difficulty.

Professor Jung: What does this mean, if the sun is the source of the difficulty?

Participant: The sun has to do with *consciousness*. One could say that the difficulty lies in consciousness.

Professor Jung: The sun always means "day." Consciousness and sun are identical. If the sun shines in a dream, this means clear consciousness; only that consciousness, of course, which is at the disposal of the dreamer. It is this consciousness that causes the terrible thirst and the danger of dying of it. He went away from the fountain of life because it was guarded by the tiger. To escape this danger he fled into consciousness, because he felt: "It is terrible down there, and man should not tempt the gods." So if the sun no longer shines in the second dream, this indicates that he has already come nearer to the unconscious. He is also already protected against the danger in an interesting way: he is wearing high boots. I do not know if the boy had heard about this, but his associations about the boots suggest that he had read that one has to put on boots to protect oneself against snakes. One might happen to step on a sand viper, and this is a nasty animal. You'd better wear boots in that case, because even tropical snakes can't bite through such a thick material. Now there are a great number of *snakes* in the dream. What does the snake mean?

Participant: Psychologically speaking, it is a *chthonic* form of instinctuality, one is in the power of the uncanny. This can easily happen in the desert, where one is exposed to many dangers. There in-

210

stinctuality appears as the epitome of the transpersonal and the uncanny.

Professor Jung: Yes, snakes are uncanny; we are afraid to step on snakes. When the dream says that the ground, the sand, is teeming with snakes, this means that the desert is *coming to life*, so to speak. Being alone then objectifies the inner state. These things really happen when we are alone—when you are alone for a long time, you may hear voices, somebody calling your name, for instance. There are actual visions and auditory hallucinations caused by solitude. When somebody with an animate unconscious—it needn't even be that animate—gets caught in solitude, all kinds of strange things may happen to him. When you are alone in your house, or when it is dark, or when the moon shines, you may think you've seen something. We also know this from the lives of the saints and the hermits, who actually often suffered from such experiences caused by solitude. These are exteriorizations[113] of inner processes. If there is a discrepancy between consciousness and the motoric and instinctual systems—that is, the cerebrospinal system with the exception of the cortex—snake symbols will appear. Basically, the snake always means the cerebrospinal nervous system. These are simply the centers of the low instincts or functions, with which we are no longer in accord. The stranger the unconscious content, the more it will be exteriorized, then occasioning these visions and auditory phenomena. This can also lead to phenomena such as ghostly apparitions, as can be well observed in such cases of exteriorization. You should consult the literature on this topic sometime. There is an interesting book by Albert de Rochas, *L'extériorisation du Sens,*[114] in which such phenomena are described, not in the light of psychology, but from a merely factual standpoint. There is mention of crashing noises in pieces of furniture, of "raps,"[115] and so on. The whole of spiritualism lives on such phenomena. We must not easily dismiss this by saying, "This is all chimera!" Naturally, one always tries to rationalize such phe-

[113] An outer manifestation of an intrapsychical content. See C. G. Jung, *The Structure and Dynamics of the Psyche, CW* 8, § 600 (ed.).

[114] Albert de Rochas, *Die Ausscheidung des Empfindungsvermögens.*

[115] This word in English in the original (trans.).

211

nomena, but if we study them closely, and under what psychological conditions they happen, we will discover that there is somebody close to the scene having an exteriorization. Such exteriorizations happen when we stand in contradiction with ourselves, that is, with our instinctual system. The exteriorization occurs when the conflict is about to become unbearable. It then shows itself to us from the outside, so to speak. These phenomena also happen to the mentally ill, in huge numbers. You may have walked through life for thirty years without taking anybody into your confidence, and then the secret exteriorizes itself: the whole town will know it, it will be everybody's secret, the record player will play its tune, and everything will leak the secret.

> There is a tragic, yet also grotesquely comic, story: An old governess had had a love affair in her youth, thank God she once did have one! She then bottled it up, sat there in her digs, old, sour, and retired, brooding over it. She began to notice that the people on the floors above and below "electrified" her. Finally the people in the street shouted after her: "Mademoiselle Desfleurs!"—the deflowered damsel—so it was already all over the town. This was a typical exteriorization.

Participant: Is this a hallucination?

Professor Jung: Yes, it is an acoustic manifestation of the most intimate thoughts, for instance, of those we never wanted to admit. This is the reason why in severe cases the voices tell you the most horrible things, the most embarrassing secrets, and it gets more and more obscene—and then you can talk about it less than ever.

> I once treated a young girl in the clinic. She was twenty years old. She was in a state of excitation, and just said out loud everything she'd ever heard. The results were the most incredible obscenities and dirtiest stories. I've heard quite a few things, but this terminology—a coachman would be no match for her. The young girl, who had been brought up and always lived protectively, just sputtered these things. Somewhere she had picked them up in passing. Her sister was very shocked and asked me: "For Heaven's sake, where did

212

the child pick up that language?" The unconscious had swallowed it with great pleasure, and then, instead of thinking those things, she pushed them aside, and that's why they had to be said out loud. But by then it was too late.

We must not entirely hide this side of life from children, even if there is the difficult pedagogical question of how to break it to them. It would be much better if we could just tell them: "Basically, you're all pigs!" Then many difficulties would disappear, but I don't know how we could break it to children, for we are no longer primitives. It makes no sense to harbor illusions about the human condition. I am all for sending kids to public elementary schools, therefore, by no means to exclusive private schools, so that they can ingest the necessary dirt. Private schools, with their cute kids and friendly teachers, are not healthy, because we are living on this earth, which simply is not clean.

The many snakes in our dream are such an exteriorization, an animation of the environment colored by anxiety. The snakes could, after all, come to you, and the strange and uncanny could penetrate you. This fear is particularly strong when you are alone in the hot desert.

Participant: At first the sand is teeming with snakes, but then something crystallizes. The chaos becomes concentrated in a primeval being, the white snake.

Participant: The multitude means disintegration. It is condensed in the image of the *boa*.

Professor Jung: Yes, now comes the really great danger, the terrible white boa with a number of black crosses on her back, a bit like an adder.[116] What does that mean? What is the *white* snake?

Participant: Now the source and the tiger, the double aspect of the unconscious, are united into one image. The snake is white and black, it is the Mercurial water, but still has a dangerous side.

Professor Jung: Yes, this is very important; the snake has to do with the water, and because it is white and black, it is really a *unification*

---

[116] *Vipera berus* (trans.).

213

of the opposites. It is as if the dreamer had had the idea that tiger and oasis are one and the same. This unification is possible because the sun no longer shines, because his conscious attitude is already shaken. This conscious attitude is somewhat darkened by the admixture of the unconscious. The dreamer has already been overcome by the tiger, and has been brought nearer to the unconscious of nature. It is an *abaissement du niveau mental*, absolutely necessary for viewing the opposites together. There is no way we could unify the opposites with clear, conscious reason—*tertium non datur*[117]—but in reality there is always a third, because otherwise we would eternally be stuck in the contradiction. Practically speaking, we are able to bring the Yes and No together, only we must not look too closely and be so terribly precise, just look the other way a bit. In this way the source has merged with the evil animal and has now become the boa, a white snake, to be precise.

Participant: White animals are those animals that don't live in the daylight, that are always underground. This clearly points toward the unconscious.

Professor Jung: Which animals are white?

Participant: The white horse in folklore, fairy tales, and myths. It also appears in a book by Kubin, *Die andere Seite*.[118]

Professor Jung: Kubin's book is actually quite silly. It was written by a modern artist keen not to think anything, in contrast with the artists of the Renaissance. He gives a description of the unconscious *tel quel* [as it is], pure raw material, a reproduction. It features a crazy horse that thunders through the vaults of the underworld. So this is such a white animal, but in this case it is a mythological one. Such animals also exist in reality. The Proteus[119] in the karst caves is white, for example, because it needs no color.

Participant: Worms and cockchafer grubs are white, too.

Professor Jung: Yes, all intestinal worms, tapeworms, and the like,

---

[117] The law of the excluded middle (trans.).

[118] Alfred Kubin (1877–1959), a famous Austrian expressionist illustrator and occasional writer. See Kubin, *The Other Side* (trans.).

[119] Proteus or Olm (*Proteus anguinus*), an endemic amphibian animal found in karst areas of the Dinaric Alps (trans.).

and in general many animals that live in the dark, are white. These are animals that symbolize the unconscious, the source just coming out of the womb of the earth. This is one of the reasons why the boa in our dream is white. But then it is not completely white, but has black crosses. This indicates that it is not just a cave tapeworm, but that its white color has still another meaning, derived from the contrast with black. What does "white snake" mean in a positive sense? Where does it appear?

Participant: In fairy tales.

Professor Jung: How does it appear in fairy tales?

Participant: Doesn't it have something to do with divination and premonition?

Professor Jung: It is, of course, the *magic serpent*; it reveals a secret, and usually appears with a little golden crown on her head to indicate that it is the queen serpent—a doctor snake. It brings wisdom and revelation, it knows about the secret treasure and the secret path. It is a helpful animal. Thus the white color is also a favorable color, obviously a color of enlightenment.

Participant: In old dream books, white animals are also favorable.

Professor Jung: Which corresponds with the fact that black animals are unfavorable. Now there are *black* crosses on the snake. What does that mean?

Participant: The unification of the opposites, of white and black.

Professor Jung: So the snake is of a contradictory nature: white on the one hand, black on the other. If we call to mind that the snake represents the cerebrospinal nervous system, it follows that a symbol of this other, uncanny, contradiction and strangeness is expressed by this image. A psychical content is expressed through it. The snake is not just a natural animal, but also a mythological animal. It not only stands for instinct, but also has a symbolic quality. We must not forget that sexuality is not just sexuality, but also a psychical experience. It has a psychical quality; it is somehow symbolic and magic. It never appears in its essence as such, therefore, but is always also a strange psychical state at the same time. Actually, the crosses don't really belong in nature; they look artificial.

Participant: Don't they actually mean a sacrifice of the natural?

215

Participant: According to an Orphic view, Hecate wears a cross on her head and is also accompanied by the snake.

Professor Jung: We have already mentioned that the symbolism of an idea adheres to this snake, that is, it is a symbolic snake. The *cross* as a symbol is very frequent in all kinds of ethnicities. In this case, of course, we have to think of the obvious, of Christian symbolism. One might speculate even further, that it could be a sōter snake, a *salvation snake*, which has a connection with Christianity, just like the source. For Christ is the fountain of life, the water of life. This snake simply replaces the source; it symbolizes the water of life. It is an alchemical idea that dragons or serpents—*serpens mercurii*—live in the middle of the earth, the imperfect metal, and are, so to speak, the anima, the soul of the metal. They are lured to the surface and then rise into the clouds, to come down again as rain; they are again absorbed by matter, and heal it. They come down as a medicine, a transforming tincture, as saviors of the being bound by the chains of imperfection, saviors not only of matter, but also of man.

At a Later Meeting of the Seminar [28 February 1939]

Professor Jung: Last time we talked about the symbolism of the snake. What did we find out about the psychological meaning of the snake?

Participant: The snake is, in general, a personification of instinct, instinctuality, of the transpersonal and the uncanny. In our dream, however, the snake not only represents instinctual nature, but is also a symbolic animal. It is white and has black crosses on its back. As a condensation of the multitude of snakes into one giant being, it also represents a synthesis of the many to the one.

Professor Jung: Yes, this is important. An example of this is the metal snake in Numbers 21:6–9. There you find the many snakes that bite the Israelites on their journey. Jehovah tells Moses to make a serpent of brass and to set it upon a pole, and whoever looks upon it will be protected against the snakes. For if you fall prey to the many, you will be dissolved. There is always the danger that an instinctual process will bring us down, and then we are dissolved in the multiplicity. We have lost the unity of the personality. If we are at one with ourselves, the other will face us.

216

Participant: Therefore, Christ is the One.

Professor Jung: Yes, just as Moses exalted the snake on the pole, Christ was exalted on the cross. That's why the Ophites said: Christ is the snake of salvation, the sōter snake. This idea persisted far into the Middle Ages. Maybe you have seen it: it is the cross with the serpent [see illustration].

You find this symbol in alchemy and in many other places. In an Indian royal palace from the fifteenth century I found a bedstead made of ebony, and there was that symbolic image, with many birds around it, and above there hovered a pelican. This piece was made by an Italian master in the sixteenth century. He depicted alchemical symbols on it, among them that snake, which can also be found in the famous book by Abraham le Juif.[120] Just as the *one* snake in the desert overcame the many, Christ, so to speak, overcame the autonomous instinctual forces, that is, the evil, and so he is the snake of salvation, the sōter snake.

Let us now proceed to the third dream. The locale of the dream is the *prairie*. What do you think of it?

Participant: In contrast to the desert, the prairie is already a bit milder; there is already vegetation.

Professor Jung: Yes, the prairie is a bit better than the desert. Grass grows there. How come the dreamer now comes into the prairie? Think of the sequence of the dreams, which is simultaneously a *causal* sequence!

---

[120] Abraham Eleazar (Abraham le Juif), *Livre des figures hiéroglyphiques*. The snake on the cross in that book is also reproduced in C. G. Jung, *Psychology and Alchemy*, CW 12, fig. 217 (ed.).

Participant: In the preceding dream the oasis and the white snake hint at something positive.

Professor Jung: Yes, the white snake is the first positive image that approached him. And because it is symbolic, a relationship with the person ensues. As a symbolic snake it is much less dangerous than if it were real. The phenomenon has been psychified, so the desert is no longer a desert, but becomes a prairie. There he is looking for a very specific *herb*. What about this herb?

Participant: In the Friday lecture there was mention of a mountain with the herb *lunaria* or *lunatica*.[121]

Participant: This herb is also found in fairy tales, where it brings life back.

Participant: The herb is also the alchemical medicine, the *alexipharmakon*, the antidote.

Participant: The expression "There's no herb for it"[122] also contains the idea of the herb as a medicine.

Professor Jung: Yes, the idea of *healing* is linked to the herb. The quality of healing already appeared with the boa, which actually is a snake of salvation or healing. If we can accept this snake, healing will follow. But as we have seen, the dreamer cannot yet accept it, although an idea of healing develops in him, by which he lets himself be led. He is looking for a better medicine.

Participant: One that he can assimilate.

Professor Jung: Yes, he could still be devoured by this giant snake, but the herb he can eat himself. This magic herb also plays a role in the Epic of Gilgamesh. Gilgamesh is seized by the fear of death, and seeks immortality by walking the path of the sun and going through the gate of the Scorpio giant. This is the [astrological] autumnal equinox of the Taurus age.

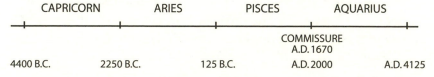

CAPRICORN	ARIES	PISCES	AQUARIUS	
			COMMISSURE A.D.1670	
4400 B.C.	2250 B.C.	125 B.C.	A.D. 2000	A.D. 4125

[121] Latin, "the lunar herb" (trans.).

[122] Literal translation of: *es ist kein Kraut dagegen (gewachsen)*; the English equivalent is: "there's no remedy for it."

218

Here we have a portrayal of the zodiacal signs through which the point of the vernal equinox went in historical times. As you can see, from the fourth to the second millennium B.C. the point of the vernal equinox went through the sign of Taurus, and then entered the age of Aries. About from 600 to 350 B.C. there were the light stars of the head of Aries. It is the age of the great philosophers all over the world: Heraclitus, Empedocles, Thales, Buddha, Lao Tse, and Confucius. Around 125 B.C., the age of Pisces began, coinciding with the beginnings of Christianity. As early as the first century, the concept of the Antichrist also came into being, referring to the second fish.[123] Our age falls in the era of the second fish, it is the *anti-Christian age*. The time of the French Enlightenment coincides with the beginning of the second fish. Voltaire's *écrasez l'infâme*[124] is characteristic of that time. Between these, there is the so-called commissure. The Renaissance falls into that transitory period, the expansion of the conception of the earth, the discovery of the earth. America is discovered, a Reformation is made, the power of the Church is shaken by the great schism. This is the first blow to the specifically Catholic attitude, although that era is still under the imprint of Christianity until the Enlightenment. From the Enlightenment onward, the erosion of Christianity as such starts, and the goddess of reason is enthroned. Now the Antichrist threatens to invade the cultural world.

These zodiacal signs are symbols that have been projected onto the sky from times immemorial, and probably reflect the structure of the unconscious.

The saga of Gilgamesh still stems from the end of the Taurus age, and was only later cast into a literary form. It was found in the library of Sardanapal, or Ashurbanipal (668–627 or 626 B.C.),[125] written on brick slabs. It is the myth of the natural hero who takes the path of the sun to unearth the secret of immortality. He goes through the columns of Heraclitus, and in the land of the West finds the old fer-

---

[123] Cf. the two (upper and lower) fish, in the zodiacal sign of Pisces, looking in opposite directions (ed.).

[124] French, "shatter infamy" (e.g. superstition, the Church) (trans.).

[125] The last great king of ancient Assyria, famous as one of the kings who could read and write (trans.).

ryman Utnapishtim, who had traveled the waters of death, and, therefore, came to live among the immortals. He tells Gilgamesh the secret. He says:

> "Gilgamesh, you have struggled hard and suffered many a hardship. What can I give you so that you can return to your land? I will tell you a secret, of a hidden magic herb I will talk to you. The herb looks like boxthorn and grows deep down in the sea, its thorn is like the spine of a porcupine, it blossoms in the freshwater sea far away. If you can lay your hands on this herb and eat of it, you will find eternal youth and life."

This is a wonderful description from ancient times. So here you have the magic herb. It is an herb with healing powers, a power that will heal forever. It is the so-called panacea, a cure-all, the elixir *vitae*, the *quinta essentia*. At the same time it is also the herb that helps the adept to produce the *lapis philosophorum*. The herb is called *lunaria* or *lunatica*; it grows on the mountain Mambracus or Mambraces, like the stone for which one should also always look on high mountains.[126]

Participant: Does it have a meaning that the magic herb of our dream is growing on the prairie?

Professor Jung: Yes, there is a connection between the herb and the prairie. The prairie is the desert that starts to turn green. Where the son of the gods, or the daughter of the gods, touches the earth, so to speak, the earth becomes green. That is why the verdant prairie indicates the imminent appearance of healing; and the green, the *benedicta viriditas*[127] appears. What would you say about that herb? What does it mean to the dreamer?

Participant: An herb has grown that bails out the dreamer.

Professor Jung: His mood is desperate. He is overwhelmed by the snake; it entwines him and threatens to asphyxiate him. It is constantly demonstrated to him that he is completely powerless. Now the dream says: "There is a magic herb, a medicinal herb." As we can

---

[126] *Aurora consurgens.* In *Artis auriferae*, vol. 1, p. 198 (ed.).
[127] The blessed green, vigor, youthful vitality (ed.).

220

see, it is no coincidence that the herb appears in this third dream. It is connected to the snake that appeared before. The snake is the healing snake that prepares for the idea of healing. In the second dream, we have related this snake to the Mercurius of the ancient alchemists. The *serpens mercurii* is the demon living in the middle of the earth. By the transformation, this *serpens mercurii* is turned into the magical herb, or the herb transforms him; he then becomes the green lion in which Mercurius disappears. The lion represents the solution in the divine water. This is also the healing water. In our dream, the medical herb grows under a *stone* that is, so to speak, transparent. According to the alchemical sources, one of the constant qualities of the stone is the *diaphanitas*.[128] What does that mean?

Participant: The stone is hard and transparent. Doesn't that stand for indestructible consciousness?

Professor Jung: As a matter of fact, it does have something to do with consciousness. Could you give more details about it?

Participant: The transparent stone refers to the diamond. It is refined earth, the epitome of refined earth. The earth is dark, gloomy, nontransparent, and starts to become transparent in the stone. Although the stone is earth, hardest earth, it assumes the character of transparent water. We speak of a diamond "of the first water." Because of its transparency, the philosopher's stone is also called *vitrum aureum* (the golden glass) or *vitrum malleabile* (the malleable glass). In the Book of Revelation it says that the streets of the new Jerusalem were like golden glass.[129]

Professor Jung: So it is the same idea as in alchemy—that the earth had been transformed into a transparent, waterlike, yet hard and imperishable, incorruptible structure. Therefore, the philosopher's stone is the expression of the highest perfection of the earthly body, and, therefore, you also find the idea that the *lapis philosophorum* is man himself, that is, his *corpus glorificatum*, his body at the Resurrection. This immortal body is the subtle body that had left the physical body and is beyond corruption. The diamond, the hardest min-

---

[128] Greek, *diaphanos* = transparent (ed.).
[129] Revelation 21:18, 21 (trans.).

eral, is synonymous with the *lapis philosophorum*. This is ancient metaphysics, old speculation in symbolic form.

What does this mean psychologically? It was mentioned that the *diaphanitas* and the stoniness, the inelasticity, could have to do with the nature of consciousness. You can find this connection in the old texts of alchemy, the idea, that is, that the stone is the product of a mental operation, the equivalent, so to speak, of *enlightenment*. Therefore the stone says in a Hermetic text: "I create the light, the light that is greater than all other lights in the world."[130] So what is actually meant is a phenomenon of consciousness, a product of human effort, and at the same time a *donum gratiae*, a gift of God's grace. It is always stressed that it is impossible to do it on one's own, it can only be given *per gratiam dei*, but man still has to make the effort to make this structure. It originally was a head, that is, a consciousness that was in the head. It is symbolized as the head of Osiris that was washed ashore from the sea and venerated by the women of Byblos. This severed head, the so-called round element, is the epitome of perfection. A consciousness has crystallized that is imperturbable, a detached consciousness, characterized by wholeness (represented by roundness).

Participant: In the legend of Perseus, too, we find this idea, in the severed head of the Gorgon.[131] Here, roundness is linked to the *mortificatio* of the mother.

Professor Jung: Yes, quite right. In the stars you find the constellation of Perseus with the Gorgon's head above the sign of Taurus. The great Gorgon's head is the horrible face entwined by snakes; it is the face of the past in front of which we are petrified. The fear it provokes can be traced back to the fear of the devouring mother, the horror of this; for this face can turn you into dead earth again. This danger was averted by Perseus by cutting the Gorgon's throat with a fiery sword, a diamond sword. This would mean that the danger is averted by the intervention of consciousness, of thinking; because it was an act of consciousness that detached him from that horror. When the flood

---

[130] *Rosarium philosophorum*. In *Artis auriferae*, vol. 2.
[131] Medusa (trans.).

of blackness is later inundating him again, he can free himself from it, because he cut the head of the horrible mother. You find a similar standpoint in the philosophy of the Upanishads; the knowledge about Atman[132] liberates from the law of the earth. So the head is that round thing, originally hidden in matter, that Zosimos called the Omega element (Ω).[133] That's why the ancient philosophers called themselves "children of the golden head." This was the opposite of the *caput mortuum* or *caput corvi*,[134] which is the sediment that precipitates, or the opposite of *nigredo*.[135] This *caput aureum*,[136] however, is the end product of the process. It is also round, it is the wholeness, and it is a transparent stone. Which consciousness is like this, inflexible, hard, detached, immortal, and can no longer be changed?

Participant: Individuated consciousness.

Professor Jung: Yes, we could say that if it is detached and no longer touched by the earth. This is consciousness attained in Buddhistic yoga, it rests, completely detached, between heaven and earth. In *The Secret of the Golden Flower* you find the idea of detached consciousness, which is like the moon, eternally untouched, and which will no longer change.[137] We could compare this state with a firm conviction or, even better, with a final psychic state that can no longer be changed. One simply has become like that. This is the effect of the individuation process, and it occurs when the flow has reached the valley, when the potential has been spent. Then a lake comes into being, which is still and mirrors only the sky. Apart from that, it does nothing. And there are also fish in it.

The symbols of the present dream have nothing to do with all that. What is interesting here is that the dreamer has an important competitor in his search for the stone, the *lion*. We have to try to understand this lion psychologically. Why does the lion also want to have the stone? What does that mean?

---

[132] Cf. seminar 2.

[133] Marcellin Berthelot, *Collections des anciens alchémistes grecs*, III/XLIX, p. 1.

[134] Latin, "dead head," "raven's head" (trans.).

[135] Latin, "blackness" (trans.).

[136] Latin, "golden head" (trans.).

[137] Richard Wilhelm and C. G. Jung, *The Secret of the Golden Flower*. See also C. G. Jung, *Alchemical Studies*, CW 13, §§ 64ff (ed.).

Participant: There is yet another possibility to get to the herb.

Professor Jung: This thought is absolutely correct, only you must not say "another possibility," but name which possibility!

Participant: Because it would be much too easy if the stone fell into his lap just like that.

Professor Jung: Yes, of course. If he succeeded in getting the stone just like that, he wouldn't need the whole life, his instinctual life. That's why the lion appears. It is a transformation of what?

Participant: Of the snake.

Professor Jung: There is a description of this transformation of the snake into the lion. Do you know where?

Participant: In the scene of Mithras's sacrifice of the bull.

Professor Jung: Yes, this scene is often depicted with a *Kratér*[138] below, and above it a lion on one side, and a snake on the other. This *Kratér* is contemporary with the famous *Kratér* of Zosimos. There is an oft-quoted passage in Zosimos, a passage where he writes to his *soror mystica*.[139] What does he say there?

Participant: "Go down into the *Kratér*."

Professor Jung: "Hurry down to the Shepherd of Men (Poemandres), dive into the vessel [*Kratér*], and hurry up again to your kind,"[140] to your *genus*, to your lineage, to your relatives, that is, to what one actually is.[141] This whole idea of the *Kratér* refers to a doctrine of the so-called Poemandres, which obviously already existed and was current then. This is the Hermetic doctrine found in the *Corpus Hermeticum*.[142] Unfortunately these things are virtually unknown; they should be known much better, because they are very beautiful. In the fourth tract it says that the Demiurge created the humans as only half-conscious beings, and that he made a vessel (*Kratér*) to help them, filled it with Nous, that is, with spirit, and sent it to earth. Those humans who aspired to achieve broader consciousness—that is, salvation—could dive into this *Kratér* to regenerate

---

[138] Greek, "mixing-bowl" (ed.).

[139] Greek, "mystic, enigmatic sister." Alchemical term for "anima" (ed.).

[140] Cf. C. G. Jung, CW 13, §§ 96–97 (ed.).

[141] *Eranos-Jahrbuch* 1937, p. 47, note 3 (also in C. G. Jung, CW 13, § 137, note 211) (ed.).

[142] The core documents of the Hermetic tradition. In English translation at www.sacred-texts .com (14 March 2007) (trans.).

224

themselves and become *énnooi* there,[143] because they were in the state of *anoia*, of nonconsciousness. The *Kratér* is the wonderful vessel that later became, in poetic adaptation, the *Grail* cup. In alchemy the vessel is also known as *vas Hermetis*. It is said to be made of water: *Vas Hermetis est aqua*. Now the lion is simply another form of the snake. In the Mithras cult it fights with the snake over the vessel, that is to say that the vessel, at that stage, is not yet with man, but still in the unconscious. It is filled with fire, and the two stages, the stage of the snake and that of the lion, are still at odds with each other. What's the difference between them?

Participant: The lion is a warm-blooded animal.

Professor Jung: Exactly, that is the difference. The lion is the snake, but on a much higher level. It is the fight between cold and warm blood, but it still takes place below consciousness.

Participant: In the *Aion leontocephalus*,[144] snake and lion are also depicted together.

Professor Jung: Yes, but there they form a unity.

Participant: It is the unity of the opposites.

Professor Jung: It is the statue of a human body with the hands resting on it. In the museum of Arles there is a wonderful *Leontocephalus*, also in the British Museum. He is lion-headed; a snake entwines him completely and lays its head on his head. Here lion and snake are identical. So this is man in the state of his spinal cord: it is unconscious man, strangely enough in no visible connection with the Mithras sacrifice. He assists, so to speak, in that act of salvation in which Mithras kills the bull. The bull is Mithras himself; he is sacrificing himself. It is a simple variant of the Christian idea, but Mithras is older. It is a pre-Christian idea.

At a Later Session [7 March 1939]

Professor Jung: Last time we talked about the symbolism of the *lion*. I already told you that in medieval philosophy the lion very fre-

---

[143] *Eranos-Jahrbuch* 1937, p. 32 (also in C. G. Jung, CW 13, § 97) (ed.).

[144] The "lion-headed Aion" is a Mithraic God-image of time (Kronos). It means eternity, world age. The Gnostics used this term to designate the forces emanating from God before the creation of the world (cf. C. G. Jung, *Symbols of Transformation*, CW 5, fig. 84) (ed.).

quently appears as a transformation symbol, namely, in the alchemical process. There it represents a stage of the transformation process, not quite the first, but rather a middle stage. The first stages can vary, depending on the starting point of the operation, but then comes the stage in which the lion appears. I will present a few examples in medieval philosophy to you, from which you can see what role the lion plays there. Because it is a kind of transition point, it is, like any other part of the transformation, also called *lapis*. The *lapis* is at the beginning, in the middle, and at the end. At the beginning it is the *prima materia*, related to chaos, then it is the green lion, later it is the eagle, then the philosopher's gold. All that is the stone [*lapis*]. One alchemical passage reads: "In this way the stone has been compared to the animals, because of the blood being their life substance, for the soul of each animal is in the blood."[145] The author goes on to say that the name *lion* was chosen because of the soul substance, and that *dog* or *camel* could have been chosen just as well, just as any other name of an animal, simply because it represents that living being which is drawn out of the first matter. It does not become clear, however, why it should be precisely a lion. The other animals to which he refers appear much less often, with the exception of the snake or the dragon.

That the lion is a dynamic phenomenon is evident from *The Book of Ostanes*.[146] It is an Arab text going back to an ancient Greek-Persian source. An Aristotle is quoted in the book—a pseudo Aristotle, of course, as it was common to use the names of the old masters. He tells the story of a man who wanted to put saddle and reins on a lion, but the lion did not obey, so he took a whip and humiliated the lion. This worked, and he was able to ride it. This is an allegory for the *transformation process*. It follows that this is the stage of unbridled instinct or untamed power, which is called lion in the alchemical process because of its inherent instinctual force. It was hardly possible to translate this into the chemical terminology of alchemy. These contents can barely be conceived chemically, unless

---

[145] "Eodem modo animalibus lapidem assimilaverunt propter sanguinem quo vivunt, nam anima cuiusque animalis in sanguine" (author unknown).

[146] *The Book of Ostanes* (*Kitâb el Foçoul*), in Marcellin Berthelot, *Chimie au moyen-âge*, vol. 3.

we think of an acid that is keen on attacking a base, for instance, hydrochloric acid and marble and such, which, by the way, the alchemists actually did. Hydrochloric acid corrodes lime. We also say that the lime has been "bitten into,"[147] as if the lion had attacked it with its teeth. The acidity of the acid is often stressed by the alchemists; that's also why they talk about the "most acidic vinegar." This would correspond to the lion: a devouring, penetrating affinity that takes possession of the object.

Another ancient author is Senior Filius Hamuelis who, however, cannot be traced back to antiquity. The original language he wrote in was probably Arabic or maybe Hebrew, but his work is extant only in a Latin translation from the early Middle Ages, around the eleventh to twelfth century. In this source there is a passage where the stone speaks: "It is through me that the secret of secrets is generated. When I recover from long illness I have the life of the roaring lion."[148] So this expresses the fact that after a longer process, in which the *prima materia* suffers, the lion—that is, a wild desire—is the result. Psychologically this would mean: there is a state of suffering, and out of this suffering comes roaring passion. This is a formula that can be corroborated by the alchemical texts.

Another alchemist also says that the philosopher's work begins with *melancholia* and ends in pleasure and joy.[149] This initial state— the *nigredo* and the *tenebrositas* are also called *melancholia*[150]—is a state of depression, which then emerges as desire. This is the libido, which had sunk into the unconscious during the state of depression, so that apparently there is gloomy apathy. If this state is dissolved, the libido comes to the surface in the form of desire—which, of course, is not yet a healed state, but an animal one, a state of the raw material.

This same author, Michael Maier, conceives the earth of chaos or paradise as the initial state, as a substance that still contains the di-

---

[147] Original: *angefressen* = eroded (trans.).

[148] "Per me enim generatur secretum secretorum: quando convalesco a languoribus, tunc habeo vitam leonis rugientis." *Aurora consurgens.* In *Artis auriferae,* vol. 1, p. 219.

[149] Michael Maier, *Symbola aureae mensae duodecim nationum.*

[150] Latin, "blackness" and "darkness" are called "melancholy" (trans.).

vine seed, and where all creatures come from. He writes: "Others have called this earth the green lion, strong and valiant in war, or the dragon that devours its own tail."[151] We see that the lion is a synonym of the dragon devouring itself; obviously it represents a similar state. Now, the dragon devouring itself is a form of libido, which runs in a circle within itself and bites into itself. The dragon forms a circle with itself, bites into nothing but itself, and even fertilizes itself in doing so. Experience shows that the libido, when it comes out of the state of depression, bites into whatever is there at the moment. What then occurs is called transference. The libido does not necessarily bite into itself; that is why one alchemist says that the lion or the dragon had to be kept in a sealed vessel, otherwise the locked-up content, and thus the whole [alchemical] *opus*, would blow up. *The lion has to devour itself*. It is stewed in its own juice, for the greatest desire, the greatest passion, does not seek the other, but itself. This is the final goal, as the ancients understood very clearly. And so this same author states, "The green lion is the medium to unify the tinctures between the sun and the moon."[152] Tincture is simply an essence, an extract of the sun and the moon; this is the classical description of the male and female. The idea is that the lion actually *unites the essences of the male and the female*, which are the primordial opposites. The essence is not the male or female *in corpore*—that is, in its actual form—but it is a fine subtle body, an extract, that is, of the male and of the female. It is not the man and the woman that are unified, but the male and the female, in a subtle, psychical form. This is the way in which the ancients did psychology. They expressed themselves substantially. Instead of speaking of a psyche, they talked about the *humidum radicale*, something humid and rooted. When we use the term *psyche* we think we have said something with that, but actually we don't express more with it than the ancients—something cool and humid, a humid breath. In this breath it is possible to keep the male and the female together. In other words, consciousness and the unconscious have to be kept together in the hermetic vessel so

[151] "Alii appellaverunt hanc terram leonem viridem fortem in proelio s. draconem devorantem caudem suam." Maier, *Symbola aureae mensae duodecim nationum*, p. 427.

[152] "Leo viridis quod est medium coniugendi tinctures inter solum et lunam" (ibid.).

that both will merge into each other. This is the goal of the process: both should function together, instead of one functioning alone, while the other is not seen or is suppressed, for example, when the head is cut off so that it floats in the air on its own, and we can no longer make use of the body at all. That's how today's eccentric psychology is; people believe anything could be done with the head.

This unification of the male and the female happens, as we have seen, in the lion. The wild desire, the greatest passion, expresses the wholeness of the human being (expressed in the symbol of the ouroboros). Although the lion is a roaring monster, a voracious wild animal, it loves the *light*, the *sun*. Another ancient author, a Jesuit of the sixteenth century, talks about the lion as a friend of the light,[153] which is also how it is described in alchemy. In astrology, too, we find this connection between lion and light or the sun. The zodiacal sign of Leo is the *domicilium solis*, the house of the sun, for Leo is the transition point of the sun between July 21 and August 21, and this is when the heat of the sun is greatest. In this sense the lion takes on a sunlike meaning. In the alchemical process the lion is also called *aes hermetis*,[154] for example, in the *Consilium coniugii*. It is said to be nothing else but the *sol inferior*, that is to say a light, a day star, which is, so to speak, beneath our feet; an enlightenment coming not from heaven, but out of the earth. Thus the lion is that enigmatic *earth containing the seed of light*. In psychological terms this would say: this devouring desire contains light in itself. It is not completely dark, but light can evolve from it, that is to say, enlightenment, expansion, intensification of consciousness. Self-knowledge, for instance, can evolve when the lion devours itself. If the desire is kept within the vessel, if it is not diverted outside onto some object, but kept within the person, a light will arise. A depression can change only if we are able to endure and accept it. We can change nothing if we haven't accepted it. If we resist, it will only get worse. In accepting the depression, we are no longer able to hold the whole world responsible for it, and then it can change. But then heat, wild desire, evolves

[153] "Leo est animal lucis amicum." Nicolaus Caussinus, *Polyhistor symbolicus*.

[154] The metal vessel (made of copper or bronze) of Hermes corresponds to the hermaphroditic transition substance (ed.).

from it. If melancholy is reversed, it will become wild *concupiscentia* [concupiscence]. That's why melancholics are such terrible egotists. The source of warmth and light is said to go bad from meat, which itself is said to be of a lunar quality. And then it is added that the meat will go bad and be eclipsed.[155] So the sun suffers an eclipse, caused by its meat. Now we can understand that old phrase of the alchemists that the philosopher's gold is made *ex sole et umbra eius*.[156] It is explained that the shadow is nothing else but the moon. The moon, however, represents the female; the female in the male, that is, the admixture of the unconscious to consciousness, is the reason why the sun is darkened. The text says, therefore, that consciousness would go bad and be burnt together with the perishable body. This is the end of the lion, when it devours itself. It is transformed by it, and the transformation is caused by the so-called warming, or breeding warmth, as the alchemists call it.

It further says in this source: "This is the reason why our ore, the enigmatic substance, is called lion, because—just like the roaring lion wakes the dead children by breathing life into them—the dead body of the ore is resurrected."[157] This passage is somewhat cryptic. In this connection we have to know that there is an ancient legend according to which the lion gives birth only to dead children, which it then brings to life by roaring at them. This idea of the lion with its four children, whom it had brought to life by roaring, is a portrayal of transformation, of the resurrection of the dead. This means: In the original matter, the *prima materia*, the dark chaotic substance, there lie sleeping seeds of life, which are brought to life by intense desire, that is, by the lion's roar.

Another alchemist, Dorneus, says in his speculative *Philosophia* that the lion is power;[158] and in the *Congeries*: "You should look for your lion in the east, and for the eagle in the meridian." The eagle

---

[155] "Leo i.e. sol inferius, vilescit per carnem. Ita leo natura per carnem suam sibi contemporaneam lunarem vilescit, et eclipsatur: Luna enim est umbra solis, et cum corporibus corruptibilibus consumitur" (*Consilium coniugii*, in *De massa solis et lunae*, in *Ars chemica*, p. 136).

[156] Latin, "of the sun and its shadow" (trans.).

[157] "Haec est causa quare aes nostrum vocatur leo, quia sicut leo rugiendo resuscitat prolem mortuam, vitam immittendo, sic corpus aeris mortuum resurgit" (*Ars chemica*, p. 139).

[158] "Leo est potentia" (Gerardus Dorneus, *Speculativa philosophia*).

230

symbolizes the stage that comes after the lion. The lion turns into a bird, into something winged, into something psychical and spiritual. The lion is, so to speak, the beginning of positive life, and the eagle is the meridian, where it reaches the highest heights.

In light of all this, we are no longer surprised to hear that the church fathers also mentioned the lion, albeit in a quite opposed manner. Gregory the Great[159] calls Christ *catulus leonis*, the lion kitten. St. Augustine[160] speaks of *agnus et leo*, of the lamb and the lion. These, of course, are opposites—the lion mauls the lamb. What is meant is that Christ carries both opposites within himself. As lion, as animal of the light, he is the *rex gloriae*, the glorious king, and as lamb he is the victim. This same Augustine, however, uses the lion also as a simile for the devil: "In his impetuousness he is a lion, and a dragon in his insiduousness."[161] Here we find again the double aspect, namely, the purely beastly aspect of wild desire, and simultaneously the love of light hidden in it. This is the lion in alchemy.

From this lion the dreamer shies away. You can temporarily repress your passion, but it will rise again. The same thing happens with the lion; it reappears. In utter despair, the dreamer cries for his *mother*. The mother comes and saves him with the aid of a *bicycle*. This is a very modern, strange ending. What is your opinion? What does the mother mean in this case?

Participant: The escape to the mother is a regression. The dreamer wants to revert to the mother, wants to be a child. He wants to revert to the time when there was no sexuality yet.

Professor Jung: The mother saves him with the aid of a bicycle. Now, I beg your pardon! Why, of all things, with a bicycle?

Participant: It is a mechanization of movement, as opposed to walking on foot, which one does all by oneself.

Professor Jung: Yes, the bicycle is indeed a mechanization; it is a factory-made object. You can get bicycles by the dozens. What does that mean?

[159] Doctor of the Church in Rome, 540–604 (trans.).
[160] Saint and Doctor of the Church in the late Roman Empire (354–430) (trans.).
[161] "Leo in impetu, draco in insidiis."

Participant: It indicates something very collective, because all the others do likewise.

Professor Jung: That is to say, in an economical and efficient way. Naturally, one advances much faster with a bicycle than by walking on foot. One follows a formula that is universally present and available everywhere. One is the nice boy, the dear mother's darling; just the way one does it. One becomes like the others. One forgoes becoming what one is oneself. This is the bicycle!

9. *Two Dreams of a Girl of Geese and of a Locomotive*[162]
PRESENTED BY HANS BAUMANN[163]

Text: *1. Seven white geese go along the street; all beings that they pass drop dead to the earth on the spot.*

2. A locomotive comes down the street. It kills, not by running people down, but merely by going past them.

Professor Jung: Mr. Baumann has assembled the archetypal material with great care, and has made very important contributions to the interpretation of the number seven. The number seven has indeed that *temporal* character, as also already implied in the dream by the sheer movement of the geese. Picture a march of geese; this is rhythm. We find the motif of movement also in the parallel dream of the moving locomotive. Usually there are a couple of carriages behind the locomotive. It is a train. We also say that the geese form a line.[164] Anything passing with a certain rhythm is a train, something going by. This is even suggested by the street; the street on which the people walk is an extension, in a way also a going by. The basic idea is obviously this *going by*. It is the nature of time to go by. It is said to go by quickly. There is an inscription on an old wooden bridge in the hilly region of [the Swiss Canton] St. Gallen: "Everything is transition," with its double meaning: transition[165] over the river and transition of time. There is a nice Arab story of a bey in Tunis. One day a question crossed his mind. He sent for the vizier and asked him for

---

[162] Session of 7 March 1939.

[163] Mr. Baumann's paper is not extant (ed.).

[164] Original: *einen Zug bilden* = literally, "to form a train" (trans.).

[165] From the Latin *trans* = from one place to another, *itare* = to go (trans.).

232

the word that changed pleasure to pain, and pain to pleasure. If he did not find out the word within three days, his head would be laid before his feet. The vizier consulted the Koran, he visited the doctors and the sages, and none of them knew the answer. Finally, he was told that if there were anybody at all to know it, this would the marabou on the border of the desert. This was far away. He had the fastest camels saddled, and sent his servant to the marabou, with the instruction to obtain the word. The marabou said: "Alright," took a ring off his finger, and told the messenger: "Bring this to the vizier!" The vizier in turn brought the ring to the bey, and there was written on it: "Everything passes." Time itself is passing, life as movement is passing.

Participant: Why are there precisely seven geese? Couldn't the number twelve also express time?

Professor Jung: That it is seven is related to the fact that the ancient time is a moon time, not a sun time. In the lunar year the months have twenty-eight days. The number seven goes back to the seven lunar days. The number twelve is a solar term for time, which we encounter only in later, more developed cultures, while lunar time is natural time. The moon is the natural clock; you can deduce the lunar time from the fullness of the moon. Thus you will often find lunar calculations in primitive cultures, and not solar ones.

The core of the dream is actually a *vision*. It is as if the child's eyes had been opened. She was shown that picture: "Everything passes." Everything is transition, here the geese passing by. This is nature, these are animals, the animal life. It passes by. The locomotive is cultural life, spiritual life, man's invention. It also passes by. And everything passes, and the people drop dead. They wither away like grass as time passes. They all drop dead.

This dream has no lysis, because it is a dream vision, not an acted dream. Why should the child have this vision? What is the one and crucial reason? Here you have to take into account what I told you about the psyche in early infancy. Where does infantile consciousness come from?

Participant: From the collective unconscious.

Participant: From the golden age.

Professor Jung: From a time when there was no time, from the *aljira*. Consciousness, time consciousness, grows out of the *aljira*. The child doesn't know time yet; neither do the primitives. And so you find that wonderful, extremely impressive phenomenon among the primitives that a child is nothing but a child, an adult nothing but an adult, and an old man nothing but an old man, and he has been it forever. He has the absolute style. Look at an old man in Arabia: he has got the absolute style of an old man, who has always been an old man, has been it for millennia, because he has never completely left timelessness. Only the cultured man has a pocket watch. He has the notion of time, he has become all time. This is what the child has to learn: that everything passes.

I would gather from the lapidary character of the vision that the child is healthy. This lapidary vision contains a colossal synthesis. In a few words a profound truth is expressed, which scares and confronts the child, and which it cannot grasp for a long time. Therefore she has to dream this truth repeatedly. It simply says: "You are coming from timelessness. Here, however, in this world, there is time." Unfortunately, we are living in time. We are no longer in the *aljira*, where there was no time yet. I would say: this is a naive child, who does not come from a cultivated family, but is a bit primitive. Naively she faces the phenomenon of the world, and possesses no real basis, so she tends to fall back into that primitive timelessness, into that dream of life, in which life is not a *somnium breve*, but a *somnium longe*.[166] The life of the primitives is actually eternal. They all behave as if they could waste thousands of years. There they sit, years go by, and seemingly nothing happens. Just try to live for a day as if you could waste thousands of years! You feel like a king. There is no hurry, no inferiority feelings. You simply *are*. For this is the highest art: to live as if we were eternal, without hurry, without nervousness: "What's the time? Is it too late? Or too early?" All this is unknown to the primitive, accounting for the natural beauty of primitive life. The primitives do not know time. Then the white man comes, and all hell breaks loose; then time is there. Of course they also know that

[166] Latin, not a "short," but a "long dream" (trans.).

234

they get older, that there is death, but it is all a bit shadowy. He who dies, dies with the right gesture. I remember the following episode: two Europeans sought shelter in a Negro hut. They entered, and there sat an old man, he sat there and looked odd. All the Negroes left, and one of them said: "He is dying." The old man had sat down alone to die, as if he had been told: "Now it's time to die." This is style, this is poise. However, they do it unconsciously. We have to fight for heroism, to acquire that style to know that now it is time to die, and to die in the right way, the way it simply has to be done. And thus the primitive can live and die, for he has no time.

4

Psychological Interpretation of Children's Dreams
(Winter Term, 1939/40)

1. General Remarks
(PROFESSOR JUNG)

Professor Jung: This year I would like to forgo a longer introduction to the technique of dream analysis, and just briefly address a few general questions. As you know, we apply a structure to the dream, that corresponds to the pattern of a drama. We distinguish four elements: the *introduction* often specifies place and time, as well as the actors (dramatis personae) of the dream action. There follows the *exposition*, which unfolds the problem of the dream. It contains, so to speak, the theme, or maybe the question posed by the unconscious. From this arises the *peripateia*: the dream action leads to increasing complexity, until it reaches a climax and changes—sometimes in the form of a catastrophe. Finally, the *lysis* gives a solution or the result of the dream.

As you know, in every interpretation of a dream we first of all ask: How does such a dream come into being? What caused it? What are the experiences of the previous day? What happened? Is there a remarkable situation? An important additional question is also whether the dreamer is conscious of anything about it; this must by no means be taken for granted. In the case of children's dreams as remembered by adults, we are only exceptionally able to ascertain the situation out of which they arose. And yet we have to try by all means to search for it, and to keep in view the question of causality, even if

236

we cannot answer it empirically for the time being. We have to reach a point where we can deduce the preceding situation from the dream itself. Our dream analysis is of value only if we can subsequently detect, from the interpretation, what caused the dream. Naturally this has to be done with the necessary care, because one can go considerably astray.

In addition, we subject each detail of the dream, its symbolic figures, and the sequence of the actions to a careful examination. Whenever possible, we take note of the *context* of each idea or image. By context, I mean the association material in which the idea is embedded. When someone says, for example: "I dreamed of a glass," do we then understand what this means? We don't understand anything yet. It could be a wine glass, a beer glass, a test-tube, a bottle, or a window pane. First we have to know in which context the image "glass" is situated. So we can't avoid asking about it, and then, sure enough, we may often hear the most astonishing answers. In the case of banal ideas—as they so frequently occur in dreams—it perhaps suffices to confine ourselves to taking note of the context; this will not always be sufficient in the case of more complicated ideas, because often precisely the very important things are held back, as the complexes prevent the person from making the statement. We also know this from the association experiment.[1] In these cases, we are forced to delve deeper into gathering information on the context, which I have called *amplification*. In the interpretation of children's dreams, too, we will have to revert to this method. As I explained last winter, we have always to reckon with the fact that the child cannot provide any associations to the dream. In addition, precisely the most important children's dreams are frequently told only much later, so there is no possibility of getting information on the context.

This method of amplification is an *expansion*, a conscious enrichment. I make the dreamer focus his interest on the image, and to bring up all associations linked to the image. This must not be confounded with *free association*, in which we glide from one association to another, without regard to the initial idea. In doing so, however,

[1] Cf. C. G. Jung, *Experimental Researches*, CW 2, and seminar 2 (ed.).

237

we lose the certainty that the final element still has a relation to the initial one. Of course we encounter complexes, but for that we need no dream, and moreover we don't want to discover complexes anyway; instead, we want to know what the dream says. Freud adhered to this method of free association, and he could do that because for him the dream is not the essential thing, whereas for me it is. For him, it is the façade, for me, the essence. In this I rely on a Jewish authority, the Talmud, where it says: "The dream is its own interpretation," meaning that we have to take the dream for what it is.[2] We should not see in the dream something different from what it expresses, but we actually have to learn to see differently—that's the difficulty. When I analyzed an Asian, I noticed the difference: he had an amazing ability to "smell" his context. Unabashedly, he said out loud what we ourselves would have noticed only with great difficulty. The natural faculties Asian people show in this respect are astonishing. They are helped, however, by their language, with its richness of images, in which everything is already given. On the other hand, they are not used to designating something precisely. Tell an Asian man, "Please, bring me a blade of grass," and he will bring you the whole meadow. We have lost the larger context, because we see only the separate details; Asians, however, always have an *overall picture*. William McDougall has something characteristic to say about this. He had the typical Western mind, stuck on details. He was interested in Chinese philosophy, and had trouble understanding the notion of Tao. So he asked a Chinese—his pupil—about the meaning of Tao, but did not understand anything of what the Chinese explained to him. So the latter grew impatient, dragged the professor to the window and asked him: "What do you see?" "Houses, cars, people; and also trees, clouds; it is raining and the wind is blowing." And the Chinese said: "Well, you see, this is Tao."

We have to try to gain such an overall picture with the help of amplification, even in the case of very simple dream images. So, for instance, what does it mean if someone dreams of a rabbit? Then we must not look at it separately, by itself, but we have to see it in the

[2] C. G. Jung, *Psychology and Religion*, CW 11, § 41 (ed.).

238

field, notice how its fur matches the earth; we must also feel that the hunter belongs in this context, and the dog, the corn in the field, and the flowers. Only then will we know what a rabbit is. In interpreting the single dream elements, I proceed in this complementary way. Only from this general view do I realize the meaning, and I've had quite a few surprises. If someone dreams of a bicycle, for example, I will ask: "How would you describe it if I had never seen a bicycle before?" The dreamer has to create an image for me, to write an elementary school composition, so to speak, so that I will know how he sees it. A downright "myth" of the bicycle can result from such a description. Perhaps we discover that it is a sun wagon, in which a ghost journey is made. The primitive mythology of the European may come to light on such an occasion.

In using this method, we are not necessarily bound to the concrete statement of the dreamer, but can amplify the dream images ourselves. In this, we have to revert to those images we all have in common, namely, the *archetypal images* of the collective unconscious, as they are found in language, myths, and so on.[3]

So we explain a dream by amplifying the range of the image for each single element, in using all our knowledge. To verify an interpretation, we must have a look not only at the dream by itself, but maybe also in the context of a whole series. Then we will often discover that the dreamer had a dream right before or afterward, in which our interpretation is already contained. In a *series* we can compare dreams with one another and thus eliminate errors. Let me give you an example for such a verification: I was told a dream in which the patient's father holds a globe, trying to divide it into two halves, such that there would be exactly the same number of people in the East as in the West. The dream reminded me of the history of creation in Genesis, in which God also makes a division, when on the second day He divided the waters that were under the firmament from the waters that were above the firmament.[4] From this I concluded that a process of growing consciousness had occurred in the dreamer, that

[3] Cf. seminar 1.
[4] Genesis 1:7 (trans.).

239

he had started to think consciously and autonomously. This hypothesis could later be verified. This person had already dreamed of the act of creation the night before; he had dreamed that God had created a world with lightning and thunder. Of this dream, however, I knew nothing. You see how we can retrospectively verify the interpretation of a single dream image in the context of a dream series.[5]

2. Dream of a Ten-Year-Old Girl of a Snake with Eyes Sparkling Like Diamonds[6]
PRESENTED BY MARIE-LOUISE VON FRANZ

Text: *A snake with eyes sparkling like diamonds chases me in a forest or in my bedroom. This dream frightens me so much that I no longer dare move in the bed, because even when awake, everywhere in the room I see the glowing eyes of the snake that wants to bite me.*

Ms. *von Franz:* As is evident from the text, the dream has often recurred. When a dream appears with such forcefulness, we have to conclude that it will be of central importance for the dreamer's psychology, indeed, that the situation here depicted will perhaps govern her whole life. Already among the primitives, recurrent dreams are accorded a very special importance.[7]

Now, the difficulty in the interpretation of this dream lies in the fact that it does not really have a plot or activity, but only contains one single image; therefore, we are not able to apply the usual dramatic schema (exposition, statement of the problem, peripateia, lysis or catastrophe). In fact, the dream takes the *form of a vision*, of an apparition, which is also confirmed by the fact that the dreamer still sees the snake "even when awake"—we would say half-asleep. She does not dare move in the bed, "because even when awake, everywhere in the room I still see the glowing eyes of the snake that wants to bite me." Thus, the image appears so intensely that, like a vision in the waking state, it is even able to interrupt the continuity of waking consciousness.

---

[5] Further examples in C. G. Jung, "Individual Dream Symbolism in Relation to Alchemy," *CW* 12.

[6] Session of 7 November 1939.

[7] Cf. Richard Thurnwald, *Primitive Initiations- und Wiedergeburtsriten.*

So we have only the image of the snake by which to orient ourselves, an image which, as you know, is so enormously widespread in all religions and myths of the world that, frankly speaking, I was able to draw only very general conclusions regarding the situation of the dreamer. A few details of the description, however, may perhaps show the path to the particular way in which the dreamer reacted—that is, the emphasis on the gaze of the snake, the eyes, described first as sparkling like diamonds, then, in a gradual increase of its evil character, as glowing, and, by the final sentence, that the snake "wants to bite her."

As far as the snake in general is concerned, it nearly always belongs to the *chthonic-female* element of religions, indeed it very often is its embodiment proper. In dualistically oriented systems, therefore, it often stands in opposition to a bright, male, spiritual world, from whose perspective it represents the *demonic-evil*. Through the story of Paradise, the snake has, as it were, taken this meaning for the whole Christian world. Philo of Alexandria in particular, probably under Persian influence, contributed to this snake symbolism and to the development of the devil concept. For him, however, it is at the same time also the most spiritual animal, of a fiery nature and of great velocity. Through its ability to shed its skin, it is even immortal.[8] But in other cultures, too, the snake plays the role of the *primal enemy* of the *upper world of the gods*: the Midgard snake, together with the Fenris wolf, threatens the gods in Asgard by creating a flood. In Greece it is Gaia, the earth goddess, who creates half-snakes, the Titans, who storm Olympus and wrestle with Zeus. Simultaneously, she is the mother of Echidna (= snake), of the Sphinx, Cerberus, and others. Leviathan, too, the antagonist of Jehovah, is a snake, a dragon at the bottom of the sea. In the Mithras cult, the snake is the animal opposed to life that, together with the scorpion and the ant, absorbs the life-giving effect of the bull sacrifice. It is the antagonist of the lion, the damp, cold, dark animal in contrast to the animal of the heat of the sun. It devours the vital force of the sacrificed bull, or it wraps itself around a Kratér (vessel), with the lion facing her.[9]

[8] Cf. Jakob Maehly, *Die Schlange im Mythus und Kultus der klassischen Völker*, p. 7.

[9] Cf. Franz Cumont, *Textes et monuments figurés relatifs aux mystères de Mithra*, p. 100, and C. G. Jung, *Symbols of Transformation*, CW 5, § 671.

It stands in a similar opposition to the lion as it does to the eagle, which is the sun-bird and spiritual principle. Thus, an eagle sits on top of the Germanic world tree, but a dragon dwells below, while the squirrel Ratatwiskr (bearer of discord) transmits mutual insults. In Indian mythology and in fairy tales, the races of the snakes and eagles are eternal enemies, and seek to destroy each other. Once, the snakes outwitted the eagles, which then had to serve them, but the eagle Garuda, Vishnu's mount, stole the soma, the drink of immortality that he was supposed to obtain for them.

A North American fairy tale recounts that a child-stealing witch seizes the hero Tsoavits, but an eagle leads him back again. At this, the witch seeks help from her grandfather, the giant snake, but is devoured by him on the spot. "Ever since all witches have been snake-like."

The snake is also closely related to the basilisk or dragon, whose defeat signals the beginning of nearly every heroic legend. I will mention only Heracles and the lernaic snake, and Siegfried and the Christian St. George, both modeled after him. In wanting to help the bright upper world to achieve victory, indeed by embodying the new sun himself, the hero stands in opposition to the snake. It is because of this that two snakes—sent by Hera, the evil Great Mother—already threaten Heracles in his crib; later she sends him fits of madness, during which he even kills his own children. A snake also steals the herb of immortality, obtained with great difficulty, from Gilgamesh, while he is inattentively bathing in a pond. The hero Philoctetes, too, a figure identical with Heracles, is bitten by a snake in the foot because of the curse from the nymph Chryse, whose love he did not requite; he slowly wastes away from the wound.[10] In a very similar way, the son god Re is poisoned, according to an Egyptian hymn,[11] by a venerable worm, formed out of his own saliva and laid in his way by Isis, who is enraged at him. She then heals him only after he discloses his name to her, but his power remains broken. Apollo also had to first conquer the python in Delphi before he could

---

[10] Cf. Wilhelm H. Roscher, *Ausführliches Lexicon*.
[11] C. G. Jung, *Symbols of Transformation*, CW 5, § 451.

create his oracles there. Strangely enough, such prophetic abilities often arise out of defeating a dragon, just as Siegfried understands the voices of the birds after having eaten Fafner's flesh.[12]

As far as the especially numerous snake and dragon fights in Greek mythology are concerned, it should be pointed out that matriarchy had ruled in the Aegean culture before the Indo-Germanic populations of the Greeks invaded it about 2,000 B.C., and that the cults of the Great Mother, later worshipped as Cybele, Agdistis, Mountain Mother, Artemis of Ephesus, and so on, stem from this time. (As a matter of fact, we know about the free status of women in Crete.) This Great Mother was often depicted together with a snake. The shield goddess Athena, too, is pre-Greek, and often the snake is her companion (compare Phidias's depiction). Hence, for the Greeks, overcoming the snake means at the same time overcoming the goddess of the ground, overcoming the unconscious reemergence of the pre-Greek layer, which in the postclassical period broke through again in the mysteries of Cybele, Sabazio, the Phrygian Mother goddess, and others, and which has inundated the whole spectrum of Mediterranean culture.[13]

It is quite clear from this compilation of images that the snake symbolizes the vital, instinctual, and drive stirrings in man, his unconscious dark side in contrast to brightness, to the conscious side of his nature. Scientifically speaking, the snake has only a cerebrospinal nervous system, and so represents all the stirrings originating in this sphere. In various Gnostic systems it is identified with the human spinal cord, proof that already then one was aware of these correspondences. This is a direct parallel to the Indian Kundalini snake in Kundalini yoga, climbing up and down in the spinal cord.[14]

In the contexts previously described, the snake plays the role of an evil *demon*, hostile to light, and represents a dark, ambiguous deity of the depths. But this is only one side of its being; at the same time it is also a *god of healing and salvation*. In the mysteries of Sabazios it represented the highest deity: according to the testimony of Clement of

[12] Cf. also the Grimm fairy tale "The White Snake."
[13] Cf. Erich Küster, *Die Schlange in der griechischen Kunst und Religion.*
[14] Arthur Avalon, *The Serpent Power.*

Alexandria,[15] a snake was pulled through the abdomen of mystics. Arnobius also testifies that a golden snake was drawn through the clothing of the initiated. The snake is the ὁ διὰ χόγπου Θεός, and the ritual signifies the mystical unification with the deity, toward whom the mystic is in a feminine position.[16] Similarly, the snake is the animal accompanying and, in earlier stages, personifying Asklepios; according to Artemidorus, its appearance in dreams of the sick signals healing and the return of vital power. A Grimm fairy tale shows particularly well how strongly it is associated with the mysterious vital power of a human being: a child who eats with a snake thrives until his mother slays the snake. From this moment on the child, too, loses weight and wastes away until he finally dies. Likewise, Porphyry writes in the biography of his revered teacher, Plotinus, that the latter's disciples had observed by his bedside, a few days before his death, how a snake came out of Plotinus's mouth and left; the master died shortly thereafter. For these reasons the appearance of a snake at the sickbed can also mean death. It was also generally assumed that the souls of the dead would live on as chthonic snake gods, as inhabitants of the underworld where they became guardians of a treasure.[17] Thus, snakes were ritualistically worshipped in holes and crevices in the ground in the Asklepieias of Ptolemy and Hygieia. At the so-called Arrhetophorias, obols[18] and cakes in the form of a snake or phallus were sacrificed in crevices in the ground.[19] An erect snake made of granite was found in the pits. Thus the snake becomes the guardian of the secret treasure, and very often also the possessor of the herb of life (compare the Indian fairy tale in which it wants to have the soma potion) with which it can reawaken the dead.

A Greek saga recounts that the hero Glaucus, sitting next to the corpse of his murdered friend Polyeides, catches sight of a snake, which he slays. Thereafter a second snake appears, fetches an herb, returns, and reanimates its dead friend. At this they disappear to-

---

[15] Protrept. II, 16.

[16] Albrecht Dieterich, *Eine Mithrasliturgie*, pp. 123–24.

[17] Erwin Rohde, *Psyche: Seelenkult und Unsterblichkeitsglaube der Griechen*, p. 244.

[18] Obol or obulus: Greek silver coin worth one-sixth of a drachma (trans.).

[19] R. Herzog, *Aus dem Asklepeion von Kos*. In: *Archiv für Religionswissenschaft*, 10, p. 212.

gether and leave the herb for Glaucus, who revives his friend Polyeides with it. This motif emerges in identical form in the Grimm fairy
tale "The Three Snake Leaves," and in numerous other fairy tales.
When the snake, as I mentioned in the beginning, steals the herb of
life from Gilgamesh in a moment of inattention or unconsciousness,
this somehow belongs to this same sphere. The snake arrives there,
attracted by the scent of the flower that Gilgamesh had fished up
from the bottom of the sea along with the herb, and, one is almost
tempted to say, takes back what is hers. Perhaps you recall the dream
series that was discussed at the end of last winter,[20] in which a boy
dreams that he is searching for a transparent stone and that a lion,
also wanting the lapis, appears at that moment—similarly, the snake
is also a lover of stone or the herb of life. (Incidentally, in that series,
a white snake with black crosses on its back appears in a dream directly preceding the former, a symbolically depicted sōter snake, the
serpens mercurii, which dwells in the earth. And earlier still, it was
the spring, the water of life, with which it is identical.)

The snake is not only the guardian of the stone or herb, however;
it is essentially identical with it, or contains it in itself. The Indians
believe that the cobra carries a diamond in its head; and an Indian
fairy tale recounts that a snake daily brings a scholar a gold piece for
reading to it from spiritual works in a garden, until the old man's
greedy son hits the snake on the head and breaks the jewel inside;
the snake kills the son in revenge and disappears, lamenting: "Woe,
who has shattered my jewel?"

The particular reason why I presented this fairy tale is because
such an association may resonate in the expression of our dream text:
"eyes sparkling like diamonds."

As already suggested, the snake and its relation to the lapis play
an essential role in alchemy. Thus, a text from the Musaeum Hermeticum says: "A terrifying dragon lives in the forest who lacks nothing; when it sees the sun's rays, it forgets its poison and flies so dread-
fully that no living animal can resist and not even the basilisk is its
equal. Whoever knows how to kill it wisely . . . will escape all dan-

[20] Cf. seminar 3, § 8 (ed.).

245

gers . . . and its poison turns into the ultimate *medicina*. Suddenly it swallows its own poison by eating its own poisonous tail. It is forced to complete all that within itself. Then a magnificent balsam will flow forth from it." A thought parallel to this is that the gold is already present in the initial situation, but that it is either old and sterile or *compositum*;[21] this gold is dissolved in a type of aqua fortis, which corresponds to the snake. Yet, the whole process is something taking its course within itself, which is why it is also said that a *punctum igneitatis*[22] exists in Mercury himself through which that (immanent) dissolution happens.

I do not want to go into this alchemical problem here any longer, but to address instead a source of alchemical symbolism, the concepts of the Gnostic sects of the Ophites and Naassenes. *Ophis* is Greek for snake. Likewise, *Naas* is the Hebrew word for snake. The Gnostics gave themselves these names in saying "that they alone could grasp the depths of God." Thus the snake is the *deus absconditus*,[23] the dark, deep, incomprehensible side of God. The so-called Perates, too, especially elaborated on the theory of the snake. "The primeval power originating from the father, the *logos*, is *a snake*; so are the stars, but they are the evil snakes. This is why Moses shows the perfect snake to the children of Israel. . . . Whoever sets his hopes on it will not be destroyed by the snakes of the desert, that is, the gods of creation. This all-encompassing snake is the wise logos of Eva, this is the *mystery of Eden*, this is the *river that flows out of Eden*."[24] This explains the meaning of the words "and as Moses lifted up the serpent in the wilderness, even so must the Son of man be lifted up."[25] The snake is the "*great beginning*," of which it is said: "In the beginning was the Word, and the Word was with God, and the Word was God. The same was in the beginning with God. All things were made by him; and without him was not any thing made that was made."[26] What is

---

[21] Latin, "alloyed" (ed.).

[22] Latin, "point of ignition" (ed.).

[23] Latin, "hidden God" (ed.).

[24] Hans Leisegang, *Die Gnosis*, p. 147.

[25] John 3:14 (trans.).

[26] John 1:1–3 (trans.).

made by it is life. The snake stands for vital power, as we have seen. Eve originated through it; Eve is *life*. This Eve is the mother of any-thing alive. The evil *materia*, however, in contrast to the logos, is also, in the final analysis, a snake. At first, it is the water to the Perates, flowing around the world as in a ring; it is Kronos. They say of it: "It is a power bright as water, and no creature can escape this power, Chronos; it is the reason why each creature is doomed to perish; it is the water of Styx." One can view the battle of these two snakes in the sky: "The logos is the constellation of the dragon; to the right and left of it are the crown and lyre. In front of the dragon kneels that pitiable man, Heracles. Behind his back the evil master of this world, the constellation of the snake, draws nearer so as to steal the crown from him. The bearer of the snake, however, keeps them together and prevents it from touching the crown." Here again, the snake is aim-ing at what is most valuable. The main ritual of the Perates, the evening meal, proceeded as follows: they piled loaves of bread on the table and summoned the snake that, as a holy animal, was cared for in a container box. The snake came near and slithered on top of the loaves. Through this the breads were consecrated. Each member kissed the snake on the mouth and prostrated himself before it.[27] Thus logos is present in the form of the snake at the Lord's Supper. It is Christ both as logos and as snake. The rituals of the Sabazios mysteries, mentioned earlier, also belong to this area; they are the *co-niunctio* with the divine logos. But in other cultures as well, the snake is the savior of the logos: Quetzalcoatl, the god of the Toltecs, is a winged snake, the son of the "cloud snake," who appears as the bearer of culture and savior. Upon Tollan's fall, he again disappears in a lake in the form of a snake. According to the Gnostics, the evil snake, too, was not evil originally, but became so as follows: Justinos re-counts that on his journey west, Heracles had united with a virgin, half snake, half human (cf. Herodotus), in order to regain his stolen horse. Elohim likewise is said to have united with a virgin half-snake and half-human, called Eden or Israel, and to have procreated with her twelve paternal angels and twelve maternal ones. He then leaves

[27] Epiphanios, Panar. Haer. 37, 5.

her and returns to the upper, good god. Out of her sorrow at having been left, she then becomes that evil power, hostile toward God. Her servant, the angel Naas (snake), later brings about the crucifixion of Christ; Christ, however, left Eden his body on the cross, with the words: "Woman, behold thy son!"[28] But these are the very words Christ spoke to Mary when he entrusted John to her. So John is, as it were, the body, the mortal part of Christ! Strangely enough, in medieval art John, too, has the characteristics of a snake. In a picture of Quentin Matsys, he holds a communion cup containing a small dragon, which he consecrates.[29] In the great division of the cosmos, shared by nearly all Gnostic sects, there are three realms, and always right at the bottom there is the snake leviathan,[30] the ouroboros, reappearing in alchemy. But the latter is Eve, that is, life. Leviathan is the master of this world, of whom it is said in Isaiah 27:1: "In that day the LORD with his sore and great and strong sword shall punish leviathan the piercing serpent, even leviathan that crooked serpent; and he shall slay the dragon that is in the sea." Alchemy also knows—besides the tail-eater who unites the opposites in itself—the image of two snakes uniting, a fleeing and a wingless one (see also the contrast eagle—snake).

I turn now to one last aspect of the snake, actually already contained in the preceding one: the snake as a *time symbol*. It is the snake that is Chronos, Greek for time. It is the ring of coming into being, the ἕν τό πᾶν (one and all). "All cults and mysteries serve it. As Oceanos or Jordan it is the humid substance, and nothing in the world—immortal or mortal—can exist without it. Everything is subject to it, and it itself is good, and, just as in the horn of the one-horned bull (Moses), it embraces the beauty of all other things . . . like the river rising in Eden and dividing itself into four origins." Simon Magus, however, says: "And it is always one and the same, that which is living in us, that which lives and is dead, and which is awake and asleep, and is young and old. When it changes, the latter

[28] John 19:26 (trans.).

[29] This picture by Quentin Matsys (*Saint John*) also in C. G. Jung, *Transformations and Symbols of the Libido*.

[30] Leisegang, *Die Gnosis*, p. 169.

is the former, and again the former, when it changes, is the latter."[31] Meister Eckhart calls this "the river flown into itself." Christ was also interpreted in this sense as the great ecclesiastical year; he was the Zodiacal snake, whose pictures represent the twelve apostles. The Indian god of creation Prajapati, too, is the world year. The idea that the snake represents time, the coming into being, and the *durée créatrice* is probably connected with the fact that it sheds its skin. Many fairy tales of the primitives interpret this as a *reincarnation*, and infer the snake's immortality from this. We have also heard that Philo regarded it as immortal. So that is probably also the reason why it is in possession of the herb of immortality. In Mithraism one has also found the figure of a god with a lion head, on whom a snake winds upward, laying its head upon his. He is the god Aion or Zervan, the god of eternal duration. Similarly, in Kundalini yoga the snake, climbing up the spine and touching the various chakras in a temporal development, stands for the vital force by which man is simultaneously put into the course of time. It stands for nature in contrast to the spirit, yet at the same time it is the principle leading to the lapis, to perfection beyond nature.

It is quite impossible to bring some order into the whole wealth of this material, and still harder to interpret the meaning and the real essence of the snake as a symbol. When I stressed three main aspects—the snake as *earth demon*, as *savior*, and as *time symbol*—this was just an attempt to organize the many aspects. When the snake appears in a dream, you basically have to take into account all three aspects. I now come back to the dream to evaluate the remaining details of the description.

The snake appears to the girl either in the *forest*, or it chases her as far as into her *bedroom*. The encounter in the woods is, so to speak, the more natural place, because the forest stands for the dark, unconscious side, where one meets one's animals and projections. Initially it looks as if the dreamer came to meet the snake. But then the situation is reversed; the snake chases the dreamer as far as into her bedroom. There exists an intense attraction between the snake and

[31] Leisegang, *Die Gnosis*, p. 99

the child; the snake becomes active and the child thinks it wants to bite her. It haunts her with glowing eyes, sparkling like diamonds. The snake is famed for its gaze, by which it hypnotizes its victims, to devour them afterward; one also says of certain women, the "vamp" type who exerts a kind of terrifying attraction, that they would have that snakelike gaze.[32] Its eyes sparkling like diamonds could be an indication that the snake does after all possess the diamond, the lapis, carrying it in its head, whereby it would not only have the pure, negative instinctual characteristic, but also, as seems to be indicated, the possibility of higher consciousness. The glowing eyes are easy to explain. As has often been said, the snake is connected with the secret fire; it carries within itself the *punctum igneitatis* of self-destruction; it is also in connection with the fiery lion. Mercury is the kyllenian fire, and many dragons in mythology are fire-spitting monsters; all of this has to do with the fact that it dwells in the depths of the earth, psychologically speaking, that it has to do with the sphere of emotional outbreaks, with the drives. By the way, the motif of the snake's eyes is sometimes accentuated in other contexts, too. You may remember the vision of St. Ignatius, from the lecture at the beginning of this summer, to whom a snake with many eyes appeared after rigorous ascetic exercises.[33] He says that a certain something appeared to him, beautiful and great, greatly comforting him. Sometimes it would have been a snake full of sparkling eyes, although it was not eyes. Later he interprets this as a vision of the devil, and wards it off. Argus, too, is such a dragon figure with innumerable eyes. This multiplicity of eyes may be connected with the multiplicity of subliminal perceptions: man is, so to speak, more clear-sighted in the unconscious than in the conscious, and, above all, sees into many more directions simultaneously. Hence the snake's power of prediction, also bestowing the gift to understand birds' voices.

The last remaining statement of the dream says: "the snake that wants to bite me." It is questionable if this is so objectively. In any

[32] Cf. Baudelaire's poem "Le serpent qui danse."

[33] Cf. seminar 2, note 96. In the summer of 1939, C. G. Jung gave, within the framework of a lecture series on "Modern Psychology," a seminar at the ETH Zurich titled "Process of Individuation: *Exercitia Spiritualia* of St. Igantius of Loyola" (ed.).

case the child supposes this, because she is frightened. *Because* she flees the snake, the latter chases her, for it just wants to get near her. Obviously, it wants to unite with her in one form or another, and chases her as far as into her bedroom, that is, into her most intimate living space. The girl rejects it, however, being frightened by its instinctual, negative, demonic aspect. Incidentally, in many Asian fairy tales we find the motif that girls transform themselves into snakes at night, or, conversely, that snakes walk as girls, or one sees how at night snakes glide into a girl's mouth. This is interpreted as possession by a demon. So we might assume that the dreamer has a conscious attitude that cannot accept this power the snake stands for, a so-called Christian attitude, which, of course, can only be the result of the milieu; or else a too orderly, well-behaved, rational scope of consciousness, which naturally provokes, attracts, and at the same time rejects the snake as its counterpart. The girl being young, the snake might well rather stand for temptations of a worldly nature, that is, for life and "the lord of this world," whom the snake after all represents. If she cannot accept it, the snake will probably poison her and create a flood, that is, an inundation of her consciousness with unconscious images. For the rest, it can be said of the problem that the child faces a rather common situation, which makes a solution more likely.

Professor Jung: In her exhaustive paper, Ms. von Franz has very beautifully pointed out the three main aspects of the snake symbol: the aspects of the chthonic snake, the sōter, and the time snake. You can now picture how ambiguous this symbol is, and how manifold its manifestations are. The snake touches on the deepest instincts of man, so that from time immemorial one thought it to be in possession of great secrets. Let us now deal with our dream in detail.

It is a *snake vision*. The girl is *threatened* by an enigmatic snake that is very intense and alive. That it assumes such a concrete form is striking and indicates that it plays an important role in the dream.

Participant: Doesn't the frequent recurrence of the image also point to its importance?

Professor Jung: Yes, we have to assume that the dream has quite a special importance for the psychic disposition of the child. What follows from the snake's assuming such a concrete form and from the intensity for the dreamer?

Participant: That the unconscious seeks to forcefully assert itself.

Professor Jung: When is this the case?

Participant: When consciousness is split off from the unconscious.

Professor Jung: Yes, there has to be a strong *splitting off* of the unconscious, probably having existed for years. There are many reasons for such a phenomenon of splitting. As a rule, they lie in the *environmental conditions*, for example, in the relationship of the parents to each other. It is not uncommon that the split in the child is a reflection of the conflict between father and mother. Here we may thus assume that there is a certain tension between the parents, not allowing the child to find herself.

Of course, there are also other reasons for the split that needn't be related to the parents or other environmental factors, but are determined purely *intrapsychically*. What could those be?

Participant: Perhaps a psychic trauma?

Professor Jung: That, too, would somehow be determined externally.

Participant: It could be an inherited disposition to anxiety.

Professor Jung: This, too, would follow from the parents' psychology. In addition, the fear of the snake cannot be readily explained in the context of inheritance; it is simply there. Either you fear a snake, or you don't. There are individuals for whom a stay in the tropics becomes a perfect hell because of their constant fear of running into a snake. After all, it is very inconvenient to suddenly discover a snake in your bed, or in your shoes, in your trousers, in the cupboard, or in all sorts of impossible places. Snakes are always where you don't suspect them. The uncanny thing with these animals is that they are completely inhuman; they aren't in any rapport with human beings. The snake wardens in the zoos know this. For some time, the snakes let one do anything with them, and one day they wind themselves around the warden with lightning speed, trying to squeeze him to death. You can make contact with nearly all animals, but there seems to be no possible psychic bridge to the cold-blooded animals any

252

longer, although they let themselves be hypnotized, as we know. No "niceties" any longer here.

But now back to our question: What would an *inner motive* for the split be?

Participant: There could be too great a stress on consciousness.

Professor Jung: But this again would be related to the environment; we have to find an inner cause.

Participant: Maybe the child is strongly determined by the former ages, through the "Bardo,"[34] and has difficulties in developing into reality.

Professor Jung: I am thinking of something else, namely, of cases in which a content emerges from within quite spontaneously, without causal involvement of the environment.

Participant: Could it be a psychic *inclusion*?

Professor Jung: Yes, that's what I mean. I am calling this a psychic teratoma. This is a term borrowed from medicine. There it refers to a kind of tumor as the result of a developmental disorder, and containing parts of a twin, for example, hair, teeth, finger parts, an eye, and so on. Teratomas are to be conceived of as an incomplete development of a fetus that is included in the other, fully developing twin. Something analogous exists in the psychic realm too; though one can't talk of a psychic twin, but rather of an encapsulated entity of inheritance. You all know what an entity of inheritance is, don't you? You know, for instance, the peculiarity of the lower lip in the Habsburg family, although it has nothing to do with a teratoma. Now, if an entity of inheritance simply grows along unbeknownst to the individual, then we are dealing with a kind of teratoma. It is like the inclusion of something alien that is not properly connected to the surrounding environment. This creates a character who, on the one hand, may have a normal disposition, but in whom, on the other, something is hidden that doesn't want at all to connect with the rest of the person. It's not always easy to identify a teratoma; when folks say, for instance, "Now that's a very nice guy; unfortunately he's in-

[34] Walter Y. Evans-Wentz, *Das Tibetanische Totenbuch*.

herited that particular family trait that ruins his whole life," there needn't necessarily be a teratoma present, but it may point to some manifest feature, such as mendacity, alcoholism, or the like. If something completely incommensurable is enclosed in the character, however, something that in no way would fit the character or could be derived from his mentality, then we can assume the existence of a teratoma. When this part of the soul becomes conscious it can cause immense disturbance. That is why one may touch this encapsulated world only with utmost caution, because otherwise there is the danger that all of a sudden a second personality erupts. Such cases can be observed in the mentally insane. Do you think that the present case could point to such a teratoma?

Participant: No, it wouldn't manifest itself as such a *general* symbol.

Professor Jung: Quite right. As I described it, the characteristic feature of the teratoma lies in the fact that it is a pathologically grotesque phenomenon, for example, consisting of only one eye, or two teeth, and so on. The snake in our dream has no such pathological character at all, but is a general symbol. So, by no means is it a teratoma. What then can, on the contrary, be concluded from this universal symbol?

Participant: That the child is not abnormal.

Professor Jung: Yes, that she is quite normal overall. Only the facts of concretism and the force personified in the snake are striking, both being strongly accentuated. So where must we locate the reason for the split?

Participant: In environmental influences.

Professor Jung: Yes, very probably there must exist *parental influences*, affecting an in itself normal disposition of the child, and causing there a split that is an adequate answer to the situation at home.

The cause of the split, with which we are obviously dealing here, is thus clarified. We now arrive at the question: "How should we conceive the character of the split?" Naturally, such a disturbance affects the child's whole behavior. Don't forget that this anxiety-triggering figure is very dynamic and contains very much energy. What does this mean for the *consciousness* of the child?

Participant: There is a certain paralysis of expression.

Professor Jung: Yes, one could say that.

Participant: The instinct is missing.

Professor Jung: Yes, *the instinctive is missing*. With what influence on consciousness?

Participant: Problems in adaptation.

Professor Jung: Well, I am thinking of a certain, and quite frequent, form of *difficulty to adapt*. The snake represents, as we have seen, the instinctive, unconscious life, which actually contains the complete expression of the unconscious. There lies in it a blind naturalness closely connected with instinct. If all of this is unconscious, the conscious personality will lack it. What impression does it then make?

Participant: An intellectual or not genuine impression.

Professor Jung: That is too negative an expression; I'd rather say: it makes the impression of an *artificial* personality, imitating what it finds in its environment. For instance, it lets itself be governed by the opinions in its environment and adapts to these with a minimum of effort. It lacks, as it were, the "real" thing. A relatively normal person can get away with this attitude for a long time. Quite a few individuals live with an artificial personality, and they also get away with it—until the point when the function of instinct is absolutely of the essence. Now, which moment is that?

Participant: When you fall in love or marry.

Professor Jung: Yes, when someone marries, or just falls in love. Then you are challenged. Because then you can't enforce it any longer with the artificial personality, then you have to be connected to the deeper sources.

If the entire snake entity is in the unconscious and therefore invisible, then the conscious personality will be more or less artificial. But there are cases in which the snake entity is, at least partially, absorbed by the conscious personality. How does such a person strike you then?

Participant: As very contradictory.

Professor Jung: Yes, these individuals have a *double personality*. On the one hand, they are reasonable and adjusted; maybe too much adjusted, you know, just a bit subdued, not very obviously, or yet a bit obvious on the one side, be it intellectually or emotionally, depend-

255

ing on their talents. In the main, the differentiated function will take over and will lead the personality. On the other hand, this is somebody who is very different. These cases are very frequent. There are also children who show this double quality to a more or less high degree; above all, it's the well-bred children who suddenly play all kinds of mischievous tricks round the next corner. In the grown-up it often takes just a bit of alcohol to make the other personality come to the fore. Then you say: "I had no idea you could be like that." Often, the person concerned didn't know it either, until it just happened to him and the other side of his personality broke through. Such individuals are often the "other" at the wrong place. It is in this way, as we know, that many things come to light. In a way, they are committing indiscretions toward themselves. In the case of these splits, the one personality often has a taste contrary to that of the other. What will happen then?

Participant: Such a person will, for instance, say at home just the opposite of what he says outside of it.

Professor Jung: Yes, a devil at home and an angel on the streets. This expresses itself in a child so that at school he shows a completely different character from at home. This expression is only too well known. Children with a striking split, for instance, behave quite atrociously toward their mothers, while they are polite and nice with other people, or, conversely, they are lovely and nice at home, and somewhere else behave like the worst street kids. Such children find special fun in deceiving the adults, and in doing so feel like little martyrs: "Oh, if you only knew how I really am. You really deserve it that you hurt me." They find it extremely attractive to think: "If you only knew how I suffer, but I just don't tell."

I remember my own school times in Basel. There was a kid who had to wear white gloves on Sundays. Once she came to the countryside; there, she raised her head, marched into the meadow in her white lace, and finally put the excrement found there into her mouth. Such piggery would never have entered the heads of the village kids. It is precisely the well-bred children who develop such obsessions. They think of the oddest things, because these belong to the side of their personality of which they hadn't had any idea. When they see something horrible lying in the street, a toad, for instance, they have to eat it. As a rule, children with such splits really develop two characters.

So, if we know about this split, what would we then tell such a child?

Participant: That he is *at odds with himself.*

Professor Jung: Yes, one could tell the child that to his face. You are at odds with yourself; you say "yes," and it says "no," or the other way round. The child actually understands such language: You want to obey the parents, and then something happens that comes in between. You should do your homework, and then you can't do it. You also should be nice in school, and then it doesn't work. These are opposites in which the split manifests itself, and which the child knows very well. He will also tell you examples of his own, and then you can quite naturally bring up the question of how all this feels for the child, and how one could possibly address this situation.

Participant: Couldn't one also ask him how and when he feels best?

Professor Jung: That is too complicated a question. I'd rather ask: "Say, how come you're so different at home from at school?" Or: "Really, how come in school you're so terribly naughty?" It wouldn't make much sense just to ask with regard to the school alone, because the school is only secondary to the child, but he may well know to tell a quite different tale about the parents.

Participant: But perhaps the child doesn't yet know anything about that.

Professor Jung: Perhaps—but a ten-year-old girl usually knows already much more than the parents would guess. In these years the question already arises: "How do I tell my parents?" I myself have unlearned being naive about children. I'm no longer naive about a ten-year-old girl.

You are pointing right to the center of the problem with all these questions regarding the child's being at odds with herself. If you focus completely on this schism, you will understand not only the dream, you will also understand the child.

The dream not only describes the situation of the child, but also allows us to say something about the prognosis. Which details of the dream could we take as a starting point here?

Participant: The snake wants to devour the dreamer.

Professor Jung: Yes, this stands for an *intense relation* between the *halves split off* from each other. What do you conclude from that?

Participant: That the dreamer wants to assimilate the snake.

Professor Jung: Of course, both attract each other with great force. The snake wants with all its might to come near her, and she is fascinated. So you can bet that both halves will come together at some point, that under favorable conditions, in other words, the split will be overcome. The prognosis of this split is good, because the child and the snake are intensely relating to each other, which, it is true, still expresses itself in the child as strong anxiety. At that moment the unification of the opposites was quite impossible for the child; but one may assume that in the course of time the mutual attraction will eventually make itself felt.

Now we still have to deal in more detail with the nature of the snake! In this dream the *eyes* in particular are very impressive. They are described as sparkling like diamonds and glowing. Ms. von Franz has, therefore, correctly stressed their importance. The eye really is the seat of fascinating fright; the attraction and the threat come from it. A good parallel to this is the snake with the many eyes in the vision of Ignatius.[35] The stress on the eyes differentiates the snake in the dream from the dim poisonous snake and points to the fact that it contains an inner light and fire. What would you conclude from that? To what could this point?

Participant: That the snake contains the light of consciousness.

Professor Jung: Yes, that it has a consciousness in it, that it is, so to speak, the second person of the dreamer who, however, has completely merged with the unconscious. What meaning, then, does the snake have here?

Participant: The meaning of the sōter snake.

---

[35] Ignatius, *Exercitia spiritualia*. Cf. C. G. Jung's lecture "On the Nature of the Psyche," CW 8 (ed.).

Professor Jung: Quite so; one could conclude with some certainty from the dream that this snake is a kind of bearer of the light, or at least a bearer of the diamond, the glowing stone. In alchemy we find the idea that the stone, the *lapis philosophorum*, can be found in the brain and is, therefore, also called the brain stone. The same idea can be found in our dream, too: there seems to be a light hidden in the brain of the snake. It announces the capability of an extended consciousness, not yet present at the moment. For the time being, there is a restricted consciousness, as is normal for the child; at the same time, the possibility that at some later point *consciousness can expand* is hinted at. The reason why we may draw this conclusion is that the snake here is a sōter snake. The chthonic snake, with its character of the earth demon, of evil, would not directly lead to a healing outcome, because it is only drive, which, as such, brings hardly any promise with it.

Participant: Could one assume that in life the child is fascinated by precisely those figures in which the quality of light is prominent?

Professor Jung: This is a quite natural conclusion, as the whole religious question is being raised with the image of the sōter snake. The sōter snake has a distinctly *spiritual* meaning. That's why Christ is often depicted as a snake. Such representations are frequent in the Middle Ages. The snake is the symbol of secret wisdom and promises the revelation of hidden things and knowledge. It offers instinctive, as opposed to intellectual, knowledge. What's the term for this?

Participant: Intuition.

Professor Jung: This is not knowledge, but a perception.

Participant: Inner view.

Professor Jung: That's right.

Participant: Illumination.

Professor Jung: That's its consequence.

Participant: Revelation.

Participant: Belief.

Professor Jung: That's quite right, but not in the sense we today conceive of belief, as *scientia fidei*, as science of belief. What I mean is *gnosis*. This is knowledge of an irrational nature, different from the arbitrary act of thinking. It is an event, a self-revelation, a mental ac-

259

tivity, the result of a quite peculiar spiritual situation. When you study the Gnostics you will find similar ideas. The Gnostics preach snake wisdom, that is, knowledge *coming from nature itself*. There is also a specifically *Christian gnosis*. You can barely trace the secret of this knowledge. Rationally, it can't be explained at all. You get an idea of this difficulty when you ask how the dogma of the trinity came into being. This is gnosis, knowledge springing from inner experience.

Participant: Couldn't one call this knowledge also mystical knowledge?

Professor Jung: That would be a metaphysical term. We view this question, however, from the psychological standpoint. Then we understand that there is still another *way of gaining knowledge* that is simultaneously a *life process*. Naturally, these things are alien to us, but they become more understandable if we make ourselves acquainted with the psyche of Eastern man. In the East, the intellectual thinking processes recede very much into the background; the whole philosophy of the Upanishads and classical Chinese philosophy, for instance, stem from life processes whose nature is, at the same time, a process of gaining knowledge. This is a thinking out of the bowels,[36] out of the depths. This stands in contrast to the academic intellect that is often empty and, as we know, doesn't always do us any good. For women particularly, it has something destructive. For what basically concerns her is not the intellect either. What concerns her is gnosis. That's why so many women are most deeply disappointed by their university studies, particularly by philosophy, because nowadays philosophy, too, is treated intellectually, in contrast to antiquity, when it was still a life process. Then it was gnosis, a drive, a fact of nature, an inner need. It was like water seeping into dry ground. Gnosis is knowledge stemming from blood. Thus the alchemists say of the stone: "Invenitur in vena, sanguine plena," that is, the stone or lapis is found in blood-filled veins. That's why it is also called *sanguineus*, or carbuncle, or ruby.

This form of knowledge is also expressed in the above-mentioned

---

[36] Greek, *engastrimythos*: designation of the person who prophesies in ecstasy (trans.).

eye snake of Ignatius. When he strove for knowledge of God, that snake appeared to him, as if it wanted to tell him: "I am the one with the one hundred eyes that see all and are all-knowing." These *many eyes* are, so to speak, as many possibilities of consciousness, corresponding to decentralized functions of consciousness. The objects of gnosis are quasi self-glowing, and reveal themselves in their own light. That is also why this process is so often described as a revelation, as an eruption by which the individual is overwhelmed. It is always a process reposing in itself. That's the meaning of the snake when one experiences it from within.

The image of the many eyes also appears in alchemy. The alchemists referred to a passage of the prophet Zechariah,[37] where it says that the eyes of the Lord run to and fro through the whole earth. They are seven eyes, and according to the testimony of the prophet, they are on the foundation-stone of the new temple. But the eye is also the self-perception of an unconscious illuminated or capable of being illuminated. This the alchemists knew and thus they also saw corresponding phenomena in chemical transformations. They report, for instance, the lighting up of the dark, simmering compound in the flask; they took this to be oriental jewels, which they described as *fish eyes*; for the so-called *piscis rotundus*,[38] too, the eyes would have been important: this fish also appears in an Arab legend,[39] where it has only *one* eye. It embodies a being living in darkness and possessing, owing to its eye, a peculiar capability of knowledge. From such inner perceptions stem the images of God. For everything originating in this inner knowledge forms the basis of such experiences. The commonness of these experiential processes has also led to the fact that we find concordant God images in the most various places. We no longer know about these connections and, therefore, think that the God images had been "invented."

That might be the essence of what one can say about this dream.

---

[37] Sach. 4:10: Septem isti oculi sunt Domini, qui discurrunt in universam Terram (Vulgate). "They are the eyes of the LORD, which run to and fro through the whole earth" (Zechariah 4:10).

[38] Latin, "round fish" (ed.).

[39] Karl Vollers, Chidher.

There still remain the details of the forest and the bedroom. The *forest* is a symbol of the unconscious. There you can see all kinds of things, but the vision is restricted, just like in water, in which you also can't look into the depths. The *bedroom* is one of the symbols of the unconscious. But what is the essential difference between forest and bedroom?

Participant: The forest is something collective, the bedroom is a symbol of the personal unconscious.

Professor Jung: Yes, that's right. The personal unconscious has an atmosphere one can humanly empathize with; it is personal and intimate. So we can very well call the bedroom a symbol of the personal unconscious. Just as the dreamer is displaced from the wide space of the forest into the narrow personal space of the bedroom, so the collective unconscious borders on the personal unconscious. A process of *separation* is under way. This separation is necessary because a clearing of consciousness cannot take place as long as the collective unconscious and the personal unconscious are still undivided.

The personal unconscious is like a laguna that is cut off from the sea by a strip of land, and is forming a little lake or a basin itself. Just like the latter, the personal unconscious is surveyable, and one can venture out without danger. Out there, however, is the ocean, the collective. This difference is crucial for the interpretation of our dream: for when the snake is encountered in the forest, this is more or less a natural phenomenon. But when it comes into the bedroom, panic arises. Why?

Participant: Because it concerns the dreamer personally.

Professor Jung: In the forest I encounter the snake "by coincidence," but in the bedroom this goes under my skin, I am most personally touched by it. This advance of the snake into the personal unconscious is another sign of a good prognosis. The possibility of a merging of the separated forms is thus hinted at.

Participant: Doesn't the frequent recurrence also speak for a good prognosis?

Professor Jung: This shows the urgency of the problem that will make itself felt in one way or another.

Participant: But if the importance of the snake is so great, why does the dreamer feel frightened by it?

Professor Jung: It often happens that one fears what has to be, what in the deepest sense belongs to one. One fears it, and yet wants it at the same time. One should really press the fear to one's heart and say: "This is, after all, precisely what I want."

Participant: Is the fear of being bitten justified?

Professor Jung: Of course, because the snake wants to penetrate her inside, wants to be absorbed in her. Simultaneously, the poison infiltrates her; the poison, however, that is also a remedy. It is fate, and that's why one fears it. In the end, one always fears oneself; I don't mean the "I," but fear of the Other in us, the *Self*. Here, one's fear is justified, because it is a superior force of which one knows: "It belongs to me, and I belong to it." They both belong together. And yet it is terrible.

3. Dream of a Ten-Year Old Girl of Sinking in the Water [40]
PRESENTED BY MARGRET SACHS

Text: *I go from the* Bellevue[41] *across the* Quaibrücke *and I'm scared, because I know what will happen. Suddenly, between* Bauschänzli *and* Quaibrücke, *I fall into the water in an upright position. Slowly I am sinking deeper and deeper, until I reach the bottom. I nearly drown. Then I wake up.*

Mrs. *Sachs*: This dream is from the same girl whom we know from the last meeting.

First let us try to structure the dream systematically:

Locale:	From Bellevue across the quay bridge; the water.
Dramatis persona:	The ego of the dreamer.
Exposition:	"I'm scared."
Peripateia:	"Suddenly I fall into the water in an upright position."

[40] Session of 21 November 1939.

[41] The mentioned locations are in Zurich. Bellevue: central square by the river Limmat. Quaibrücke: quay bridge. Bauschänzli: public square on the other side of the river Limmat, opposite Bellevue (trans.).

Lysis: The dream shows a possible solution only with the word "nearly." So something is there that saves the dreamer from the final catastrophe; some yet unknown eventuality might still occur, a backdoor for an escape has been left open.

The frequent recurrence of the dream—it was dreamed "innumerable times"—indicates its importance and its certainly fateful meaning.

To start with, let us try to have a closer look at the *locale*: "I go from Bellevue across the quay bridge." Zurich seems to be the home town of the dreamer, so she does not cross just any bridge in some unknown environment, but the dream is situated in her city, in a place well known to her—an indication that the dream also concerns her own affairs. She comes from "Bellevue," a beautiful square in Zurich, which is called "beautiful view" to boot. For a ten-year-old child, the place with the beautiful view—now lying behind her—might be her past childhood, the security she felt within the family. From there she comes, and now she crosses the bridge. Although she does not mention that she has to cross the bridge, she wouldn't do it if it were up to her, because she is scared. This is probably a process at the mercy of which she fatefully is; her whole behavior in the dream is also completely passive. She has already left the place with the beautiful view, the place where life and future seemed "beautiful."

She is already on the bridge. Three particular characteristics can be found for "*bridge*": it connects two banks, two places of solid ground; it forms a secure way across the water flowing underneath it; and, third, it is not a natural formation, but man-made. Bellevue, the bygone beautiful childhood, was solid ground for her. So there would be adulthood on the other side, and the bridge would represent the transition from childhood to adulthood, namely, puberty. But Bellevue could also represent any other beautiful point of departure, a secure place, from which she has to move on. Because of its frequent occurrence, however, the dream can not only stand for a momentary slight difficulty that has to be "bridged," but has to create an image that throws light on a fundamental situation of the dreamer. We have to resort to interpretations, therefore, that do justice to the dream's importance. For this purpose let us have a look at some examples from history and mythology concerning the keyword "bridge." The following examples have been taken from the seminar in the winter term of 1936/37.[42] It is said that in a text of the Koran a bridge over hell is mentioned, thin as a string and sharp as a sword, which only the righteous can cross. A Muslim legend further tells of a bridge between the Temple of Jerusalem and the Mount of Olives, between the East and the West. Below is hell, into which the unrighteous fall. From the songs of praise of the later "Avesta,"[43] in the compilation of Schaeder,[44] we quote the passage about the "Chinvat bridge, made by Mazda." It is the place of the spiritual deities, the point of transition through the ordeal of fire. "The comely, strong, shapely maiden drags the souls of the bad and deceiving into the darknesses, and leads the souls of the truthful over the Hara brzati and lets them cross the Chinvat bridge. The 'Good Sense' rose from his golden throne and said: 'How did you get here, oh you truthful one, from the sorrowful existence to the sorrowless existence?'" As you can see, this bridge leads from this world to the nether world. Life, too, is the bridge between the cradle and the grave, the bridge between the past and the future. Thus the bridge takes on a cosmic and religious meaning.

In *Gnosis*, Leisegang gives an account of the ophitic sect of the Perates, whose name means "traversing," derived from the Greek word *peran*. Philo of Alexandria writes: "We alone, who have realized the necessity in creation, and the ways in which man came into the world, have also profoundly learned it—to traverse—and are also able to cross transience." It is an interesting fact that the sect of the Perates venerated the serpent as an expression of the Logos. Thus we have found a connection to the vision of the child with the snake, which, there too, means Logos or sōter. As a result, the problem with which the dreamer will certainly be confronted in the long term will revolve around "traversing transience" to reach the "sor-

[42] Cf. seminar 2, § 5 (ed.).
[43] Cf. seminar 2 (ed.).
[44] Hans H. Schaeder, *Urform und Fortbildungen des manichäischen Systems* (ed.).

rowless existence," revolve around being reborn, not only of water, but also of the spirit, and revolve around the snake of salvation, the sōter snake.

Another mythological concept of the bridge is based on the idea that a spirit or a water demon, a bridge ghost, would be underneath it. By building the bridge we would have escaped his direct influence, but various sacrifices were made to him, human beings at first, and later man-shaped dolls, among other things. In ancient Rome, in the month of May, a yearly procession led to the Pons Sublicius, the oldest and most famous among Rome's bridges. On the way, twenty-four chapels, the *Sacella Argeorum*, were visited, and from each an *Argei*, a doll representing an old man, was taken along. Chanting hymns and prayers, the Vestales threw these dolls into the Tiber. It is assumed that this is a relic from an older epoch, when old men, who were no longer fit for military service, were sacrificed as a yearly tribute to the river god, who had been affronted by the building of the bridge (*Encyclopaedia of Religion and Ethics*). London Bridge is said to have been made durable by being sprinkled with the blood of little children, and legend has it that human sacrifices were made in a bridge building, of the bridge in Arta in Italy, whose pillars collapsed until the bridge builder walled up his own wife in them. The last relics of these ideas are the chapels built on the former sacrificial sites on the bridges. On the Spreuer bridge in Lucerne, adorned with pictures of Holbein's *Dance of Death*, a sanctuary lamp is still burning today in a small altar niche, built in a little oriel above the river Reuss, and many a passerby raises his hat, makes the sign of a cross, or even murmurs a prayer in passing by.

The bridge phobia is a well-known form of phobia, in which even today people are seized—despite all their enlightenment and all the ferroconcrete—by sudden and inexplicable fears, nausea, and pallor when they have to cross a bridge, because the demons of the depths have come to life again for them.

Let us summarize: the bridge is a place of danger for the deceiving and the bad, because they might fall down; but it also symbolizes the situation of a transgression of transience, the path to sorrowless existence. Significantly, the Pope has taken over the name of Pontifex

Maximus, supreme bridge builder, which previously was carried by the Roman emperors.

In the light of psychology, the bridge represents a dangerous, precarious part of consciousness, a path that offers few possibilities of giving way. The fact that it is man-made, not a natural formation, may indicate that active forces will have to play a part for the "bridging" to be successful. The bridge arch, stretching from one bank to the other, from one solid place to the other, can also represent that psychic capability which moves on with certainty, with strength, and with confidence about the unknown, as a movement out of itself, into the future to a new task.

Künkel[45] talks about the "suspense arc" [*Spannungsbogen*] of children, which must be big and long enough to carry the child from one developmental stage to the other, from one difficulty to be mastered to the next. If the suspense arc is too small, and is insufficient, the child will shy away from his task, will hole up in previous positions, drop back in his development, fall into a great introversion, or even into a regression.

It is for a very good reason that the primitives have their puberty rites, which help "bridge" the transition from childhood to adulthood, from the security in the ritual house to strife and freedom, from innocent ignorance to responsibility. The separation from the mother, the fasting of many days' duration, the painful tattoos, the inflicting of pain, for example, knocking out the teeth, and then the bestowing of a new name, as well as the rituals of being devoured and eaten up, with the ensuing salvation and rebirth, as reported by Lévy-Bruhl, Frobenius, and others, all these symbolize the transition, the passing into a new phase in life. The performance of these rites of passage helps to safely master the transition into the new life situation. Although our dreamer is not devoured by a giant monster, only to be dragged out of its belly again, she falls prey to another uncanny element that scares her: the water. The dream situation shows that for the moment she is stuck in the monster's belly. Her psychical abil-

---

[45] Fritz Künkel (1898–1956), psychotherapist, originally of Adlerian orientation. He emigrated to California (ed.).

ities of bridging, of walking across, are obviously insufficiently developed. Her bridge fails, it does not stretch to the other side, and she is afraid, "because she knows what will happen." She is in the middle of a process that befalls her with fateful irreversibility, she is at its mercy. Her failure can either be determined by a lack of vitality, caused by an artificial attitude toward life, a one-sidedly accentuated persona stemming from an incorrect education, or it can be determined by the fact that the child's problem makes such great demands that involuntarily she flinches from addressing it, because she is not yet able to cope with it.

It seems that the indication of the sōter snake in the child's vision discussed earlier, symbolizes the problem of growing up, the transition in puberty, and at the same time the religious problem of transgressing transience to immortality, from sorrowful to sorrowless existence, and also being reborn of water and the spirit. The child is afraid "because she knows what will happen," the unconscious senses the danger, the inability to cope with the problems she is confronted with.

"Suddenly, between Bauschänzli and the quay bridge, I fall into the water in an upright position." For the dreamer, these are not the bright waters of the river Limmat, but the uncanny floods with their frightening depths and dangers, commonly seen as a symbol of the unconscious. Like the unconscious, the water is the element of being transported away, of change, of the secret. It wells from unknown depths, floods with torrential force, possesses overwhelming power, devours its victims and covers them. Because of its unfathomable depth, the water is a symbol of the unconscious, and a symbol of life because of its flowing changeability. In this dream, the accent is on its depth; therefore, we may reasonably assume that here it is rather a representation of the unconscious.

The waters of the rivers Styx and Acheron carry the dead to the other side, from the upper world to the underworld. The dead haunt fathomless lakes, such as the Mumel lake or the legendary Pilatus lake.[46] According to Virgil, the entrance to the realm of the dead is

---

[46] Two lakes in Germany (Black Forest) and in Switzerland (trans.).

at the Lago d'Averno. Poets and fairy tales tell of the dangers of the depths; the Lorelei draws ships into the vortices of the river Rhine, "half drew she him, half sank he down."[47] The water is also the place of transformation: Proteus, the water god, turns into a lion, a snake, a tree; Thetis, the Nereid, transforms herself into a bird and a tree while courting Peleus.

As far as the situation of the dreamer at that moment is concerned, it seems as if only the negative aspects of the water would have to be taken into account; for just as she fled from the snake in her vision, she here is afraid of the water and nearly drowns in it. At the moment it has, just like the snake, a frightening and nearly destructive influence. If we focus our interest on the possibilities of a later solution of the problem, however, we will have to consider also some positive aspects of the water, above all its changeability and healing power. In Zimmer's book *Maya* we find the following passage referring to this: "The waters are the *Gegenwelt* [counterworld] to the dry sphere of the waking day, into which the eye looks outward; in them the hidden nature of things is mirrored to the inner view. . . . Down into the water means down into knowledge. The ageless waters, taking all forms of nature, circulating as its life, know everything, they have been present since the beginning and conserve everything in their liveliness—nothing is forgotten. Thus Vishnu speaks to the holy Naranda: Immerse yourself in water, and you will know about my Maya." In another place he writes:

> The waters of life are the womb of all forms of the world, as well as
> their grave in which they are reborn, they circulate in and build,
> they carry and dissolve every form, they are the palpable element of
> the all divine Maya, whose nature the saints and seers tentatively try
> to grasp. They hold the secret of this Maya as the force of their own,
> versatile nature, and do not yield it, but let it be tasted when some-
> one opens up to them. How the world comes into being, every hour,
> outside as world *gestalt* in the flow of coming into being and happen-
> ing, coming to the fore, as *gestalt* of the inner world, from the dark-

---

[47] From Goethe's poem "The Fisherman," set to music by Franz Schubert (trans.).

ness of the unconsciousness into the light of consciousness—all this can be experienced, but how could it be fathomed?

Zimmer also quotes the wondrous motif of someone who immerses himself in water and emerges into a new life, sinking from life dream to life dream in doing so:

The Brahmin Sutapas went into the sacred waters in Benares. The Brahmin turned into a girl of a Chandala family[48] that dwelled near the sacred bathing place at the mouth of the Koka. The girl was beautiful, grew up, and was married to an unsightly man. She bore him two sons, who were both blind, and later a daughter, who was deaf. Her husband was poor. The young, naive woman went to the river, and there she always sat and cried. Once, however, when she had gone to the river to fetch water with her jug, she went down in the water to bathe—and out of the water reemerged that Brahmin Supata, the pious, agile ascetic. The Chandala came to look for his wife and wept for her; the Brahmin comforted him and taught him also to dive into the metamorphosed waters; he had barely dived into the water when he was freed of all stigma, thanks to the magical power of the sacred bathing place. On a carriage of the gods he went heavenward before the eyes of the Brahmin, light as the moon. The Brahmin, however, full of sorrow, also went into the waters of the Koka, and ascended into the highest heaven, only to come to earth again and live in a middle-class family. Being ill and suffering, he recalled his former life, went again into the waters of the Koka to ascend into heaven, to be reborn again, and to tell this story as Prince Kamadamana.

The cleansing, healing power of the water is also known in Christianity, as the baptismal water that washes away original sin and admits the baptized child into the Church, the Corpus Christi. The Jews also baptized, and admitted the proselytes into the community. The Gospel of John quotes Christ's words to Nicodemus: "Verily, ver-

[48] The Chandala or Black People were the lowest caste, or "outcasts," in the caste system (trans.).

ily, I say unto thee, Except a man be born again [of water and the spirit], he cannot see the kingdom of God."

Above all, however, we would like to refer to the Revelation of John: "And he shewed me a pure river of water of life, clear as crystal . . . on either side of the river, was there the tree of life, which bare twelve manner of fruits, and yielded her fruit every month" (22:1–2).

So far the water, into which our dreamer fell, showed only negative aspects for her. The possibility is open, however, that what she fears will change and bring her salvation.

Between the *Bauschänzli* and the quay bridge she suddenly falls into the water in an upright position. We see from this that she crossed the bridge on the right side.[49] Could this suggest that she has always been conscious of her difficulties and of her failure? Or that her failure lies in the field of outer reality?

It is striking that she falls into the water "in an upright position," which she expressly mentions. This can be interpreted in two ways: it can mean that, despite everything, she "keeps her head held high," or that the heavy weight that pulls her down is not in her head, but rather in the instinctual sphere. I do not know if we may interpret that circumstance—her falling into the water in an upright position—in this way.

"Slowly I am sinking deeper and deeper." This might symbolize a slowly progressing process of being flooded by the unconscious. "I nearly drown" has a parallel in the story about the vision of the snake: "I no longer dare move in the bed, because even when awake, everywhere in the room I see the glowing eyes of the snake that wants to bite me." Her light consciousness of the day is flooded and disturbed by the frightening snake image from the unconscious, so she is deprived of her freedom of movement. Here, she nearly drowns—the capabilities of her senses are minimized by the unconscious content entering in her ears, nose, and mouth. She is prevented from seeing, hearing, and speaking, and can hardly breathe at all. So she is in an extremely reduced state; there is hardly any possibility left to contact the outer world, life. Psychologically speaking, this could indicate a

---

[49] See, for instance, www.gis.zh.ch/gb4/stzh/default.asp (14 March 2007) (trans.).

nearly autistic state, or a very great introversion, which severely restricts the possibilities of her moving or expressing herself.

Without the word *nearly* (she says: "I nearly drown") we would have to fear the worst. This little word, however, extenuates the seriousness of the prognosis a bit—it leaves a door open, and is a mere hint of the possibility of salvation. We can't exactly deduce the dreamer's difficulties from this dream, but it can be assumed that she will have a hard time in her fight against powerful psychical forces, not only as a child, but also in her later life. The dream indicates, by its frequent recurrence and by the intensity of the images and the danger, that this is not about just a temporary difficulty in finding the way from childhood to adulthood; these elements symbolize the fateful meaning of a great life task, and grave problems that touch on her innermost being. Her future prospects may well be alarming, being threatened by the archetypal powers of the snake and the water; both of them, however, also hold great possibilities of healing and rebirth. There is legitimate hope that she will reach the other side after all.

Professor Jung: The dream is of the girl whose snake vision we discussed last time. Again it is a dream that has a surprising effect in its simplicity. But precisely these "simple" dreams are not simple at all. Here we will practice the art of making simple dreams "complicated." To do so, we first of all have to take into account the language of the *images* used in the dream. We do this with the help of mythological parallels and amplifications, which may sometimes seem somewhat superfluous to us. We so often believe that children think in a very simple way, but that is precisely the error. The language used by children is much, much older than they themselves. The whole mental and spiritual culture is handed down in language, and in language lies the whole prehistory of man. When we speak in this language, we also speak this prehistory. So if we do not find out and are not clear about the meaning or the connotations of the images in this language, we won't be able to approach the meaning of the dream. It is not always easy to comprehend these linguistic images, the more so as the German language shows a certain primitiveness: its most important terms are ambiguous and fluoresce in all kinds of colors. You can imagine what happens when these images are dreamed to boot, the various meanings coalesce, and a complex mix-up of images ensues.

So if, for instance, as in our dream, the quay bridge appears, at first it seems natural to us to assume that this is the quay bridge—and nothing else. But we forget that this is a dream image that emerged from the richness of the unconscious. This makes even our unpretentious quay bridge a *bridge*, a bridge of a highly general meaning. In dreams, that is, in the language of the unconscious, even the best-known and most mundane bridge, and be it a little footbridge, is after all "the bridge." The same is true of many concrete objects we are dreaming of: banal as they may seem, they refer to all kinds of philosophical and religious problems, or to dark places in human nature. We can observe this phenomenon also in psychopathology; in cases of schizophrenia, psychical problems of a definitely complex nature are often expressed in quite banal images. The patients can't help but think that way; they have only their appalling platitudes at their disposal. If we were able to understand the general meaning of these images, however, we would be able to grasp the meaning of the psychoses.[50] We could even heal a patient if we succeeded in making the general meaning of his images clear to him. Then we'd have to tell him, for example: "Well, look, this isn't about this quay bridge at all, it's about the bridge as such." And what does *bridge* mean? This idea refers to a great multiplicity of possibilities of psychic experience. It can mean: "To get to the other side," "Crossing the great water," or "Everything is transition." It can contain the simplest meaning as well as the deepest wisdom. If a general symbol like the bridge appears, we must not let ourselves be misled by any commonplace views. But then, are we actually familiar with anything else but commonplace views today? Who is crossing the quay bridge, thinking: "Everything is transition"? In the Middle Ages this was different. At that time, people still had a relation to the symbol. So a chapel was built on the bridge, and a sanctuary lamp was put in it. There was

---

[50] Cf. Jung's papers "The Psychology of Dementia Praecox," CW 3, § 198, and "The Content of the Psychoses," CW 3, § 317, where the expression "*Sinn im Wahnsinn*" [meaning in madness] is found (ed.).

273

a Saint Nepomuk[51] and other saintly figures who guarded the bridge. They reminded the people of the fact that each bridge is "the bridge," that everything is transition. At that time these things were experienced as real. They gave the medieval mind a strange aura, which we can no longer completely understand. Anything banal was, *at the same time*, also something general, and a part of the whole. For them, a stone is not just a stone, but it can also be the soul of an ancestor, ancestors can live in it; and an animal is not necessarily simply an animal, but it is also an ancestor, a totem father. The whole landscape is like the open book of your unconscious. Everything is ensouled by the unconscious of the people. When you walk through the landscape with a Negro, you don't just take a walk in the "topography," where everything is abstract and scientific, but you will experience mythology. When you climb a mountain or go into the bamboo woods with him, this is no ordinary venture, because you will come into the realm of the secluded spirits. In the soundless, green silence of the wood we feel as if we were immersed in the water of the sea. Then there is no more botany; the whisper of the bamboo leaves, the gentle murmur of the wind—these are the voices of the spirits, and they give people the shivers. This is an awe-inspiring experience. We all know this magic from childhood, when the world still had a certain golden glow and everything was still very strange. For the child, the world is mythology, as it is for primitive man, and this is also the atmosphere out of which dreams have to be understood. For this reason, I insist that in each dream analysis the whole spectrum of the linguistic symbol be staked out. This method is not without danger, because at first it leads you away from the personal psychology of the dream, and we are in danger of going astray. The wealth of the material can seduce us to such an extent that we no longer know where we are. We have to be very sure of our ground, otherwise we will become enmeshed in a formidable entanglement of possibilities. The dream analysis has eventually to come back, after all, to the child

[51] Patron saint of Bohemia, a martyr (d. 1393). He is also called John Nepomucen. He was vicar general of Bohemia under King Wenceslaus IV (later Holy Roman Emperor Wenceslaus). When the king wished uncanonically to convert an abbey into a cathedral, St. John opposed him, in spite of torture. The king had him drowned in the Moldava (trans.).

who dreamed these dreams in order to assess the meaning of the individual contents.

The *particular motivation* of the dream cannot be derived from the general spectrum of meanings of the images, but can only be deduced from the personal amplification, from the context, and from the *individual situation of the child*. Only if we know the whole psychological situation of the child will we be able to deal with the decision about practical questions. As I mentioned already, it is only in the most exceptional cases that we are in a situation to ask the child him- or herself about the context, considering that we are dealing with a remembered dream or that the child is still too little to answer. From a certain age onward, however, children are indeed able to answer. I once had a consultation with an eight-year-old girl. She came dolled up like a little monkey with a little purse, and told her dreams with all the tricks of the trade. With this little girl it was quite possible to have a conversation.

So let us suppose you are told the present dream by the child herself. What would you say to her? Of course, you must not disclose your mythological knowledge to her, for these are just your theoretical tools, and the practical side is quite a different thing. So imagine her to be an intelligent girl. What would you ask the child?

Participant: If she were afraid of the water?

Professor Jung: It would be more to the point if you asked her whether she were afraid of bridges.

Participant: If she had ever nearly drowned, or if she had ever had a frightening experience on the quay bridge?

Professor Jung: Yes indeed, we do have to ask such *practical questions*. Often it is only because of dreams that our attention is called to such experiences. If, for instance, an anxiety dream—and this is a typical anxiety dream—always happens at the same location, we have to ask ourselves why this place is so emphasized, if there is perhaps something special about it. Let us assume that this is not the case here. Then our next consideration has to be that the child's route leads from Bellevue to Bauschänzli. What questions could be tied to this fact?

Participant: I'd ask where she lives.

275

Professor Jung: Yes, it would be important to know if she is leaving home or going home.

Participant: Or could one also ask: "Where do you actually want to go?"

Professor Jung: Yes, this could make her recall special experiences. But we don't know anything about all that. So we can't ascertain the specific meaning that the dream had for the child at the time. Something else can probably be stated about the dream, however. With what justification?

Participant: The dream recurred repeatedly, although the specific situation was different each time.

Professor Jung: Yes, we have to conclude that there is an *inner constellation* that did not change over the years. When a dream recurs so frequently, I usually refrain from searching for the specific motives. Moreover, I quite generally take the view that a neurosis is not of traumatic origin, that is, that it can't be traced back to a singular frightening experience; I try to understand it in the context of its present meaning. For what lives and takes effect today is also recreated today, again and again. I also relate frequently *recurring* dreams to what is *currently* going on, therefore, and to what is *recreated* over and over again, and not to something that lies many years back. So this dream, too, refers to an inner constellation, which has not changed over the years.

We already know from the previous dream that there exists a certain splitting in the dreamer, that is, that consciousness and the unconscious are split off from each other. We further saw that the unconscious and consciousness even attract each other, as expressed in the threat that the snake poses to the dreamer. This dream goes a step further than the mere threat; the *danger becomes manifest*: the dreamer falls into the water, in which she is, so to speak, completely swallowed by the monster of the unconscious. We have to take into account a peculiar detail, the fact that she falls down in an upright position. This is very unusual, because usually one falls sideways one way or the other. When someone, as in this case, falls down with the hands on the body and with the feet first, this expresses a certain stiffness, as if one were enclosed by something. The feeling of suffocation

276

the dreamer experiences when sinking also points to this tight enclosure. It is as if she were pulled into the mouth of a monster and swallowed. Myths express the sucking and suffocating aspect of water by populating it with monsters, dragons, or other water creatures. Many primitive heroic myths also tell the story that the hero is devoured by the dragon, complete with his ship. In the monster's belly he is pressed to such an extent that, so as not to be crushed, he pushes the remains of the ship against the walls of the stomach. The experience of being pressed is a very important motif. In our dream it also finds expression in the feeling of suffocating. To what does this refer? From where do we have such a direct experience?

Participant: From birth.

Professor Jung: Although the newborn is not consciously aware of it, the nervous system registers these events. Dreams that refer back to birth, and seem to be based on a perfect knowledge of anatomy, are not infrequent. This led Rank[52] to the assumption, for instance, that all neuroses can be traced back to the trauma of birth. Birth is indeed a trauma, an impressive moment, and it is also possible that such an impression continues to have an effect throughout life, especially if there were complications at birth. But we must not generalize this fact.

Participant: Is this dream not about a "reversed" birth?

Professor Jung: That's right, it is like a *retrogressive birth*, a going back into the womb, into the prenatal state. This immersion into the unconscious actually represents a *figurative death*, a frequent motif of the transformation process, standing in close connection to the symbolism of rebirth. This is not at all evident from the dream at first sight, but we may add it from our knowledge. The dream itself describes only the danger; it shows that in each *transformation*, and whenever a *transition* occurs, the ground may cave in, so that we fall down into an unconscious state. When are there such transitions in practical life?

Participant: At the beginning of school, at the development from childhood to adulthood, at the beginning of professional life.

---

[52] Otto Rank (1884–1939); see his *The Trauma of Birth* (ed.).

Professor Jung: These are transitions, transformations in life, in which we change from one state into another, from a previous situation into a new one. This we can only achieve if we are at one with ourselves. A *split personality* will have *difficulties* in all these *transitions*, comparable to a sinking in water. What does this mean in concrete terms?

Participant: That we are in over our head.

Professor Jung: Quite right. We also say: "I can't keep my head above water," or "In such a situation you'll go under." The difficulties may vary greatly, it could be overwhelming affects, or experiences we can't cope with, but these are always very deep experiences into which we sink, so to speak. It is a fact, by the way, that persons with splits are particularly destined to have such very deep-going experiences. Why?

Participant: So that the split may be overcome.

Professor Jung: Yes, fate imposes hard experiences on them, to hit them in their innermost being, where they are still at one with themselves, that is, in the instinct. With their split, such persons will always blunder into split situations. They will have to endure things that stand in sharpest contrast to each other. So, for example, they will have friends of completely different characters. In all these cases, those persons never know who they actually are. They don't know: Am I white or am I black? I'm actually both, because I'm the friend of A and of B. Something is bound to happen here. This situation downright invites fate to intervene with a blow, so that deep regions are touched and may grow again as a unity. Split persons always generate split situations, conflict situations. To such persons in particular, to those who do not know who they are, it happens that they are particularly confronted with decisions, whereas other people can go on living in their unambiguous situations. The treatment of such split persons is not easy. We often simply do not manage to reunite the halves, which have come apart, into a whole. We can only say: Hopefully something really overwhelming will happen to them, so that they realize who they are.

So this dream points to the fateful necessity of having ultimate experiences, so that the point is touched where the person is still one.

278

Such a person has to be completely torn apart at first to recompose himself anew. This last unity has to be found, and this will happen only if the person is wounded in his innermost being, most often by someone chosen by fate to be the hammer, because as a rule he can't do it on his own.

4. Dream of a Five- to Six-Year-Old Boy of a Pyramid and a Glass House[53]
PRESENTED BY ANIELA JAFFÉ

Text: *I see a pyramid in front of me. On its top there is a house made of glass. There is somebody in it. As I come nearer, I realize that it's me.*

Mrs. Jaffé: In this dream we have to distinguish between a vision, as also stressed by the introductory words ("I see . . . in front of me"), and an action, which confines itself to seeing—approaching—realizing.

The locale of the events is not specified. Certainly a strange or remote place is implied, because pyramids are quite unfamiliar in the boy's environment, and still completely unknown to him at this age.

Dramatis personae:	The dreamer and his ego.
Exposition:	"I see a pyramid in front of me. On its top there is a house made of glass. There is somebody in it."
Peripateia:	"I come nearer."
Lysis:	"I realize that it's me."

If we let ourselves be affected by the dream image, we will get the feeling that nature somehow speaks with friendly irony here. Seen from an inner perspective, that is, from how the little dreamer experiences it, something extremely important happens to him: he encounters himself; he sees himself far away, at the top of an immense edifice, and, moreover, in a glass house, a veritable castle in the air— and yet at the same time he is standing below. From an outer perspective, that is, from a reflective or critical observer's view, the image of the little "Johnny Look-in-the-Air"[54] gives us the impres-

---

[53] Session of 28 November 1939.

[54] *Hans-guck-in-die-Luft*, a character in Heinrich Hoffmann's *Struwwelpeter* (Shock-Headed Peter), a classic children's book (trans.).

sion of a little helpless child, who will perhaps soon trip over some minor obstacle, with his eyes astray up on high. And when this same little child is simultaneously enthroned on top of the pyramid, even as if imprisoned in a very transparent, though not fully comprehensible glass house, we can leave aside the seriousness of the events for the moment, and take pleasure in the serenity of the image, the meeting of the great and the little, of the above and the below.

Obviously, this vision of himself is meant to convey to the dreamer an insight into his own nature. This image seems to tell him: This is you. Leaving aside all amplifications, the image and the language say something like this: You are sitting up there, high in the sky, and it's terribly difficult, perhaps even impossible, to come up and reach you. It is also doubtful if you yourself can come down; you may be doomed to stay up there forever in your proud solitude, and to spend your life in this all-too-bright little attic room.[55] In addition, you are imprisoned in a glass cage, which protects you from all direct contact; but woe betide you if you move too suddenly in it, or, as boys do, throw stones—everything will go to pieces. When the sun shines it will probably get unbearably hot in your hothouse, and you will start to sweat and suffer. Certainly you can look far into the distance from up there, and no light will be able to conjure up your shadow on the walls of your castle; and should it appear far down below on the ground, you will probably not be able to make it out. It is beautiful and important to live on top of this mysterious giant edifice, and yet it is remote, lonely, and enigmatic. And, on top of all that, you must not forget that you are actually standing down there, helpless and little. But now the uncanny question arises: where is reality to be found here?—So that's what the image and the words seem to suggest.

Now I would like to come to the amplificatons. We are dealing with the symbols of the pyramid, the glass house, and the encounter with oneself.[56] Let us deal with the *pyramid* first. In the dream text it

[55] In the original: *Oberstübchen*, literally "little upper room," a slightly pejorative colloquialism for head or brains (trans.).

[56] Cf. C. G. Jung, "Individual Dream Symbolism in Relation to Alchemy," *CW* 12; "Religious Ideas in Alchemy," *CW* 12; and Hans Baumann, "Betrachtungen über die Symbolik der Pyramiden."

only says: "I see a pyramid in front of me"—no further details about its form or dimension are revealed. But we will hardly prejudice the meaning of the dream if we assume that this is a building of immense proportions—there is room for a whole house on its top, and in most cases the term *pyramid* generally indicates, in common usage, a high building that rises above a quadratic base. In addition, most often there is still another qualification: a pyramid as it is found in Egypt is a tomb of a Pharaoh. Pyramids as sacred buildings, however, have been erected not only in Egypt, but also in Mexico, China, and Java, in completely different cultural environments. They are an expression of an archetypal image. Of the many observations that have been made on the construction of those pyramids, so mysterious to this day, I would like to single out only those that seem to be important for the understanding of the dream, acting on the assumption that this is about the Egyptian pyramid. It has been observed that the pyramids, in whose interior the mummy of a Pharaoh was conserved in a burial chamber, had a glossy, polished, and reflecting surface. The rising triangular areas acted like gigantic mirrors that during the day reflected the sunlight onto the land like a gigantic cone of light, and at night showed the stellar constellations. The hieroglyph for certain pyramids,[57] therefore, means source of light, and various inscriptions indicate its light symbolism. Something very strange or even contradictory seems to lie in the fact that these of all buildings symbolize light and radiance, because with all the impact of their completely unstructured, immense surfaces they seem to represent the impenetrability of stone and the epitome of structured matter. This double aspect is also expressed in the composition of the form: with their greatest width, the surface areas solidly rest on the ground, and then narrow more and more toward the top; they seem almost to dematerialize. Finally, coming from four sides, the surfaces meet in one single point of no square dimension at all. This point has always been considered the crowning feature of the whole edifice, however, its most sacred and mystic place. Often the tops of Egyptian pyramids were gilded or made of a specially gleaming stone. It was assumed that

[57] Belbel: a sun disk with three rays or arrows (trans.).

after the Pharaoh's death his soul, that is, his image, the Ka soul, would travel through the underworld and then be transformed into the god Osiris, or rise to Atum, the highest god of light, exactly at this top of his grave. In the pyramid of Borobudur in Java, the picture of Buddha is clearly visible on the lower terraces, surrounded by scenes from his life. On the middle terraces it stands alone, without any narrative framework. Higher up still, its portrayal is hardly visible any longer, and finally completely eludes the human eye on the uppermost terrace. The pyramids are huge central edifices rising above a quadratic base, with a strong emphasis on the top as the actual center of the towering rock mass. Such a central edifice is a body mandala, that is, a sacred area that offers not only protection, but also a place in whose center the god is born or has his home. These royal tombs, deliberately built for eternity in the third millennium B.C. (the Cheops pyramid was built around 2800 B.C.), make an immense, if remote, impression even today; they are perfect and inaccessible at the same time, and, like something final or absolute, extend from the dim and distant past into our age. In such a perfect form, which cannot be surpassed in its simplicity, there is no twilight zone in which fairy tales or legends could emerge. As if in awe, neither language nor popular belief have taken possession of these monuments, and dealt with or shaped their meaning. With great aplomb, however, Goethe wrote to Lavater in 1780, at the age of thirty one: "the desire to acuminate the pyramid of my existence, whose base was given to me as a foundation, as high up into the air as possible, prevails over everything else, and makes immediate forgetting nearly impossible. I must not tarry, for I am already far advanced in years, and perhaps fate breaks me in two in the middle, and the Babylonian Tower will remain blunt and unfinished. At least it should be said: He was of audacious design; and if I live the forces shall reach, God willing, up to the top."

To conclude, the symbol of the pyramid provides the following indications for our dream: it is an archetypal image, a body mandala, in whose depths the body of the king rests as a mummy, and at whose summit the glorification of the soul takes place. The composition of the form displays how matter becomes dematerialized, and the arrangement of the reflecting surfaces shows how mass reflects the Eternal Light.

Before I consider the psychological conclusions for the dream or the dreamer's personality, I would like to say a few things about the house of glass on top, because this house will not alter the meaning, but only reinforce what has been found out so far.

Referring to the eternal Jerusalem, lying quadratically on top of the mountain, it says in the Revelation of John: "and the street of the city was pure gold, as it were, transparent glass" (Revelation 21:21). As Professor Jung told us last year, this corresponds to the alchemical idea of the *vitrum aureum*, the golden glass, by which the *lapis*, the eternal stone, was meant. We remember that the tops of the pyramids were gilded in antiquity, or made of a gleaming stone, and we are surprised that a child's unconscious puts the glass house of the eternal city at the one and only correct place. Just as the enormous mass of the pyramid leads up to the highest point, whose nature was experienced as spiritual, there occurs the slow transformation—as we learned last year—of the heavy, dark earth into the diamond, which in its transparency and invariability stands for the true nature of man, his eternal home and his boundary, his self. Seen as a whole, the pyramid and the glass house with someone in it on top become a symbol for man in his uniqueness. I envisage it as follows: deep down, far below the burial tomb of the king, there is a cistern, remotely connected to the river that bestows growth and life upon the land, following the changing rhythm of the river's rising and sinking—an image of man's deepest roots in the unconscious, which also connects him with transhuman life, far beyond his personal boundaries. Above this there rests the body of the king, man's image of his ancestors, of his totem that is indestructible and lives within him like the mummy. The externally visible edifice rises in four planes (corresponding to the four functions) that eventually come together at *one* point at the top—an image of the bodily here and now, of daily material existence which, however, reflects the sun, the light, and the stars as a medium, thus bearing witness to them. The point at the top has no dimension, and yet it is of the hardest, indestructible quality, a crystal, a glasshouse, both an expression for consciousness of individuated man in its most developed form. By its astronomical orientation the edifice of the pyramid is set in time, yet its five-thousand-year-old existence seems to transcend time and announce eternity.

This image also roughly corresponds to the developmental line that Professor Jung mentioned in his lecture: the pyramid rises as a mountain, or as the world mountain Meru, from the quadratic base that corresponds to the division into four quarters. On its top there is again a rectangular base, the *quaternitas*, the glass house, the monastery, in which there lives the child of the union, the living being, the "someone" of the dream.

But now back to the dream text, in which it says: "as I come nearer, I realize that it's me." What occurs here is the following: what up to that moment had been intuition, a vision of someone, of *homo*, now suddenly concerns the dreamer directly. It is no longer a general problem, but his own. Simultaneously, the image changes in that it no longer represents something absolute, or some final state, but is subject to the dynamics of life and of change. To understand this image better, we have to revert once again to the meaning of the glass house. It is not only the eternal house in celestial Jerusalem or the *lapis*, but also means—as in the developmental line I just mentioned—the vessel, the *vas*, the retort, in which the transformation of man happens. In fairy tales this vessel also appears as a glass casket, in which the soul slumbers, waiting for salvation (Snow White in the casket of glass). In the *Visio Arislei*,[58] an alchemical text, a triple glass house is the place where the heroes are condemned to death in great heat, only to find new life again. This vessel corresponds to the uterus, the place of realization, in which the homunculus, the light man, is created, and which is often depicted at the center of a mandala. In the language of symbols, triangles standing on a base—in our case, the surfaces of the pyramid that rise from a broad base up to the glass—are licking flames; and thus the vision says that flames erupt from the earthen depths of man, giving birth to the spiritual body, to what is eternal within him. For the child, this

---

[58] Cf. C. G. Jung, "Religious Ideas in Alchemy," CW 12, §§ 435, 437, 449. The *Visio Arislei* is contained in *Artis auriferae*, vol. 1, § 3, pp. 146ff (ed.).

image seems to be like something that points to his own future. A comparison with the suffering of the heroes in the glass house of the *Visio Arislei* shows how much pain and sacrifice of light day consciousness this process will cost. Another parallel may confirm this. The Aztecs had the following custom: a man had to slowly climb the steps of a temple pyramid, symbolizing the slow rise of the sun. Once he reached the top, however, he was sacrificed: the sun begins to set.

With the insight in the dream: "I realize that it's me," the problem of the dreamer and his double also arises, and with it, finally, the whole spectrum of questions concerning the current situation of the child and the dreamer's peculiarities and difficulties. As Professor Jung explained to us last winter, in the first years of life the child still lives in a very close relation to the prenatal stage, the Bardo life. The child is, so to speak, not yet fully born into reality, but still much closer to the primordial ideas than the adult, the realistic person. Invasions of the unconscious may happen, and images or symbols may appear, which far exceed the comprehension of infantile consciousness—like the image of the vision of the pyramid in our example. As we heard last winter, because of the great susceptibility of children, such invasions of the unconscious always represent a grave danger of splitting and of disintegration. The child is so fascinated by the archetypal image that hardly any other reality can exist beside it. If looking into a mirror[59] appears in a dream after such archetypal images, in most cases this will signify a way of rescue, leading into reality. The mirror is the rational intellect, which clarifies and structures the seemingly overwhelming situation; when you look into it, you will have to believe in your own existence and will no longer be able to lose yourself. It seems strange that in this dream the healing look at oneself looks like an enormous split, so that doom and salvation coincide, so to speak. This may be due to the following: although the child below sees his ego far removed from himself and at a very great height, this ego is in a very special place, namely, at the center of a mandala, which not only offers protection, but—similar to the North Pole in a dream discussed in the last seminar—also has cen-

[59] The French homonym to *Glas* (glass) is *glace* = mirror (trans.).

285

tralizing power and thus averts the danger of splitting, although it may not eliminate it altogether. But what does this image mean, the image of the child appearing at the top of the pyramid while simultaneously standing on the ground? We are reminded here of the Germanic figures of the Fylgjas, the "following spirits" that accompanied a person either as his double, or sometimes in the form of an animal, and which protected him or warned him of danger; we are reminded of accounts of witches who slept in their beds at night, yet were seen to ride to the Brocken;[60] of appearances of persons who in reality were somewhere else entirely; and of reports of persons living or dead. The idea of a double ego is not alien to children; when they illustrate their dreams, for example, they often draw themselves not only in the dream scene, but also a second time on the side as they sleep in the bed. The Egyptians, according to whose belief the soul consisted of about fourteen parts or forces, know a part of the soul they called the Ka soul. It was immortal and its body, conceived as half physical and half spiritual, was absolutely identical with the person, even after his death. It was his double, his *Doppelgänger*. The hieroglyph for *Ka* shows the hands raised in prayer, which perhaps already indicate the desire for height and light with their movement.

Paracelsus, too, hypothesized another body besides the physical one, called the sidereal body by him, a half-material body that represented the reversed image of its counterpart. In *De lunaticis*, he writes: "so there are two bodies in man, one composed of the elements, the other of the stars; therefore, these two have to be well distinguished from each other. In death the elementary body is buried together with its spirit, the ethereal ones are consumed in the firmament, and the spirit of the God-image goes to Him of which it is the image." Paracelsus assumes that even after death a person's sidereal body will roam, and simulate the appearance of the dead person. It is like the inner mirror image of man, a body whose flesh is, in his words, subtle flesh, and which does not depend on doors or holes, but walks through walls without breaking anything. Long after the dissolution

---

[60] The Brocken, or Blocksberg, is the highest peak (1142 m) in the German Harz Mountains. It has long had associations with witches and devils. Also mentioned in Goethe's *Faust* (trans.).

of the elementary body in the earth, this sideric body will be slowly consumed by the stars.

The alchemists also knew about this second body, the incorruptible body, which is taken out of the physical body in the *opus* and transformed to perfection. Here I would like to quote a passage from Professor Jung's "Representations of Redemption in Alchemy." There it says: "Ruland[61] says, 'Imagination is the star in man, the celestial or supercelestial body.' This astounding definition throws a quite special light on the fantasy processes connected with the *opus*. We have to conceive of these processes not as the immaterial phantoms we readily take fantasy-pictures to be, but as something corporeal, a 'subtle body,' semi-spiritual in nature." And later it says about this imagination, according to an alchemical text: "since divine wisdom is only partly enclosed in the body of the world, the greater part of it is outside, and it imagines far higher things than the body of the world could conceive (*concipere*). And these things are outside nature: God's own secrets. The soul is an example of this: it too imagines many things [. . .] outside the body, just as God does." And, finally: imagination is, therefore, not "a question of actualizing those contents of the unconscious that are outside nature, that is, not a datum of our empirical world, and therefore a priori of archetypal character. The place or the medium of realization is neither mind nor matter, but that intermediate realm of subtle reality that can be adequately expressed [only] by the symbol."[62]

When we apply this to our dream we could say that the Ka soul, the sidereal or subtle body of the child, sits on top of the pyramid: in general terms, the desire for perfection and boundlessness, for salvation and immortality, embodied in the dreamer.

But let us not forget that at the same the child is still standing on the ground, in all the reality of his little helpless body, looking up at himself. The result is an image of the insoluble tension between limitedness and eternity, reality and dream, actuality and ideal, body and soul, mortality and immortality. From time immemorial the motif of

[61] An alchemist (ed.).
[62] *Psychology and Alchemy*, CW 12, § 394 (trans.).

man's encounter with himself has existed, of the fateful and ominous appearance of the *Doppelgänger*. While the dual motif, for example, of the Dioscuri or the two friends in the Upanishads, also expresses this dichotomy, these myths also give an indication of how the conflict can be sustained, even show that the two poles actually belong together, and that the two can form a unity only with each other, despite their dissimilarity. Both unite their forces in a joint act, in which each of them does what he can do best, and the two complement each other. Together the Dioscuri fight for the cattle herds, and despite all vicissitudes evoked by their past, Zeus grants them the final victory. In the Upanishads, for example, the two connected friends embrace one and the same tree; one eats the berries, while the other just looks down, to experience the tree in that way. It is different if the problem is expressed by the double; this always indicates that the problem is experienced in all its tragedy, nearly without a possible solution: the person who encounters his own ego no longer actually knows where his own reality is, but tries to identify first with the one ego, then with the other, only soon to experience the painful disappointment that he is at home neither here nor there, neither above nor below, neither within nor without. It is probably no coincidence that in Romanticism a great number of stories about doubles came into being. Tieck, Jean Paul, E.T.A. Hoffmann, Chamisso, and Heine write about this topic as an expression of the suffering from outer reality, which stands in a seemingly irreconcilable contrast with the experienced inner world. Unfortunately, it would lead too far to list all the *Doppelgänger* motifs here, and to give an account of the partly comical, partly tragic experiences and entanglements of the heroes and their mirror-egos, shadow-egos, or wax figure-egos. I would just like to mention that there was a renaissance of the literature on the *Doppelgänger* or double ego around the turn of the century; Dostoevsky, Oscar Wilde, Stefan George, later Franz Werfel and, in modified form, also Herman Hesse and Hofmannsthal wrote about this topic. While the romanticists seem to have identified rather with inner reality, the turn of the century was a time when the development of consciousness "peaked" (to stay in the image of the vision), when one was about to tackle the solution to the riddles of the world with the intellect, and the intellect *only*, and when man, blinded by the results, identified only too readily with this efficient consciousness. In such one-sidedness, however, the double appears and will again have to lead man to the other side, which lies in the shade, in the night, in the unconscious.

To conclude, I would like to try to draw inferences from the dream image regarding the personality of the dreamer and his problem situation. As the dream recurred repeatedly, we are justified in assuming that something of special importance to the dreamer's life is expressed in it, something that the unconscious repeatedly shows him by this. This importance is further underlined by the location where the child has the vision in the dream; although it is not specified, it is surely a remote and alien place, where important and meaningful things happen. I have tried at first to draw conclusions from the image of the vision alone, without any amplifications, regarding the child's personality and his difficulties. This could be summarized as follows: this is a child who is up very "high," in the glass house, meaning he is not yet fully in reality, but still very close to Bardo life. He is, so to speak, still in a supernatural uterus, with the possible effect that he lives in his fantasies and intuitions. To his environment the child will perhaps not let show too much—in the dream he is *also* standing on the ground. Basically, however, his adaptation to reality is only superficial, a pseudo-adaptation, because his soul is somewhere else entirely. But this inhibits the whole development of the personality, so that the child seems infantile. Being enclosed in the glass house intensifies the importance of the isolation. He will have difficulty getting in touch with other children, and he will radiate a chilly atmosphere, which in turn will make it difficult for others to reach out to him. Naturally the child will suffer for it, but in a way he will also feel important. He may be one of the many children who believe that they secretly descend from a royal couple, which gives them an inner feeling of superiority. The glass house could also indicate that the enclosure was reinforced by the parents' spoiling the child, by an all-too-pointed education, which spoils the child—the glass house is also the hothouse—and produces a delicate, shrinking violet, instead of letting the child see the world of street life early enough. Soon enough the fear of his own evil will rise in the dreamer; for in his glass house he can be seen from all sides, he is under constant observation, and he does not have that wonderful place where children keep their secrets. This is his actual poverty.

From the frequent recurrence of the dream we may probably conclude that the tension between the two egos, between inner and outer reality, expressed therein, will still remain the problem of the grown man in much later years. When, in the development of this child, the great amnesia will have obscured the Bardo world with its primeval images, such a dream will shine like a spark from the lost paradise, and remind him that he, who lives down on earth, also has an immortal, versatile soul of divine nature. From the image, in which he sees this soul out there, far away, split off from him, and nearly unreachable, we might conclude that later on in life he will identify too one-sidedly with the conscious ego. Then, in the revealing look up to the high ego on the pyramid, however, he will be fascinated like a Narcissus by his own mirror image and by inner reality, blinded by the boundless possibilities of the soul. In fantasies and daydreams he will, for instance, climb heights that are denied to him by reality. Such a superior, light, and yet outwardly experienced image of the inner ego, however, will act as a frightening and ever-present demand for perfection, that is, to adjust to his height as well as possible. Each deviation from that will be experienced as a painful disappointment, through which the remoteness and dreamlike unreality of the ideal will be felt again and again. The results will be a feeling of his own inferiority and fear of life.

This image of the oppositeness of inner and outer reality, of ego and double-ego, however, also expresses the dreamer's potentiality to reach greater consciousness despite all the dangers. Novalis says that no one knows himself if he knows only himself, and if he is not also somebody else. As Professor Jung said at the last meeting, each creation is preceded by being split in two. Here the dream has portrayed the soul in its two great opposites and, in addition, has indicated the way to change. Thus we may hope that this tension between the two souls will lead the dreamer—or has led him already—to the place where he will be able to tolerate the dichotomy, that is, to himself.

Professor Jung: The dream was told by a man whom I came to know when he was between forty-five and fifty years old. He was a man who had been on the "quest"[63] all his life, and in the course of this search finally had come to me. Already when he was a child he was unable to take the world as completely real, but was eccentric and dreamy. Later he had difficulty in choosing a profession; he finally chose jurisprudence, but only half-heartedly, and only because he had to do something, after all. He then was a judge in the colonies for a couple of years, and worked in this capacity after a fashion and with more or less success. He greatly suffered in this life, because basically he was not interested in his job. He did not want to accept that being a jurist or a judge, with more or less chance of promotion, would be the great thing about life. So he never put his heart and soul into it. It was as if he had more than one string to his bow. After much hesitation, he married; the marriage was not a good one, however, but full of difficulties. But then he only put half his heart in it, and who knows where he put the other half. Generally, deep down he was unconscious of this whole other side. Only sporadically he had some little philosophical adventures, in which he looked for what his profession did not offer him. On one of these occasions he came across one of my books, which made a great impact. So then he came to me.

The dream clearly shows the other side of his nature. He himself, however, never made the connection to his state. From this you can see the extent of his split. With one foot he seemingly stood in eternity, with the other in reality. As the dream recurred many times, we may assume that it was very important to him and quite characteristic for the course his life took. It is actually a vision that contains, similar to the dreams already discussed, something completely unchildlike. The dream is very *abstract* and of a very general and extremely *typical* character. What do you think this implies for the dreamer?

Participant: That he has a normal constitution.

---

[63] This word in English in the original (trans.); here referring to the inner process of self-discovery as described in many fairy tales (cf. Hedwig von Beit, *Symbolik des Märchens*, vol. 1, pp. 335–36) and medieval knight romances (e.g., in Wolfram von Eschenbach's *Parsifal* or Hartmann von Aue's *Iwein*) (ed.).

Professor Jung: Yes, that is correct. Or, in case there should be a neurosis, it would certainly not be serious, because the vision is not chaotic at all. On the contrary, the archetype is expressed with remarkable precision. But what is the difference from the previous dream of the bridge, which also was of a general nature?

Participant: Here the connection to everyday life is missing completely.

Professor Jung: Yes, this is an image you won't encounter in reality; it is completely unreal, as opposed to the image of the quay bridge, which in its entirety is taken from the experiential sphere. The vision of the glass house is taken from a completely different experiential world, and even appears to be fabricated. If I hadn't known the man personally, I'd be in doubt whether the image hadn't been invented.

Participant: Does the dream perhaps stem from such a deep psychical layer that it is hardly possible to link its images with the outer world?

Professor Jung: Yes, the dream is a pure product of the prenatal psyche, and belongs, so to speak, to a virginal layer that hasn't had any contact yet with the outer world. In such cases the images persist in their original form. This glass house does not correspond to any experience; otherwise, the dreamer might perhaps have rather talked of a "lantern," and then tried to make a connection between this strange object and some known form. Here, however, it remains completely unreal. Even if he had once seen a pyramid, there certainly was no glass house on top.

During this winter term we will deal with some more of those abstract dreams. The dream in which four gods rise from the four corners also comes from layers that had not been in touch with the world before. In all these cases with such remote images, we have to consult an extremely multilayered symbolism to reach an understanding. Let us only add some few remarks to the exhaustive paper of Mrs. Jaffé.

It was mentioned that the *glass house* standing on top of the *pyramid* represents its *center*. We also find this idea of the vessel as the center of the pyramid elsewhere, for example, in the Maya culture.

During the excavations of the great pyramid, a lime vessel was found beneath the altar inside, there where the ancient temple had stood. It contained a wonderful work of art in the form of a mandala, made of about three thousand small turquoise stones. It portrays four snakes aligned in such a way that they point to the four world regions.

The *vessel* also plays a crucial role in alchemy, where it appears in the most varied forms. As you have heard, it can also be a glass house, the *domus vitrea*. Often an old man sits in it, the *senex*, sweating, for the glass house is a sweat house. In the *Visio Arislei*,[64] the king's daughter and son are imprisoned in the triple glass house under the sea. It is unbearably hot there. In this *heat* the *transformation* of the dead prince takes place. To perform such transubstantiations, the alchemists often used round glass bowls, called *uteri*, whose roundness indicated perfection.

A beautiful parallel can be found in the Mountain Chant of the Navajo Indians.[65] It is a healing ceremony to which they subject themselves when they have had a bad dream, for instance, or do not feel well for some other reason. In this ceremony, a circle of about 650 to 1,000 feet in diameter is staked out. In the center of this circle, which represents a mandala, there is the *medicine lodge* with the *sweat lodge*[66] at its side. The latter is a little round hut built of branches and earth. Often the rainbow goddess is drawn with colored sand on its top, leaning over the hut as over her own uterus. The hut is heated up and the man to be healed crawls into it and starts to sweat. Do you know of a parallel in the heroic myths?

Participant: The night sea journey in the womb of the whale.

Professor Jung: Yes, there the hero sweats so much that he loses all his hair[67] and reemerges bald-headed, like a newborn child. As a matter of fact, he is reborn indeed.

In India the sweating corresponds to the *tapas*.[68] This is a kind of *self-brooding*. By the concentration of the soul powers on this one

---

[64] C. G. Jung, *CW* 12, 3, §§ 437ff.

[65] Washington Matthews, *The Mountain Chant*, pp. 379–467.

[66] Italicized words in English in the original (trans.).

[67] C. G. Jung, *CW* 12, 3, §§ 440ff.

[68] C. G. Jung, *Symbols of Transformation*, *CW* 5, §§ 589f.

point, on the central point of the self, it is hatched like an egg. One is enclosed in it oneself, as in the retort or in the uterus. Where do we find similar ideas on transubstantiation?

Participant: In the Christian church, in the ritual of consecrating the baptismal water.

Professor Jung: Yes, this ritual of the *benedictio fontis* was performed on Holy Saturday. It goes back to the seventh or eighth century and is full of mysterious things. The regulations for this ritual are laid down in the *Missale Romanum.*[69] After certain preparations of the water, for example, separating the water in the form of a cross, exorcizing, and benediction, there follows the fertilization with the help of the Paschal Candle. It is thrice dipped into the baptismal font, which contains the sacral water, the third time down to the *fundus,* the bottom of the font. This imparts the *facultas regerandi* to the baptismal water, the power to give new birth to man. Man is *reborn* into a new childhood through being touched by this magic water and is completely *purified.* This fertilization of the *uterus ecclesia* is a veritable *coniunctio,* because the candle represents Christ Himself, and the baptismal water the *mater gratia,* the Mother of Grace. In this union the transformation of the water to the *aqua permanens* occurs, the eternal divine water, as it is called in alchemy.

So here, too, we find that wondrous vessel in which a transformation takes place. Do you know of another parallel in the older literature?

Participant: The *kratér* of Zosimos.

Professor Jung: Exactly, we find this vessel of transformation in the writings of Zosimos, an alchemist of the third century A.D.[70] It probably goes back to the fourth tract of the *Corpus Hermeticum,* in which it is said that God had sent a vessel from heaven to earth, in which the humans could submerge in order to reemerge renewed in the state of *ennoia.*[71]

---

[69] *Missale Romanum:* Die Weihe des Taufbrunnens [The Consecration of the Baptistry].
[70] Cf. seminar 3 (ed.).
[71] Greek, "thinking mind, knowledge, insight": a way to reach higher consciousness. Cf. C. G. Jung, "The Visions of Zosimos," in CW 13, § 97 (ed.).

A medieval variation of this *kratér* is the *Grail*. It is a miraculous bowl from which Christ is said to have taken the Last Supper. Another legend says that Joseph of Arimathea had collected Christ's blood in it. It is also a blood vessel, filled with the blood of Christ, with the spirit of God. The power of giving man new life by filling him with its spirit is inherent in both the *kratér* and the Grail. Wolfram von Eschenbach brings another version of the story of the Grail.[72] Do you know about it?

Participant: He talks about the Grail as a stone.

Professor Jung: Yes, for him it is a stone. Wolfram von Eschenbach quotes a very strange expression in connection with the Grail, namely, *lapsit exillis*. Now this is bungled Latin; he himself did not understand Latin. Philologists have tried their hands at its interpretation in all kinds of ways. One of them interpreted it as "ex illis," "from those" (i.e., "from those eternal stars"); another as "ex coelis," "from the heavens." In my view, however, this "lapsit exillis" could refer to the *lapis*. There is evidence for this. Arnoldus de Villanova, a doctor living around the year 1250, left some alchemical texts, in which the stone is called "lapis exilis" in a hexameter, meaning that the stone is one that can be had *vili pretio*, cheaply. It is found everywhere, in the streets, in dung, in toilets. An alchemist held that people would sell it at a quite different price if they only knew its value. This stone is, of course, the *cornerstone* that was discarded by the builders, and that is an *allegoria* Christi. The Christian Church also knew about the secret similarity between the stone and Christ. In the ritual of striking fire, the new fire, which is an image of Christ, is struck out of the cornerstone, the *lapis angularis*.[73] In 1330, Petrus Bonus for the first time expressed the idea that the stone was an allegory of Christ.[74]

So this enigmatic expression, "lapsit exillis," can be interpreted as "lapis exilis," that insignificant, unimportant stone, to which nobody pays attention, although it is the greatest treasure. Do you know about a passage in the Old Testament where the stone plays a role?

[72] Wolfgang von Eschenbach, *Parsifal* (ed.).

[73] *Missale Romanum*: Karsamstag-Feuerweihe. Cf. C. G. Jung, CW 12, 3, § 451.

[74] In *Bibliotheca Chemica Curiosa*, vol. 2, pp. 1–80.

Participant: The rolling stone in the dream of Nebuchadnezzar in the Book of Daniel.[75]

Professor Jung: Yes, that dream speaks about a great, tall, and bright image of a terrible form. It was made of four different materials—gold, silver, brass, and iron—and its feet were of clay. While the king looked at the image, a stone rolled down the mountain and smote the image upon its feet, so that this great being collapsed. The strange thing about it is that the stone broke away from the mountain "without hands," without being touched by anybody. In the Book of Daniel this stone became a great mountain, and filled the whole earth. Daniel's prophecy that this stone will smite and destroy all kingdoms, but shall stand forever itself, might well have been why Christ was compared to it in the patristic literature. Where else does the mountain appear in connection with the precious stone?

Participant: In your lecture[76] you mentioned that the city of Meru is on top of the mountain.

Professor Jung: Yes, this connection is found in the Indian *Shri-Chakra-Sambhara Tantra*. We also find it in alchemy, where the city, the *vas hermeticum*, is lying on top of the *mons*.[77]

Often the image of the *vitrum aureum*, the golden glass, appears in connection with the idea of the eternal city. As you have heard in the paper, it says in the Revelation of John: "and the city was pure gold, like unto clear glass" (21:18). What does this glass indicate?

Participant: Something hard and indestructible.

Professor Jung: This is characteristic not of the glass, but of stone in general. The wondrous thing about *glass* is the *diaphanitas*, its *transparency*. One has also tried to express the *spiritual nature* of the stone or the vessel with the help of this characteristic. The same is true when we talk about the *lapis spiritualis*, the *lapis invisibilitatis*, or the *lapis aethereus*, or about the diamond stone light as water. All these expressions are meant to illustrate the spiritual existence of the

---

[75] Daniel 2:31–35 (trans.).

[76] Seminar on *Modern Psychology*: "The Process of Individuation [Eastern Texts], Notes on the Lectures given at the ETH," 1938/39.

[77] Latin, the "hermetic vessel"; the "mountain" (trans.).

stone; they are about an object that is a body, yet at the same time transparent.

The glass house in the present dream also points to this spiritual existence. Mrs. Jaffé quite correctly interprets the *Doppelgänger* in the glass house as *corpus subtile*, as a subtle body,[78] a spiritual mirror image, so to speak. One creates oneself in this transparent vessel; the double in the glass house is like a second one, who is also there, and who awaits his preparation there. This is a vision of what we have to call the Self. There the *transformation to one's own self* occurs, the other within us is consolidated there. This other has miraculous qualities: he is transparent and has a subtle and incorruptible body. For the time being, he is still in a suspended state; he has not yet become. Through the union with the human being, he is clothed in matter, thus acquiring actual existence *in actu* and is saved from his potential existence. This idea is also at the base of the homunculus, that miraculous being that, so to speak, creates himself in the stone.[79]

In the dream, the glass house is on top of the pyramid, and so there is also a connection between the double and the king, resting in the tomb as a mummy. The *lapis* is thus related to the grave, to death. Do you know anything from alchemy about this?

Participant: Before the *lapis* comes into being, the old king, the old sun, has to die.

Professor Jung: What does that mean—the old king, the old sun?

Participant: The prevailing opinions have to be overcome before something new can be adopted.

Professor Jung: Yes, what has ruled until then has to die and be buried so that the *lapis* can come into being. A basic idea in alchemy is expressed therein: *the ruling principle*, that which had been sun, consciousness, the *aurum vulgare*,[80] *has to sink* like the grain of wheat in the earth, so that it will be *transformed* into the *eternal substance*, into the *incorruptible body*. This suffering ruling principle is very often personified in the king, who, for example, calls from the depths: "Help

---

[78] "Subtle body" in English in the original (trans.).
[79] Cf. seminar 3, § 2 (ed.).
[80] Latin, "the vulgar, common gold" (ed.).

me!" Often he greatly suffers from water, be it that he suffers from dropsy, or be it that he lies half-drowned in the sea. How do we have to conceive this state in psychological terms? When are we saturated with water to such an extent?

Participant: When we are unconscious.

Professor Jung: Yes, when we have sunk completely into the unconscious we suffer from "dropsy." It can also happen that somebody sort of drowns himself by drinking a vast quantity of water. This happened to the king in the *Aenigma Merlini,* for example. Before he rode into the battle, he drank so much water that he dissolved himself. Afterward he was put together again by Egyptian doctors.[81]

These are illustrations of the fact that what rules has to go under, to make room for a different, renewed consciousness. As we have seen, this other consciousness is personified by the double, enclosed in the glass house. As you know, it is crucial that the dreamer unite himself with this *corpus subtile.* What does the dream tell about that?

Participant: The child stands on the ground beside the pyramid, so he is far away from it.

Professor Jung: Yes, there is a *split.* The dreamer has never really known who he is, where he actually belongs. You will find such a doubleness in those numerous people in whose soul prenatal remnants still exist. These may rise in visions or dreams, but mostly sink back into the unconscious again. It is only in a psychological treatment that these images are again remembered. The dreamer told me the dream more or less as a curiosity, but I could infer the core of his whole life from it. He lacked precisely this self-realization, the spiritual existence. His change subsequently showed that this was exactly what he had needed. The proof was that he then became a contented man. When he was told the meaning of the dream, both currents flowed together. Up to then they had never come together, and he had never really known: am I in this one or in the other one? Now he became a *whole.* He had found his soul. The two halves that were united were the man of consciousness, the ego, the mortal being, so to speak, and that other side, that complex of emotional values and

---

[81] In *Artis auriferae,* vol. 1, § 9, Merlinus. Cf. C. G. Jung, *The Practice of Psychotherapy, CW* 16, § 472 (ed.).

attributes which accompanies us as a vague anxiety as long as we have not extracted the eternal being, the spark, the *spinthēr*[82] in it.

Such a dream can be an experience of the greatest importance for somebody. If he grasps its meaning, it will become an experience for him that he will value more than all the kingdoms on earth. These are experiences we cannot rationalize. Neither can we argue about them, just as we cannot argue about Paul and the great vision he had on the road to Damascus. The transformation occurs when that inner growth, with all its original values and implicit meanings, enters into the empirical world. The experience of this wholeness can be so all-embracing that it has actually been called the *medicina catholica*, the panacea, the *alexipharmakon*, the antitoxin against all toxins. The highest attributes have always been ascribed to this idea, not out of rational consideration but because it expresses the deepest inner experiences of man.

5. Dream of a Five-Year-Old Boy of the Beloved Girl[83]
Presented by Dr. Emma Steiner[84]

Text: He sees a girl in the toilet, washing her hands. He loved her very much, but was very shy. He feels a pain of separation. The dream recurred again and again until his thirtieth year.

Dr. Steiner: This is not an actual dream, but a vision. Let us make a note of the fact that the dreamer himself only watches, that he is passive. This passivity will be the starting point of our interpretation in the second part. The dream has no lysis, therefore, and that is probably the reason for its perpetual recurrence.

Locale: The toilet.
Dramatis personae: The dreamer and the girl.
Peripateia: The dreamer watches the girl wash her hands.

Let us proceed to the amplification. In the *toilet*: Even if we have to assume that it is a modern, hygienic, sparkling restroom, the place is

---

[82] Spark of light (Latin, scintilla), a Gnostic concept; see Jung, *Psychology and Alchemy*, CW 12, § 131 (trans.).

[83] Session of 12 December 1939.

[84] To avoid repetitions, the end of the paper was abbreviated (ed.).

still somehow suspect. The toilet has always been considered a gloomy and uncanny place, full of dangers, full of uncanny events. This is one of the reasons, apart from the obvious hygienic ones, why our ancestors did not include the toilet in the main house; a separate small hut, the *Hüsli*,[85] was erected in the yard. Gradually, the toilet was built nearer and nearer to the house, until it became an annex. But even so, the toilet was considered a haunted place, where ghosts and devils were up to their tricks, and which one did not dare to enter alone at night. In Iceland, Scandinavia, Germany, and Arabia, too, to mention only a few examples, the toilet is seen as the place where the spirits of the dead and the devils appear.[86] In an Irish monastic regulation the toilet is described as such a place, and the monks are given a blessing formula that they have to speak when entering it. This concept of the toilet as an ominous place can also be found in various Nordic myths. In the saga of Thorstein, King Olaf expressly warns his guest against going to the toilet alone at night. Thorstein does it nevertheless and has to survive a dangerous adventure with a devil, who reveals himself as the spirit of a dead knight fallen in battle. Thorstein is saved only by the fact that at the last moment the church bells begin to ring. In a Sigurd legend, too, the shadows of death spirits appear in the toilet. The same idea—that this place is full of spirits—is widespread in Germany. A report by Thietmar von Merseburg[87] tells how uncanny demons rose from the toilet in the sickroom of a monastery, much to the horror of a gravely ill man. In the Canton of Aargau, people often say that if you let the child sit alone in the toilet, the *Hoggema* will come and get it. Healing magic and popular medicine also have often made use of the toilet.

But let us come back to our modern [German] word *Toilette*.[88] In

---

[85] Swiss German, a diminutive of *Haus* = house (trans.).

[86] The following examples are taken from H. Bächtold-Stäubli, *Handwörterbuch des deutschen Aberglaubens*; *Encyclopaedia of Religion and Ethics*, ed. James Hastings; Jakob Grimm, *Deutsche Mythologie* (ed.).

[87] 975–1018, bishop of Merseburg and noted historian (trans.).

[88] When referring to history, ethnology, and mythology, Dr. Steiner used the German *Abort* (etymologically derived from *abgelegener Ort* = secluded place), a now old-fashioned synonym of the word used in the dream text, *Toilette* (from the French *toilette*, a diminutive of *toile* = cloth, later euphemistically used for lavatory = *cabinet de toilette*) (Duden, *Herkunftswörterbuch*) (trans.).

German it is synonymous with *Abort*, while in French it has a different meaning. *Toilette* is derived from *toile*, a small linen blanket, which originally probably covered the lady's dressing table and referred to her dressing room.

Despite the modern term used by the boy, and despite the sparkling hygiene associated with the word today, this place is still taboo for us. Even today, refined and enlightened persons who otherwise speak quite explicitly about biological processes talk in paraphrases or enigmatic abbreviations about this place. There are the elegant foreign words *Toilette* and *water closet*,[89] there is the *flüsternde Örtli*,[90] the *Locus*,[91] or, in the mysterious language of runes, the WC or the AB,[92] still whispered today like the blessing formula of the Irish monks. So even today this place is something suspect, mysterious, taboo, forbidden, a secretive place one avoids mentioning by name, because it serves the lower needs of man. What does the boy see in the toilet? He sees a girl. He does not give more details about the girl in the dream, in this vision, but the context and the explanations the young person later gives about the girl show that he sees a specific type of girl before him. She is a girl with dark-brown hair, with a tinge of red, with a skin and blood complexion that is characteristic of certain Englishwomen, and considered, I dare say, the ideal by the average Englishman. A person from the continent knows this type from the illustrations by Rackham, and also from the portrayals by the Pre-Raphaelites, in which this type tends to have decadent features. So what the boy sees is not an everyday figure, but a kind of fairy-tale creature, an elfish being. According to Jung, these elfish beings are a preliminary stage of a magical female being that we call anima. *Elfen*, or *Elben* in Middle High German (from the English *elf* or *ælf*) are often creatures of the light with both human and divine features. According to Grimm, the blessed virgins can be classified in this category, the wise women who sunbathe, comb their hair, and bathe; the Lorelei, the Greek Sirens, the mermaids and fair

---

[89] This expression in English in the original (trans.).
[90] Swiss German, literally "the whispering room" (trans.).
[91] Latin, "the place." In common usage: "the john, the loo" (trans.).
[92] The origin of the abbreviation could not be traced; probably short for *Abort* (trans.).

water beings[93] who are in need of salvation. These elfish beings, these elevated fair ones, however, have nothing to do with the fairy figures that rather indicate a mother symbol. The word *Fee* (fairy) is derived from *feie*, fine; *fata*, fate. These are goddesses of fate, the Nornes, who hold the life string in their hands. Our elves, however, are beguiling, enchanting beings who often dance at night in a clearing in the woods, moving seductively to a sweet melody, beguiling young people, pulling them toward those light regions where there is neither death nor sin. Certainly these beings are very often able to change; the fascinating attraction emanating from this light creature can give way to the *lamia*,[94] to the *empusa*,[95] to those man-eating monsters, to those succubae who consume men from within and put straw and wood in place of their hearts.

With this description we have at the same time characterized the archetype of the anima; it is not identical with the dogmatic notion of soul.[96] Soul, in Gothic *saivalo*, is movement and oscillation par excellence, in short, everything that constitutes life in all its aspects. It is this moving and lively force in its roguishness and artfulness that drives man, and this mixture of wisdom and roguishness appears, to quote Jung, as one and the same in the elfish being.

We have shown the connection between the nature of the girl and the elves. Elves don't have souls. In her playful way, the girl now does something very significant: she washes her hands.

Washing one's hands has always been connected with a great and magnificent ceremony. At first, washing one's hands was probably done out of politeness and custom, but it is also a symbolic act. Thus the priest in Catholic mass prays for moral lustration during the washing of hands, the introductory part of mass. In Matthew 27:24, there is the well-known passage: "When Pilate saw that he could prevail nothing, but that rather a tumult was made, he took water, and washed his hands before the multitude, saying, I am innocent of the

---

[93] *Huldinnen* (pl. of *Huldin*), female personifications of grace (trans.).

[94] Latin, child-eating monster or witch; in folklore a corpse that rises at night to drink the blood of the living (trans.).

[95] In ancient Greek mythology, the Empusa (or Empousa) was a supernatural monster or demoness (trans.).

[96] *Anima* is Latin for "soul" (trans.).

blood of this just person: see ye to it." Something similar is found in Deuteronomy, where the following is demanded after a manslaughter: "And all the elders of that city, that are next unto the slain man, shall wash their hands" (21:6). In Cornwall, according to the biblical tradition, washing one's hands was the sign of innocence of a certain crime. An Icelandic prayer says: "I remove my enemies and adversaries from me by washing." In this context let us also remember the statement of Lady Macbeth: "A little water clears us of this deed: How easy is it, then!" Who can forget the scene in which Lady Macbeth enters the hall after the bloody deed at midnight, watched by the doctor and the gentlewoman: "Look, how she rubs her hands— It is an accustomed action with her, to seem thus washing her hands."

In ancient customs, too, washing one's hands is considered necessary in extraordinary circumstances, for example, in Silesia, one has to wash one's hands after a burial to avoid dying or losing one's teeth. In the Rhineland, you should wash your hands after a sudden fright to prevent lasting harm. In Southern Germany and in Switzerland, special blessings by washing the hands are customary, which impressively show the importance of this act. In all cultures, washing one's hands is a symbolic act, an integral part of the ritual. The Egyptian priest, for example, is called *uibu*, the washed one, or *uibu totui*, the clean one with both hands. In alchemy, too, we know of the *ablutio*, when the pure white color emerges after the *nigredo*, the blackness.

The boy felt a *pain of separation*. This pain felt in separation is not an unambiguous feeling, because one would like to, indeed would have to, separate from such an elfish being—this would be the quite appropriate, instinctive feeling of the dreamer. At the same time, this pain of separation generates a half-lustful, half-world-weary feeling, and a wish to remain in this state.

In contrast to the previous dream of the pyramid, this dream absolutely corresponds to the scope of the boy's personal experiences. Seen superficially, this is nothing but a very banal vision, explicable by the boy's personal unconscious, but the enrichment of the dream material should disabuse us of this assumption. Despite its banality— "washing her hands in a toilet"—this dream reaches far down into the collective unconscious. For one, it was shown that the girl in her

303

elfish nature is an instinctual, preliminary stage of the anima; and this playful, elfish being does something very meaningful, symbolic, and ritualistic: she washes her hands, and she does so in a somewhat suspect place, in a forbidden place, for which we may substitute the unconscious here. This place, where the lower functions of human life happen, is taboo. What we have here is also a pair of opposites: black–white; the haunted place where spirits and devils dwell, where black demons rise, on the one hand, and the light figure, the elf, who washes her hands with an ironic smile or in a gesture reminiscent of Pilate, on the other.

We now come to the interpretation of the dream. To begin with, we have to ask why it recurred so often. For one, the dream does not have a solution, and is dreamed again and again to demonstrate to the dreamer that he should finally deal with his anima. This the dreamer does not do; he remains in his passivity, and this passivity gives us the key to understand the vision. There can be no solution in this vision because the dreamer does not confront the elfish girl, his anima; thus, the archetype of the anima becomes autonomous. What is fascinating in the elf—to fascinate derives from *fascere*[97]— actually becomes a decisive factor. Metaphorically speaking, the oscillating, elusive, effortless quality turns into something beguiling, a *lamia*, a fiend, an *empusa*. To stay in the picture: it turns into the *succubus* that sucks the marrow out of the young man's bones, or, to put it psychologically, the anima turns into an autonomous being that exercises an absolutely dominating influence.

Professor Jung: The dream is of an approximately five-year-old boy. It has recurred for a long period of time in one version or another, and the cause for these recurrences was always the motif of the separation pain. This went on until about the thirtieth year. Then something happened that we could have guessed already from the dream itself: he fell in love with a girl who absolutely resembled the dream figure. This love affair dragged on for quite some time, up and down, back and forth, with great indecisiveness. One moment he thought

---

[97] A doubtful statement; it rather derives from the Latin *fascinare* = to bewitch, to jinx (Duden, *Herkunftswörterbuch*) (trans.).

he should marry her, the next he shied away from this thought. She was a fairly enigmatic girl, and he could never find out any actual details concerning her family and her background. Eventually it all ended with a break-up after all. He suffered greatly from this fascination, and the relationship gave him many a sleepless night. She also caused him great difficulties with his parents.

This girl resembled the above-mentioned English type. Such girls usually radiate something fairylike or elfish, that certain something that makes a man feel at a loss. To characterize this type I'd like to tell you a story: A Danish pastor once went across the moor; there was only one path leading through it, and whoever deviated from it would drown in the mud. He had a long way to go across the country, because he had been called to a dying man. When he was on his way back in the middle of the night, he faintly heard some music, and wondered: "What is this?" Then he saw two little figures coming toward him on the moor, going where no human being would have been able to. When they stood in front of him, he realized that they were elves. They asked him who he was. He answered: "The pastor." They asked what a pastor was. "Someone who has to pray with the people so that their souls are saved." They moaned that they had no souls, to which he replied that he could not help them; they would have to ask God to give them immortal souls. He wanted to teach them how to pray and said to them: "Our Father which art in heaven . . ." They said, however: "Our Father which art *not* in heaven . . . "—They simply could not repeat it otherwise. So he had to dismiss them again. And that is why they never received immortal souls. We have to imagine the girl in the dream as such an elfish being.

In contrast to the dream discussed in the previous session, this is not an *image*, but a vision; because a vision usually has a synthetic character and is a kind of composition. Each part derives from the other, so that all of them together form a complete synthesis. The present dream, however, is essentially composed of material drawn from experience, which stems from the most varied sources, and is not connected by inner evidence. It does not follow at all from the character of the dream image that the girl necessarily had to be in the toilet.

We can distinguish three elements in this dream: first, the *memory* of

305

this girl who historically is not linked with the toilet at all. She had made a deep impression on the boy, and had perhaps for the first time aroused a certain feeling in him—the pain of separation. This emotional situation is repeated in the dream: the dreamer does not approach the girl, but, if there is movement at all, this movement is nipped in the bud, and, therefore, he experiences the pain of separation.

The second element is the *toilet* with all its concomitant associations. It is a place around which the erotic fantasies of the boy revolve. This is quite normal, because the beginnings of sexuality lie in the cloacal area. These two sources, the memory of the girl and the toilet, originally have nothing to do with each other, because the dreamer did not associate any sexual fantasies with this girl until he was an adult. So we have to state that it was not the girl who was the object of his sexual fantasies, but the toilet. It is very important, therefore, that these two elements appear together in the dream.

The third element is *washing the hands*. The girl washes her hands because she has used the toilet. This is a completely natural activity, appropriate for this place. It shows that a functional relationship has been established between the anima and the toilet. For the time being, we are not able to give more details about this, but instead will deal more closely at first with the dream.

The *toilet* is a very meaningful place, and I am glad we can once seize the opportunity to speak about it. True, it is not a very savory subject, but it is of great importance to children. That place is always haunted because the functions that are exercised there are the *natural functions* par excellence. In every place where humans are natural, and can't help but be natural, the ancient natural demons are also still nearby. It is quite understandable, therefore, that the toilet becomes the *taboo place* par excellence, in which obsessions, phobias, and a plethora of neurotic symptoms have their origins, because it is precisely the natural functions that are disturbed in the neurotic. The fascination of this place is also immensely increased by the fact that the first beginnings of sexuality are linked to these functions. Now, there is always a close relation between instinctual processes and the collective unconscious, which reaches deep down into our nature and offers a view, so to speak, of our primordial nature. So we are completely justified in calling the toilet the collective unconscious, as Dr. Steiner has quite correctly interpreted. Now we also understand that the anima, that enigmatic figure of the unconscious, just like a spirit, a devil, or a fiend, is up to her mischief in exactly this place. Are there other places where one is afraid of apparitions?

Participant: The cemetery.

Professor Jung: Yes, cemeteries are classic haunted places, because death also is part of the natural, irrevocable processes. This is also the reason why dying is accompanied by fears and psychical phenomena. There, too, nature simply forces its way, and we cannot avoid it, just as we can't avoid dealing with all the other natural bodily functions. Do you know in which cases the dream language makes use of these processes?

Participant: In case of natural necessities.

Professor Jung: Yes, if we dream, for example, that we have to pass water in the company of other people, or that we have to get up immediately and go to that place. This means that nature cannot be stopped. It must get out after all. If, for instance, someone constantly avoids talking about certain things, about which he should talk, he will perhaps have such a dream sometime, in which he suddenly has to go to the toilet or something like that.

In alchemy, too, the toilet plays a not inconsiderable role, insofar as the *prima materia* or the *lapis* can also be found in the privies or in excrement. Meyrink reports on one of his own alchemical experiments in the translation of a tract that has been attributed to Thomas Aquinas. For this purpose he had bought an old privy, had it emptied, and put the base, the "peculiar juice,"[98] into an alchemical pot. On this he applied a coat of clay and sealed it "hermetically"—obviously quite well, because when he slowly heated the pot over the fire, the lid of the pot all of a sudden blew up. He claimed that a strange, yellowish matter had formed in it. The experiment still did not convince him that one couldn't make gold out of the sediment of a *sterquilinium*[99] after all! When we study these things we shake

---

[98] Cf. Mephistopheles in Goethe's *Faust*: "Blood is quite a peculiar juice" (trans.).

[99] Latin, "manure pit" (trans.).

our heads and think: there has to be something in it after all, if people are so fascinated by it unconsciously. We have to consider the claim, therefore, that the *prima materia*, that earth of paradise, that primordial chaos, is hidden in the fecal matter, as a significant contribution to the psychology of this place.

In our dream the *anima* appears in the *toilet*, in precisely that taboo place. Is this alright? Does it fit?

Participant: No.

Participant: Perhaps it does after all, because the toilet represents the unconscious. And the anima mediates between consciousness and the unconscious.

Professor Jung: But doesn't it strike you as extraordinary or strange that the anima appears in this of all places?

Participant: That's all right as it is, but it still seems to me that the anima belongs more in nature, while the toilet is like a distortion of nature, which gives the situation a moralistic aftertaste.

Professor Jung: Let us disregard the unpleasant and repulsive character of this place for the moment, and focus on the fact that it represents the unconscious. We can then simply state that the anima is in the unconscious. Is that abnormal?

Participant: On the contrary, it is the *place of creativity*, where something is created.

Professor Jung: Yes, this is quite in order, or at least it can be in order, because the toilet isn't just "nothing but," but, on the other hand, it also has the meaning of a creative place. As a matter of fact, something is really created there. Children know this very well. One of my children once stayed in the toilet for a long time. When my wife asked: "What're you doing in there?" a voice answered: "The carriage and two ponies!" You probably know the so-called *Dukaten-scheißer*.[100] The relation between the absolutely worthless and the absolutely valuable is, as we already saw in the previous meeting, a basic idea in alchemy: it is the *thesaurus thesaurorum*,[101] and at the same time the cheapest of all objects that you can find even in the street. If we keep this in mind it is not surprising that we come across

[100] Literally, "shitting ducats"—an inexhaustible source of money (trans.).
[101] Latin, "the treasure of all treasures" (trans.).

308

the anima in this place of creativity and of the unconscious, because the anima is a figure of the collective unconscious.[102] It is the soul image of a man, that inner personality that is compensatory to the conscious attitude. As long as it remains unconscious—as it usually does until the second half of life—it is experienced in projection only. But how is it experienced by the child?

Participant: The child at first projects the soul image onto the mother.

Professor Jung: Yes, the *mother* is the female figure that plays the greatest role in the lives of children. Children project their unconscious onto her. But as they are still completely living in the collective, they cannot experience the mother as real, but above all as an archetype, by which she gains that superhuman, fateful importance.[103] She can become the witch, the demon, the all-powerful, all of which she is not in reality; or also the all-loving and all-understanding mother. In dreams she often appears as someone menacing and uncanny, as a ghost or some other monster. Naturally, it may also be the case that projections of such archetypal images are facilitated by the psychical structure of the mother. I remember the case of a mother driven by instincts, who could not understand her children at all. She was infatuated with both her daughters, and the daughters adored her. But at night they had terrible nightmares in which the mother appeared as a witch, a persecutor, or as an evil animal. The younger girl once told her fourteen-year-old sister about it, who confessed to having similar dreams of their mother. Later it turned out that these dreams did not come out of the blue, but were in fact related to the mother's psyche. In menopause she fell ill with a depression with fugue states, in which she turned into the same wild animals the children had dreamed of! She crawled on all fours and accused herself of being a wolf, a bear, and so on. So the dreams of the children had been a reflection of the mother's instinctuality, which she would have to realize. The mother had been too much "up

---

[102] Cf. C. G. Jung, "The Relations between the Ego and the Unconscious," CW 7, §§ 296ff; "Archetypes of the Collective Unconscious," CW 9, §§ 51ff (ed.).

[103] Cf. seminar 3, § 7; C. G. Jung, "Psychological Aspects of the Mother Archetype," CW 9, § 156 (ed.).

there," and had played the role of saintly motherhood. Her daughters had reinforced the mother's attitude. The depression was meant to bring her down to earth again. But even if the dream figures were facilitated by the mother, we must not overlook that they belong to the archetypal world of the children; they are their own archetypes, and must not be taken away from them.

In the present it is not the mother, but a girl who appears. Why is the anima shown as a *girl* here?

Participant: Because the anima already appears in connection with sexual fantasies.

Professor Jung: Exactly. What consequences does the emergence of the sexual fantasies have for the relation of the boy to his mother?

Participant: These sexual fantasies separate him from the mother, because he cannot approach her with them.

Professor Jung: Yes, otherwise incest would be the result.[104] But why can't he simply have an incest fantasy? Why can't we commit incest?

Participant: Perhaps the father prevents us from committing it?

Professor Jung: No, for one, the father isn't always at home. One could commit incest twenty times if one really wanted. Incest is something quite doable, and it does happen. But why should it not be committed? What is the reason?

Participant: There is the incest taboo, isn't there?

Professor Jung: Of course. Where does this incest taboo, which has been there for thousands of years, come from? It cannot be observed, as such, in animals, but it exists in all kinds of variations in humans. The main reason is a psychological one, because this is a highly symbolic matter. If it were possible that a man could commit incest just like that, he'd have everything at his fingertips and would never leave his home. His initiative would be completely paralyzed, and a psychical incapability would be the result.

The primitive, of course, does not have such considerations. His own nature stands in the way of incest. The attraction of something new is so overwhelming that it will always chase him out of his

[104] Cf. seminar 3, § 4 (ed.).

cramped nest. Primitive man created his marital laws and customs out of his inner needs, such as the marriage castes, the custom of abducting the women, and so on.

We can assume that in children, too, such instinctual forces are effective, so that they do not become involved in incest. How does their sexuality normally develop?

Participant: It is transferred to a person who does not belong to the family.

Professor Jung: Yes, this also happens with our dreamer. He had seen this girl in reality, she made a strong impression on him, and in the dream he then brought her up in connection with the toilet, with his cloacal, sexual fantasies. This helped him circumnavigate the dangerous cliffs of incest. This connection is only correlative, however, not interdependent. The latter would have to be expressed by a movement toward the girl. In the dream the boy feels only separation pain with regard to her, because his sexual fantasies are still attached to the toilet, and will remain split off from the girl for some time to come. Why?

Participant: Because he is still attached to his mother.

Professor Jung: For such a child the mother is not real at all, as we have seen. She is the bearer of the soul image, she is anima. So we have to investigate the question why the boy splits off his sexuality on the basis of the psychology of the anima.

Participant: Perhaps another girl is the reason.

Professor Jung: No, these things pose many riddles. I have to point out that we have to be very cautious in the case of little children, when we think in terms of the personality and try to find a rational explanation. We must never forget that the infantile soul is no *tabula rasa*—this would be the greatest misconception—but we always have to keep a door open—to what?

Participant: To the collective unconscious.

Professor Jung: Yes, quite right. This is also the reason why the anima does not unite with the cloacal fantasy. Can you tell me why?

Participant: Perhaps the dreamer is too self-centered?

Professor Jung: He certainly is. The toilet represents his autoerotic attitude. Like so many children, he is curious what adults do in the toilet, and this arouses distinct sexual feelings in him. But this merely confirms that he got stuck in his cloacal fantasies and was not able to reunite them with the anima figure.

Participant: Would it have been alright for him to link the sexual fantasies with the girl?

Participant: No, because the anima is a figure of his soul.

Professor Jung: Yes, this girl has actually all the advantages of a soul image, and the noblest feelings have been associated with her. So it was impossible for him to associate her with the other side—his anima image would have been soiled. This is also the deeper reason for the anima to wash her hands. She shows him that she cleanses herself of all impurity. It is as if she said to him: "Your sexual fantasies are about unclean things, with which I don't want to have anything to do." Naturally, this also throws some light on the dreamer's sexuality. We have to conclude from his behavior that the image of the anima is, a priori, such that it does not want to merge with the other side, that is, with his budding sexuality. This actually causes the beginning of a *split* between the lower and the higher spheres in him. He has to part with what is high and pure, and it is because of this separation pain that he remembered that dream. Why is this separation necessary?

Participant: Because otherwise he would never be able to approach the dark side.

Professor Jung: What would happen if he could not separate from the girl? He would for ever have remained the little boy in whom an image lingers on, and his instinctuality would remain completely undeveloped. He has to be separated, therefore, from the anima image. In the dream it is the anima herself who keeps the distance. She actively intervenes. We must not conceive of the anima as a passive image that the dreamer could control as he wishes; she is autonomous to a great extent. When she appears in the projection, she is usually extremely overpowering, and the man in question falls prey to her hook, line, and sinker. Rider Haggard clearly saw this: "She that must be obeyed."[105] The anima can be a terrible tyrant!—Pierre Benoit

---

[105] Rider Haggard, *She*. Quotation in English in the original (trans.).

has also described this anima type in his *Atlantide*. In a woman, the analogous figure is the animus, which can dominate her and completely bring her to ruin. The fatefulness of the soul image announces itself very early. Whenever the anima figure appears in a boy's dream we have to be careful, because she represents life as such: that which moves herself as well as the dreamer.

In the present dream, the anima washes her hands, which psychologically means that she doesn't want to have anything to do with sexuality, but wants to preserve her purity. This attitude of the anima has played a great role in the later life of the dreamer. The ensuing split between sexuality and the anima is, by the way, frequently found in men, and often manifests itself as a *neglect of Eros*, which is the essence of the anima. Men are rarely split off from sexuality, because it is too evident for them, but what they lack is Eros, the *relational function*. Men often think they can replace the relational function with reason. They are proud that they don't let themselves be controlled by affect, because this would be womanly, tantamount to weak. No Eros, for God's sake! This lack is what women most complain of in marriage, and is what so disappoints them. For what they seek in a man is the Eros, the capacity to relate.

This is exactly what is missing in our dreamer! The anima withdraws; she does not want to mingle with the unclean place, does not want to enter into the instinctual turmoil. But then this is a quite natural attitude for someone whose sexuality is still bound to the cloacal sphere. At this age it is not yet possible to have a different attitude; sexuality cannot but develop out of this cloacal sphere. It is the place in which it originates, in which man is born. "*Inter faeces et urinas nascimur*,"[106] as St. Augustine put it. For the boy, sexuality belongs in this region, and he should not feel otherwise because then he would be in danger of becoming obsessed. By what?

Participant: By the soul image.

Professor Jung: Yes, precisely by the anima. And this would have the psychological consequence that he would remain the cute little boy, tied to his mother's apron strings, a nice kiddie who never gets

---

[106] Latin, "we are born between feces and urine" (trans.).

into mischief, and to whom the mother says: "Promise that you will never hurt your mommy and kiss a girl." Then the little boy is a puppet on the anima's strings. This is the sweetness we have to renounce over and over again. The result would be that sad, nice boy who is good for nothing, whose sexuality is repressed and therefore remains confined to the privy pit. These are men who foolishly might be taken in by prostitutes, maybe even acquire syphilis. And why? Because they didn't notice anything and have never developed out of this toilet into the world. Then they cannot distinguish between what is dirty and what is clean. Doctors see all kinds of things in this respect.

Homosexuality plays a great role in these men, because a homosexual is identical with the anima, which brings about his aesthetic femininity, with all of the virtues of the feminine. He sees a heterosexual relationship in the light of the aspect that exists within himself, which is that undeveloped sexuality—and acts accordingly.

I saw a typical case, a very refined, cultured, amiable adolescent, who was identical with his anima. Of course he was affectionately attached to his mother, who had taken him on her lap too much when he was a child. Unfortunately he agreed to undergo a treatment, lost his homosexuality, and wanted to be a "real man." But what did that get him into? He fell for a terrible woman, a potential whore suffering from lues, who was afflicted with a bone syphilis in the nose, a syphilitic ozena, a "stinky nose," that suppurated all the time. This was the "toilet" alright, and this was the woman he married and had a child with, who then suffered from hereditary syphilis. These terrible things could happen because this boy suddenly fell out of the perfumed atmosphere of the mother—she herself an anima child—and into his undeveloped toilet-manliness. His wife reeked of the stench that had fascinated him.

It is part of the normal instinctual development of man that it begins in the cloacal sphere and has to pass through this dark valley. The instinctual development is a development "*per vias naturales.*"[107] If it only concerns sexuality, however, without the inclusion of Eros,

[107] Latin, "along natural ways" (trans.).

314

this will be the source of the most bitter disappointment in women. Most men, however, are not aware of this.

So when the anima says in our dream: "I'm not coming with you," this means that the dreamer *has to develop into the world*. Fortunately, he cannot give up the toilet fantasies, and fortunately he cannot transfer them onto the anima figure. Unfortunately, he later succeeded in doing so, leading to bitter disappointment. Life had to demonstrate to him that he must not transfer sexuality onto the anima. In falling in love with the anima, he forcibly tried to circumvent the laws of development. This was a concession to his mother complex. He was not man enough to withstand seduction, partly due to the fact that he also had a father complex. His father never allowed him to assert himself against him. The father was too powerful and did not leave enough room for the son to develop into a man. As a consequence, the latter was forced to that side of his feelings where he fell victim to his own weakness, and no longer had the strength to escape the anima. A man proves his moral strength by running away from the image of his anima. When he falls prey to the anima, he has lost a battle. This is also the reason why most normal men flee the anima by marrying a woman who does not correspond to that type.

The constellation of this anima type always entails the risk of a concession to the mother complex, but it also brings about the danger that the anima itself will violate its bounds and come out of the unconscious to enter into the world. *The relational function with the unconscious must not be transformed into a relational function with the conscious world!* The anima must always establish the relation with the unconscious, even when the man begins to consciously experience it as a function. If it tries to represent the relation to the world of consciousness, however, the person concerned will become effeminate. Unfortunately, their insecure social status forces many men today to function via the anima, that is, to use the anima as a relational function with the environment. An employee has to know about the whims of his boss, know what to say to him, and so has to acquire quite feminine traits. Such a man has to become a nice "office sissy"! This femininity is of no advantage to him, but secures his

315

existence. That's the reason why so many men are so unconditionally enthusiastic about the war, because finally they can—"thank God!"—swear, hit, and be real men. For how can one be a man in a pussyfooting, moralistic society? Vice versa, the same is true for today's woman, who is often forced into an animus adaptation. She would prefer to be feminine, and not to take possession of the world head first.

For the boy, the whole extent of the anima problem is hinted at in the dream, but of course his consciousness at that age is not capable of understanding the problem. The dream image does evoke a certain feeling, however, leaving at least an emotional imprint: here my toilet fantasy and the attached sexuality, there the beautiful child from whom I have to separate.

Let us return to the previous question: why this *separation pain*? Why does his anima indicate from the very beginning: "Alas, I have to leave you?" The moment he has discovered her, he has to leave her again. What is the reason? Something must have happened before, something occurring entirely in the unconscious, which might provide the explanation for why he has to take leave from this figure.

Participant: He has the inner conviction that the anima is too grand.

Professor Jung: Yes, that's what I meant. The first anima experience of the boy is a very high idea, something incomprehensibly grand and beautiful. It is so beautiful that he just knows that he can only lose it. It is like the *farewell to paradise*, that wonderful thing, just beginning, filled with the pain: it is lost! This is connected with those golden memories, those prenatal images, which are still sensed by the child. The boy's separation pain shows that he is attached to those magical images, that he comes from that world which, however, he has to leave behind. The dream shows him that now he has to choose the dirty path, just as *eating dust* comes after the loss of paradise. It is outright dangerous to remain attached to this lost world, because in that case one refuses to get in touch with the earth—and will never be born. Quite recently I met such an unborn man, who constantly had to dream of his own birth. He had got stuck in his anima. Such people give the impression of a strangely arrested development. They cannot touch the world and take it into their hands—but if we want to live we have to take hold of it, and not be anxious about getting our hands dirty. The world isn't clean. Our dreamer has the greatest difficulties imaginable in touching the world, because he has been fascinated by the anima over and over again. This arrested his development and he became inefficient. He couldn't take the dream's repeated warning to heart.

Participant: It is not clear to me why the girl is a collective figure. Isn't she rather a personal figure?

Professor Jung: Yes, it is a girl he knows. However, she has certain traits of the Anglo-Saxon race and, therefore, represents a type that he will frequently come across in his later life. This is crucial in this case. Women, as it is, like to act a type, for instance, that of the coquette; in this respect, one woman is like another, they are interchangeable. This is only possible, however, if it concerns the man's anima, and not the *woman as a personality*. Men with some insight into their eroticism can easily tell what their anima looks like. The can say: this is she, and nobody else.

It is strange that there are not many kinds of anima in a man's soul, but only *one* anima. Women, on the other hand, have a *multiplicity* of animuses. Often they appear in combination. There is an excellent description in the book by H. G. Wells, *Christina Alberta's Father*. There a whole "court of old men"[108] is concerned with the moral behavior of the young woman. The same phenomenon is described in the occult literature. Among the spirits of William James's well-known medium, Mrs. Piper, there was a special group of controls,[109] called the "Imperator group" by her. The animus very often appears as a power animus. In contrast, the anima is essentially a unity, at least in a man whose development proceeds normally. Such a man will get married and have sexual relations with his wife. In addition, he will perhaps have the image of a woman whom he adores from a great distance. If his quiet course of life is unsettled, whether by in-

---

[108] This expression in English in the original (trans.).
[109] This word in English in the original (trans.).

explicable mood swings or by external events, doubt about the past will arise. He is thrown back onto himself, and has to try to solve the conflict within himself, meaning that he has to establish a relation to his unconscious, and this is only achieved if the *anima becomes conscious*. The result of its becoming conscious is that *distinctions* are being made: the paradoxical and, as it were, completely amoral anima has to be split, because otherwise it would remain inexplicable and not comprehensible for consciousness. Then it occurs that the man experiences the white and the black anima, the saint and the witch or the evil Circe. The anima is an absolutely *paradoxical* being which, however, is basically always *one and the same*. It is precisely her ambiguous nature that fascinates man, attracts him until he perishes, and that he has to escape. Read the novels of Rider Haggard[110] and you will get an impression of what the anima is. Once he met her in South Africa; he was so impressed that he had to write a large number of books about her. He accurately sensed that a supernatural being is concealed behind this phenomenon, and that it radiates that strange and powerful magic that also was effective in the ancient goddesses. These divine figures live on in the anima, with all their attributes of motherhood and pleasure, as well as with all their demonic features, their depravity and magnificence.

Participant: Does the anima remain the same throughout a man's whole life?

Professor Jung: No, the anima is by no means unchangeable. If the individuation process sets in, for instance, the anima, too, is subject to a *change*. She is a personification of the unconscious and consequently modifies her character when the conscious attitude changes.

Participant: Does this change of the anima coincide with the *climacteric period*, the age between thirty-six and forty?

Professor Jung: This is indeed so, or, I'd better say this would normally be the case, if only the transformation processes were uncomplicated. In the primitives, these processes are made much more *concrete*, so that they can be read, so to speak. I'd like to tell you an example from the Indians. A very bellicose chief dreamed in his for-

---

[110] Rider Haggard, *She*; *She and Allen*; *Wisdom's Daughter*.

tieth year that he turned into a woman, and had to dress in women's clothes and eat their food—in our eyes an absolutely ridiculous transformation. But he followed the dream's command and nonetheless remained as respected in his tribe as before, enjoying the reputation of being surrounded by magic. It was a great dream, a dream of being called. Old men are considered sages by the primitives. They are the guardians of the teachings of the tribe, of the great secrets that alone make the existence of the tribe possible. If this wisdom is lost, the tribe will dissolve. Old Jews had a similar position. In the Old Testament it says: "Your old men shall dream dreams."[111] They had a wise anima who could open their inner ears.

You see what natural forms the inner transformation assumes in the primitives. In our own case, this is usually much more complicated, because we are no longer able to make the inner processes as concrete. The reason for this lies partly in the fact that the cultural process inhibits natural development, causing certain shifts. This has the effect that we cannot live what we would have long lived already under primitive circumstances. Thus a man of fifty or sixty may have to make up for what he should have experienced at the age of twenty-eight. Then highly infantile things come to the fore in an unnatural way; these are, so to speak, worn out children's shoes—all this because conventions prevent a natural realization. Then such belated developments happen. As you can see, it is difficult to lay down the general rule that this change is always linked to the turn of life, as it can also happen much later or not at all. In the case of a highly civilized man in particular, it is possible that he goes on leading an absolutely abstract, unreal existence, and that the whole development takes place in the unconscious. This nevertheless makes itself felt in consciousness, for example, in the form of a nervous breakdown[112] or of depressive phases. It can also have the effect that such a person goes under, becomes demoralized, a snivelling woman, full of resentment and with all the symptoms of "female logic." He then is nothing but anima. In creative persons we can observe changes in the

---

[111] Joel 2:28 (trans.).
[112] The words *nervous breakdown* in English in the original (trans.).

form of their creative production during these phases. Nietzsche, for instance, had the dramatic Zarathustra experience at the age of thirty-eight, which stood in remarkable contrast to his previous intellectualistic manner. True, it is hard to find the female element in *Zarathustra*, but if you read the work with a critical eye, you will discover the anima at the end. This experience, however, led him into insanity. All his anima eroticism is contained in the texts that were found in Turin by Overbeck,[113] and were burned by Mrs. Foerster-Nietzsche because she found them too unsavory. From a psychological viewpoint, it would have been extremely interesting to learn something about his development in precisely this period.[114]

The Gnostics already knew about the transformations of the anima. In their writings we find a kind of development of the anima, from its most primitive stage up to wisdom. The most primitive anima is *Chawwa*, the earth. She is Eve, who represents the all-motherly and the receiving. At this stage, the anima is still a purely sexual being, a kind of earth goddess in a nearly prehuman developmental form. A further stage is *Helen*. According to a Gnostic legend, Simon Magus discovered a girl in a brothel in Tyrus (Phoenicia), in whom he recognized a reincarnation of Helen of Troy, and whom he therefore named after her. Helen of Troy was an adulteress and the lover of many a hero of those times. She was actually the type of the "femme qui se fait suivre."[115] The link between these two women is that both of them carry a light within them, regardless of their bad reputation. Helen of Troy means beauty to the man, the Gnostic Helena *ennoia* (consciousness). At this stage, man still experiences the anima as a collective figure, but a certain concentration on the *one* woman has already taken place. This is a very human stage, partly conducive to cultural development. The next stage of the anima is *Mary*, who was also an extraordinary person. She was the lover of the Holy Spirit and so become the mother of God. The humiliation by illegitimate moth-

---

[113] F. Overbeck (1837–1905), Lutheran theologian and pastor in Basel, a friend of Nietzsche's (ed.).

[114] Allusions can already be found in the poems in *Zarathustra*, by the way, for example, in "Dudu and Suleika."

[115] French, roughly "the woman who makes others run after her" (trans.).

erhood is compensated by the symbolism of her being the mother of God. Although this stage still bears human traits, it already points to the spiritual. For the Gnostics, the highest developmental stage of the anima is *Sophia*. She is one-half of the divine syzygy (Greek, "pair," "yoked together"; conjunction and opposition of sun and moon). She is the most spiritual form of the universal mother. Any human or personal aspect has disappeared.

The anima as a friend or *soror mystica* has always played a great role in history. In the *cours d'amour* of René d'Anjou she even takes precedence over the wife. The term *maîtresse* actually means mistress or master. In the Middle Ages, for example, the worship of the anima led to courtly love, in which the knight was committed to his lady and was at her service. In later history we know of women such as Madame de Maintenon, Ninon de Lenclos, or Madame de Guyon. The latter was a woman of the highest spiritual eroticism and of a strangely deep wisdom. She deserved being called a saint. It is no sign of culture if a woman is only a daughter, or only a pregnant mother, or only a whore. The primitives and also the apes do act out this one-sidedness. But should she become the *femme inspiratrice*,[116] oscillating between goddess and whore, representing all the doubtfulness and diversity of life, the highest skills and the highest Eros are called for. Such women are manifestations of a much more developed culture, and this was known in the Middle Ages and also in Greece in its heyday. You know, of course, about Aspasia, the mistress of Pericles and of many cultured men of her time.

Participant: Is it a specific quality in a woman that makes such relationships possible at all?

Professor Jung: Many anima types have something masculine about them. But then, it is after all the soul image of a man. It is probably the unconscious feminine side in man which, however, does not completely lack maleness. That's why a man projects his anima onto a suitable woman who shows some male characteristics. For then she can also be a friend; the relationship is not just a heterosexual experience, but also *friendship*, and this is very important.

[116] French, "inspiring woman" (trans.).

Participant: But then we cannot say in general that it is a sign of strength if the man flees the anima.

Professor Jung: No, this only refers to the *young* man. He has to flee this type, so that he may develop into the world. The real confrontation with the anima is one of the problems of the second half of life. What was right before now dies down; the former ideals are burned. This is also how we have to understand Nietzsche's dictum of the revaluation of values: man destroys the values of his youth and prepares his own descent.

6. *Dream of a Seven-Year-Old Boy of a Dead Girl in the Water*[117]
PRESENTED BY MRS. A. LEUZINGER

Text: *I went to the lake to the steamboat jetty. There two tree trunks were rammed into the ground to moor the ships. I had already fished at this place. When I looked into the water, I saw a schoolmate, on whom I had a bit of a crush, in the water. She lay dead in the water. Her face was still completely fresh. She was dressed in a red and white checkered apron. When I kept on looking, I saw that her face disintegrated. It got criss-crossed with wide red cracks. I didn't have an uncanny feeling at all, as I later had when I dreamed of corpses.*

Mrs. Leuzinger: The dramatic structure of this dream is as follows: the beginning indicates the situation and the locale: the lake, at the steamboat jetty.

The persons are the dreamer and the girl in the water. The exposition shows the dreamer's activity and the topic: earlier the topic had been fishing, now it is looking into the water. The peripateia: the face disintegrates, there are wide red cracks in it. The lysis is contained in the sentence: "I didn't have an uncanny feeling at all, as I later had when I dreamed of corpses."

The dream could also be divided into two halves or dream images: in the first part, the dreamer stands on the steamboat jetty, looking into the water. In the second part, the focus shifts from the dreamer to the girl in the water; the dreamer becomes only an onlooker.

Some of the symbols, for example, the steamboat jetty and the girl,

[117] Session of 16 January 1940.

322

come from the dreamer's personal experience and state of consciousness. Around the eighth year there is a transition to ego consciousness, as we have already seen in previous children's dreams. The child
breaks away from the extremely close relatedness with the familial
milieu; he has already acquired a certain experience of the world, and
the libido, which had up to then been tied to the parents, detaches
itself from them and often is introverted.

In our dream there are already some indications of this experienced reality: the girl in the water is a schoolmate—the one he's got
a bit of a crush on. The steamboat jetty is a place known to the
dreamer, where he had already gone fishing.

Seen from the perspective of consciousness, the *steamboat jetty* is
a place that exerts a great attraction for boys at the age of seven or
eight in their first school years; it has a touch of life in foreign countries and adventure, ships moor and cast off, fishermen cast out their
lines or prepare their nets. It is also possible to stand there oneself
with a fishing pole and fish. There are also other strange and exciting things in the water at the steamboat jetty: bicycles, old tires,
things made of tin or iron, sometimes there are also dead fish at the
bottom; in short, for an enterprising boy who seeks his first adventures, the steamboat jetty exerts a great attraction.

In the dream, the boy goes to the lake, to the water. The *lake* or
the *water* are among the most common symbols for the unconscious.
So I would just like to mention its two main aspects: first, the *destructive* quality of water—we can sink and drown in it; second, the
aspect of *healing* and salvation, of transparency and spirituality, cul-
minating in the rebirth out of water. The dreamer approaches the
water, but stays at or on the steamboat jetty, as can be deduced from
the fishing.

The steamboat jetty has some similarity with the symbol of the
bridge, with which we have dealt in detail in one of the previous children's dreams. If the bridge stands for the continuity of consciousness, however, the steamboat jetty indicates a certain state of consciousness: while the bridge connects two sides, the steamboat jetty
abruptly ends in empty space. The only possible further connection
is by boat, with which one can travel the waters, the unconscious

depths. The steamboat jetty that ends in empty space is like a still-isolated fragment of consciousness, which could be flooded by a wave of the unconscious, just as the pier could be flooded in a storm by the waves of the lake. The steamboat jetty is a much less secure place than the bridge; we also say: on shaky ground.[118] It is suspended between the sky and the water, one no longer has firm ground under one's feet, but stands above the water in a slightly elevated position. It is a place in consciousness from which one can easily sink into the unconscious.

The steamboat jetty is a kind of link between the ground and the water. All this leads to a kind of suspended situation, which beautifully illustrates the psychological situation of the dreamer. A child at his age is indeed suspended between consciousness and the unconscious; he does not yet have a firm foundation of consciousness. The child is still rooted in the unconscious, just like the pilings of the pier that are rammed into the bottom of the lake.

What Professor Jung said about consciousness in the primitives is also true for children: their consciousness is still insecure and rests on shaky foundations; it is still childlike, having just emerged of the primordial waters. A wave of the unconscious can easily run over it.

The dreamer is a contemplative onlooker, which is in perfect line with his uncertain, suspended situation. The actual drama, the action, begins in the water, in the unconscious.

This time the dreamer does not fish, but looks down into the water, that is, he immerses himself in the unconscious, being attracted by the depths of his own unconscious.

Looking into the water is equivalent to going to oneself. Professor Jung has elaborated on this process at length; let me quote the relevant passage here:

> True, whoever looks into the mirror of the water will see first of all his own face. Whoever goes to himself risks a confrontation with himself. . . . The meeting with oneself is, at first, the meeting with one's own shadow. The shadow is a tight passage, a narrow door, whose painful constriction no one is spared who goes down to the

[118] Original: *ein schwankender Steg*—a swaying, shaky footbridge or jetty (trans.).

deep well. But one must learn to know oneself in order to know who one is. For what comes after the door is, surprisingly enough, a boundless expanse full of unprecedented uncertainty, with apparently no inside and no outside, no above and no below, no here and no there, no mine and no thine, no good and no bad. It is the world of water, where all life floats in suspension; where the realm of the sympathetic system, the soul of everything living, begins; where I am indivisibly this *and* that; where I experience the other in myself and the other-than-myself experiences me. . . . Our concern with the unconscious has become a vital question, a question of spiritual being or non-being. All those who have had an experience like that mentioned in the dream know that the treasure lies in the depths of the water and will try to salvage it. As they must never forget who they are, they must on no account imperil their consciousness. They will keep their standpoint firmly anchored to the earth, and will thus— to preserve the metaphor—become fishers who catch with hook and net what swims in the water. . . . Whoever looks into the water sees his own image, but behind it living creatures soon loom up; fishes, presumably, harmless dwellers of the deep—harmless, if only the lake were not haunted. They are water-beings of a peculiar sort. Sometimes a nixie gets into the fisherman's net, a female, half-human fish. Nixies are entrancing creatures.[119]

According to Grimm's *Teutonic Mythology*, the *mermaid* is a magical water creature that has much in common with wood nymphs, elves, water and fountain ghosts, Mrs. Holle, sea nymphs, virgins, and so on. As is shown in many fairy tales (of the water nixie, the nixie in the pond,[120] the little mermaid,[121] the beautiful Melusine,[122] etc.), these are all creatures in need of salvation. The nixies appear as they sit in the sun, comb their long hair, and with the upper part of their bodies—which is of great beauty—rise out of the water. When they

[119] C. G. Jung, "Archetypes of the Collective Unconscious," *CW* 9, §§ 43–52.

[120] Two fairy tales collected by the brothers Grimm (trans.).

[121] By Hans Christian Andersen (trans.).

[122] Melusine (sweet as honey), the heroine of a fairy tale of Celtic origin, who, as the daughter of a king and a sea-nymph, on certain days had to assume the shape of a fish or a water-sprite (trans.).

go ashore, they are dressed like human maidens; they can be recognized only by the wet hemlines of their skirts or the wet tails of their aprons. Like the siren, the nixie draws the listening youth into the depths with her singing. According to German fairy tales, children who fall into the well fall into the hands of the water nixie, and have to spin matted flax as in the fairy tale of Mrs. Holle. But nixies also appear as helpful beings and accompany the drowned humans into the home of the water nixie. Characteristically, the nixie beguiles man with her singing, fascinates him with her beauty, renders him weak-willed, and pulls him down to her. Something iridescent and seductive is inherent in the nixie, as was convincingly portrayed by Böcklin in his *Mermaid of the Calm Sea*. Professor Jung defines the nixie in the Eranos Yearbook of 1934: "The nixie is a still-instinctual stage, a preliminary stage of a magical female being, which we call anima."

This nixie-elf-anima represents the soul in its entirety, uniting the good and the bad; it is moving, iridescent like a butterfly. The soul is a life-giving demon, and plays its elfish game beneath and above human existence.

So what the boy sees at the bottom of the lake, and what fascinates him so much that he loses himself in it, is his unconscious soul, his anima. Before this sight he stands as if spellbound. It would only be natural for him to try to rescue and pull this girl up to him, this girl who is his classmate and with whom he has an emotional bond, his "crush." But he remains as if paralyzed, unable to actively intervene—a motif often found in dreams.

Nevertheless, he registers the details of her appearance: the still-fresh face and the red and white checkered apron.

The *apron* is a somewhat strange dress for the anima, who otherwise prefers ancient dresses. Moreover, it is the girl's school apron, a somewhat dowdy piece of clothing. It is an exquisitely feminine piece of clothing, designed to protect one's dress. In popular superstition (according to the *Handbook of German Superstition*), the apron has various meanings: on working days it is worn as protection, on Sundays as an adornment. The color of the apron is not without significance: in many regions girls, brides, wives, and widows are distinguished by the color of their aprons; in Upper Austria, bride and bridesmaids are dressed in white aprons as a sign of their innocence. Very often the apron has a distinctly sexual meaning, as in the case of the "pubic cover," called *Skamskyte* on the Swedish island of Öland. The loss of the apron means loss of virginity; that's why we talk of a "skirt chaser,"[123] who is after the skirts like the devil. The apron has become the attribute of the feminine as such.

Sometimes the apron has a protective and exorcizing function. According to an Upper Austrian legend, the Holy Virgin catches the pilgrims who fell in the Danube in her apron, so that only one soul is left for the devil who had made the whirl. When people, and in particular little children, fall down somewhere without getting hurt, the Magyars say that they had fallen into the apron of the Virgin Mother; such an apron is called the "lap of the Virgin Mother."

The apron is also the place of transformation: in fairy tales it often turns leaves and wood, which had been carried home in it, to pure gold. In the apron of St. Elizabeth, the food for the poor turns into roses.

The apron is also the place where girls hide something. I remind you of the dream of the little girl who rode on a lion and had the magic mirror hidden in the pocket of her apron.[124] On that occasion Professor Jung called the apron the region of the Muladhara, the dark instinctual region, the lowest psychical center.

The *Schürze* [apron] is also a synonym of *Schoß*[125]; in dialect we call the *Schürze* "*d'Schoß.*" *Schoß*—lap or womb—has a maternal meaning. "To rest in the womb of the earth" is an expression we use for the earth as the Mother of All Living Beings. So a maternal secret is hidden in the apron.

In summarizing, we can say that the apron has a protective and transforming meaning that refers to the female sex.

The *color* of the apron is also important in our dream; the girl wears a red and white checkered apron. White and red are a *pair of opposites*. The queen in "Little Snow-White" wants to have a child white

---

[123] The German equivalent, *Schürzenjäger*, literally means "apron chaser" (trans.).
[124] See seminar 2, § 4 (ed.).
[125] *Schoß* can mean both "lap" or "womb" (trans.).

as snow and red as blood. *White* symbolizes innocence, *red* instinct and passion. In alchemical symbolism, white means the feminine, the *femina alba*;[126] red means the masculine, the *servus rubeus*.[127] In our discussion of Peucer, we came across a dream from antiquity in which the pair of opposites white/red appeared. An old woman, a Sibyl, who kept the old religious sacrificial laws, had to be found between a yew (taxus), which has red berries, and a myrtle with its white blossoms. The maternal secret lay hidden between the pair of opposites.[128]

I think that the apron in our dream, checkered red and white, refers to something similar. Checkered red and white means that the red and white lines intersect, so that the pair of opposites of male and female is united in these crossing lines, so that the opposites are united in a center. In this unity there lies the secret of the maternal womb, in which all new life has its origin.

The dream continues: the girl, the classmate, lies dead in the water, but her face is still completely fresh. Through the transparency of the water, the dreamer looks at the bottom of the lake, where the girl is lying like Snow-White in the glass coffin, of whom it is also said that after three days, "she still looked as if she were living, and still had her pretty red cheeks." But whereas Snow White lay in her coffin for a long time without decaying, in the dream there is a sudden change: "When I kept on looking, I saw that her face disintegrated. It got crisscrossed with wide red cracks." Here something starts in the dream that Jung calls enantiodromia, the fact that the events take an opposite course. In the philosophy of Heraclitus, this term signifies the play of opposites in an action, the assumption that everything that exists will turn into its opposite. What lives will become dead, what is dead will live, what is young will become old, the old young, what is awake will sleep, and what sleeps will awake. The flow of creation and destruction never ends. One moment the face of the girl was fresh and her colored apron glistened in the water, the next her face starts to disintegrate, and there are wide red cracks in it.

---

[126] Latin, "the white woman" (trans.).
[127] Latin, "the red slave or servant" (trans.).
[128] Cf. volume 2 of the English edition (ed.).

Disintegration is an eerie process. Children generally dread these processes of decay and dying. The cracks in the face remind us at first of old paintings with their cracks and tears; these, however, are wide red cracks, rather reminiscent of the stigmata of saints, which are linked to suffering and death. The cracks, signs of disintegration and decomposition, bring the process of dying as it were to life and make it observable to us. Dying means to pass from the living state into the dead state. The dead body unites the opposites of life and death in itself. In popular belief, the corpse still shows signs of life; there are still connections between the living and the dead, which are only severed as the dead person undergoes several transitional stages. In the *Tibetan Book of the Dead*, this transitional stage is expressed by the symbolic forty-nine days, which is the period of time between death and rebirth. It is significant that the greatest chance of salvation occurs in the direct process of dying. So here we have to conceive of the dead body as the direct expression and the symbol of the magical transformational capacity of the soul, the anima.

This leads us to the actual meaning of the dream. The steamboat jetty portrays the psychical situation of the dreamer. Looking into the water is his approach toward the unconscious.

The figure of the girl on the bottom of the lake means that the dreamer's anima is entirely situated in the unconscious.

The attribute of the apron signifies that, with regard to the figure of the girl, the emphasis lies on instinctuality and sexuality. This is also the reason why the anima has been separated from the mother and transferred onto the classmate.

As Jung has explained in the definitions in *Psychological Types*, the soul, our inner attitude, is represented in the unconscious by certain persons who show the characteristics that are commensurate with the soul. The character of the soul would in general complement the outer character and contain all those attributes missing in the conscious attitude.

In his consciousness the dreamer has "a bit of a crush" on the girl, thus something entranced and ethereal; the unconscious, however, shows him exactly the instinctual, sexual side of this figure.

Jung says that the personification of the anima (here represented

329

by the classmate) psychologically always denotes a relative autonomy of the personified content. Such a content spontaneously either reproduces itself or withdraws from consciousness. Such a split may develop if the ego and a certain complex are incompatible. Experience shows that this split often occurs between the ego and the sexual complex.

In the case of a seven- to eight-year-old boy, this will probably not concern a repressed content; the boy was not yet consciously aware of the content at all, and the content now confronts him for the first time in a different form, the form of the anima.

The present dream could be seen as complementary, because it stresses the other side. The dream brings to light a very specific aspect of the unconscious, the instinctual character of this anima—in this sense it is probably a direct expression of the opposition between the dreamer's ego and his instinctual nature.

The anima makes the dreamer look down into the water, where the unconscious reigns, and where human consciousness wanes like the notion of time in the realm of the water spirits and nixies. Here a natural process—*dying*—takes place; viewing it in this light, we could also characterize this dream as a process in which something is partially brought into consciousness, as the nixie/anima is hidden wisdom and secret knowledge.

One moment the girl, with her fresh face and the red and white checkered apron, has all the attributes of freshness and liveliness; the next she turns into a corpse and disintegrates and decays. This dying is not a completed process, however, but a transition and a transformation, and also includes the possibility of a rebirth. This is why the nixie/anima of the dream also has the aspects of life and transformation; her element, the water, is at the same time the element of rebirth.

The disintegration and death of the anima demonstrates that what had been valid before—the old still-infantile position—is now dying to be changed into something new. The dream represents the tensions between the opposites of above and below—between the dreamer's ego, which stands above on the steamboat jetty in a somewhat insecure and precarious state and is threatened by the danger of the unconscious, and the anima, which haunts the bottom of the lake and leads her own spectral life there.

By looking into the depths and approaching himself, the dreamer has probably chosen the right path, although, like so many heroes in fairy tales, he stops halfway, entranced by the all-powerful anima. When he says of his dream: "I didn't have an uncanny feeling at all," he obviously sees the process of dying as something natural and inevitable. For the time being, he remains observant and assimilating in his attitude, and does not interfere. His problem, in all likelihood the confrontation of his ego with his instinctual nature, as it is represented by the anima, is actually not tackled and solved, so the later dreams of corpses are much more threatening.

Professor Jung: In the paper we have heard about interesting mythological parallels to the single symbols. The real message of the dream, however, seems not to have become entirely clear yet in my view. What might the message of the dream be?

Participant: The boy is told that his little friend is dead.

Professor Jung: At least you have to say: "Well, something has happened." You have to imagine the situation: the boy has a crush on somebody. He has the first presentiments of tender feelings, and now he discovers his little friend dead in the water. This should actually frighten him, and the astonishing thing is that this is not so. Isn't it a bit suspicious when he states that it made no impression on him, because especially when they were scared shitless, boys usually say: "Oh, that was really nothing."—But the dream shows us that a little drama actually happened, and that the girl lies half-rotten in the water. What does that mean? You'd best approach this dream with as little prejudgment as possible, and ask yourselves: what does the dream tell? What it says is: wherever you may go fishing, you will discover that the girl whom you love is lying dead in the water. That is the message, but how do we interpret it? The dream is like nature: it puts a bug in your ear, but you just dismiss it—"Yuck, that's a bug!" And you forget how complicated this actually is. Just try once and exhaust all the secrets of a bug! We will never understand this secret of life and this cosmos, it is much too complicated, and the same is true for dreams. They fall like nuts from the tree of life, and yet they are so hard to crack.

So in order to understand the meaning of this seemingly simple message, at first we have to take a look at each detail. Let us begin with the locale of the events. The *steamboat jetty* connects the firm ground with the water. The former is the place where we feel that we are standing on firm ground, and where we can see and breathe. The fact that the boy is on the steamboat jetty in the dream means that he approaches the *border* between consciousness and unconsciousness. What does this mean for the dreamer in reality? We have to keep it very simple and stick to the image: he is on the land and comes to the brink of a large lake or the sea. What will happen if he keeps on going?

Participant: But he can't go further.

Professor Jung: Well, but if he went further anyway?

Participant: He'd come into a new world.

Professor Jung: You call that a new world when someone falls into the water? He comes into the beyond. There is a danger, and therefore the dream says: here you're coming to the *edge*, to an end. Now it's getting hot and you'll have to be very careful. Here the risk begins, the uncertain element of water. This is the first statement in the dream. But then he stands on a jetty on which steamboats can land, which adds a new twist to the situation: it contains the possibility of leaving, of traveling the unsafe waters and of cruising the lake. This is the primordial image of the courageous *venture*. For the dreamer this implies that he must do something. He has come to the edge of the steamboat jetty, in other words, to the edge of his consciousness; just as we say that we are on the "brink" of something. At that very moment, what was common and usual ceases and an adventure starts. What has he done so far?

Participant: He went fishing.

Professor Jung: And what does this mean for a little boy?

Participant: He hauls out images of the unconscious.

Professor Jung: At this age, *fishing* is more like a game, it is a game and nothing professional. Up to that moment he has played with it, and in doing so has hauled out various objects, various possibilities, from those vague and indefinite regions. Fishing, and also hunting, are old symbols of a more or less playful involvement with adventure. This continues until it gets serious. Do you possibly know an example where hunting went wrong and became serious?

Participant: The story of St. Hubert.

Professor Jung: Yes, this gives you an idea. It is the story of a hunter who on a Sunday sees a white stag, which he wants to bag by all means. All of a sudden he perceives a shining crucifix between its antlers. This is a prey he hasn't dreamed of: it is the Holy Spirit itself whom he meets in the forest. The same story is told of St. Eustace, another Hubert, so to speak. Many people interact playfully with their unconscious. They are like fishermen who daily fish in the unconscious and even "nourish" themselves on it: they take all kinds of good and evil things from the treasure of the unconscious, they can have a cultured conversation about them, can philosophize this or that and even write newspaper articles about them. One day, however, it happens that they catch a golden fish, just as in fairy tales. What can that mean?

Participant: It could be the anima.

Professor Jung: Yes, it's the old story of the nixie or the mermaid who gets caught in his net. It is the being that has no soul and therefore strives after it. And that's where the problem begins.

In the dream, too, the boy's fishing is a playful occupation with something of which he is not yet aware that this is an adventure and involves danger. At this moment the dream tells him: "Attention! Today you won't catch any fish, today you will *see* something for a change, something wonderful." What can we see in the water that is so fascinating?

Participant: We can see ourselves.

Participant: When we look into the water we see our own images.

Professor Jung: In hydromancy, for instance, a dark bowl filled with water is used, as is still today the custom in India. Little boys have to look into a water bowl, whereupon they fall into a trance and report what they see. A similar fascination can be observed in looking into a crystal. There is a parallel to this *self-mirroring*, the strange vision in the Gnostic myth of nous and physis.[129] Nous is the divine spirit that comes from above and looks down into the mirror of physis. He sees his own wonderful picture in it; at that moment physis clasps him and does not let him go, he is captured in her. The physis is like the mirror of the water, into which he looks. She is the waters with the thousand arms, the danger of the unconscious. Now our dreamer does not see his own mirror image in the water, but the girl on whom he has a crush. With that the water reveals its secret; the girl is the physis that wants to pull him down with a thousand arms.

But the girl is dressed in a very rustic apron. What kind of apron is this?

Participant: A *cooking apron*.

Professor Jung: Yes, the cook at home probably has such an apron. But why does the girl wear the apron of the cook and not, say, of the mother? What is the cook in contrast to the mother?

Participant: She is the countermother and subordinate to her.

Professor Jung: Yes, she is the one at whom the boy's affection is directed. She secretly gives him the forbidden candy that the mother wouldn't give him. As Wilhelm Busch has put it:

> "Each young laddie will get hooked
> on the beautiful kitchen cook."[130]

The cook is a subordinate woman who can on certain occasions perfectly correspond to the anima. The cook also prepares the food in the *kitchen*, and this is the place where everything is prepared in mysterious ways. It is the *uterus*, the place of coming into being, which is often brought into connection with cooking, baking, or roasting in folkloric tradition. Just think of the oven or the cooking pot in which the little children are made! So the cook is a maternal figure, who can represent the anima figure to the boy at a certain age. At our last meeting we saw that the mother is the bearer of the soul image. Normally she remains so until the beginnings of sexuality make themselves felt, and the boy has to go down a step. Then he will often go

---

[129] C. G. Jung, "Religious Ideas in Alchemy," CW 12, § 410.
[130] Original: *Jeder Jüngling hat nun mal / Den Hang zum Küchenpersonal* (trans.)

334

into the kitchen, because there he finds something more appropriate, something which corresponds to his level of relationship. He finds it easier to deal with the cook than with the mother, because there is no incest barrier. As a result, however, the mother is more and more elevated, until she rises into heaven, so to speak. But the boy also looks for someone less difficult to deal with—no education, for God's sake! It is extremely convenient for the boy to be spoiled, but not educated, by a woman. That's why boys get so easily attached to the kitchen personnel; the kitchen is *le lieu de raccrochage*[131] for them. Later, of course, it is the school; there are female classmates among whom one can find a suitable one. The figure in the water was also a little schoolgirl who, moreover, wore the kitchen apron as a distinction. With the apron she also possesses the whole secret hidden behind it. But the child is *dead*. We might therefore say that this whole hopeful development breaks off. What does this mean?

Participant: It is like in the previous dream: the dreamer has to separate from the anima.

Professor Jung: Of course, it's exactly the same here. The previous dream gives us the key to this dream. In both cases, the dream is about the farewell to the anima. In the previous dream, the dreamer had to separate from the anima he met in the toilet. This is even farther down than in this dream, which is about the kitchen. From a certain, perhaps more liberal, viewpoint we could consider this development of such an anima relation as something desirable. Exactly this development is stopped, however, and a strangely longing atmosphere ensues. The image of the dead girl seems to tell him: "The sweetest dream of your life"[132] is lying down there and is shattered.

The girl wears that mysterious kitchen apron, checkered *white* and *red*. Mrs. Leuzinger has rightly traced the meaning of these two colors. Red and white are a *union of opposites*. Among others, they are the symbol of the medieval mystical marriage, which represents a union of these two, of the white and the red. There are alchemical tracts in which this union takes place in the depths of the water, for

[131] French, "the place of attachment or clinging" (trans.).

[132] *Deines Lebens schönster Traum*—a crypto-quotation from Wilhelm Busch's *Max und Moritz* (trans.).

335

example, in the *Visio Arislei*.[133] There the couple, Thabritius and Beya (that is, the red slave and *Albeida*, the white one), are locked into a triple glass house on the bottom of the sea. It is terribly hot, and they sweat profusely. This is done with the help of Arisleus, the ancient natural philosopher (*Arisleus* is *Archelaos*, the disciple of *Anaxagoras*), and his companions, who are also locked in the glass house. They have to bring the couple to life again.[134] The philosophers describe consciousness, which activates the latent opposites in the unconscious and leads them toward the mystical union. As a place of rebirth, the glass house is a symbol of the uterus. To understand the colors white and red, we also have to take into account something else: they are also the colors of the underworld, as we know from the so-called Apocalypse of Peter. In the *Mabinogion*,[135] there are white dogs with red noses and eyes in the underworld. Just like the uterus, the underworld is also a symbol of the unconscious. Both indicate a state of unconsciousness that, however, simultaneously represents a potential state—*in utero*—before birth. The dichotomy of the two colors is contained in yet another detail in the dream, namely, in the peculiar disintegration of the corpse, in which red cracks appear. This is a very graphic image: the white skin dissolves, and the red flesh appears. We might say that the whole girl herself becomes that apron, representing the *dissolution of the opposites*. She returns to the state of dissolution and is now herself like a white and red being of the underworld. This process of decay also occurs in alchemy, where *putrefactio* leads to rebirth. Putrefaction is linked to *nigredo*, blackness; like the darkness of the underworld, it is a state of complete unconsciousness. If we apply this to the dream, we could say that the girl simply dissolves into the unconscious. This seems to be a negative ending but, quite to the contrary, this end means something positive: it is only by this that the dreamer can sep-

---

[133] C. G. Jung, "Religious Ideas in Alchemy," *CW* 12, § 435. See also *Artis auriferae*, vol. 1, p. 146, and Julius F. Ruska, *Turba Philosophorum*, p. 23.

[134] In a certain version, the bridegroom, the *servus rubeus*, completely disappears in Beya during the intercourse, and dissolves into atoms in her body. Cf. C. G. Jung, "Religious Ideas in Alchemy," *CW* 12, § 439; and *Rosarium Philosophorum*, p. 246.

[135] A collection of stories based on the oral tradition of the Welsh bards (trans.).

arate from the attachment to the anima. Why did he have to have such a dream?

Participant: Because he was in danger of being possessed by the anima.

Professor Jung: What would that have meant for him?

Participant: He would have got stuck in the anima image and he would not have developed into the world.

Professor Jung: From what does the boy suffer so that he has to receive this message?—It is a *mother complex*; he is still much too attached to the image of the "mother." This is a typical dream of a boy with a mother complex. It could lead to the strongest anima possession. The more somebody clings to the "mother," the more dependent he is on the processes going on in his unconscious, the stronger their archetypal power and their demonic power will become.

In girls something analogous happens. In their case, however, it is the father who can become such a demonic power, while the mother plays a different, although not unimportant, role. For a woman the mother is not the anima—for the anima is always the object of longing desire—but actually the sexual organ, the uterus. In the case of a negative mother complex in a woman, there often are various disturbances of the sexual function, for instance, menstrual disorders and similar disturbances.

In our dream there is too much of the mother in the anima. The boy has "too much mother." For him to be able to distance himself from the "mother," the dream has to tell him: Now you're coming to the edge. Now comes the adventure of life, with which you have just played so far. Now it could be expected that this would cause him great pain. But we should not be surprised that this is allegedly not so; as we have already remarked, many boys won't admit—God forbid!—that they were impressed by something.

Participant: But if the mother is meant, why does the classmate appear in the dream?

Professor Jung: This is due to his age. I have shown you how the anima gradually becomes this classmate. For certain reasons, the mother can no longer represent the anima figure; the cook takes her place, or any other female being wearing an apron, thus also that girl.

337

As a representative of the mother, she has to die. And this is desirable. If it were not for that apron, that ridiculous detail, we might well doubt whether this lysis is desirable. Then we could ask ourselves, if it hadn't been preferable that the boy had fallen into love with this little girl after all, and if it weren't sad and alarming that such a normal expression of love had been cut off. This would truly be a problem—if the girl did not wear this apron! The apron reveals the secret connections, reaching to the mother via the cook. Obviously, the girl is his anima, and this constitutes the difference from a normal relationship. An anima relationship is never a normal relationship, but always something fantastical. A man sees his female face in the anima, and that is dangerous; the anima transforms everything it touches. Wherever it is active, it visualizes one's own image, a man's own image, and this is his female being, an invisible minority that he carries inside himself.

7. Dream of a Three-Year-Old Girl of Jack Frost[136]
PRESENTED BY DR. WALLER[137]

Text: *Jack Frost*[138] *is coming. She is scared. He pinches her everywhere in the belly. She awakens and realizes that she has pinched herself.*

Professor Jung: This dream is connected to early masturbation, which already started at the age of three, but then stopped again soon afterward. The dream was dreamed by a three-year-old girl and is the earliest to be remembered. There are some medical questions involved. The dreamer has a strong hereditary taint. An aunt suffered from schizophrenia. Her own psychosis remained latent for many years, and first surfaced in the form of a severe obsessional neurosis. An obsessional neurosis is one of the most distinct phenomena of dissociation we know of. It can mean a complete split of the personality, in which one part wishes as passionately to stay healthy as the other wishes to remain ill.

---

[136] Session of 23 January 1940.

[137] The text of the paper is missing (ed.).

[138] Jack Frost is a figure believed to have originated in Viking folklore, an elfish creature who personifies crisp, cold, winter weather. He is said to leave frosty crystal patterns on leaves and windows on cold mornings. It is also thought that the English derived the name Jack Frost from the Norse character names, Jokul ("icicle") and Frosti ("frost") (trans.).

338

The dramatic structure of the dream has been described quite correctly, but the question of the lysis has not yet been cleared up. Can we speak of a *lysis* here?

Participant: Perhaps it lies in the fact that the dreamer wakes up from pinching herself.

Professor Jung: No, because this no longer belongs to the dream action.

Participant: Is it the anxiety the child feels?

Professor Jung: No, because this would mean the exact opposite of a lysis. The final thing the dream expresses is just anxiety, and surely anxiety can't represent the solution of the problem. Moreover, it is nothing extraordinary to wake up from a dream in a state of anxiety. Many anxiety dreams can have an actual lysis, often, however, it is only hinted at, for instance, if in the dream we know that it is an anxiety dream. But sometimes the lysis is completely missing, and this is the case in this dream. Do you remember what we said about dreams without a lysis?[139]

Participant: They point to an unfavorable prognosis.

Professor Jung: Yes, but we must not generalize this. Not every dream without a lysis has an unfavorable prognosis, for instance, if the danger does not reach you in the dream, or if there is something like a comforting allusion. But why do we have to suspect an unfavorable prognosis here, after all?

Participant: It is a dream from earliest childhood.

Professor Jung: Yes, and it has been remembered throughout her whole life. If such an *important dream* has *no lysis*, we will have to be attentive, because then a *vital problem* of the dreamer has found *no solution*. Naturally, a dream without a lysis always gives an unsatisfactory impression, particularly if it is of a catastrophic character. When we hear such a dream, we are actually frightened and would like to maintain silence. In the last seminar on children's dreams we discussed two such dreams,[140] and I also told you about two catastrophic dreams of a fifteen-year-old girl that ended without lysis. In all these dreams, the climax, the catastrophe, coincided with the end.

[139] Cf. seminar 3, § 5 (ed.).
[140] Cf. seminar 3, § 5 (ed.).

In addition, the present dream seems rather unremarkable, and such meager dreams often have an unfavorable prognosis. But we must not avoid such examples, because they do happen in reality. When you ask: "What kind of a lousy dream is this?" you have already noticed something important. Then, however, you have to go on asking: "Why is this so?" Only if we take the simplest things seriously will we have the key to wisdom. A dream is like a piece of nature, and of course we have to react to it. So we may well swear now and then and say: "Such a piece of shit of a dream. That's really pathetically poor; such poverty is enormously saddening." We have to let this poverty of nature affect us. Dreams are not always full of fancy details. If a rich fantasy had blossomed, we could say: "All hell broke loose." Here nothing broke loose, which confirms the unfavorable prognosis. The dream contains hardly any possibility of appropriately reacting to it. It is much too meager compared to its importance.

The figure of *Jack Frost* appears in the dream. He is a figure from English folklore, and there are similar figures in German popular belief. There is St. Nicholas, the icily gray and cold one; he is the old man symbolizing the beginning of winter. St. Nicholas, however, is a benevolent figure. Why?

Participant: He's like the Erinyes, who are evil and benevolent at the same time.

Professor Jung: Yes, often a good name stands for an evil cause.

Participant: St. Nicholas is also split into two figures. He usually is accompanied by *Knecht Ruprecht*, who represents the devil. He comes with a rod and a sack, in which there are the children he has already taken.

Professor Jung: Where does he carry the bad children?

Participant: Into the forest.

Professor Jung: Yes, into the forest. And what happens there? What is the forest?

Participant: It is a dark place, full of dangers.

Professor Jung: You know the saying "To hell with him!" This means that the devil takes you to the place of darkness and terror, actually to the place of the dead. St. Nicholas, too, takes the children to the place of darkness. As the gray one, who appears at the beginning of December, he is also *death*, who takes man into the world beyond. He is a kind of judge of the dead, who punishes the bad and rewards the good, similar to Osiris, the judge of the underworld. So a very serious meaning is concealed behind the figure of St. Nicholas. Jack Frost corresponds to St. Nicholas, although he is much less incorporated into folkloric culture. He, too, appears at the beginning of winter and represents *coldness*, which implies a *memento mori*. A white *ghost*, he seems to be covered by the shroud of snow. What does Jack Frost in our dream signify?

Participant: Death wants to get to the dreamer.

Professor Jung: Yes, it is not yet spring, and winter is here already.

Participant: Do we have to see the figure of Jack Frost in such a negative light? If he wants to take the dreamer into the forest, this might perhaps only mean a state of introversion, out of which a new content could arise.

Professor Jung: Such an optimistic interpretation is not appropriate here. We must not forget that the dream has no lysis, and that it is extremely meager. It is impossible to conceive of the figure of Jack Frost, therefore, as positive. Even if the *Samichlaus*[141] appeared in his place, it would be misleading to think of a joyous children's party or any other merry event. We have to try to grasp Jack Frost in his ominous meaning, as the one who freezes all life.

We also have to stick to the dream, in which the child does not experience joy, but fear of the ghost of coldness. And this figure *touches her*!

Participant: This increases the negative effect of this figure. It is similar to the *Erlking*.

Professor Jung: Yes, the Erlking is also such a ghost. In Goethe's poem the increasing anxiety of the child is beautifully expressed, until the moment where he says:

"Dear father, oh father, he seizes my arm!
The Erlking, father, has done me harm!"

Then the child dies.

---

[141] The Swiss equivalent of St. Nicholas (trans.).

Participant: It also seems very dangerous to me that Jack Frost touches the girl on her belly.

Professor Jung: Yes, the *belly* is the kitchen, the stove, radiating warmth. In the belly we are sheltered as long as we are embryos. If we are cold, we'd like to crawl into our own belly to warm up. This place of warmth is also the origin and the center of all life; this is expressed in the word "liver," the main organ in the abdomen. It is "the liver," he who lives.

Participant: Can we see from the dream if this is about a psychical or physical death?

Professor Jung: This is not easy to see. Let us assume that the child told this dream at the age of ten, that is, at a time when there was no visible sign of a neurosis yet. In this case, I would really have been in doubt whether it referred to a physical or a spiritual death. I would have been able to say only that the dream indicated something extremely alarming, but I would not have been able to decide if this would later lead to an obsessional neurosis, to a psychosis, or to suicide. But then the dreamer took her own life at the age of thirty-six in a mental institution! The psychosis began with extreme anxiety states that intensified until the fatal end. The dream does contain a detail that could point to the suicide. She *herself* intervened in her life with a *cold* hand.

Participant: Was this the reason why she escaped into masturbation? Was it an attempt to keep herself warm?

Professor Jung: Yes, for her it was a defensive move, an apotropaic magic, a stress on life *in aspectu mortis,*[142] just as people may become sexually aroused when they are in mortal danger or confronted with hopeless, life-threatening situations.[143] There was ample evidence of this desperate eroticism in the earthquake at Messina.[144] It is as if the life instinct asserted itself, and as if life tried to affirm itself in a *quand-même.*[145] So, you see, the dream is very tragic. I would not hesitate

---

[142] Latin, "in the face of death" (trans.).

[143] Cf. Marie-Louise von Franz, *Alchemy,* p. 59 (ed.).

[144] A catastrophic earthquake in Sicily and Calabria on December 28, 1908, in which approximately 75,000–100,000 people died and Messina was almost totally destroyed (trans.).

[145] French, "nevertheless, in spite of everything" (trans.).

342

to make a connection between the fact that the dreamer pinched herself and the suicidal outcome. Any more questions?

Participant: You mentioned that the dreamer at first fell ill with an obsessional neurosis, which masked a latent psychosis. How did the psychosis become manifest?

Professor Jung: Behind each classical obsessional neurosis a psychosis is hidden. In the dreamer the mental illness broke out when the voices began to become audible. From then on the process could not be arrested by anything.

Participant: Doesn't emotion also originate in the belly?

Professor Jung: Yes, of course, it is the seat of the *solar plexus*, where the psychical and the physical are still one. But you must not conceive of the belly as too complicated. It is merely the center of warmth, the seat of life. Because the psychical and the physical are still one in it, it is hard to tell if it was a physical or a psychical illness that prematurely destroyed the dreamer. The unconscious actually does not seem to care one way or the other. Moreover, the unconscious has a different relation to death than we ourselves have. For example, it is very surprising in which way dreams anticipate death. Often this does not happen the way we look at death, but in a completely different manner. You will find something analogous in astrology or also in chiromancy and other ancient "mancies," in which the indications for death are also very questionable. It is as if death was something other than what we think. That is, approximately, how we could put it. It might be linked to the fact that the unconscious has a different relation to time than we have. In the unconscious there exist, so to speak, an elastic space and an elastic time. It seems as if these deeper layers of the psyche were characterized by particularly strange features, and this, of course, is also expressed in dreams. So I would not have dared to predict from the dream's character if a physical or psychical death was implied.

Participant: Wouldn't it have helped the dreamer if she had later gone to a female analyst? What she missed was probably primitive, vital warmth. Perhaps she never received enough maternal love; moreover, the dream expresses a very negative attitude toward men.

Professor Jung: If we are dealing, as in this dream, with such deep-

343

reaching and life-threatening affairs, the sex is no longer of importance. In these cases, a physical force has to intervene, a force that pulls the person out of the predicament and saves her from drowning, so to speak. These fine details no longer play a role, and it doesn't make any difference at all if it is a man or a woman who tries to come to the rescue.

8. Dream of a Ten-Year-Old Girl of a Transparent Mouse[146]
PRESENTED BY CORNELIA BRUNNER

Text: The Transparent Mouse. *In the dream I imagined a mouse; once worms came into it, and the mouse turned gray, then snakes, and it turned red, then fish, and it turned blue, then people, and it turned into a human being itself. That's how all men and women develop.*

Mrs. Brunner: This is an extraordinary dream, seemingly childlike at the beginning, and then purely archetypal. The details, seen for themselves, could be based on day residues; the context and the structure, however, do not correspond to any experience of the outer world, but, down to the last detail, to experiences of the inner world. This "development of man" cannot be the phylogenetic development, because the sequence—mouse, worms, snakes, fish—does not correspond to the biological line of development. Biologically speaking, the fish would have to appear before the snakes, and the mouse afterward.

Let us try to structure the dream:

Locale:	In a world of envisaged images.
Time:	Once (as in fairy tales, "once upon a time," thus again in the realm of the prenatal imaginary world).
Dramatis personae:	Mouse, worms, snakes, fish, humans, one human being.
Exposition:	"In the dream I imagined a mouse."
Peripateia:	Animals and people enter into the mouse.
Lysis:	The transformation of the mouse.
Final realization:	"That's how all men and women develop."

So it actually is a drama in four acts, with a prologue and an epilogue.

[146] Session of 30 January 1940.

I will now provide the amplifications to each single dream phase, and then try in each case to deduce the meaning of the respective dream part. Regarding the fourth act, in which the dream deals with man, I will be very brief, but instead provide a few parallels to the whole of the dream, by which the meaning of "man" will be circumscribed.

The girl gave the dream the title "The Transparent Mouse." This mouse awakens a special emotion in us. *Mouse* is a highly suggestive name for a little girl. Many mothers involuntarily use this term of endearment. It seems to me that this is a name for a certain kind of child. *Mouse* suggests the image of delicate, gray little fur, of a dainty, swift little creature, which scurries past before disappearing into a corner again, of a friendly, warm, and lovable being, shy toward strangers. That's how I imagine the little dreamer.

Now to the amplifications: Brehm calls the mouse the most faithful companion of man, which follows him to the farthest north and to the highest Alpine huts. He describes it as charming, amiable, also curious, crafty, and very skillful. It runs, jumps, and climbs even on a blade of grass. It can even run on two legs like a human. It is very fertile; each year it gives birth to about thirty young, and a newborn female casts its young already after forty-two days. Young mice are extremely small and nearly transparent, says Brehm.

According to Schrader, the word *mouse* is derived from an ancient Indian word, *mush*, which means "to steal." Vice versa, *mausen* means "to nick" in our dialect.

As to the mythology: it says in the *Handbook of German Superstition* that dwarfs and elves often turn into mice or slip into mouseholes. Earth-, mountain-, and house spirits help man in the form of mice, and guard treasures. Bewitched virgins or wise women sometimes appear as mice. The transformation into a mouse is often a punishment, for instance, because of a fondness for sweet things. Peucer saw the devil in the form of a mouse, running back and forth underneath a woman's skin. Witches try to escape from the fire by turning into mice. While the girl witch is dancing with Faust on the Brocken, a little red mouse jumps out of her mouth. Innocent children's souls and the souls of the just appear as white mice, those of the godless as

345

red ones. The souls of unborn children, too, appear as white mice. There is a very widespread notion that the soul leaves the human body during sleep in the form of a mouse, sometimes to quench its thirst, sometimes to cause nightmares in people, animals, and trees— in that case, it is usually the soul of a girl. If the mouse does not return, the girl will die. To whistle after mice means to lure the souls into the afterworld. Mice are often signs of death. Gray and black mice generally indicate disaster. They spread the Black Death and other diseases. The white mouse appears as a fever demon but, on the other hand, also attracts fever. It is said that mice are created out of earth or putrefaction, or are made by witches. Because of their gray color they are seen as tempest animals, coming from the clouds or the fog, or being brought by the wind.

The Teutons, Greeks, and Romans named the muscle after the mouse—*mus*. The uterus is called mouse sometimes. There are also etymological links between *mouse* and *girl*.[147]

Now let me try to interpret: the mouse is a soul animal, an image of the psychical reality that is difficult to grasp (it disappears into holes). It is a form of the soul closely connected with muscle, flesh, body, sexuality and fertility, and the devil. This is probably the reason for the extraordinary fear and excitement it arouses in many women. As a *transparent* mouse, it has obviously just been born, something still very little and clumsy. Let me also give you the amplifications to "transparency." When we talked about the glass house on the pyramid, Professor Jung mentioned that transparency would be the expression of a spiritual being, of a disembodied, spiritual existence, of the subtle body in a still unmaterialized state. In India, the subtle body is represented by the *lingam*, the phallus symbol. Thus the mouse, in its meaning as a uterus, is also an analogous female symbol of the subtle body.

We may probably interpret the transparent mouse, therefore, as the subtle body of the dreamer. The girl sees her own, still hardly born soul. *Transparent* brings to mind *glassy*. The transparent mouse probably corresponds to the glass vessel in which the *homunculus*, the lit-

---

[147] Original: *Maus und Mädchen* (trans.).

tle man, is to come into being, "the Tom Thumb who dwells in the hollow of the heart."—The fairy tale "The Glass Coffin" tells that the servants of the bewitched princess are captured in glass vessels as blue smoke or as colored *spiritus*.

"Once *worms* came into it, and the mouse turned *gray*." Worms represent one of the lowest possible stages of animal life. They are segmented and their nervous system consists only of chains of ganglia. They impress us as a bunch of muscles with a mouth and intestine. We can hardly feel into such a low stage of nervous life. They blindly devour the fertile ground, in which they originated, and probably know, besides that greed, only a vague feeling of life and movement, and a blind feeling of being confronted with the resistance of matter. Worms are found in dead bodies, in putrefaction and decay. African myths explain that the soul stays in the body until the first worm, the soul worm, comes out of it.[148]

As to the interpretation: for a naive observer, the worms eat earth and transform earth into life, into movement, into greed. They transform matter into soul. They are life originating in death. Worms symbolize the first, unreflected movements of the soul—contents that are still colorless, still completely undifferentiated and incoherent, without feeling, without reason, the stirrings of the blind life instinct. Worms are the most primitive forms of psychical reality, hidden in matter. They belong to an unconscious level, in which the soul is still completely projected onto the outside, onto objects, and in which we experience the world only by blind devouring, by the resistance of the matter, and by involuntary innervation. Soul is here still little more than a physical-chemical substrate.

The entering worms are the soul of the matter; they take their element, matter, into the transparent mouse. This means that the soul, driven by greed, begins to "eat the world," to get entangled in the world. The subtle mouse becomes a real, gray mouse. Darkness, impurity, the gray shadow enter into the pure vessel.

"Then *snakes* came into it, and it turned red."—The snakes are hermatocryal, scaled reptiles; they breathe with their lungs and have

---

[148] Erich Küster, *Die Schlange in der griechischen Kunst und Religion*, p. 63.

a cerebrospinal nervous system. According to superstition, "a man's marrow, especially from the backbone, turns into snakes."[149] When someone makes a fire at night in places with many poisonous snakes, he will soon experience how the snakes will be attracted by the fire and come crawling from all sides, so that he will have his hands full for hours fending them off. Snakes feed almost exclusively on living animals, which they attack and devour *in toto*. Snakes are of various colors and markings: green, yellow like sand, depending on their habitat. Those living underground are often characterized by a beautiful metallic luster.

The Teutons used the same word, *ormr*, for worm, snake, and dragon. In the primitive view, the snake is a bigger worm, which creeps out of the earth toward the fire.[150] Regarding the appearance of the snake in *mythology*: you remember what Ms. von Franz told us about the snake as an earth demon, as soul of the dead or the heroes, as a dark god of the Ophites, as the snake of the river bed, as movement, as vital force, as time, and as the snake of salvation.

Philo says of the snake that it would be the most spiritual among the animals, that it would move with exceptional speed, and that its nature would be that of fire.[151] Ninck points to the fact that the expression, "sparkling snake," is often used for the eye of the hero. He says of the dragon, "that fire sparkles out of its eye and mouth." The dragon blood has the properties of fire: weapons melt and steel is hardened in it.[152]

The mouse turns red because of the intruding snakes. Red is the color of fire, of blood, of wine, the color of embers and of inebriation. In the *Handbook of German Superstition*, red stands for life and death, for fertility and danger.

According to the Hermetic tradition, red is the color of the spirit, of gold, and of the sun.[153]

---

[149] Hanns Bächthold-Stäubli, *Handwörterbuch des deutschen Aberglaubens*.

[150] Martin Ninck, *Wodan und germanischer Schicksalsglaube*, p. 157.

[151] Jakob Maehly, *Die Schlange im Mythus und Kultus der klassischen Völker*, p. 7.

[152] Ninck, *Wodan und germanischer Schicksalsglaube*, p. 153.

[153] Cf. C. G. Jung, *Mysterium Coniunctionis*, CW 14/I, § 130 (ed.).

Let me again try and interpret: snakes force their way into the gray mouse. Where life stirs in the dark womb of the earth, it will soon come to the light of day and assume a color, that is, the psychical stirring assumes a certain emotional color, which will at first still be identical with the respective environment, just as snakes show the color of their environment. The snakes force their way from the outside into the mouse. It is as if it were attacked by the instinctual stirrings that seem to intrude from the objects into the being in the retort. What comes into being feels attacked, assaulted, devoured, and, at the same time, invaded by sudden, forceful impulses, by sudden wishes and compulsions. It has no wishing and feeling of its own, but rather wishes and compulsions that attack it from the objects. These wishes and compulsions finally reach consciousness, because the snakes open up, with their cerebrospinal system, the possibility of a connection between the sympathetic nervous system and the brain. A knowledge about the wishes is added to the wishes as such.

The more snakes intrude, that is, the more instinctual wishes are accumulated in the retort, the hotter it gets in it. The black mouse turns red, the blood warms, the fire of passion erupts. Here alchemy speaks of the "red slave," and rightly so, because the being in the retort is at the complete mercy of the heat; it does not yet have a countermagic with which it could fight or control the fire. Erupting passion calls for action, for attack, assault, and devouring, snake-wise. The snake symbolizes the freeing of the energy, the aim at an object, aggressiveness, and drive. The turning red of the mouse shows that the heat of the soul develops out of the material soul, so that passionate wishing is no longer experienced as imposed by the outside, but as an inner compulsion. Before, the shadow entered into the mouse, now the *animus* is revived; the male instinctual force is awakened, which wants to conquer the world to possess it. And each new conquest feeds the fire and the heat.

"Then came fish, and it turned blue."—Fish are cold-blooded vertebrates with a barely developed cerebrum, but with gill breathing. Brehm says that fish perhaps surpass all other animals in their endurance. Salmon can cover a distance of twenty-six feet in one sec-

349

ond, and up to 15.5 miles in one hour. It can cut like an arrow through the water. Most fish are predators, voracious, and audacious. When they rest—the state corresponding to our sleep—their lidless eyes never cease to be receptive to the environment. The fertility of fish is enormous. A codfish lays up to nine million eggs. Fish change their color according to their psychical processes; when sticklebacks, for instance, get enraged or want to conquer a position with regard to the females, they change from a greenish, silver-speckled, matte coloring to a crimson to reddish-yellow and shiny green color. The habitat of fish is the sea, down to the deepest depths, from the Pole to the equator, and up to the mountain rivers and lakes.[154]

Let us have a look at their *mythology*: In the fairy tale "The Fisherman and His Wife," the flounder appears as a wish-fish. It fulfills all the wishes of Ilsebill.[155] But when she wants to be God Himself, she plunges back into her old misery. In Hofmannsthal's *Woman without a Shadow*, seven little fish are the souls of unborn children. The little children, who are gotten out of the well, live as little fish in it. Three wise women dressed in blue coats appear to an Icelandic wife of a count, and order her to go to a nearby river, to lie down and drink, and to take the trout she will see into her mouth, and then she will become pregnant.[156]

During the Annunciation, Mary is described as fetching water from a well, or as eating a fish.[157] The fish is Christ, so called after the constellation of Pisces, in which the vernal equinox entered after the beginning of Christianity.

In the mystical epitaph of Bishop Aberkios, there is a passage: "Belief (impersonated as a woman) always went ahead of me and gave me a fish to eat from a well, a gigantic, pure fish that a holy virgin had caught. This fish she always gave the friends to eat, with well-watered wine, together with bread."[158] Aberkios speaks about the Last Supper or about the fish meal on Fridays, an ancient custom that

[154] Alfred Brehm, *Illustriertes Tierleben*.
[155] The fisherman's wife in the fairy tale (trans.).
[156] Robert Eisler, *Orpheus the Fisher*, p. 265.
[157] Ibid., p. 265.
[158] Ibid., p. 249.

350

originally was dedicated to Venus (*Venerdi*),[159] to Ishtar, or to a Babylonian fish goddess.[160]

In the fish sanctuaries of Western Asia, the fish were kept in sacred ponds, sometimes adorned with golden jewelry, on which formulas or whole poems were engraved. A Babylonian god was called fish as well as "writing stone of Bel."[161] In an Irish myth, the "salmon of wisdom" plays a great role. He who eats it will become the wisest seer in the world. To this day, Irish peasants say: "They will not be able to do justice to the cause unless they have eaten from the 'salmon of wisdom.'"[162]

The Greek alphabet was ascribed to the mythical Orpheus, whose name is translated as "fisherman" by Eisler. In a Merovingian liturgical mansucript we can see how the thoughts are held by letters in the form of fish.[163]

The mouse turns *blue* because of the intruding fish. The pure clear water is blue, the mountains are blue, the sky is blue. Romantic longing searched for the "Blue Flower." The little boy described by Maeterlinck[164] searches for the bluebird and finds the way to the primordial images. Blue coats are worn by the wise women who, as swan virgins, are linked to the water, to the mist, and to the sky. Mist rises from the water, rises up into the blue sky, to fall back on earth as rain. In alchemy and tarot, blue is the color of the moon, of silver, and of the soul.

Now to the interpretation: fish come swimming, they surface and disappear, effortlessly they float in the waters and slip away, fish of all colors and forms; inconceivably fantastic are the creatures of the deep sea, enchantingly beautiful in their colors, fabulous the goldfish; some of them shine, others are transparent like glass, others dark and dangerous, silent, lively images that chase one another, devour

---

[159] "Friday" (*Freitag* in German) is derived from the German goddess "Freyja," goddess of love and beauty; Romance languages derived from "Venus," hence "Venerdi," "Vendredi," "Viernes" for "Friday" (trans.).

[160] Eisler, *Orpheus the Fisher*, p. 221.

[161] Ibid., p. 31.

[162] Ibid., p. 47.

[163] Ibid. (picture).

[164] *The Bluebird* (*L'Oiseau Bleu*), a play by Maurice Maeterlinck (1908); cf. the "bluebird of happiness" idiom in Western culture (trans.).

one another, playing in the boundless element. They bring their coolness, the diversity of the various colors and forms, the unborn potentialities, into the red-glowing mouse. Thoughts emerge, ideas, premonitions, and feelings, hard to grasp, vague in their origin and where they go, one idea devours another, new ideas emerge, enormous sowings of clearly contoured images in the indeterminate, undulating change of the spiritual element. And the voraciousness of the fish? How easily an impression, a feeling, is swallowed by another content, how easily we ourselves fall prey to an "ism," an ideal, a primordial, overwhelming image.

The blue, cool flood flows into the mouse with the fish swimming toward the light and with the "salmon of wisdom." It turns blue, blue glass or ice, a sapphire, a cleansed mirror of life.

Where previously wanting and compulsion reigned, now the wish and the idea emerge, where the impetus was caused by and directed to the outside, now the nature and the action of the environment intrude, the imaginary world of the unconscious, the thinking that is in the air. Feeling is no longer bound to the environment; it now becomes a living form of the content, a psychical expression. Where previously there was fighting and activity, now there is also feeding and passivity. In the blue mouse the soul becomes the *anima*, which mirrors the contents. Life flows in and assumes a solid form. The thoughts become cool and clear.

"Then *people* came, and it turned into a human being itself."— Now what shall I tell you about the humans, about the species *homo*? That they have an erect posture and thus display their double relatedness, to above and to below? Or, as Pico della Mirandola says: "So he is free to sink to the deepest layer of the animal world. But he can also rise to the highest spheres of God."[165]

And which of the myths is the right one here? In legends, the hero kills the dragon and wins the virgin; frogs, lions, and bears turn into princes. Deer and swans turn into virgins, fish into nixies, and then new complications arise, bringing suffering with them and calling for decisions.

---

[165] Giovanni Pico della Mirandola, *Ausgewählte Schriften*, p. 18.

What is it that distinguishes man from animals? Is it his reason that makes him tell right from wrong? Is it his eros, his potential for faithfulness and loyalty, or for unfaithfulness and treason? Is it the freedom of will that makes him say yes to all that wants to exist? Is it consciousness that experiences: all that is, and I am——? And the *one human* into which the mouse is transformed?

To begin with, let me give you some parallels to the gradual structure of this dream. You will then understand that I have little to say about this final, most crucial transformation.

First, an Australian myth: The ancestor of the Unmatjera tribe was a lizard. He was lying in the sun, stretched his legs, and as he looked around, there was a second lizard beside him. Surprised, he called: "But this is my spitting image!" And again he was lying there, and again he looked around, and again there was a new lizard. In this way he multiplied his existence by watching. They all came out of his body without his realizing it. And as he was again lying still, he became a man.[166]

The myths of the Zuni Indians are more elaborate. They know of four cave worlds, lying on top of one another, through which the humans climb up on a plant from the dark to the light of day, in order to take off their slimy and scaled clothes. In one version, these worlds have the following names: the inner world of raw dust, the inner world of soot, the inner world of mist, and the inner world of wings.[167]

I think there is a very elaborate parallel in Tantric Yoga.[168] This visualizing yoga knows seven mandalas, situated one above the other, which correspond to certain body parts, and which are successively to be awakened and meditated by the ascending Kundalini serpent. The lowest of these mandalas is the *earth lotus*. It corresponds to the gray mouse. It is the place of the world-bound souls. In its center there is the *lingam*, colored like a fresh sapling, perhaps reminiscent of a worm. Coiled around the lingam, the Kundalini serpent sleeps. In it sleeps the essence of the highest experience. When it awakens,

---

[166] Bächtold-Stäubli, *Handwörterbuch des deutschen Aberglaubens*, s.v. anthropology.

[167] C. Baumann, lecture: "Zuni Origin Myths."

[168] *The Serpent Power*, ed. Arthur Avalon.

it ascends, passing through all lotuses to bring them to life. It is the driving force, the compulsion to become conscious. The animals in our dream can be seen as a transformational form of the Kundalini. The *dragon* in the second lotus corresponds to the snakes in our dream. Above, there is the *fire circle*, the center of emotions. This is the navel lotus, in the region of the solar plexus. The fish correspond to the *heart-lotus*, with a fleeing antelope. Nearby there is the place of the "divine wish-tree." In this lotus thinking begins. Then follows the *ether airspace* or *firmament-lotus*, which reveals its connection with the blue mouse by its blue ovary and by its name, "circle of purification and ablution." Above, in the two-leaved, winged *circle of knowledge*, there are no longer any animals. There the yogi sees the highest, eternal god, the incarnate, primordial man. And finally, in the highest, *thousand-petaled lotus*, the yogi receives the "knowledge of one's own self." The name of this place is "eternal blessedness," and some call it salvation, Atman knowledge, or knowledge of existence itself.

Another parallel is given by *astrology*, in the sequence of the historical ages. About six thousand years ago, the first historical written records were made in the *Age of Taurus*. The earth element is assigned to the constellation Taurus. In ancient Egypt, the spirit found its expression through the medium of matter, the stone, and the earth.

Two thousand years later, the vernal equinox entered the constellation *Aries*. With that, a fiery age began, as witnessed by Moses, when he sees God in a fiery bush, or when God appears to His people as a pillar of fire.

Around the birth of Christ, there follows the *Age of Pisces*. Pisces is a water sign. That is probably why we have to look for the spirit in the water, in life's flow of images, and in the unconscious.

And now we are on the threshold of the sign of Aquarius. The air element is assigned to it, and it is symbolized by an angel or a human being, instead of an animal. Here the spirit is meant to become something subtle again, and man to become who he is.

This juxtaposition shows what is meant by man in general and by the one person in our dream. These final stages correspond to the lotuses of Atman-, Purusha-, or God-knowledge. It is a union with

Christ and an experience of the self, or an anthropogenesis that will be fully realized only in the coming Age of Aquarius.

I am not able to make this reaching of the final stage[169] clear to you. Let me quote instead from Meister Eckhart's sermons. You surely know the words of Meister Eckhart: "All nature means man." And another one: "All creatures feel an urge to rise from their lives to their inner nature. All creatures carry my reason within themselves, so that they may gain reason in me. I alone again prepare all creatures for God!"[170] (All creatures—thus also man!)

And about the final transformation: "When the soul has to realize that no creature at all can come into the Kingdom of God, it begins to feel itself, goes its own way and no longer seeks God. Only then does it die its highest death. In this death the soul loses all desire, all capability of thinking, all form, and is deprived of all essence. Now at last it finds *itself* in the highest primordial image, in which God lives and is active, where He is His own kingdom." Here the soul has found out that it itself is the "Kingdom of God."

That is why the Church Fathers particularly stress "that the humanness of Jesus must not be just adored separately from the deity, but both have to be worshipped together in one single act."[171]

Now let us consider what the dream wants to tell the little girl. Look, it says, look at this little mouse, this little, subtle, fragile being. This is the origin of all humans. This is not about the growth of the body, because it does not start with the parents. Neither is it about the "Spirit from Above," because the image of God does not stand at the beginning. What it is about is something very little, the mouse, that elusive, pilfering, devilish little animal. And for a long time it goes through many transformations. At first come the worms, disgusting and voracious. Through greed the soul becomes entangled in the world, it becomes earthen, dark, and evil. It is touched by the objects and the humans, and everything is gray and dark. Then come

---

[169] Original: *Erreichnis*, a neologism condensed from *erreichen* (to reach) and *Ereignis* (event) (trans.).

[170] Meister Eckhart, *Predigten.* See Herman Buettner, *Meister Eckeharts Schriften und Predigten.*

[171] Georg Koepgen, *Die Gnosis des Christentums*, p. 214.

the snakes, uncanny and dangerous. Fast as lightning they dash forward, devour their victims and disappear in the fire. Possession by the instincts, obsession, and heat of the blood lead to fiery desire and fervent compulsion. And now the magical beauty of the playing fish, colorful, shining, transparent, veiled. They bring the blueness of the sea with them, the feasts of heaven. Endless are the possibilities of being, the varieties of wishes. Whence they come we do not know. Accept them, for they bring coolness, clarity, knowledge, and wisdom. And then the humans: young and old, men and women, ancestors and grandchildren, each burdened with his or her experience, fate, and cross. Take them into your experience and behold, this becomes the one, the all-encompassing, the all-representing human being.

So this is a reversed *Bardo Thödol*, beginning with what is lowest and smallest, to bring all creatures home to the blessedness of the soul. The Tibetan teachings about the dead, however, incessantly remind us: "Realize that you are looking at yourself. This is you. Everything depends on your reality and that image becoming one."

We know that the little girl died one year after this dream. The dream does not reveal anything pathological to me, it has a lysis. Although all the animals that appear in it are considered souls of the dead, they stand in logical connection with the inner development. What is alarming is only the absolute completeness of the archetypal vision, and this at an age when the archetypal images should be covered and suppressed by her own perceptions and experiences. This openness to the invasion by the unconscious indicates that she is endangered, that the infantile consciousness was profoundly shaken for reasons we do not know.

In our amplifications to the mouse we have heard that the soul leaves the body at night in the form of a mouse, to quench its thirst; it is said that in most cases this is the soul of a girl, and that if the mouse does not come back, the girl will die. In our dream, the girl sees her soul mouse, but it does not turn toward her. None of the animals comes to her; all pass by as in a film, and in no instance is she addressed directly or involved in an active way. On the contrary, it is as if everything *living* left with the animals for an afterworld of images; thus a process takes place that is appropriate for old age, not for this early childhood.

We can perhaps draw only one conclusion from the amplification for the inner situation of the girl: that her soul is thirsty—thirsty for living water. And this dream originates in the living water, only she is not able to grasp it. That is why she confides in the father: maybe he can grasp it.

Parallel Motives

Dream	Psychology	Tantrism	Astrological Age
glass mouse		(*lingam*)	
worms		germ	
gray	shadow	world circle	Taurus, earth
snake		dragon	
red	animus	fire circle	Aries, fire
fish		gazelle	
blue	anima	firmament circle	Pisces, water
		ablution	
humans		circle of knowledge	
		seeing Purusha	
the human being	self	thousand-petaled circle	Aquarius, air
		knowledge of Atman	(human being, angel)
		vision of one's own self	

And when we look at it now in retrospect, we are most unsettled by what she conveys with it: "Father, here you have your little mouse. I am going to the beyond of the images, and I am leaving you this dream so that you know what happens and how it happens. I am becoming a subtle vessel, your point of crystallization. It is still only a pending possibility, but death and dissolution can make real what is only imagined now."

At a Later Meeting of the Seminar [5 February 1940]
Professor Jung: This dream was dreamed one or two years before the death of the child. I have chosen it from a series of twelve dreams,

357

and we will hear about still another dream from this series. All of them are extremely peculiar; I have come across only a few such dreams, and was surprised when I read them for the first time. At first I did not know at all what this might be about. We have to go through such dreams very thoroughly and carefully to find out approximately what they might tell. For this, the only appropriate method is amplification, because nothing of relevance can be deduced by reduction from the relatively meager visual language of the dream. This Freudian method would lead nowhere; we would finally arrive at some banal conclusion, perhaps something generally known. Some little misery or other would come to light.

If we conceive of this dream as a message of the unconscious, however, made in an oracular language, so to speak, we make a certain presupposition: we assume that the dream has a *meaning*. But as we cannot easily make a coherent whole out of the few visual notions, this meaning remains hidden to us for the moment. So it will not be immediately evident to us that this dream of the transparent mouse refers to the development of man, although its meaning seems to be expressed in the final sentence: "And that's how all men and women develop."

At first this ideational connection strikes us as very strange. If we did not know anything about the child, it would be hard to realize that there lies a destiny behind this dream, and that the dream does indeed refer to the end, which has already cast its invisible shadow. I saw the child myself at that time. She looked fragile, but was in no way ill. I would have never guessed at the time that an *exitus letalis*[172] might happen in the near future. The only thing I can say is that the child impressed me as a bit precocious. There was no neurosis, no hereditary taint by mental illnesses. I know the father and the mother and practically all the details about the family, so that I can exclude such a possibility. In the case of such strange dreams it is by no means absurd to think of a schizophrenia and to inquire after the hereditary taint; in any case this is a sign to be careful! Such dreams, which surprise us by their strangeness, also occur in other cases, namely, in children who have a touch of genius themselves or come from fami-

---

[172] Latin, "lethal ending" (trans.).

358

lies of geniuses. But in that case the dreams are of a different kind, and show a greater richness. The series from which this dream was taken, however, is not characterized by a very powerful fantasy; every single dream is actually meager and not drawn from the abundant wealth of the unconscious. It rather seems as if the child had sunk into the unconscious with a part of herself—perhaps favored by her weakness—and was subsequently permeated by thoughts and images that she then could grasp only in her childlike language.

In this dream, the essence is expressed in the final sentence: "That's how all men and women develop." This is the leitmotif of the dream, so to speak. Without any doubt this is a *general* idea, a conclusion that the dreamer herself draws. We now have to ask ourselves: What does it mean for the child when such an idea rises from the unconscious? What psychical state does this imply?

Participant: Perhaps the child's development did not proceed undisturbed, so that it has to be brought to her attention somehow.

Professor Jung: At first we have to take the generality of the idea as our starting point, and disregard the particularity of the development for the moment. Obviously, it is the dream's tendency to acquaint the child with the general idea that all humans develop. What does this mean for the child's consciousness?

Participant: The dream sounds like a primitive myth.

Professor Jung: This is correct, but this refers to the "how" of development, and not to the fact that development, as such, takes place. What could this mean: "That's how all men and women develop"? What meaning does this have? What does it imply? You always have to imagine a dream as like a conversation you overhear on the radio or the phone. Somebody says something, you hear a sentence of conversation, then the conversation breaks off again, and now you should reconstruct what had been said. That's how you should think of dreams. It is always a "listening in."[173] You just overhear something for a moment. Something becomes clear subliminally. You wake up with a sentence on your lips, but perhaps you've even forgotten the dream, too.

---

[173] This expression in English in the original (trans.).

We have to try to understand such a dream as an *answer* to the *conscious situation* of the child. What question may have preoccupied the child? Perhaps she asked herself: "How do people actually come into being?" Do you think that this is the question here?

Participant: No.

Professor Jung: Why not?

Participant: Because the sequence of the images in the dream is no biological developmental line. If this were the question, the dream would have to start with the parents.

Professor Jung: Yes, this is not about the question: where have I come from? The dream does not show a biological, but a completely different developmental line. At first we have to clarify the psychical situation of the child, because none of all that existed in her consciousness.

Participant: It seems as if she hadn't had the time to wait for the real development.

Participant: Perhaps the child felt she was somebody special, so that she had to be told: "You, too, are just one of all those."

Participant: Often persons whose death is imminent undergo an accelerated development. A whole life unrolls in a very short time. So it could be that the dreamer has experiences that anticipate her development, because she is marked by death.

Professor Jung: I have already mentioned a couple of times that we cannot apply our notion of time to the unconscious. Our consciousness can conceive of things only in temporal succession, our time is, therefore, essentially linked to the chronological sequence. In the unconscious this is different, because there everything lies together, so to speak. To some extent, in the unconscious we all still live in the past; in a way we are still very little children, and often only very little is needed for the "child" to come to the surface. At the same time, we are standing in the shadow cast by a future, of which we still know nothing, but which is already somehow anticipated by the unconscious.[174] So if the child is going to leave this world in the relatively near future, it is conceivable the unconscious has already in some way

[174] Cf. seminar 1 (ed.).

anticipated death. We can assume that the closeness of death has already cast its shadow on the soul of the child, and has raised questions in her such as: "Why did it come into being in the first place, if it will end anyway?" Or: "Why did it come into being? For what reason?" It must have been a *philosophical* question, because the answer is also philosophical. It is a question that we ask before we die: "Now what was this really all about?" Like the question that Newton himself answered on his deathbed—he said that he had played on the beach with the other boys, and had found a shell more beautiful than those of the others. This is such a philosophical answer to a philosophical question. The dream, too, also leads a kind of philosophical conversation, and the philosophical answer is: "That's how all men and women develop," meaning: "That's how humans, as such, come into being."

If we apply this hypothesis to the other dreams of the series, we will realize that actually each of the dreams is of a philosophical nature and contains the answer to a philosophical question. There is a dream, for example, that the dreamer titles "Heaven and Hell," which goes as follows:

> Once I went to heaven with a man. There were people there who danced heathen dances. Then we went to hell. There were angels, who did all the good.

This dream contains the idea of the relativity of good and evil. In a similar manner, this peculiar philosophical character recurs in all the dreams of this dream series, so that we find confirmation of our assumption that the present dream contains an answer to a philosophical question. The single dreams of a series are logically linked to one another, they express a common content and refer to one and the same psychical situation. When we have the key to one of these dreams, we will usually understand the whole series.[175]

What is surprising in this series is the strangely impersonal character of the individual dreams. The events are observed as from a distance of a million light years. It is very hard to feel into this; but then

[175] Cf. seminar 1 (ed.).

the dreams are so instructive precisely because they demonstrate man's existential questions without any reference to the ego. This is especially clear in the dream titled "The Evil Animal," which we will discuss in our next meeting. Also the dream called "The Island" by the dreamer has this strange, objective character:

> Once I was on an island, and it was full of little animals that crawled in all directions. This really scared me. Then they got terribly big, and one sassy bastard ate me up.

In all these dreams, the dreamer states quite matter-of-factly that that's how it was. But the situations are such that we would have to expect a much stronger emotional reaction, if, that is, there had been a connection to ego-consciousness.

How does the present dream portray the way men and women develop? It gives a description as we might find in the tribal lore of the primitives. A primitive cosmogonic fairy tale could sound quite similar. The dream is along the lines of ancient patterns, and, therefore, Mrs. Brunner has quite correctly traced these correspondences. Four different forms of transformation are distinguished, to which different colors are attributed. They correspond to a certain sequence of stages from animal to man. Here these stages are characterized by the gray mouse with the worms, the red mouse with the snakes, and the blue mouse with the fish; the final stage is man, to whom no color is assigned any longer. This sequence is quite imperfect, and seems to be a bit contradictory at first sight. So the stage of the fish, for example, comes after that of the snakes. What might be the reason for that?

Participant: For children and primitives the worms and the snakes belong together.

Professor Jung: Yes, of course. In former times the snake was also called worm, as, for instance, in *lindworm*.[176] Certain superficial similarities may have been the reason for this: they are of similar shape, they creep in the earth and in secret holes. Both are chthonic animals. Their equation is an expression of a very primitive view, how-

---

[176] A large serpentlike dragon without wings (trans.).

ever, because the anatomy of the snake is much more sophisticated than that of the worm. In phylogenesis, the snakes come after the fish, in accordance with their more highly developed nervous and respiratory systems.

The transformational forms of the mouse imply the idea of different worlds: the worms live in the earth, the fish in the water, and man actually belongs to the air world, because he carries his head in the air (what is missing, however, is the world of fire). Man's erect posture has already given rise to many philosophical reflections. It is not easy to classify the snakes in this context. Apparently, they did not always creep with their bellies on the ground, but were only later cursed to do so, as it says in the Bible: "Upon thy belly shalt thou go, and dust shalt thou eat all the days of thy life" (Genesis 3:14).

But why is it the mouse, of all animals, that is the medium of the development? We cannot give any compelling reasons for this, but Mrs. Brunner has given you enough evidence that the mouse is a *soul animal*. She has also quite correctly pointed to the transparency of the mouse and interpreted it as spirituality. Transparency is a criterion for the spirituality of matter. So the *lapis philosophorum* is also called *vitrum* (glass), precisely because it is of a spiritual nature, or *lapis aethereus*. So we have to imagine that the mouse, by virtue of its transparency, can form the spiritual vessel, in which the various transformations from animal to man take place. The starting point of this development is the gray mouse. The gray mouse is, as Mrs. Brunner has mentioned, an animal that stands in connection to the *darkness of the soul*; it represents that fleetingly glimpsed, dark nature of man that makes itself unpleasantly felt from time to time, above all at night. Mice are also allegories of *gnawing thoughts*, therefore, of pricks of conscience, that haunt us like spirits at night. These are chthonic animals with a certain relation to *death*. As deathly animals, they are brought in connection with Apollo. The Greeks worshipped *Phoebus Smintheus*, that is, the Mouse-Apollo, in whose temple mice were kept under the altar. There they were looked after and cared for, and in a way this had the meaning of apotropaic magic. We might ask what, for heaven's sake, Apollo, the sun god, should have to do with mice. Now we know that Apollo is not only the god of

363

light, but also the bearer of death, because his arrows can bring the plague, which is an illness that is spread by animals such as mice and rats. The mouse in general is an uncanny, deathly messenger. A great mouse plague is an evil omen for a country. This is understandable, because there were times when veritable mice epidemics broke out, when they multiplied in great numbers, destroyed all the crops, and caused famine and illness.

Participant: In *Faust* the mice also appear as *spirits*.

Professor Jung: Where?

Participant: When the pentagram prevents the devil from crossing the threshold.

Professor Jung: Yes, there Mephistopheles calls his assistants, the rats and the mice, that they should gnaw through the pentagram:

> "The Lord of Rats and Mice,
> Of Flies, Frogs, Bugs, and Lice,
> Summons you to venture here,
> And gnaw the threshold here."[177]

Participant: The gray color of the mouse is also the color of the spirits.

Professor Jung: Yes, it is the color of darkness and of the spirits. So, you see, for all these reasons we may understand the mouse as a dark and enigmatic starting point of the development. In Greek antiquity, for example, the mice that crept out of graves were considered the spirits of the dead, and were, therefore, taken care of and fed.

The same was true of the *snakes*. If such a snake from the grave came into the house, the whole family moved out, because the *spirit of the dead* had taken possession of the house (the same can also be found in certain primitive tribes!). In their capacity as spirits of the dead, snakes were even publicly worshipped in Greece. The snake that was worshipped in the Erechtheion on the Acropolis was considered to be the spirit of King Erechtheus or Erechthonios, who was buried there. Usually the living spirit of the dead was fed by sacrificed food offered to it through burial holes. The snake cult also had an

---

[177] *Faust 1*, lines 1516–19 (trans.).

apotropaic meaning, because snakes are animals that suddenly appear out of the darkness and, therefore, frighten people. Moreover, man is incapable of establishing a rapport with them. They are as enigmatic and frightening as the unconscious, so, since time immemorial, man has protected himself against them as he has done against the unconscious. Primitives, for example, wear amulets on each joint, and their whole life is completely regulated by an immense number of practices governed by fear. They live as if imprisoned within walls they have erected out of fear of their unconscious, for it might well play a sudden trick on them.

Snakes, and particularly red ones, are not only spirits of the dead, but can also represent *emotional* states, as you have heard in the paper. They stand for the heat of the soul, the fire of passion, and thus represent a more intense stage of development.

The *fish*, the next transformational form of the mouse, represent the water element. Here the chthonic quality recedes into the background, and the spiritual begins. Mrs. Brunner has quite correctly pointed out that fish are like thoughts and premonitions that rise from the unconscious. There is an analogy in alchemy: when the primordial water, the *humidum radicale*, is sufficiently heated up, something like fish eyes (that is, steam bubbles) appears in it. This is what is most precious in fish, that which is capable of being illuminated. We may here interpret the fish, therefore, as the transition into *spiritual* element, into the air. In creation there was only the primordial water at first, which also contained the air. Then, it says, God divided the waters which were under the firmament from the waters which were above the firmament.[178] The lower waters border the underworld, but the upper waters are the spirit. According to alchemical philosophy, the spirit of life becomes visible here, the Holy Spirit. The upper waters form the body of the *pneuma* and are a kind of *corpus spirituale*, or a *spiritus corporalis*, a subtle spirit. At the final stage, humans come into being.

As we have heard, different *colors* correspond to the four stages. We mentioned already that the color *gray* is the color of ghosts. Gray

[178] Genesis 1:7 (trans.).

is a combination color; it is semidarkness, in which light just starts to emerge from complete blackness. In alchemy, *nigredo* is the initial state, in which death reigns, absolute *unconsciousness*. Then follows the *albedo*, that is, whitening. The alchemists call it the rising sun that brings the morning and the crack of dawn. In this respect there is a certain analogy to the stage of the gray mouse.

In alchemy, *red* comes after white: after dawn comes sunrise, and after sunrise the full sun. In Greek alchemy, the complete constellation is called the "midday position of the sun." When the sun reaches its zenith, the meaning of the day is fulfilled. What has been prepared during the night has now reached its highest perfection. In other contexts, too, the finished body is called *rubinus* or *carbunculus* in alchemy. It is a more intense state than *albedo*. Red, as it is, is an emotional color and stands for *blood*, *passion*, and *fire*.

The *blue* color is assigned to the following stage. Blue stands in stark contrast to red and indicates a cool and calming state. Blue is the color of Mary's mantle in heaven. She is the womb in which Christ was born, and has always represented the symbol of a spiritual *vessel*. Blue is also the color of water and can thus represent the unconscious: just as we see the fish in the clear blue of the water, the spiritual contents contrast with the darkness of the unconscious. The color blue cannot be found in alchemy, but it is found in the East, where it takes the place of black and actually represents a color of the underworld. In Egypt, too, Osiris in the underworld is portrayed in black or blue. It is more a bluish-green color that characterizes not only the underworld (Osiris as the "Master of Green"), but also the water world. This world corresponds to the "lower waters," in which the animals live as disembodied spirits. Thus blue is also the bluish-green sea that houses the spirits of the dead. The fourth stage is man, to whom no color is assigned.

So the development occurs in *four* stages, and this is no coincidence. This is the most frequently found structure, as, for instance, in a basic law of alchemy, according to which the process of transformation occurs in four stages. This gives expression to the idea that everything human develops out of something *divided into four*. In the legend of paradise, the river that flows out of the Garden of Eden parts and becomes

366

four riverheads.[179] This image has been taken up by the Gnostics to illustrate the development of the inner human being. According to Simon Magus, paradise is the uterus, and the Garden of Eden the navel. Four flows emanate from the navel, two air- and two blood-vessels, so to speak, through which the growing child receives its food, the blood, and the *pneuma*. In antiquity, the world was classified into four elements, to which also four temperaments corresponded. Four reemerges in the work of Schopenhauer in the theorem of the Fourfold Root of the Principle of Sufficient Reason. In Christianity, the division into four is expressed by the symbol of the cross. Where else does the division into four appear in Christianity?

Participant: In the *benedictio fontis*.

Professor Jung: Yes, in it the priest divides the water in the form of the cross, he seemingly divides it into four parts. In this way he repeats the beginning of creation. By this act the water becomes the mysterious, eternal, and divine water, by which man is cleansed of all sinfulness and impurity. The ablution, as it were, puts him back into the primordial state of innocence.

Apart from the four there are, of course, still other sacred numbers, but in each case of totality *quaternity* plays an important role, be it about the most primitive or the most elaborate ideas. The four always expresses the coming into being of what is essentially human, the *emergence of human consciousness*. Thus, the alchemical process also begins with such a division into the four elements, by which the body is put back into its primordial state and so can undergo transformation.

9. Dream of a Ten-Year-Old Girl of the Evil Animal[180]
Presented by Dr. Jolande Jacobi[181]

Text: The Evil Animal. *Once I saw an animal in a dream, and it had very many horns. With these it gored other little animals. It coiled up like a snake, and was up to its tricks. Then blue smoke came from all four corners, and it stopped eating. Then came the Good Lord, but actually there*

---

[179] Genesis 2:10 (trans.).
[180] Sessions of 20 and 27 February 1940.
[181] Dr. Jacobi's paper is missing (ed.).

were four good gods in the four corners. Then the animal died, and all the eaten animals came out alive.

Professor Jung: As you have seen, this dream is rather difficult and, given the young age of the dreamer, really remarkable. It is a product of the unconscious such as we rarely come across. As in the dream we discussed last time, the expression is basically simple. But that is precisely the astonishing thing. At first glance we are nearly unable to form a picture of what it might mean. Initially one does not have the courage to draw such far-reaching parallels as Dr. Jacobi, and to assume the presence of such fundamental problems of the history of mankind in a child's mind. But there's absolutely no way around it, because we can be sure: the simpler a dream is, the more we are confronted with general and fundamental problems. For it is only a deceptive simplicity, due to the fact that the dream, despite the importance of its content, has not found enough substance to express itself. We could compare it to a framework of archetypes, for which there is already a disposition at the beginning of life, and which is gradually filled with substance in the course of development. If a primordial image forces itself onto consciousness, we have to fill it with as much substance as possible to grasp the whole scope of its meaning. Basically, in our dream only *axes* are hinted at, which express the *core content* of the image in a very general way. The poverty of the composition strangely contrasts with the importance of the content. At first there is a horned animal, a kind of dragon, which gores all the other animals. It is a destructive monster that brings death to all living beings. We could say: this is death. Then the deity appears, actually divided into four gods, and reverses the whole process. The monster dies, and the little animals can come out alive again. This is a typical *enantiodromia*, which is already contained *in nuce* in the two extreme figures of the deity and the dragon. This is about the age-old confrontation of man with god and devil, these two poles of the world into which he is put. It is a deep-rooted dream of mankind, which reaches down into unfathomable depths. Here it could not assume a more complete form, however, because there is still too little experiential material in an infantile mind.

We could ask ourselves: How come a child has such a dream? It is a completely pagan dream, whose symbols can barely be still detected in Christianity. We do find such images in the apocalypse, but there they are in such a complex context, and in such cryptic form, that today we are hardly able still to understand them. So we may assume with reasonable certainty that the child did not get these images from the New Testament. Moreover, she grew up in a family that did not attach much value to religious education. The ancient historical images, so immensely attractive to children's fantasy, no longer play any role at all today. This is a loss for our souls, because we don't give the soul a language to give expression to its contents. In religious instruction, we more and more refrain from making children acquainted with these images, and instead offer them moral teaching, in which the devil is ignored altogether. But as this dream concerns an evil animal, which obviously represents the devil, we can be rather sure that the child did not get this image from school. So we may probably exclude an influence on this picture from the outside. The infantile soul is no *tabula rasa* at all, as presumed by modern psychology, but the ancient images are always already there a priori.

Mrs. Jacobi has assembled excellent material, which enabled her to give a nearly complete explanation of the images. I have nothing basically new to add, and would just like to make a few amendments. What is remarkable is that the dream is divided into two parts. We can distinguish a first, "descending" part from a following, "ascending" one. These two parts correspond to the earlier-mentioned polar structure of the dream. The dragon as representative of the first part symbolizes the organism in its two aspects of life and destruction. It represents the being that in China is expressed by the yin principle. The ascending part, in contrast, leads into the blue smoke, into the air, which by its nature corresponds to the yang principle. It is the smoke that rises from the earth, and which contains the gods as spiritual beings or smoke figures. Through them rebirth takes place. The primordial image of the division into two, preceding each creation, is also found in Genesis; there, the darkness of the depths—the lower waters—is incubated by the spirit of God hovering above it. Thus they are impregnated, and the creatures of the world emerge from them.

369

The first, descending part of the dream takes place, so to speak, in the lower waters, that is, in the unconscious. The dragon gores the *many little animals*, so they are doomed. The feature of *multiplicity*, here in combination with the animals, is an essential characteristic of all inherently unconscious life processes. This phenomenon is also frequently found in illnesses that are on the border between the psychical and the physical, for instance, disorders of the sympathetic nervous system or also states of intoxication. In the hallucinations during a delirium tremens often a great number of mice, insects, or also people, appears. This multiplicity is closely connected to the nature of the sympathetic nervous system, because its function is neither centralizing nor unifying, but branching and disseminating into the individual life of each cell. The image of the many little animals that are devoured thus indicates a dissolution and a destruction of organic life in this child. A death is taking place, so to speak. This process of destruction, by the way, is also hinted at in other dreams of this series, in which there is also a mass of animals, as in the dream entitled "A Severe Illness" by the child. It goes as follows:

Once I dreamed that I had a severe illness. Suddenly many birds came out of my skin, and they all sat down on my legs and on my whole body.

The phenomenon of multiplicity does not necessarily appear only in the case of an organic problem, as in this case, but can also indicate a *dissolution of the person, the individual,* into the collective environment. Multiplicity, as such, is characteristic of any inherently unconscious life process. The more unconsciously a process takes its course in a person, the stronger it is dissolved in the sphere of multiplicity, in the region of the many, of the others, of the mass, of the collective. In these cases it is often difficult to prove that such a process still belongs at all within the sphere of the individual. It is rather as if it were "in the air" and belonged to the many; therefore, it is also represented by the many. I would like to illustrate this with a typical dream:

Someone dreams that he comes to me in my practice. On the way, he meets lots of acquaintances and relatives, which annoys him. Now every-

body knows that he is going to Dr. Jung. Then he enters my room, and
again there are lots of people, so he can't speak.

Here the unconscious state of the dreamer is hinted at by the multiplicity. He is "scatterbrained," not centered, that is, not brought together into one. When someone is in such a state, every psychological process is contagious and leads to peculiar phenomena of participation.[182] On the one hand, deep psychical stirrings in the individual may then affect the whole environment, and, on the other hand, the individual is carried away when the environment is seized by some psychical momentum. When you are in a crowd that gets agitated you will be infected, even if you do not share the people's conviction. You can't do anything against it, because nothing is passed on more easily than emotions. It goes straight into the unconscious, and then it is nearly impossible to hold out as an individual. This is also how religious collective experiences work, in which each individual at the same time experiences the many, the others. All are united with one another, and in all the same state of multiplicity predominates. There is something destructive in this multiplicity; it turns against the unity of consciousness and dissolves it. Wherever the multiple occurs, there is a *conflict* between the unity of the ego and the multiplicity of the persons in the environment. The person is, in other words, under too much pressure from the environment, from the opinion of other people, and from what is written in the newspaper. It can very frequently be proven that "the many" represent as many resistances and prejudices, which thwart the unity of the individual. So in the dream some aunt may say: "Oh dear, now what are you doing, going to Dr. Jung?" Or the father and the priest raise their objections. The psyche will then be decomposed into many single units, and we actually will have to put the person together again so that he regains his unity. So there is a great deal of collective psychology in the motif of the many little animals.

Thus our dream not only concerns the soul of this single child, but it pertains to much more, namely, to her parents, siblings, and the

---

[182] This word in French (or English) in the original (trans.).

whole environment. I have to add that the child is from a German family, and that the father was very active politically. So there is no doubt that there is a great emphasis on the environment, and when exciting things happen there the child will be forced to take part in the emotional state of the family.

The first part of the dream represents the dissolution of the individual into multiplicity; the second part shows the complete reversal of the process: the dissolution is followed by the *synthesis*. It occurs in the upper layer as represented by the blue smoke. It says in the dream: "Then blue smoke came from all four corners," and then: "Then came the Good Lord, but actually there were four good gods in the four corners." The deity is something like vapor or smoke, rising into the air from below. Simultaneously the principle of *fourness* appears: it is the *tetras*, the quaternity, which is always the symbol of composition, of bringing order into the chaos. We saw already last hour that dividing the chaos into the four elements is the primeval act of the seeing spirit; it is the attempt to bring order into the chaotic plenitude of phenomena. The division into four is a *principium individuationis*; it means to become one or a whole in the face of the many figures that carry the danger of destruction in them. It is what overcomes death and can bring about *rebirth*. In our dream, the appearance of the four gods causes the death of the evil dragon animal, by which *life* can *begin again*: the many little animals all come out again.

The dragon as the dominating power in the first part of the dream prepares for the advent of the deity. It is the devil, the devouring animal of the underworld that swallows everything. But when it has devoured enough, it will have eaten its way into its own demise. Events turn, and the second phase reestablishes order. Thus the devil is a preliminary stage of individuation, in the negative it has the same goal as the divine quaternity, namely, wholeness. Although it is still darkness, it already carries the germ of light within itself.[183] Its activities are still dangerous and deadly, but at the same it is like the darkness of earth in which the seed germinates. In the dream it is, therefore, followed by the blue smoke, which rises from the depths

[183] Cf. seminar 3, § 8 (ed.).

in the four corners, and in which the divine quaternity, the whole-ness, becomes visible.

The fact that *deity and devil belong together* also plays a great role in alchemy. There the devil appears in the form of the *serpens Mercurii*, which, however, is at the same time the serpent of the Nous. For the Naassenes, too, the *nachash*,[184] the serpent, is the Nous, or the Logos. Psychologically speaking, the fact that the Logos at first manifests it-self as a poisonous snake means that whenever a powerful content emerges from the unconscious, which we cannot yet grasp with our consciousness, there is a danger that the whole ego-consciousness will be pulled down into the unconscious and dissolved. This intro-version process can eventually lead to mental illness. Consciousness is completely emptied, because its contents are attracted by the un-conscious as by a magnet. This process leads to a complete loss of the ego, so that the person in question becomes a mere automaton. Such a person is actually no longer there. He makes the impression of a piece of wood that lets itself be pushed around. He has completely lost his initiative and spontaneity, because his consciousness has been dissolved by a content of the unconscious. In the process of in-dividuation, too, new contents can announce themselves in this de-vouring form and darken consciousness; this is experienced as a de-pression, that is to say, as being pulled downward. As the unconscious has a tendency to project itself into the outer world, there is a dan-ger that one might get dissipated in the environment, instead of stay-ing with oneself. That's why the alchemists stress again and again that the alchemical vessel has to remain hermetically closed during the *opus*. If the lid springs open, vapor will escape and the process will be disrupted. Only when we bear our situation and accept our de-pression will it be possible for us to change internally. Then the de-vouring animal will be deprived of its power, and the new content can be grasped by consciousness.

In the dream, the dragon animal appears as a *horned figure*, al-though the child does not specify the number of horns. The image of the horned serpent is very frequent in mythology. *Seven horns* stand

---

[184] Hebrew word for "serpent," from which the Naassenes received their name (trans.).

in connection with the seven days of the week, to each of which a planet is assigned; in seven days the moon completes one phase (one week), and in four times seven days queen Luna, accompanied by the seven planets, wanders across the sky. The idea of the seven planets also plays a great role in alchemy. There they sit together in a sub-terranean cave; they are the seven that are hidden in the womb of the earth. Here the seven are representatives of the metals. When the dragon has *twelve* horns, this corresponds to the twelve months or the twelve signs of the zodiac. So we can say: the animal in the dream carries on its head, like a diadem or a crown, either the *hebdomas*, the seven planets, or the *dodekas*, the twelve signs of the zodiac. In antiquity the image of the horned serpent was projected onto the sky. It appears in the well-known image of Draco, which meanders as a shining ribbon of stars, as *sky serpent*, between the Great and the Little Bear and, while always visible, moves around the pole.[185] The world fire burns in this place, and, therefore, it is also called the fire pole. There the dragon rotates, eternally watching the objects in the sky. Now, we must not think that the ancients actually saw bears and snakes in the sky; this is a mythology inherent in all of us, which everybody can, therefore, reproject onto the sky. Thus our science has started with the stars. There our world consciousness came into being, and from there we took our science. Our deepest inner layers are hidden in the stars. When it is said that old Aratus interpreted the constellations mythologically, this is nonsense. He did not interpret anything, but everything has always been as it is. This sky serpent, the Draco, is the reproduction of a primeval image within ourselves.

Later, at the begin of the Christian era, Gnostic natural philosophers tried to incorporate these projections of the serpent into man, and to conceive of them as a part of the human structure. The body of the serpent became the spinal cord, its head the brain. This anatomical localization of the archetype contains an excellent interpretation, insofar as the lower psychical centers of the spinal cord

---

[185] In astronomy, the constellation of Corona (crown) is not directly above the head of Draco, but this is irrelevant for the mythological interpretation.

are without doubt the seat of the unconscious. Already the sky serpent, which winds around the mysterious North Pole, was based on
the idea of the *serpent as the seat of the unconscious.*[186] It revolves as
if around its own center. The world axis goes through the pole; it is
in some sense the center of the world, but also the center of the unconscious around which everything revolves. There the deity, the
ruler of the pole, moves the whole firmament as if he had it on a handle. The same idea can be found in the Mithraic liturgy, in which
God swings the shoulder of a cow in his right hand. This is the Great
Bear, which rotates around the pole like the dragon. A similar image
of rotating serpents is found in the so-called Tantric Yoga, in which
the Kundalini serpent winds three and a half times around the *lingam*,
the phallus of Shiva.

So if we take a very close look at the dragon with its mysterious
horn, we will see that it also represents the *deity*, only in a different,
dark aspect. In the dream the dragon is followed by the blue smoke,
rising out of the four corners, and thus being divided into four. It represents the positive aspect of the deity. To conclude, I would like to
make some additions to the important notion of quaternity. We often
find it portrayed in Christian images, although it actually does not
belong to the dogma; the latter is the Trinity, the threeness. Quaternity is basically a pagan notion and much older than Christiantiy.
Originally it goes back to Pythagoras, who saw in quaternity the root
of eternal nature. It is a number that expresses the inner essence of
nature. This meaning has remained preserved through all times. In
Christianity, for example, we have the picture of the *rex gloriae*, the
triumphant Christ, who sits enthroned amidst the four Evangelists.
Frequently their animal symbols are found instead of the Evangelists;
three of them are symbolized by an animal, and only John, the fourth
Evangelist, by an angel. There are pictures from the Romanesque age,
in which the Evangelists are portrayed with the heads of their respective animals: Mark with the lion head, Matthew with the eagle
head, Luke with the head of a calf or an ox. The four symbols of the
Evangelists have also been condensed to *one* animal, so that a *tetra-*

[186] Cf. seminar 3, § 3.

morphous emerged, a fourfold being, which served as the mount of the Church.

In the Gnostics, too, we find a portrayal of the Son of God on a platform on four pillars, the *tetrapeza*. The four legs are the four pillars, which represent the four Gospels. The Gnosis is rich in portrayals of quaternity. You know, perhaps, the Gnostic "Anthropos," the primordial man, who is symbolized by the city with the four gates. He is the Autogenes, the one who gives birth to himself. He is also surrounded by two parental couples, that is, four persons. Moreover, in Irenaeus we find the idea of the upper mother (Anometer), the Barbelo. She is the female appearance of the deity. Her name is interpreted as "in the four there is God."

In numerous Gnostic systems there are such and similar ideas, sometimes in the form that three further principles are deduced from a basic one. Or the ideas are more Aristotelian, meaning that originally there are four elements, and the fifth, the *quinta essentia*, is their center. For Aristotle this is the ether. So the four is thought of as 3 + 1, or simply as 4, or as 4 + 1. In the latter case, however, the result is not the five—which would be an expression of the state of unconsciousness—but the *quinta essentia*, which is always the extract or the origin of the four. In alchemy, the idea of a month is a basic principle. It is also called the *prima materia*, and the four elements develop out of it. Out of these, in turn, the *monas* develops, which represents the spiritual unity of the four.

Here, too, quaternity is the unfolding of the one; it becomes a *system of orientation for consciousness*. An example is the division of the horizon into four parts. In addition, the four elements provide a first orientation in the world, and the four temperaments are an orientation in the chaotic psychical nature of man. In accordance with these, the principles of human life were localized in the body in a kind of system of *chakras*, namely, in the brain, in the heart, in the liver, and in the genitalia. So, amongst others, reason and the sanguine temperament were associated with the brain, courage and the choleric temperament with the heart, the warmth of life and the melancholic temperament with the liver.

In alchemy, the division into four plays a very special role insofar

376

as the nature of Mercurius is the cross. In his fourfoldness he expresses the *unity of the opposites*. Mercurius is the most peculiar and paradoxical being imaginable; he is also called the *servus* or *cervus fugitivus*,[187] he who can never be caught and who runs through the fingers like quicksilver. Mercurius is composed of four *mercurii*; their names are:

1. *mercurius brutus*, the brute Mercurius, that is, common quicksilver (mercury);
2. *mercurius sublimatus*, Mercurius as a spiritual being;
3. *mercurius magnesiae*, magnesium as the *vera alba*, the pure substance, the shining wisdom, and the great light;
4. *mercurius unctuosus*, the unctuous Mercurius, which gives expression to the darkest darkness that we find in the interior of the earth and of matter. It is thought of as slimy, gooey, viscous, unctuous matter.

This Mercurius divided into four parts is in accordance with the idea of Mercurius as a hermaphrodite. For he is the Re-Bis, the male-female, who holds the new light. In the Middle Ages we find the idea that the unharmed virgin, who in turn is Mercurius, is living in the interior of the earth. The alchemists were convinced that God had put a spiritual substance into the world, so that it would be transformed by man into the substance that brings salvation.

Regarding the polar appearance of the deity, there is a parallel in the meditations of Przywara,[188] in which God appears as *concurrence of the opposites*. When He manifests Himself, this happens in a *conflict*, on the cross. Here you can see the whole symbolism. The conflict situation seems to have been the origin out of which *consciousness* developed, and *still develops anew again and again*. We still witness this nowadays, day after day. Nobody will ever become conscious if he does not hit his head on something.

Now why should the child dream of such problems? This I don't

---

[187] Fugitive servant or deer (trans.).

[188] Erich Przywara, *Deus semper maior* (ed.) See www.helmut-zenz.de/hzprzywa.html (14 March 2007) (trans.).

know. We can only state that this is what happened. The child has been told a truth, the absolute, basic truth of humankind, for which there is no proof, of course. The proof lies in the truth itself. It is expressed by the soul and by what human beings have thought since time immemorial. These are the truths that live forever.

Seminar on Children's Dreams
(Winter Term, 1940/41)

A. CHILDREN'S DREAMS
Further remarks on the interpretation of dreams[1]
(PROFESSOR JUNG)

Professor Jung: We are dealing here with children's dreams of a particular kind, which are very often not understood correctly, because it is thought that these dreams are being observed in children—that is, are directly recorded by the father or the mother. We are not dealing with such dreams, however, but with children's dreams that have been remembered by adults. So a selection of these dreams has already been made. These are dreams that have stood the test of time and persisted. If someone had written down the dreams of your childhood, for instance, and you read these notes again later, they would be completely foreign to you, and you yourself would not be able to remember them. But *some* of the dreams have lingered on, as fresh as on the first day. This is the kind of dreams we are dealing with here. Partly I have collected these dreams myself, partly they have been told to me by participants in the seminar. As soon as the problem of a dream is no longer acute, that is, it is solved and outgrown, the dream vanishes from memory. If it still persists in memory, however, the problem has not been solved, or the dream touched on something that one perhaps still hasn't understood yet, or never will. Phenom-

[1] Meeting of 29 October 1940.

ena and contents are touched on that are completely unconscious for ordinary mortals. And these things exert an enormous influence on the shape of subsequent destiny and, therefore, get stuck in memory. Such dreams are of special importance, because in a way their content anticipates a problem of later life. These dreams in particular make us understand why the ancients attributed a pronounced prognostic meaning to their dreams. Throughout the whole of antiquity, and to a large extent still in the Middle Ages, it was believed that dreams foretell the future. Our consciousness is directed only outward, light only falls onto this world, but it throws no light backward, on the thinker of the thoughts and the doer of the deeds. If consciousness does do it, however, it throws light on the basis of consciousness, on the unconscious, and there things may be brought to life, just as we can enliven reality by observing it.

As far as the work with the dream is concerned, we first of all structure the dream as a story, as a course of events; the dream is a drama taking place on the inner stage, and a true drama of course always has—like any course of action—a beginning, a middle, and an end. So, to begin with, we determine the *exposition* of the dream, in which the specific place, the time, specific persons, and a specific problem are exposed. Usually you can already find it in the first sentence of the dream. For you have to break down the text into sentences and thus work out the problem—it is about this and that. This is the first part. The second part is the *development of the problem*. This means: the problem stated at the beginning starts to have an effect, it gets complicated, the plot thickens, a certain development occurs. This leads, in the third place, to the *peripateia*, a certain escalation that may become truly dramatic: it leads to a climax in which the turn of events then happens. The latter constitutes a change—it can be a decision, for example, or something occurs that throws a completely different light on the problem. This leads us to the fourth part, the *lysis*, the result of the dream that, of course, is not final or complete as in a conscious drama. Most of the time, the end is somehow enigmatic, not really satisfactory to our taste. But, in any case, this is the result for that moment. In series, the end usually presents a new problem. One is dead, or somebody else is dead, or something completely

380

out of the way has happened. This then remains as a question. Some impossible situation presents itself, and then we have to ask ourselves: what will happen next? What can be done? An answer is given by the next dream, perhaps the same night, after a hiatus. The second dream takes the problem up again in a different form.

Once this structuring has been done, we can start to truly work on the dream, that is, to look for the corresponding context for each motif. This is not the same as free association, which just leads you from one thing to another; one doesn't need a dream for that, but one might as well let someone associate about a button, and one will of course also arrive at the complexes. This does not prove at all that these complexes are also represented in the dream. By free association we won't know yet what the dream means; because the dream does not consist of the complexes, but represents the way in which they are dealt with. It represents what the unconscious does with the complex and how it tries to solve the dilemma. Our look at the complex is a look at the associative *connections* to the dream image. We have to know what it means for somebody to dream of an elephant, not what *I* as an analyst think about an elephant, but what connections it has for the person who had the dream. Perhaps one had been to a zoo the evening before, the other had been in the wilderness and had an experience with an elephant, or a third had been told by his wife: you are such a clumsy elephant, and so on. For each of them the elephant means something different. You have to carefully inquire about the events of the previous day. In recording these contexts, you have to encourage the person whose dream you analyze not to make *free* associations, but always to stay with the image. For the dream image is nothing accidental, otherwise we'd have to say that anything in nature is accidental, a chaos, and that there is no explanation. We have to assume that the dreams take place in a world according to laws, that there exists a certain causality, not just pure arbitrariness. There are specific reasons why the dream is precisely what it is, and not something different. Now when you investigate the single dream images with regard to the context, you will find that certain contents—not in all dreams by far—are of an archetypal nature, meaning that these latter forms of ideas are of a collective na-

381

ture and can be found everywhere. Naturally, you will not be able to recognize them if you aren't already knowledgeable about such ideas. One has to have the corresponding material at one's fingertips in order to recognize archetypal figures. This gives the dream an additional, very special character. You can then determine into which depths the dream reaches. The archetypes always appear as mythological figures or motifs.

The final act consists in the *interpretation*: one formulates a hypothesis about the possible meaning of the dream. This formulation has to be concise. You have to insert, in other words, the expressions you found into the dream text, to reformulate the dream, but this time with the found expressions. Then you will find the meaning of the dream.

> 1. *Dreams of a Four- to Five-Year-Old Girl of Her Father*
> *as a Menacing Giant, of a Pergola and a Dachshund,*
> *and of Exercising in a Barn*
> PRESENTED BY DR. IGNAZ REICHSTEIN[2]

Text: 1. *I'm lying in my bed and watch how the door to my parents' bedroom slowly opens. My father appears in the opening, but it's a mighty giant; he looks ferocious and threatens me with a club. I wake up frightened.*

2. I'm standing in front of an endless pergola; a little dachshund jumps out of it and comes toward me. I am so scared that I wake up.

3. I am in a very big, high barn, and under the roof I climb from one beam to another.

Dr. Reichstein: In the first dream, the locale and the persons are: the dreamer's bedroom beside the parental bedroom, the dreamer herself, and her father as a giant. Peripateia: the door to the parents' bedroom opens, the father appears in the form of a giant and threatens the dreamer with a club. The lysis is missing.

The dreamer is in her bed next to the bedroom of the parents, usually a very protected, intimate place, in immediate proximity of the parents. We are in bed before or during sleep, thus in a state in which the unconscious is particularly activated.

---

[2] Session of 29 October 1940.

382

Then the dreamer sees how the door to the parents' bedroom slowly opens. She catches sight of the place where the unconscious of the parents is activated. Above all, this is the sphere of sexuality and the place of procreation.

From there the father comes in the form of a mighty giant, threatening her with a club. The *giant* is an archetypal figure. In German mythology, the giants are described as follows: they are primordial natural beings, mostly appearing in groups, displaying little individual character. In the *Edda*, Ymir, a primordial giant, develops out of the primordial waters, out of whose body parts the world was built. The giants stand in contrast to the gods; they are coarse creatures, indifferent to morality, who know only fleshly pleasures such as getting drunk and overeating. On the other hand, as the eldest beings, they possess a knowledge of primordial things, an uncreated and traditional wisdom. Utgard, their dwelling place, lies outside the circular earth, along the sea coast, or beyond the world ocean, which was thought of as a small strip—thus, in a place outside the world. According to another myth, they are underground, in the womb of the waters or of the hollow mountains. The gods had erected a protective barrier, the fortress Midgard (the land of man), against the attacks of the giants. Gods and giants constantly fight against each other, as is particularly evident in the *Götterdämmerung*, the twilight of the gods, in which giants and gods destroy each other in a final battle.

In ancient mythology, giants and dragons often turn into each other, and enforced human sacrifices had to be made to them. Later heroes, who took the place of the gods, put an end to these sacrifices by defeating the giants, freeing the treasures guarded by them, and saving the princesses who had been destined to be their victims.

In Greek mythology, the giants are also sons of the earth and adversaries of the gods. In the *Gigantomachia*, the battle between the gods and the giants, the latter can be defeated only with the help of a mortal, which task falls to Heracles.

The *club* is the primitive weapon of the giants, but often also of the gods. Grimm writes: "Stones and rocks are the weapons of the race of the giants; they use only stone clubs, stone shields, no swords."

The god Thor, too, the main opponent of the giants, is armed with a hammer or a club. It also corresponds to the thunderbolts and the flash of lightning, by which the club also assumes a fertilizing character, as can already be seen from its typically phallic form. In *Frauenlob*, Simrock mentions a passage in which a virgin says about God the Father: "the smith from the upper land threw a hammer into my lap/womb."[3] The lightning also throws wedge-shaped thunder stones as deep into the earth as church towers are high, "nine fathoms deep," which rise again to the surface of the earth after seven or nine years.

To summarize, the giants can be characterized as follows: they are chaotic, untamed, natural, instinctual creatures; insatiable and destructive in their carnal greed, if they are not reined in by the gods to be more benevolent.

We can now see in what form the father approaches the girl. The figure of the father comes out of the sphere of the parental bedroom, with which all kinds of awakening ideas are associated in a child of this age, but he is very different from how he is during the day. Defenseless and undressed, she is lying in her bed, in precisely the place where she otherwise feels protected. The father, the person who alone could protect her, is no longer present, only the monster that threatens her with a club. It is remarkable, by the way, that the mother does not appear at all. Only the mention of the parents' bedroom lets us think of the mother, and if we envisage the situation—the father, who comes out of the parents' bedroom as a mighty giant with the club—we will involuntarily think: either the mother, too, is helpless against this brute, or he has killed her already. As the dream is not about just any giant, but precisely about the father, we may assume that the dream uncovers the father's unconscious attitude toward the daughter. So the father places extreme demands on the daughter. As the dream has no lysis, we are all the more justified in concluding that the child is in an endangered position.

The second dream goes: *I'm standing in front of an endless pergola; a little dachshund jumps out of it and comes toward me. I am so scared that I wake up.*

---

[3] On lap/womb, see seminar 4 (trans.).

Locale and persons: In front of an endlessly long pergola, the dreamer, and a little dachshund.

Peripateia: The little dachshund jumps toward her.

The lysis is missing.

The dreamer stands before a long pergola. A pergola is a walkway in an arbor, resting on pillars, which are often entwined by vine branches. The term is of Italian origin. It is a civilized setting, a cultivated piece of nature with a southern flair, where one goes for leisurely walks. If one is standing before such an endlessly long pergola, however, one's gaze will necessarily be directed in a certain direction, into the endlessness out there. In temporal terms, we could interpret it as a look into the future. From there a little dachshund is jumping toward the dreamer. Ordinarily, a dachshund is a droll and cute animal, of which one is usually not supposed to be afraid. So why is the dreamer so scared by it?

As a dog, that is, as an instinctual animal, the dachshund represents the instinctual sphere of man. According to Brehm, it is the most peculiar and curious of all dogs. Despite its smallness, it is strong and courageous. It is intelligent, quick to learn, but also crafty and malicious. It is not afraid of other dogs, even bigger ones. It is single-minded when hunting, and with unequaled greed and determination pursues its way until it reaches its goal. It especially likes to rout out other animals that live underground, like the badger or the fox, which it drives out of their holes with unbridled ardor and hardly controllable hunting fever. Its body shape, nearly without legs like a worm or mole, is reminiscent of the shape of the club in the first dream. Again it is the natural instinct that confronts the girl from the outside, as if in the future. This time it takes a less threatening, more domesticated form, not monstrous and brutally destructive, but still eager to hunt, scenting out and inexorably chasing its prey. There is still another antagonist to the giants besides the gods: Tom Thumb, or the youngest child, who is always more than what he seems. The dachshund, the smallest among the dogs, can so be seen under this aspect with regard to the giants. Because of its quickness, craftiness, and smallness it can get into anything and seems to be

385

everywhere. By this it compensates for the enormous dimensions of the giant. Under certain circumstances, Tom Thumb himself becomes a giant, as is the case in a Grimm fairy tale. So the anxiety of the girl would be understandable. While the giant represents the coarse and inert side of the instinct, the dachshund embodies the small, agile, and all-penetrating instinctual principle. It is impossible to get out of its way, therefore, which is symbolized in the dream by the arbor walk bordered on both sides, where one can move only forward or backward, just like in life itself. So she finds herself between these two opposites. Just like the first one, this dream also ends without a solution.

The third dream goes: *I am in a very big, high barn, and under the roof I climb from one beam to another.*

Locale and persons: The barn, the dreamer.
Peripateia: The dreamer climbs from one beam to another under the roof.
The lysis is missing.

The *barn* is where the crops are securely stored, it is part of every farm. Mostly it is a simple, plain building, where the corn is also threshed.

According to the *Handbook of German Superstition*, it is a place favored by demons. The beams, too, are favorite places of the spirits. The roof protects against rain, snow, and coldness, but not against the dreaded stroke of lightning. In *Rheinische Volkskunde* [*Rhenish Folklore*], Wrede describes various rituals to ward off strokes of lightning.

In this dream, the dreamer is alone in a place that is more primitive than, for instance, a pergola. In contrast to her previous passive behavior, she now moves from one beam to another. At first glance this activity seems to be pointless, because it resembles a swinging to and fro, which always takes one back to the starting point. Although she is in a relatively secure place, she is in a highly insecure position and, moreover, in constant motion, always in danger of falling down. The barn is incredibly high, maybe so high that not even a giant could reach the top. As near to the roof as possible, perhaps comparable to the firmament, she is in the sphere of the demons, far re-

386

moved from the ground, in constant motion from one beam to another, in which ghosts dwell, as if she were forced forward and backward by them.

This dream also leaves the girl without lysis in a dangerous situation. If we interpret the barn as an anticipation of her own adulthood, however, we can conclude that she will prefer always to remain in the upper regions of her own person, and anxiously avoid descending into her instinctual sphere. This tense and labile state clearly shows us the dangerous aspect of the situation.

*　*　*

If we now have a look at the three dreams in context, we can state the following: The first dream reveals to the dreamer the unconsciously split-off, chaotic, instinctual nature of her own father, which frightens her very much without showing her a way out. In the second dream, she takes a look into the future, so to speak, from where the inevitable natural instinct comes toward her. Although this is seemingly less threatening (particularly expressed by the contrast between the little dachshund and the mighty giant), she herself has in the meantime become isolated from her parents and is afraid, again without finding a loophole. Finally, in the third dream, she has fled from the house and the well-kept pergola to the barn, where she seeks shelter from the menacing earth creatures high above the ground. We could possibly view the whole dream as an unsuccessful attempt at a lysis to the two previous dreams. She moves to higher regions, to the spirits, which, however, do not leave her alone either.

In short, the meaning of the three dreams is approximately the following: The dreamer is confronted with a conflict—which, as we may assume, stems from the unsolved problem of the parents, and particularly of the father—in such a way that she will subsequently not be able to assimilate her own instinctual sphere. She is forced to live in the upper regions, which might find an expression, for example, in a one-sided intellectual or social activity. This is a very insecure situation, however, in which one is constantly in danger of falling down into one's instinctual sphere.

*　*　*

387

Professor Jung: What is interesting is that there is no lysis in any of these dreams. Now if we have a dream series without lysis, how would you interpret this?

Participant: The conflict persists.

Professor Jung: Yes, this is the case in this dream series. Although there are three dreams about the same topic, there is no lysis. What does this mean for the prognosis?

Participant: There is no solution.

Professor Jung: No, it means only that for a very long time there will be no lysis. This is a problem that will not be solved for a very long time. These are remembered dreams that got stuck, so to speak, and that are still valid; and from the fact that the lysis is missing, we know that no correct answer to this problem will be found for a long time. Have you noticed anything else?

Participant: I would perhaps stress even more the contrast between the father and the dachshund, and maybe say: the instinctual frightens her off; it seems to have become the same as the father to the dreamer, but with a different quality. The first dream is about the destructive problem in the father; then she shies away from something constructive, from something that lures foxes and badgers out of the underworld. This means that there is something extremely constructive in her, after all.

Professor Jung: Yes, absolutely. This proposition of the dream gives rise to high hopes. This confirms what Dr. Reichstein said: the following dreams are an attempt at a lysis. This is the example I mentioned before, in which the following dreams take up again what had been left unfinished by the previous one, but again without achieving a lysis themselves. So I definitely agree with Dr. Reichstein: what strikes us in the first dream is the menacing giant, and in the next the dachshund, which is such a cute little dog of which one really needn't be afraid, and yet, strangely enough, it frightens her. I would have added in the third dream: here, too, there is the giant motif, that is, an enormous, high barn. I recommend that you keep these motifs clearly in mind. If the topic is a giant, we will look out for the motif of something too big or too small also in the following dreams, because archetypal ideas are always ambivalent, no Yes or No. What is right is also left; what is up is also down; what exists also does not exist. All statements about supernatural phenomena, therefore, have to be of a paradoxical nature, the biggest is also the smallest, and so on, which shows that we have reached a transhuman sphere. So the giant turns into a dachshund, which gives rise to hope.

Participant: The third dream represents progress. It is a barn, not a skyscraper. The barn is nature.

Professor Jung: Yes, you are quite right. The third dream further pursues the euphemistic course. Already the dachshund is a remarkable euphemism. It is a very significant change in the dream that the absolutely frightening and terrible is transformed. In the first dream it was still impossible to cope with the giant. Then it is exactly as if the unconscious said: let's try it the other way around. How could we tell the child? With a dachshund. The dachshund contains everything the giant has, too: *primordial nature*, but it is also the animal that has gotten closer to man, a domesticated animal, and thus not dangerous.

Participants: This is reminiscent of the dream of the little boy who went into the robber's den.[4] There we find the same opposites: one giant has the power, the other, the thin one, has the wisdom of nature—as in our case the giant and the little dachshund. Both represented the two world powers that threatened the little boy from the world of the adults.

Professor Jung: In that dream there are *two* giants, which indicates: the giant is archetypal, which means oppositional. "Long and thin, devil within."[5]

Participant: In the second dream, the motif of the very big is also there, in the long pergola. So in the first dream nature predominates, while in the second one time already plays a role.

Professor Jung: Yes, and with it also culture. You were right in pointing out that there is something positive in this dream: what had been destructive has turned into something harmless, into a little dog. Moreover, this scene is no longer nocturnal and uncanny, but it

---

[4] Cf. seminar 3, § 4 (ed.).

[5] Original: *Lang und dünn steckt der Teufel drin*; German saying (trans.).

is about a pergola. We picture it in the green, with flowers and a garden, where there is no evil, wild, mythological, primordial nature at all. The dreamer noticed that, of course, because unfortunately she is frightened even here by the dachshund, which shows that she must have recognized the giant in the dachshund. Now what does the motif of a skillful euphemistic guise mean?

Participant: It aims at making the dreamer accept the giant.

Professor Jung: Yes, the giant is a mythological figure that represents chthonic nature, a purely natural being, against which one cannot protect oneself except by cunning. But the child is helplessly at his mercy, and yet this being, this exemplar of menacing nature, has to be accepted and has somehow to be translated into the child's structure—because obviously the giant represents an impulse that is present in the child herself. Of course, we are inclined to think of the father, and a brutal father at that. But he need not be brutal at all. In the case of a given disposition in the child, he can impress her as frightening without actually being it. After all, there are idiosyncrasies: a loud noise may frighten the one, but only tickle the other; the one is hurt by a certain remark, the other isn't. I have already noticed that completely harmless things can frighten children, if there is a certain susceptibility or if something fateful is active. But we may assume that the father was very impetuous, which had a frightening effect. We would assume a causal relation with the father; the father would be to blame for the child's having suffered this trauma. We would then have to suppose that something got into disorder. This is correct thinking, but we also have to take the child's reaction into account. We have to take the child into consideration. We have to leave the blame on the individual, because it is more correct to say: unfortunately, wrongly, the child reacted to something that actually is also in her nature—because it was *her* nature, the child's nature, that turned the father into the giant. The unconscious of the child did this. It turned the father into a giant, so to speak; for if we do not express it in this way, we actually say that the being into which the father was transformed was not accepted. But the child has to integrate precisely this impetuousness, something that is also in her own nature. It does not matter in the slightest whether this once came into her from the outside, or whether it was there from the beginning. If it is in her, it has also to be accepted. We can never avert such an effect by eliminating it. The dreamer will be truly healed only if this natural force is assimilated. This is what the unconscious tries to help with by the second dream. To this end, the second dream transforms the giant into something quite acceptable, because in reasonable anticipation we might suppose that one would not be frightened by a dachshund. But even this does not help, because the child has again sensed the dangerous natural force in the dachshund.

Now comes the third dream, of the enormous, high barn. This dream has taken up the second one: the motif of bigness, but no longer in the active form. We can presume, therefore, that the third dream, too, is trying to get her acquainted with the gigantic, which is also represented by the barn. The barn roof has something *protective*. The barn is a dry place for storing supplies. It is part of the stable where the cattle are. Many barns have big roofs, something quite homey, protective, which covers them. So absolutely nothing aggressive remains to be seen, and the giant motif has turned into a building that accommodates the dreamer. So what happened with the natural creature?

Participant: It has become a protection.

Professor Jung: Yes, it already represents a pact with the giant: Help me, protect me! That's how far the dream goes in the euphemistic transformation of what causes fear and is dangerous. Now, however, one would expect that she has a nice roof and feels secure. But then it happens that she climbs under the roof beams. Dr. Reichstein explained this by the secrets of the roof timberwork. Who dwells there?

Participant: Bats.

Professor Jung: Yes, bats, something secret, nocturnal, spiritual. "The wind is sighing through the roof, the voices of the spirits" (*Ossian*). In the house of the spirits of the primitives, in the tribes of the headhunters and similar ones, the heads of the killed are hung on the roof beams, because the spirits rise into the air as smoke and "subtle bodies."[6]

---

[6] This expression in English in the original (trans.).

Participant: In Barlach, in *Der tote Tag* [*The Dead Day*], the evil spirit of the mother also sits on the beam.

Professor Jung: Yes, *Steissbart*. So what does it mean to climb on the roofs?

Participant: If she cannot come down to the ground, she will remain a spirit herself.

Professor Jung: The attempt of the unconscious failed, because instead of a solution of the problem she is climbing in the beams.

Participant: Don't we have to take into account that all children would love to do that, but aren't allowed to? There is some mischief in this.

Professor Jung: What do we call this mischief? Who does this? Who climbs in the roofs? Haven't you ever seen this?

Participant: The apes.

Professor Jung: The lysis is in the ape house! Where did the dachshund go, the life that was in the dachshund?

Participant: It went into herself. It is a gradual assimilation of what had been terrible and frightening. It is assimilated like a shell shock, that is, only step by step.

Participant: The roof is something constructive.

Professor Jung: Certainly, the giant, the dangerous, has turned into the protective roof. But through this the life of the giant has disappeared, and also the life of the dachshund, and so what happens to it? It has to be somewhere: it has gone into herself. She is changed; she now climbs like an ape, so to speak, in the timberwork.

Participant: She gets to know the giant from the inside.

Professor Jung: Yes, at first in the form of a dachshund. The giant is a superhuman being, but we can understand a dachshund. The ape is the next stage, which one could use for a comparison. In many respects, humans are like apes. I have recently read of an ape that looks after a whole dog kennel of English foxhounds. When the dogs want to fight, it keeps them apart; it behaves like a servant, so one can easily let the ape be in charge of the dogs. So in a way man approaches the dog's nature via the medium of the ape. For this he needs a kind of atavistic memory. He is nearest to the ape where he best understands the dog. That is why it is so very satisfying to keep an animal, because our animal nature is constantly warmed and sustained a bit by this. This is the secret of the love of animals.

Participant: But the ape is still removed from the ground of reality.

Professor Jung: This dream is more positive than the other dreams, but the fact that the ape nature emerges is not yet a solution.

Participant: It is a regression to the animal stage.

Professor Jung: But into which stage?

Participant: It is unconscious.

Professor Jung: Yes, a certain unconsciousness regarding this problem sets in.

Participant: This dream is more dangerous, because the dreamer may fall to her death.

Professor Jung: No, not with the ape nature. She does have the ape nature, doesn't she, the strength and the skill to hold on to these beams and climb on them? Others would fall down, but not she.

Participant: The barn is also not the house in which people live, it is an unconscious situation. It is actually there where the animals are, where the bats live, and so on.

Professor Jung: Yes, it is nearer to nature, something between farmstead, stable, and barn, and from there it leads out into nature. So it is primitive, too.

Participant: Perhaps she enters the intellectual sphere with the libido.

Professor Jung: Exactly. When a house appears in a dream, it plays an important role anyway, regardless if one is in the basement, on the uppermost floor, or on the roof. Here you must always think of the stories of the human body. Bats that live in the roof, for example, have given rise to a proverbial saying: "bats in the belfry,"[7] for someone who is "bonkers." He then has bats, so to speak, up there in the attic. Attic and roof are the uppermost parts of the house and of the body. The stomach is often compared to the kitchen; Paracelsus said: Everybody has an alchemist in his belly. The digestive organ is the alchemical kitchen in us. So in our case the inevitable conclusion would be that instinct, which had been triggered in the child by the

---

[7] This phrase in English in the original (trans.).

393

effect of the fright, is a head instinct, a spiritual instinct. The girl is pulled upward, unconsciously pulled upward, into the sphere of the head; this is by no means done deliberately, because this is an unconscious state. Unconsciously, instinctually, she is pulled upward. And she simply prefers to wander around in the timberwork, to enter into the intellectual sphere; all this because of that first shock.

Participant: The father already had this problem.

Professor Jung: Was he intellectual?

Participant: No.

Professor Jung: Not at all, he lived on the emotional level. The club, the shattering instrument, had to do with an emotion that had caused the shock and had a shattering effect.

Participant: Perhaps the father suppressed the instinctual nature in particular?

Professor Jung: Not necessarily. What we can see from the dream is only that some emotionality has to be present, which has a shattering and crushing effect.

Participant: Isn't it so great precisely because it is split off?

Professor Jung: Yes, that could be. Or the emotionality is unnaturally exaggerated by being mixed with a thinking that does not differentiate; if someone, for instance, should think, but does not, this energy passes into the emotions. Emotions are always there where we are not adjusted. They are always a sign of maladjustment. At the point where we fail, we have emotions.

Participant: So he is intellectual after all?

Professor Jung: No, he needn't be, if he does not think. We will leave the question open whether this is a case of repressed emotionality, which acts like an explosion, or of a secondary emotion due to a non-differentiation of a necessary function. In this case, if such an intellectual course manifests itself in the child, we rather have to assume that the latter is the case. This is shown by the hidden solution: if the emotionality had been repressed in the father, it would have surfaced in the child, as her task. This I have often observed in families. I know generations! I really had to struggle with the emotions of children of people with repressed emotionality; these children had been given the task to live these emotions. But here this does not

394

seem to be the case; here the result is an intellectualizing effect, even the destiny of an intellectual activity that is inescapable and fateful, a legacy taken over from the father. We have to infer this *causa* from the effect.

Participant: Couldn't the *causa* lie in the patient herself? For instance, because of an ambivalent attitude toward the father: she loves the father, but at the same rejects the giant father?

Professor Jung: It is indeed good always to take the patient herself into account, not only the ascendancy,[8] and not to constantly blame the latter for having caused anything that's wrong with the child. If we did that, we would have gone much too far. This girl, however, is a four- to five-year-old child. For therapeutic reasons we have to consider the father, because at this age the relation with the father is of vital importance. The child still lives in *participation mystique* with the parents and is exposed to the effects they have. Let us suppose that a young girl who comes to me for analysis is still living in the house of the father: in this case I would consider the father by all means. So if the dream says, "father," and the child lives with the father, we, too, normally have to say, "father." We must not assume that nobody had said anything about the father. He is mentioned. Here too. The *father* appears; it doesn't just say: the giant.

And it makes perfect sense that the father has precisely such an intellectualizing effect and can provoke, with this shock, an intellectual reaction. An intellectual talent has to be present, because otherwise the girl could not react as she did. A father's legacy for the daughter is always a spiritual one; that is why fathers have such an enormous responsibility for the spiritual life of their daughters. If they give them a political philosophy, this is a crime against the spirit, because this will go to their head. But here the result was an effect that we have to consider constructive.

Participant: So the last dream would be the only resort, at least for the next ten years? One would have to see dreams from puberty, then.

Professor Jung: You may think of an even longer time period.

[8] I.e., the parents and the relatives (ed.).

Participant: So if this is a remembered dream, and one remembers a certain time period, the problem is not yet solved?

Professor Jung: It is still active.

Participant: Would this mean that it is still active at the moment of remembering?

Professor Jung: It could also be the case that one had lived this consciously. Then one remembers dreams even when the situation has already been solved. We have to expect that this content remained below the threshold of consciousness. What will be the effect, if it has subliminally remained unsolved for such a long time?

Participant: Consciousness will be detached from the world.

Professor Jung: Not necessarily. We can put the question as follows: What will result if a content is constellated? What can happen then?

Participant: There can be complex-related reactions.

Professor Jung: Yes, dissociative phenomena.

Participant: Slips of the tongue, forgetting.

Professor Jung: But emotionally?

Participant: Anxiety.

Professor Jung: Yes, symptoms of anxiety neurosis in general, mood swings, bad temper, not being at one with oneself. This is the root. This comes because one feels two things in oneself: above, one is one thing, and below, something else. One is not able to be identical with oneself; there is a second one rumbling below the threshold. One is discontented with oneself, with the mother, with the old man, with the Good Lord, and with the political situation. Nothing suits one, because one doesn't suit oneself. The situation in the last dream is the condition under which a certain discontentment may arise, whereas the dream itself occurs quite fatefully. It is a fateful situation. Nothing can be argued against it. There are different tasks in life. Everybody is one-sided, and one has to live with one's one-sidedness and accept it.

2. Dream of a Five-Year-Old Girl of a Tiger
PRESENTED BY WALTER HUBER[9]

Text: *I am standing on the porch of a pile house. Then a tiger jumps over the balustrade and wants to attack me, but he gets caught in the jump and*

[9] Session of 5 November 1940.

is torn into two pieces (like in The Adventures of Baron Munch-hausen).

Mr. *Huber*: I made the following classification:

Dramatis personae: Child, tiger.
Locale: The porch of a pile house.
Peripateia: The tiger jumps over the balustrade and wants to
                     attack the child.
Lysis: 1. The tiger gets stuck; 2. the tiger is torn into
                     two pieces.

The beginning of the dream shows us a situation with which we are familiar from the very frequent persecutory dreams. The dreamer is to be attacked and killed by an overwhelming being. Very often in such dreams there is a process that turns the terrible monster into a milder form, or some help appears, a miracle happens: the dreamer is given some magic with which he can face the enormous monster. If this is not the case, the feeling of anxiety usually increases to a state of horror, and the dreamer awakes from the excessive oppression. But none of this happens in our dream. The association of the girl, "like in *The adventures of Baron Munchhausen*," gives us a clue which is very appropriate for this persecutory situation. A great number of his travel adventures show Munchhausen in a dangerous situation, in which an ordinary mortal would be at a complete loss, and then he emerges as a *deus ex machina*,[10] and magically and in the most incredible way brings about the far-fetched, lucky ending. Munchhausen is a show-off and braggart with a sense of humor. He saves himself from danger in a way one would never anticipate. Let me say at this point that a similar magical ending will occur in our dream: the persecuting animal gets stuck and disintegrates.

The beginning of the dream shows us the little girl on the porch of a *pile house*. We may conclude that such a house is not unfamiliar

---

[10] Latin, "god from the machine." In some ancient Greek drama, an apparently insoluble crisis was solved by the intervention of a god, often brought on stage by an elaborate piece of equipment. The phrase has been extended to refer to any resolution to a story that does not pay due regard to the story's internal logic and is so unlikely that it challenges suspension of disbelief (trans.).

397

to the child, as she grew up in India. She also knows about the tiger from conversations in her environment. In India houses are often built that way, because it is advantageous not to be too near the ground. Various dangers are lurking there; one can never be sure what will sneak up at night from the jungle or the rain forest. Usually one keeps the domestic animals there. So this locale has the features of an environment familiar to the child.

"The *tiger*," says Brehm,

> shows all the customs and habits of cats; but in its case they are in correlation to its bigness. Its movements are as graceful as those of little cats, at the same time extremely fast, deft, and persevering. Prowling soundlessly, in its predatory pursuits it easily covers hour-long distances, moves very fast at a gallop, and is an excellent swimmer. It can jump a distance of about five meters.[11] With the exception of the strongest mammals (elephants, rhinoceroses, wild buffalo), no animal of its class is safe from it. The natives of India say that young tigers are trained in the predatory craft by their mothers, and have to creep up to the clever, watchful apes and peacocks under her guidance. In whole regions of India the tiger is regarded as a god, and the natives, when talking about it, commonly call it by all kinds of names, but never by its real one. We distinguish three kinds of tigers: hunters of wild animals, hunters of domesticated animals, and man-eaters. The strongest point of its attack is the moment of surprise. It is extraordinarily strong. It is said that eyewitnesses have observed a tiger pull an ox of 1,800 pounds through the bush for a couple of hundred meters.

In the mythological context, the natives regard it as an animal with an extraordinarily strong *mana*. Warneck, who closely studied the religion of the Batak tribe, writes about this:

> It is the task of the wise man to conserve his *tondi* (that is, his *mana*), to strengthen it, to enrich it by supplying additional soul content, and to keep it in good humor. The *tondi* is a kind of man within man, with its own will and its own wishes, which it can enforce against

---

[11] Actually up to ten meters (cf. www.tiger-online.org) (14 March 2007) (trans.).

man, causing the most unpleasant feelings in him. Man's fortune depends on it. It inhabits all parts of the body, but unevenly; most of the *tondi* is found in the head, the blood, and the liver. It can make the body ill by leaving it; according to the Batak, in death it is even said to turn to the *begu*, the death spirit. *Tondi* is found not only in man, but also in animals and plants, and most of all in the most feared animals, such as the tiger, and in the most useful and nutritious plants, such as rice.

The belief in werewolves also belongs in this context. A human can turn into a rapacious animal—a wolf in our regions, a tiger in South Asia, a leopard in Africa—and in this form can kill his neighbor's animals or a personal enemy. A similar view is reported by Ivor Evans in *Studies in Religion, Foklore and Customs of British North Borneo and the Malay Peninsula*:

> As far as I could establish, the Sakai on the Malayan peninsula consider all tigers to be human beings who have taken animal form. The Mantra of Johore (even those converted to Christianity) believe that a tiger they encounter can only be a human being who had sold himself to the evil spirits and was bewitched to take the form of the predator, to give free rein to his cravings for revenge or his malice. They claim that whenever one encounters a tiger, one would have seen a human being disappear in the direction from which the beast attacks, or at least could have seen one.

In his book *The "Soul" of the Primitive*,[12] Lucien Lévy-Bruhl gives a number of examples as evidence of the mystical view of primitives that certain humans and animals are actually one and the same. All of the Naga people (a people living in the northeast of India), at least those belonging to the western group, claim that humans and tigers have a common origin. When the village people of Angami killed a tiger, the chief ordered a day of rest in mournful memory of the death of an elder brother. All Nagas are very afraid of tigers. They all view it as a being that is very different from the other cats of prey, and particularly closely related to humankind.

[12] Lucien Lévy-Bruhl, *The "Soul" of the Primitive*, chapter 4 (trans.).

399

The figure of the tiger in our dream is an eastern symbol, assigned to the *yin* principle. In the *Tibetan Book of the Dead*, the *Bardo Thö-dol*, the tiger symbol appears twice to the departed during his Bardo existence, on the thirteenth day, when he is in *samsara* and the eight wrathful deities appear to him, the *kerimas* and the *htamemnas*: "from the south, [there appears] a red, tiger-headed [goddess], crossing her arms downward, staring hypnotically and gnashing her fangs," and, again on the fourteenth day: "from the south dawns the yellowish-black, tiger-headed Rakshasi, a blood-filled skull in her hand."[13]

In the ancient Japanese religious traditions, in Shinto, the tiger is deferentially worshipped as a sacred animal.

In summarizing, I would like to describe the figure of the tiger in our dream as follows: it is the devouring, bloodthirsty, man-eating beast of prey, which soundlessly prowls out of the dark thicket of the rain forest or the jungle into the well-guarded areas of human civilization, by which it is attracted, exposes its mauling paw out of its velvet enclosure, and gets ready for its terrible strike. It is the insatiable animal, sparing nothing, mercilessly lunging in devilish craving at the five-year-old child on the porch.

The child stands on the *porch*. So she is no longer fully in the house, but in a somewhat exposed place. One can see things from the porch; there is a view of the environment, the wildness of the rain forest, in our example. Maybe the girl, curious as children are, is lured by the manifold magical attractions of the tropical landscape. We could also say that she met the tiger halfway. The girl is helpless. Let us consider for a moment the developmental stage in which the child is. She is in the stage of the very first phase of consciousness. We know from many children's dreams, which we already discussed here, that it is not the attitude of the young child to bear the labors of becoming conscious readily and willingly; basically, this runs counter to nature. Rather, there are resistances to adapting to real life. The unconscious of the child instinctually senses the painful process that lies ahead of her after having left the paradise of childhood. Now if the process of becoming conscious and adapting is painful and diffi-

---

[13] See reluctant-messenger.com/Tibetan-Book-Dead_Houston1.htm (trans.).

cult for the child in the first place, the child's environment will make this process a particularly tricky problem. Why? Although she has been raised in a European way by Western parents, the surrounding air, the psychical space, so to speak, is pregnant with the magical, demonic atmosphere of the Indian belief in the supernatural and its effects. The world of the unconscious thus appears to be like a reality whose effect is also felt from the outside. Europeans often have native wet nurses for their children, who have to take care of them; they tell them their legends and fairy tales, so the children get in ever closer touch with this primitive world, are fascinated by it, and get stuck in this fascination. This is what standing on the porch means. As we know from numerous examples, it is difficult even for adults to resist the magic and the demonic attraction of the foreign earth.

Participant: In the chapter "Mind and Earth" of *Civilization in Transition*,[14] Professor Jung says the following (although this passage deals with America, it follows the same psychological laws):

> Thus the American presents a strange picture: a European with
> Negro behavior and an Indian soul. He shares the fate of all usurpers
> of foreign soil. Certain Australian primitives assert that one cannot
> conquer foreign soil, because in it there dwell strange ancestor-spirits
> who reincarnate themselves in the newborn. There is a great psycho-
> logical truth in this. The foreign land assimilates its conqueror. . . .
> Everywhere the virgin earth causes at least the unconscious of the
> conqueror to sink to the level of its indigenous inhabitants.

Mr. Huber: Woe betide the European who is not safeguarded against the onslaught of demonic, magical forces! He has no inner "skeleton" with which he could withstand the gravity that pulls him down, and no "muscles" that would enable him to maintain his equilibrium in the face of these forces. Little wonder, then, if he is attacked in this state by that world as if by a mauling tiger. He simply seems to be doomed. In our dream something extraordinary happens. Evidently something should be demonstrated to the child. I frankly confess my embarrassment and difficulty when I search for an inter-

[14] *CW* 10, § 103 (ed.).

401

pretation that would sufficiently explain the fact that the attacking beast gets stuck and disintegrates. The rescuing hero who undoes the force of the attacker and dissolves its devouring might is completely missing in our dream. What could it be? To tackle this riddle, the association "Munchhausen" may be illuminating. You remember that in his adventurous tales there is a horse that breaks into two parts. The rider notices this when he lets the horse drink and sees the drunk water run out again at the back without refreshing the animal, because the horse had been severed from its hind quarters. The disintegration into two halves calls to mind the creation myths in which we are told that the world was created when the creator divided a primeval state or being into two halves, by which the pairs of opposites came into existence.[15]

So if we may relate the archetypal symbol of the dismembering of the tiger to the creation myth, we may further assume that the annihilation of the attacker, the complete undoing of its potency, is caused by its being fragmented into its opposites. The dream does not tell this directly; as already mentioned, there is no visible light god who would divide the beast of prey coming out of the darkness of the jungle. Or could it be that, precisely because he is invisible in the dream, his real nature is revealed, namely, ubiquitous and nowhere, as in the well-known circle symbol?[16]

Let us now come to the end of the dream's message. It roughly says the following: the child is in a dangerous situation. The danger appears in the form of the tiger that symbolizes the alien earth with all its demonic reality. In this situation a rescue appears. It is expressed by an act of creation, or, psychologically speaking, a development of consciousness. What does this mean for our case in practical terms? In the further course of her development the child will have to consciously confront the problem of this world, with which she is living, so as not to be devoured by it. This confrontation will presumably last for a whole developmental period; it is a process in whose course,

---

[15] Here follow detailed comments on the Babylonian creation myth from the library of Assurbanipal (ed.).

[16] *Deus est sphaera infinita, cuius centrum est ubique, circumferentia nusquam* [God is an infinite circle, whose center is everywhere and circumference is nowhere] (ed.).

so to speak, two opposite religious principles come up against each other and collide, and in which one is overcome by the other. It is as if the rescue by the invisible god, as it is manifest in the dream, will have to be realized by the life of the child. Here the dream has a meaning very similar to religious visual language in general. It may be understandable that this language speaks in the past tense and gives an historical account, so to speak, as if an act of creation had indeed taken place, but needed the human willingness to develop consciousness for its realization, and for manifesting itself anew over and over again.

In Professor Jung's lecture we learned how tremendously important the development of consciousness is. If the rescue from the mauling beast is to take place in our dream, the act of becoming conscious will be inevitable. It will become a requirement, we could say the essential task as such. It is true that we could shirk this task if we wanted, but we would then have to bear all the consequences of this avoidance with inexorable logic. An exceptionally good description of this task, with which I would like to close my talk, was given by Nietzsche:

> The hidden imperious something, for which we for long have no name until at last it proves itself to be our task—this tyrant in us exacts a terrible price for every attempt that we make to escape it or give it the slip, for every premature act of self-constraint, for every reconciliation with those to whom we do not belong, for every activity, however respectable, that turns us aside from our main purpose, even indeed for every virtue that would like to protect us from the severity of our most personal responsibility. "Illness" is always the answer when we begin to doubt our right to *our* task—every time we begin to make things easier for ourselves. How strange and how terrible! It is our *alleviations* for which we have to make the severest atonement! And if we afterward want to return to health, we have no choice—we must burden ourselves more heavily than we have ever been burdened before.[17]

---

[17] Friedrich Nietzsche, *Human, All Too Human* (1879). English text at www.geocities.com/thenietzschechannel/mom.htm (14 March 2007) (trans.).

Professor Jung: In this paper you were fascinated by the material. You have read interesting things concerning it. But this is a temptation. If you present all that, we will get completely dizzy. We will drift away and move too far away from the dream. Therefore, you have to restrict the material to the bare essentials; we have to think of the poor audience that will get completely drunk. It goes too far when you read us such seductive texts. This is dangerous. In the case of such a simple dream, we have to stay as near the material as possible. Otherwise we will have an enormous balloon that will take us over countries and peoples, until we finally no longer know where we took off and how to find our way back home. I recommend that you use a hydraulic press to condense the material. You have presented too much, although we may include it as a *sous-entendu*. But when you present it you have to withhold the best and give us only the juice. There is still much too much cover, and too little core.

Now as regards the dream itself: the essential thing, which Mr. Huber has quite correctly stressed, is that the child was born and raised in India. He has rightly pointed to the fact that these children absorb the atmosphere, and when they also have an Indian wet nurse they will take it in with the breast milk. Very often there will be serious disturbances. Adults, too, get under this influence when they live there for a longer time. This is so well known there that everybody will tell you. Europeans in India are much more interesting than the natives, because their primitivity emerges. The primitive is also still in us. If I want to meet "negroes," I can go to the Lötschen valley.[18]

The *tiger* is, of course, part of the atmosphere in these regions. The tiger is the personification of the night horror, the night anxiety, as is the leopard in Africa, for example. Because this is what is always on the prowl. If you pitch a camp in the bush in Africa, the leopard will come every night and eat the bones you have thrown out. The next day you can see the imprints of the paws, and if a man eater is among them, which is fortunately not the rule, you can even be de-

[18] A Swiss valley in the mountains between the Valais and the Bernese Oberland, still very isolated at that time (trans.).

404

voured. When you go to the countryside in India, the tiger will be what is talked about. And if it is a man-eater,[19] a werewolf or a were-tiger, it will be the talk of all the villages. Nobody living under these circumstances can escape this local atmosphere. And naturally this is absorbed by the children—thus, this dream. I was surprised that Mr. Huber did not draw this analogy. What would it be in our regions?

Participant: A bear.

Participant: The wolf.

Participant: Little Red Riding Hood.

Professor Jung: Yes, Little Red Riding Hood would be the appropriate analogy. The child is in the situation of a Little Red Riding Hood who is eaten by the wolf, which is simply replaced by the tiger here. For us the wolf has the same meaning. Of course only in fairy tales, because we no longer know what wolves are. We no longer know the horror of the winter night, when no human dared to go outside because wolves were at large. But that is the experience of our ancestors. And the tiger is the corresponding animal in the East. You drew a parallel to Mephistopheles, but there I'd have rather said: the dog gets bigger and bigger, and swells behind the oven.[20] What does that mean?

Participant: That it gets more dangerous.

Professor Jung: That is exactly the representation of ever-growing anxiety; one gets more and more oppressed. One is completely driven to the wall. A typical childhood dream is, for instance, of a light or an object or a ball, which gets bigger and bigger and eventually so big that the child wakes up in horror.

Participant: In Gottfried Keller's dream, it is a snake.

Professor Jung: Right. So the swelling of the dog makes it suddenly expose itself; and what does Faust say?

Participant: "So this then, was the kernel of the brute!"

Professor Jung: Yes, the disguise vanishes, and Mephistopheles appears. Here you also have the motif of division: the anxiety suddenly

---

[19] This expression in English in the original (trans.).

[20] Jung refers to a passage in the seminar that is missing (ed.). "But what's this I see! / Can this happen naturally? / Is it a phantom or is it real? / The dog's growing big and tall. / He rises powerfully, / It's no doglike shape I see!" (Goethe, *Faust I*, lines 1247–52) (trans.).

gets divided, and out comes a different figure. The other motif is *division*. This is an archetypal motif that you encounter in various forms. Mr. Huber has quite correctly taken into account the cosmogonic parallels.

Participant: The pile house stands in contrast to the rain forest, as the boundary of consciousness. The tiger wants to jump there.

Professor Jung: We will come back to that. For the moment, let us stay with the division: we can actually observe division most clearly in the cosmogonic myths, for instance, in Genesis.

Participant: The division of the light from the darkness.

Participant: The division of the waters under the firmament from the waters above.

Professor Jung: This is a typical division, such as the division into heaven and earth by Tiamat, for example. In Egypt, Geb, the earth god, is below; Nuth, the firmament, the star woman, above. In between is the air god Shu. This is the most primitive idea of division; we find such a division, for instance, in a myth of the Yorubas on the [African] west coast. Frobenius mentions the myth of the primeval parents Obatala, heaven, and Odudua, earth.[21] They live in a gourd, squeezed close to each other. Suddenly they feel that they are forced apart and are actually two: a son was created between them who forced them apart. He is the analogy to Shu in Egypt. In the Babylonian myth there is more violence. Marduk, the god of light, kills Tiamat. How does he kill her?

Participant: He inflates her with wind.

Professor Jung: He blows the power of the storm into her, so that she swells; then he can kill her. He kills her by inspiration, so to speak.[22] This is the inspiration of consciousness. It is always the god of light who kills the dragon. The dragon is always cut open in other contexts too, and then everything he had devoured comes to light again: at first, usually father and mother, then the treasures and whatever else time had devoured. By this the hero restores what had been destroyed by time. This division is connected to the development of

[21] Cf. Leo Frobenius, *Das Zeitalter des Sonnengottes*, p. 269.
[22] From the Latin *inspiratio* (n.), *inspirare* (v.); "to breathe into" (trans.).

consciousness, and the dream says: the moment the seemingly destructive force of the unconscious reaches the threshold of consciousness, the latter is forced to disengage from its base.

Participant: The tiger wants to get in.

Professor Jung: In psychological terms, please. What is the tiger?

Participant: The unconscious.

Professor Jung: Yes, that which it devours. Of course it also possesses motherly qualities, but that is not important. This is mere decoration. It is the unconscious *tout bonnement*.[23] What does it do?

Participant: It jumps up. It wants to eat up the child.

Professor Jung: Yes, the house is the child's region of consciousness. The tiger wants to eat the child. The unconscious is overcome by desire to eat the child. You have also drawn a parallel between the unconscious and the devil, who goes around, "like a roaring lion and looks whom he will devour." The unconscious is overcome by desire for the light of consciousness. There is a Gnostic view, according to which the devil is hungry for and desirous of light. He thinks he will get the light if he devours man. Isn't that what we also think? There are people who want to gain knowledge. They eat from a cultured person, marry a cultured woman or a clever man. This is still primitive. One thinks that something will rub off. The primitives simply kill you and spoon out the brain or eat the heart to give them courage. One thinks that if one had the object, one would have "it." With the piano you have music in the house. We desire somebody to get his qualities, and think we will have them if we succeed in taking him in. The tiger is also bitterly mistaken: that it would fall onto the balustrade—this it didn't reckon with! This is a miracle, of course. Usually when it jumps it knows where it will land.

Participant: The interpretation has to start before, with the *pile house*. It is built in a way that animals cannot intrude.

Professor Jung: It is not that high; a tiger could jump five times higher. This is meant only as space of consciousness above the primitive earth, a space one gets only indirectly through Aja[24] or the jun-

[23] French, "pure and simple" (trans.).

[24] In Yoruba mythology, Aja is an Orisha, patron of the forest, the animals within it, and the herbal healers, whom she taught their art (trans.).

gle. It makes an enormous impression to see how little white people touch the earth in the tropics. Whenever possible they behave as if they were in the English countryside. The etiquette is much stricter than at home. One speaks and thinks about nothing but what is happening in England, and unconsciously one is completely eaten up by the earth. A woman I had to treat suffered from anxiety states, which simply expressed that she wanted to protect herself against India. I told her: please read a book about India, invite Indian ladies and let them tell you about it, then you needn't be afraid of it any longer. The anxiety stems only from the fact that people do not confront themselves with the ground on which they live. But they are not able to, for if they touched the ground they would be pervaded by the psychology of the ground. The ground poisons them in a way. There, of course, thoughts completely different from ours have developed. In India we are at a total loss with our Christian ideas. We can only defend ourselves, but if we touch the Indian ground, we have to know why Shiva and similar gods exist. And such contents are then absorbed by the children, and that is the dangerous thing.

The balustrade is what establishes the child's border; on the other hand, it is also the magical barrier, so to speak, for anything that comes from the outside.

Participant: In alchemy one has to divide the dragon, or it will eat its own tail; then it disintegrates into its opposites. This is like the splitting of the tiger. The opposites dissolve into each other once they reach consciousness.

Professor Jung: Yes, Mr. Huber has rightly asked himself why there is no hero who splits this lion. This really poses a question. It does not look as if the tiger would disintegrate all by itself. Which means: we simply have to accept this as a fact, it just so happens in the dream. When the unconscious intrudes into spaces of consciousness, it is automatically split into its *pairs of opposites*. When it appears, it becomes two. The motif of two-ness, the motif of two of the same, which appears here, is of general importance: the Dioscuri, the Açvins,[25] two

[25] Twin horsemen, helpers of men in distress on land or sea, in Greek mythology identical with the Dioscuri (Castor and Pollux); also in Hindu mythology (trans.).

fruits, objects, and so on. These notions are always on the border of consciousness, *in statu nascendi*; they are about to be perceived. Then they are two, that is, they dissolve into a pair of opposites: bright and dark, right and left; because we cannot identify anything without its opposite. It is a *conditio sine qua non* of knowledge. We can see white only if we also know black. Thus, no statement about a content of consciousness can dispense with pairs of opposites. This is the meaning of the fact that the tiger sort of breaks into pieces the moment it reaches consciousness. The remarkable thing here is that this disintegration takes places spontaneously. Mr. Huber has rightly dwelt on this. In our case, some help would have to appear, a hero who would kill the monster. In India, however, it happens by itself. How do you explain this?

Participant: The girl has received the right instruction. It is the fence, the balustrade, on which the tiger breaks apart.

Professor Jung: Obviously, she is well protected. But what is really magical is that the tiger disintegrates by itself.

Participant: The Indians are more familiar with the magical powers.

Professor Jung: One could also say the opposite. But we have to understand that this child was under a favorable influence in India, that the same processes occur in this child as in the Indians. For that's how it is in the East—there the unconscious can enter into consciousness without disturbance. You will see in the dream of the young Indian, which we will discuss later on, in how positive a way the unconscious flows into consciousness. In contrast, the dream of the big snake—what an affair this is for us!

Participant: Is it because the archetypes are concretized?

Professor Jung: In India everything spiritual has grown out of nature. The unconscious flows absolutely freely into consciousness. Indians have no thoughts that would prevent consciousness from functioning, no devils that could devastate consciousness.

Participant: It is strange that the tiger, which jumps into consciousness, is no longer a tiger the moment it is in it. The whole story is harmless, with a touch of Munchhausen.

Professor Jung: This is, after all, a remembered dream. Munchhausen is a later association.

Participant: For us, an analogy would be Rumpelstiltskin: if one gets to know his name, the enraged dwarf is torn in two.

Professor Jung: In India they already have the names that make things burst; we don't.

At a Later Meeting of the Seminar

Professor Jung: We are still discussing the dream of the tiger. Mr. Huber, could you please tell us in two words what the dream says.

Mr. Huber: It is a situation of persecution: the tiger wants to attack the girl, but gets stuck and breaks into two pieces.

Professor Jung: You should not tell the dream, but describe the situation. What did you find with regard to the house and the child and the balustrade and the tiger, or to the breaking apart? Please insert this into the dream, in the dreamer's words if possible, only already interpreted.

When you have accumulated material, you will then have to think and insert what you found as if into an equation. The result has to be that you are able to repeat the dream, but now with the interpreted expressions. You have to do that now; then I will know if you have understood the dream.

Mr. Huber: The tiger is a symbol of the dangerous aspect.

Professor Jung: Now you're already talking *about* the dream. Talk *in* the dream, but in the interpreted terms. You have to begin with: a child is in the bungalow . . .

Mr. Huber: A child is sitting there in her consciousness or her spiritual state, which corresponds to the bungalow.

Professor Jung: Let us abbreviate this and simply say: the child's "consciousness." The child in the dream stands for the child's consciousness, her ego-consciousness. When I dream, for instance, that I go down the stairs, this means: my consciousness goes down the stairs in the dream. Now what does that mean, "down the stairs"? My consciousness goes down into the depths of the unconscious. Now continue!

Mr. Huber: The child's consciousness is attacked by a tigerlike unconscious.

Professor Jung: I would also leave out the "tiger."

Mr. Huber: By the devouring, destructive aspect of the unconscious.

Professor Jung: This is a crucial point: the destructive, the devouring. Well, the unconscious with its destructive quality—with this we recapitulate a great area of experience. What do you call this in a few words? What motif is touched on?

Mr. Huber: The mother.

Professor Jung: Yes, the maternal aspect too. And what is the maternal in Chinese philosophy?

Mr. Huber: The *yin.*

Professor Jung: Yes, this is the most abstract term we have for this. It is the maternal, the specifically feminine; besides, it is, of course, also a philosophical principle that applies to physics and all sorts of other things.

So we may say: this tiger represents the devouring aspect of the feminine. Now go on!

Mr. Huber: If this unconscious, with this quality, reaches consciousness, it will automatically become bipolar and thus be deprived of its devouring tendency.

Professor Jung: Yes, it therefore loses its dangerousness. Well, have you got any further questions about this interpretation, which is quite perfect in its shortness?

Participant: The child is standing on the porch, isn't she?

Professor Jung: This is not absolutely essential, but it greatly helps to illustrate the situation, in that the child's consciousness is represented twice: first by the presence of the ego (as the center of consciousness, the ego is a *conditio sine qua non* of consciousness as such), and, second, by the fact that the consciousness occupies a space, in most cases represented by a room or a house. This is the range of consciousness; a dog's olfactory field, for instance, is its world of consciousness, and so for the child the inner rooms of the bungalow naturally represent her world of consciousness. The porch with the balustrade is the place where children play. In Africa you can't let the children go outside in the blazing sun, because there is the danger

411

that they might pull off their topees[26] and get a sunstroke. So that's why they are on the porch. This is a kind of garden, a playground, the space of consciousness of the child. So when they go outside and come to the balustrade, they about reach the border of their world. And that is a significant detail. Formulated more precisely, it would read about as follows: consciousness is nearing the extent of its range, its boundary. At the border comes the dangerous moment when something different and completely alien, namely, a devouring, feminine, instinctual unconscious, comparable to the animal because of these features, comes to the child in a threatening manner.

Participant: Why must this destructive and devouring quality a priori be feminine?

Professor Jung: This I don't know.

Participant: It is the tiger, after all. Is the tiger feminine in Chinese?

Professor Jung: Yes, it is a cat; in the whole of the East, the tiger is feminine. The cat is the symbol of female deities. Of which?

Participant: Sekhmet is lion-headed.[27]

Participant: But you said it would be the wolf in our regions. The wolf is not the representative of the feminine.

Professor Jung: Not under all circumstances, but still—think of Romulus and Remus and the she-wolf. It does appear as something feminine. We have no big cats, otherwise we would surely use cats. In Chinese, the tiger is a symbol of *yin*, and the dragon a symbol of the masculine. So what would you say about this division? As Mr. Huber saw it, the division in Genesis is a quite appropriate image. A division into two always means capability of consciousness. In this capacity we find the division in many places, in the cosmogonic myths and also in Hermetic philosophy, whenever it deals with the development of consciousness. But now a further question: why does the child have this dream? What does this mean? So far we determined the content, but now we must address ourselves to the meaning.

Participant: Something has to be shown to her.

[26] This word in English in the original (trans.).
[27] Sekhmet ("She who is powerful") is a powerful ancient Egyptian goddess (trans.). Cf. the Egyptian cat goddess Bast (or Bastet) (ed.).

Professor Jung: Here you have to be careful. You must not off-handedly ascribe the parental role, the role of the godfather or -mother, or certain intentions, to the unconscious. It is pure nature. It just happens this way; whether these events are of a benevolent nature is another question. But there has to be a sufficient reason for this dream.

Participant: There is a concrete danger; the child is surrounded by threatening powers.

Professor Jung: What would be the danger then? It would be an unconscious danger, of course.

Participant: The nanny.

Professor Jung: Yes, or the mother. We see such dreams, for instance, when the mother is devouring, eats the children up, and thinks the children are there to feed her own sensations.

Participant: But would it be the eastern symbol in that case?

Professor Jung: There is no talk about the mother at all here. Therefore, I would think that it is not the mother. If the tiger came out of the house, I'd say: the source of destruction is within the house. But when the tiger comes out of the darkness, of the jungle, we may not assume it to be the mother.

Participant: Another possibility would be that this is a common developmental stage. The child is five years old, at an age when the unconscious has to be made conscious. So it would simply represent progress in her development. Something could have been dammed up that is discharged in the form of this dream, illustrating the inner process in the dream.

Professor Jung: You are justified in thinking that this could be a developmental phase. But why must it still be dreamed? Why doesn't it simply happen?

Participant: The dream is a compensation for conscious processes.

Participant: There is a factor in the conscious situation of the child that has an inhibiting effect and brings about the tension, so the tiger has to jump, as if over an obstacle.

Professor Jung: This is correct. It lies in the nature of infantile consciousness, and of consciousness in general, that it always lags behind. As a rule, consciousness is late. Therefore, something violent

413

has to happen. If consciousness were fast enough, it would already have a certain readiness to contain those tensions and integrate them. This can be proven. We often see this in analytic treatments. As a rule, at the beginning there come dreams full of tension, followed by banal and undramatic ones. When one anticipates the unconscious by descending into the unconscious on one's own, one could spare onself dreams altogether. There's no need for them. In case of a far-reaching familiarity with the unconscious, dreams will mostly be rare and undramatic. The beautiful, great dreams, however, mostly occur only when something lies completely outside of consciousness. The tensions of the unconscious can then smoothly flow into consciousness. There is no longer a need for dreams.

Participant: Perhaps this child has not yet developed in her structure the readiness to accept the tiger image?

Professor Jung: This is the necessary boundary of the space of consciousness, only a bit more accentuated than in our regions. We would say: "You may go as far as the garden hedge," then comes the street. In the tropics, of course, this is much more pronounced; most often there is only a tiny little door leading to the outside, because there naturally is the danger of reptiles, particularly snakes. I remember an incident that I was told of by Englishmen in Guinea: their two-year-old child was on the porch. They heard tender noises. When they went there, a puff adder was lying in front of the child, a very dangerous animal, thick as a salami, with strong teeth. But these are extremely inert critters. You have to step on them for them to bite. They then carefully removed the child and killed the animal. So if the dream really represents a developmental process, what developmental process is it?

Participant: An expansion of consciousness.

Professor Jung: By what?

Participant: By incorporation.

Professor Jung: What enters into consciousness?

Participant: The primitive unconscious.

Professor Jung: This is much, much too vague.

Participant: There is a realization that what is feared is not so terrible after all.

414

Participant: It is something female.

Professor Jung: Yes, the female instinctual world, that's what begins there. There the child starts to become a female, so to speak. In later life, too, whenever something is about the female instinctual world, these feline animals reappear, or bears, or snakes. In Switzerland, after all, we had a bear goddess. In the Historical Museum you can see a *dea arcto*.[28] Long before the Berne Zofingia, there was a Gallic-Roman bear cult in Berne. The believers of Artemis call themselves *arktoi*, the bears. The bear represents the female instinctual world. Well, how would you formulate the purpose of the dream? How does the dream function in the psychic balance?

Participant: From the tension that something should appear in consciousness.

Professor Jung: Wouldn't this be expressed much more clearly if the tiger jumped in and knocked the child over?

Participant: The dream wants to say: there is more to this dangerous thing, an insight. This is what lies hidden behind it.

Professor Jung: Without doubt, this intrusion of the tiger is an intrusion of the female instinctual world, with a frightening aspect. This could prompt the child to flee the female instinctual world, but that would be a danger for the child's consciousness. The dream is comforting in that it says: although the tiger jumps at you, it breaks into two parts. This expresses a basic, fundamental truth. Which?

Participant: You are a human being, a woman, but there are also men, because everything is bipolar.

Professor Jung: There are polarities in the dream. Which is the first one?

Participant: Inside and outside.

Professor Jung: The first polarity is the ego and the instinctual world. The second polarity is what? The divided tiger. It has a frontside and a backside. And the front and the back of the tiger is a wonderful polarity, which couldn't be conceived in a better way. It says: the instinctual world has a front and a back, for it is an animal. If it is split, it will be deprived of its potency. This means that it is still to-

---

[28] Latin, Arctos (sing.), Arctoe (pl.), the two Bears in the northern sky (trans.).

415

gether, but shows that the instinctual world has a double aspect. This is a wisdom of the dream, a particular finesse. What is the double aspect of the instinctual world?

Participant: A physical and a spiritual aspect.

Professor Jung: Yes, exactly, for there is also a spiritual aspect to the instinctual world. It has a head, a tiger-head, just as man is also actually split into an above and a below. In vulgar terms, the spiritual aspect is above, and the instinctual one below. Man himself is a double, split animal. He is no animal, but a human being, but as such he is actually split. He is no longer an animal, but—what does he foolishly do?

Participant: He thinks.

Professor Jung: Yes, he reflects. It is better to say: reflect, because we also *feel* in a reflecting way. Thinking is too specific. Above there is the *anima rationalis*, to use the medieval term, and below the *anima vegetativa*, only life as such. The moment it becomes conscious, the two aspects will reveal themselves. So what enters into the soul of the child? A whole tiger or a half tiger?

Participant: Two halves.

Professor Jung: Yes, two halves. What consequence does this have for the child's consciousness?

Participant: It is not dangerous.

Professor Jung: Well, to have eaten two tiger halves—that's quite something. What would happen, for instance, if the child ate one half, the half of the head? What does that mean? This half is assimilated to the head, the lower or rear half is assimilated from below. What has happened by this? Well, look: for us the child is actually unity par excellence. With the eaten tiger, however, *conflict* moves into the soul of the child. The conflict had hitherto still been in the unconscious, but now it jumps at the child's consciousness. If she assimilates the tiger, the split will be transferred into consciousness. From that point there will be the Yes and the No. Here the moral conflict comes into being, the distinction between good and evil.

Participant: But wouldn't there be a rescue in this case?

Professor Jung: This is not about rescue, just that something happens. An image happens, and the image tells what is really going on.

416

This means: "From now on you are divided. Now the instinctual, the female instinctual world has penetrated into you, and so you are now a divided being, that is, a human being." Before it was just a dream, an infantile paradise. If I knew what later became of the child, we would see many more things in her later life, for this was the first dream that foretold her later destiny.

3. Dream of a Five-Year-Old Girl of the Devil in the Garden Shaft[29]
PRESENTED BY DR. EMMA STEINER[30]

Text: I am seeing my father at a shaft in the garden. The earth moves, and I think: there's the devil down there. And I call my father for help. But my father laughs and pushes me down. I land in a tool shed with a cold frame full of seedlings.

Professor Jung: What is the difference between this and the previous dream?

Participant: Here the child must go down, in the other dream she had to go up.

Professor Jung: Both are girls five years of age. Now here you see a very different picture. What do you think about the situation of this girl's consciousness?

Participant: The child thinks too much like her father.

Participant: There the child has no premonition of what will come; here she has.

Professor Jung: Yes, isn't that so? In the first case, in the dream of the tiger, consciousness is quite childlike and completely paradisial, and then something suddenly comes. In this case, the moment the earth moves, it already knows that this is the devil. What does that mean? In any case this consciousness is much better prepared. What does this mean in practical terms?

Participant: She is not an anxiously well-cared-for child; she is a precocious child.

Participant: She is healthier.

[29] Session of 12 November 1940.
[30] The text of the paper is missing. The dream text is roughly the one given in the text (ed.).

Professor Jung: First of all, I'd say that she is not that naive, but has already sensed quite a few things with her five years; she is not all that stupid. She already more or less knows how things go. In this respect, a prepared consciousness is better than an unprepared one, and such an important fall into the instinctual world can be much better absorbed. But there are difficulties here, too. What is the conflict in this case? This is a state of consciousness already characterized by conflicts. This is a child who already has a premonition of conflicts; the tiger episode already lies behind her.

Participant: There are already typical projections onto the father, for example, his connection to the devil.

Professor Jung: Yes, sure, but what is the conflict?

Participant: The difficulty in really accepting the devil.

Professor Jung: No, the conflict is stated in the dream itself. In what does it consist?

Participant: That the father is in cahoots with the devil.

Professor Jung: She calls the father for help, but the father does not give it to her, quite the contrary: with diabolical laughter he pushes the poor child into the abyss. Well, isn't this a conflict? If the dream took a different course, for instance, something we'd quite naturally expect—that the father would hurry toward her to rescue the poor little thing from the devil—what would this be then?

Participant: A regression.

Professor Jung: Then the father would be the all-good one. According to consciousness, he would be perfectly alright. He would be the one who gives protection, who nurtures and holds. And the child would be completely contained in the father. What would then show in later life?

Participant: There would be more conflicts.

Professor Jung: There would be a father complex as high as a house, a *fille à papa.*"[31] What psychology does such a girl have?

Participant: She turns against the mother.

Professor Jung: An anima type would probably develop, a woman who always knows how to twist the father round her little finger

[31] French, "daddy's girl" (trans.).

418

so that he opens his fatherly arms and protects the poor little soul from the world. Naturally, there would be a number of complications with the mother, and so on. What happens in the dream is the normal process, namely, that the father already stops an attempt at a father complex at the outset; because in this dream a rudiment of a father complex is visible. The child's plea is: I want you to protect me. How do you conceive of the shaft into which the father pushes her?

Participant: As a descent into the unconscious.

Professor Jung: But a shaft?

Participant: It is reminiscent of birth, a precipitate delivery, so to speak.

Participant: It reminds me of a mine.

Participant: Something has been arranged so that something can go up or down.

Professor Jung: Yes, something has been prepared. So there already exists a shaft, as if a mine were down there. What does this indicate?

Participant: We would have to assume that the father is in possession of the communication with the unconscious.

Participant: It indicates that this, too, has been arranged in the garden, a shaft into the unconscious, that is.

Participant: A helpful force is present.

Professor Jung: Yes, above there is the garden. How would you interpret it?

Participant: As the state of the child's consciousness.

Professor Jung: Yes, this is a certain state of the child's consciousness. This is already a space of consciousness. And what is the garden? It is not the woods, the open countryside, but a garden of all things. What does that mean?

Participant: This is culture.

Professor Jung: Yes, there exists a cultural atmosphere in the child's space of consciousness. And characterized by what? Something very specific.

Participant: That the father is working in it.

Professor Jung: Well, isn't that nice. But it is a prerequisite that the father has something to do with culture. That's why the daughters take over the father's spirit, the animus, but here there is something special.

Participant: The garden is not only above ground, but also cultivated subterraneously.

Professor Jung: Yes, but what would you otherwise expect to find in the underworld, where the devil dwells?

Participant: Hell and fire.

Professor Jung: Yes, seething chaos; but there is only a tool shed down there, and a cold frame with seedlings to boot. What has happened here?

Participant: There is order in it.

Professor Jung: Exactly, there are shovels, axes down there, anything you need to cultivate the garden in preparation for cultural work. And what is a cold frame, exactly?

Participant: Again a preparation.

Professor Jung: Of course, there you grow the seedlings. Thus a preparation again. But there the devil is in a very strange place indeed. What place is it actually? Where is room for the devil there, where can he spend the night? What's the matter with the devil?

Participant: He isn't in the right place.

Professor Jung: Yes, if he is indeed the devil, he is completely out of place. So we cannot but assume that this is no longer a real devil at all. He is so out of place that he has no hell, and thus can't do anything, and so we have to presume that he is a modified devil.

Participant: He is a vegetation demon.

Professor Jung: Yes, this is absolutely correct. His hell consists of a garden, and later of a cold frame. Who appears in a cold frame?

Participant: Osiris.

Professor Jung: Yes, this is a classical figure. In the British Museum you see the figure of Osiris stretched on a canvas, covered by wet sand in which grass was planted; then Osiris sprang up in the form of grass. Thus, every year Osiris sprang up again from the earth. He was also depicted as wheat springing up from his sarcophagus. He himself reappears as young corn, as its first green seedlings. He was really a vegetation god, and as master of the underworld he actually bears a certain resemblance to *our* god of the underworld, the devil. Al-

420

though he is the good one, his brother Seth-Typhon is the bad one, the brother who was born with Osiris as his opposite in the same pregnancy. He is simply the shadow of Osiris, and by virtue of this shadow he has a relation to the underworld and consequently is a *chthonios*. One can actually no longer correctly classify this devil that appears here, because he has become a vegetation god. And the initial horror of the devil, where does that come from? Why the horror? The cry for help to the father?

Participant: The devil has been condemned by the Christian Church.

Professor Jung: There is a Christian influence that speaks of the evil, which naturally gives consciousness an infernal fright. But the dream saves the dreamer from this shock in showing her: If you do fall down to the devil, there will be a tool shed where one is prepared for cultural work: there is a cold frame with seedlings. Then one will lie amidst the seedlings. The child falls down into a cold frame with seedlings; she herself is planted like a seedling into the fertile earth. The cold frame is a kind of incubator. The whole aspect of these images of hell has changed, not in the Christian sense, but in the antique one.

Participant: We can then view the underworld as some sort of realm of the blessed spirits.

Professor Jung: The dream says: what impresses you as evil is the fertility of earth and nature.

Participant: But isn't the earthquake something threatening after all?

Professor Jung: The child is in a secure place. Instead of intruding from the outside, the disturbance comes from out of the earth, and the child also knows already: this is the devil. An earthquake always means that one's standpoint is shaken. "The earth is trembling under my feet" means that one is confronted with something one cannot cope with. So it is as if the earth were shaken. It is assumed [by the girl] that this is the devil. This interpretation comes from a consciousness influenced by Christianity, for the child does not know that a shaft has already been provided. And who made this shaft?

Participant: The same people who made the garden. The tools are

421

there anyway. The person who made the garden even took his tools from that tool shed.

Professor Jung: Yes, the father provided that, and uses this room as a tool shed. How do you understand that?

Participant: It is a well analyzed father who treats his daughter properly.

Professor Jung: Exactly. Everything has been provided so that the children will immediately fall into the fertile earth in case of an earthquake.

Participant: As a counterpart, a dream of a child comes to mind in which a witch comes out of a chimney and gets the little girl out of a crowd.

Professor Jung: This means that the child is possessed by the unconscious for a longer period of time, that she is dissolved in an unconscious state. You know the story of Jimmy, who was killed in a tiger hunt. The bagged animal was then brought to his relatives with the remark: "Jimmy inside the tiger!"[32]—This is a case in which no lysis occurs. The child is "inside the witch." The child is gotten by the devil. You know, there are children who live in hell for years, who are preternaturally bad or feel themselves that they are in a hellish state, who are terribly unhappy and tormented, children for whom childhood is one big hell. These are children who are captured in the unconscious. This child, for example, is a child who for a long time is not herself, but something evil and enigmatic. Such children are "inside the tiger." They are surrounded by a cloak of demonism. I remember such a boy: he was an evil spirit who tormented everybody else. But once during a school outing, when by chance the two of us were alone, he told me: "I know I'm really bad, but here, where there are no people, here I'm completely alright." He was fourteen years old. There it vanished—anything vanished, that is, that had been imposed on him by the environment. Such events do not take place naturally, but are caused by the atmosphere resulting from the unresolved unconscious of the parents. A thick wall separates these persons from their own souls, and the child then falls into it, is born out

---

[32] "Jimmy inside the tiger" and "inside the witch" in English in the original (trans.).

of this atmosphere and then bewitched by it, possessed by the darkness of which the parents have never wanted to be aware—and also have not been able to. Such dreams result from such conditions.

Participant: Here the devil is a gardener in the garden of God.

Professor Jung: The devil is not the gardener, the father is the gardener. The devil here is the vegetation god, dweller in the prepared earth. He is the one who lives in the cold frame. He is the life demon of the budding, future life, quite like an old Osiris.

Participant: I once read of a Roman goddess, Lavinia, the terrible mother. Just like Kali, she is present at each birth of a child to prevent the decision to lay the child quickly onto the earth, by which it would be saved from her.

Professor Jung: You see, this is actually the planting into the earth, the being brought in touch with the earth as an inhabitant of the earth. One falls down to the earth, where one becomes fertile oneself. "Be fruitful, and multiply,"[33] for we are planted into the earth like a tree. The image is so clear and simple that there is no need to further abstract the dream.

Participant: I wonder what happened to the child at the time?

Professor Jung: Nothing special; after this dream nothing special at all was to happen, for everything is perfectly alright.

4. Dream of a Six-Year-Old Boy of Rotating Grids
PRESENTED BY DR. KENOWER W. BASH[34]

Text: *We, that is, me and a boy of the same age, have been captured by the witch into a middle-sized cave with her. The cave has a round form and blood-red walls. The only exit is a narrow and low passage, a kind of tube. The passage starts on the ground of the cave; at first, it slopes gently down, and then gently ascends again. In its last part, two interlocking rows of iron bars protrude from the wall; these two grids rotate, so that for one moment they open the exit and then block it again. Going, or better creeping, through the exit is particularly dangerous here. I wake up with very great anxiety, so I wake up the nanny sleeping beside me to tell me that it is just a dream.*

[33] Genesis 1:22 (trans.).
[34] Session of 3 December 1940.

Dr. Bash: The locale here is the witch's cave, middle-sized, round, with blood-red walls, whose only exit is a narrow, low, tubelike passage that starts on the ground, at first slopes down and then ascends. This passage is blocked by rotating grids that alternately lock and open it. The persons are the dreamer, a boy of the same age, and the witch by whom these two are captured. I think that in this case I will have to dispense with the usual dramatic structuring of the dream events, because not only is there no lysis, but also no real action. The dream is more like a vision; frightened by this vision, the boy awakes with a cry of fear. We will later come back to the meaning of this fact.

The symbolism of the *cave* is generally known. It is the breeding ground, the womb, the place of birth, rebirth, and change. Its middle size is conspicuously stressed: conspicuous, so to speak, precisely because it is not conspicuous. As a rule, the extremes are eye-catching, not the middle, which is not mentioned in particular. That the cave is middle-sized must, therefore, have a special meaning. An enormous cave would suggest the underworld of the dwarfs or gnomes, or maybe the shadowy underworld in which Pluto sits enthroned, the hidden, spacious treasure chambers of the fairy tales, in which immense riches are kept, in short, what is uncanny, monstrous, supernatural, and hardly known about the unconscious as such, should it once reveal itself directly. The hollows of such a cave would lie in the shadows that veil the inscrutable. Man would, then, stand there either as a presumptuous intruder or as a captive of chthonic powers, on foreign soil before the last secrets that transcend anything personal, beyond the individual and the temporal. A small, narrow cave, on the other hand, would remind us of the incubation caves or huts of the Greek mysteries and various primitive religions, in which a candidate has to await a dream, or at least stay there for some time until he has been filled by the spirit. In contrast to the previous example, he searched for, and found there, a personal confrontation with the unconscious. For him as an accomplished but still undeveloped personality, the main problem was his position, his relation to the unconscious, whereas his individual personality hardly mattered in the gigantic dimensions of the enormous cave. Our dreamer now stands between these two possibilities. To interpret his position we have to take his age into account. At the age of six, he is beyond early infantile unconsciousness, which feels carefree and sheltered in the collective, but still far from the complexity of the adult, in which one firm point, so to speak,[35] a core personality, has been developed, with reference to which he can confront the collective. It is exactly the transition that is a main problem at this age, in which the child first learns to venture out of the shelter of the house and the parents, goes to school, begins to adjust to organized society, and starts to enter into relations with the foreign object world. His world is no longer completely within himself. Hetzer[36] draws attention to this change, which can be easily ascertained by the *Vienna Development Tests*, edited by herself and Charlotte Bühler, and writes:

> Subjectivity and objectivity . . . are partly a criterion of development. Until the fifth year, subjectivity is normal. It shows in the fact that children are not really willing to comply with the circumstances: they arbitrarily interpret the content of a picture, their own drawings and constructions; they do not exactly repeat or draw what has been said or done before, but willfully make additions or alterations; they do not accept the fact that the examiner has won in the competitive game, but claim the victory for themselves, regardless of their obvious loss. Children at the age of five and older have a certain objectivity and are capable of assimilation, which is, for instance, shown by the fact that they tell stories about pictures that correspond to their contents, or that they build a copy of the model building. It corresponds to their stage of development that they comply with given tasks. If they do not show this objectivity we may conclude that there is very little willingness to submit to given facts, an inadequate awareness of reality, and an overemphasis on instinctuality, which cannot be reconciled in a normal way with the demands of the outer world.

The child leaves the inner collective and now has to differentiate himself in order not to lose himself in the outer collective. His psy-

---

[35] Allusion to Archimedes, who used to demand just one firm and immovable point in order to shift the entire earth (trans.).

[36] Hildegard Hetzer, *Psychologische Untersuchung der Konstitution des Kindes*.

chical perimeter, daily expanded by new contacts with the environment, is restricted at least quantitatively, if I may say so, on the other
side in that the collective contents recede into the background. It
becomes middle-sized. The problems occurring there have their roots
in the collective, on the one hand, and in the personal, on the other.

The cave is *round*, which gives the problem a certain contour. It
does not reach immeasurable dimensions. The content of the situation is directly given and apparent. The hidden things are outside,
not in the causal situation itself. Insofar as they are inhibitions (as
indicated by the confinement), they are on all sides and concern the
whole individual. They are also self-made—a natural cave is not so
well-rounded.

In addition, this cave has *blood-red* walls. Here, too, we are rather
inclined to think of something artificial than of a natural color. There
are indeed red rocks, but hardly blood-red ones. Red is the color of
passion, of excitement, of aggressiveness, of fire and anything fiery in
general. The devil—who also lives underground and embodies the
evil powers of the unconscious—is almost always depicted as dressed
in red. Blood stands for pulsating, pushing life: blood-red is thus the
color of the vital instincts and of the overwhelming emotional turmoil they bring about. From what we have said about this scene we
may probably conclude this: the child is in a highly affect-laden situation, which probably lies in the normal way of psychological development, but which has not been caused by the normal inner developmental processes alone.

Let us now turn to the persons of the dream. First of all, we come
across a not clearly specified "we." Of the unknown person we only
know that he is as old as the dreamer and completely shares the latter's fate, as it seems. Therefore this figure cannot be interpreted with
certainty; I am most inclined, however, to see it as a kind of *double* or twin who establishes a connection to the collective for the
dreamer, and at the same time provides him with a possibility to differentiate himself from it. The fact that the dreamer is almost two,
the same and yet not the same, very probably indicates that the problems concerning this double figure are of a collective nature; all the
more so as the resembling boy stands in no distinct contrast to the

426

dreamer, characterologically or otherwise, as is so often the case when this double is to represent the shadow side. That this indication of the collective is restricted to a mere duplication, instead of a multiplicity, probably corresponds to the mid-sized cave, that is to say that neither the personality of the dreamer, nor the impersonal forces of the unconscious, necessarily prevail in the present problem. At the same time, the fact that the comrade is undoubtedly experienced as a different person makes the dreamer realize his individuality and so provides him with a starting point for further individualization.

The second figure is the *witch*, who also is not described in more detail. We need not go into the symbolism of the witch at length. She is a force of the unconscious that exerts a magical pressure here. The boy is captured here as part of a collective, with which he does not feel completely identical, however. If we may attempt to interpret the dream on a personal level, it seems reasonable to suppose that this is about the mother. As is so often the case in fairy tales, the mother is replaced at least temporarily by an evil stepmother or a witch, who is nobody else but a mother that insufficiently fulfills, or willfully neglects, her duty and obligation toward her children. And who else would be in a such a position to hold back the child in a primitive developmental phase and in the womb of the collective? As we have already mentioned, there is evidence that the child was forced by something from the outside, that the situation he is in was created by someone from the outside, and this could most likely be achieved by a maybe all-too-loving mother. This is also confirmed by the round form and the red color (the color of the intestines) of the cave, which might indicate the uterus, and also by the winding path, first sloping downward, then ascending, and the especially stressed "creeping through," reminiscent of the birth canal and of birth. We need not interpret these factors in this restricted sense at all, however, because they could equally well, on a general level, stand for rebirth and for coming to a developmental stage yet to be reached. The subterranean cave and the red color, which was spilled around the child, remind us a bit of the Mithraic taurobolium,[37] which was ex-

---

[37] "The sacrifice of a bull, usually in connection with the worship of the Great Mother of

pressly conceived of as a rebirth. So we roughly have the following situation: the child is at an age in which he should normally begin to differentiate himself, and to go out into the world as a budding individual. This means stepping out of, on the one hand, the vegetative-collective existence of the infant, and, on the other hand, also the permanent care of the parents and the identification with them. A first step toward that has already been made; nevertheless, the child is still detained by a force effective in the unconscious, which probably does not originate in the child's own soul alone, but creates an oppressive situation around him. This corresponds to remaining in the maternal womb, as seems to be indicated by the condition of the cave. The most probable assumption may be that it is indeed the mother who inhibits the boy in his development in such a way.

We have not yet dealt with the most peculiar and most characteristic part of the dream, the blocking of the exit by the rotating *iron grids*. Iron grids are the usual barriers in prisons and mental institutions—in any place where one is held against one's will. On the other hand, they also offer a view of the outside, of possibilities lying beyond the barrier. This confirms our assumption that the child's situation was not created by him alone, and that he tries, more or less, to fight against it, or at least senses that he should not be content with it. The specific feature, however, is that creeping through is only possible at a certain, well-chosen moment. Here we encounter a motif that is well known in mythology and literature, although it has not appeared very frequently in the dreams we have discussed so far in the seminar. Thus, I'd like to give you a few pertinent examples. Most likely we will probably think of the passage of Aeneas between Scylla and Charybdis, or of that of the Argonauts between the Sym-

---

the Gods, though not limited to this. Of oriental origin, its first known performance in Italy occurred in A.D. 134, at Puteoli, in honor of Venus Caelestis." Prudentius describes it in Peristephanon (x, 1066ff): "the priest of the Mother, clad in a toga worn cinctu Gabino, with golden crown anti fillets on his head, takes his place in a trench covered by a platform of planks pierced with fine holes, on which a bull, magnificent with flowers and gold, is slain. The blood rains through the platform on to the priest below, who receives it on his face, and even on his tongue and palate, and after the baptism presents himself before his fellow-worshippers purified and regenerated, and receives their salutations and reverence" (http://en.wikipedia.org/wiki/Taurobolium; accessed 14 March 2007) (trans.).

428

plegades, the gigantic rock formations at the entrance to the Black Sea, which clashed without warning and crushed the poor seafarer. The doves, which bring ambrosia to Zeus, have to fly between two rocks that suddenly clash and regularly crush the last of the consecrated birds. In later times we find something similar in Dante's ascent from hell, when he has to go with his guide Vergil under the flapping wings of Satan at the moment in which they are raised. Frobenius offers a great deal of material on this motif of the clashing rocks in his book *Das Zeitalter des Sonnengottes* [*The Age of the Sun God*], from which I quote:

> When Maui descends into the underworld, he has to pass the rising and falling rocks, and only repeating the saying he learned from the mother keeps the god from being crushed. When Bogda Gesser Chan travels to the ogres to visit his wife, he will have to pass the clashing rocks. The rock gate closes in North Korea and in ancient Mexico, and for the North Indians the clashing rocks thunderously smash together behind the blessed spirits that levitate into the beyond. Sometimes this motif may be varied; in Northwest America, a biting door replaces the clashing rocks, and the collapsing tree trunk—which can be found there as well as in Japan as one of the hero's ordeals—may also belong to this group. Moreover, it is interesting that the motif is split into groups in Samoa and by the Navahos in America. On his journey into the underworld, Tiitii has to pass the reeds; his magic spell makes the reeds part. Then he has to pass the rocks, and the rocks open upon his spell. For the Navahos, those wandering toward the sun first have to pass through the rocks, then over the cutting reed, then across the field of cactuses that tear everything to shreds, then over the boiling barren land of sand; and only then do they pass the various gate wardens who face each other with their mouths wide open in trembling rage: two bears, two snakes, two winds, and two flashes of lightning. All these they have to pass, and in this sense this is the highest evolution of this motif.

In almost every case, therefore, this is a journey into the beyond, or the quest for a precious treasure that is difficult to obtain, and which assumes a value of immortality. It is a rebirth, as is unambiguously in-

429

timated by the whole present dream situation. Frobenius goes on to say:

> The climax of interest in this myth is only reached, however, when the motif is amplified by a little addition, when it is told how the hero gets through the clashing rocks by a hair's breadth, while the back part of his vehicle is crushed. . . . Although the famous ship in the journey of the Argonauts luckily succeeds in gliding through between the equally famous rocks, a little accident occurs, however. For not even birds were able to fly through, and so Phineus gave the advice to let a dove fly before them and, if it came through, to follow with all their might—otherwise they would have to abandon their journey altogether. And really the dove passed through; only its tail feathers were crushed when the rocks smashed together. So the Greeks waited until the gate opened again, rowed with all their might and shot through, and only the ornamental tip of the rudder was crushed. When Maui flies into the underworld on Mangaia to visit his parents and to get the fire, on an ogre journey, that is, he also has to pass the clashing rocks. Maui has borrowed the red dove Tanes, and on it he rides into the beyond. To his delight, the rocks open upon the magic words that Maui had learned from the mother, only to close again when Maui passes through. He luckily succeeds in getting through but, alas, the resplendent tail of the beautiful dove has been crushed.

This means: for the goal to be attained and the transformation to be completed, a sacrifice has to be made. To achieve the new, the old has at least partly to be abandoned. This is the age-old "die and become"![38] Here the boy has to leave the mother's protection to differentiate himself in accordance with his age. Above all, it is important that he seize the right moment that must not be missed; because already he is a bit past the point at which he ordinarily should have found his way into the objective world in a normal development. Hesitation is dangerous. If he gains insight into the line of life, how-

---

[38] "And as long as you lack this / True word: Die and Become! / You'll be but a dismal guest / In Earth's darkened room" (Goethe, "Blissful Yearning," *West-Eastern Divan*) (trans.).

430

ever, into the rhythm of life as symbolized by the alternating closing and reopening of the gates, into events dictated by time, then he will be offered the possibility to pass through successfully without severe losses, although not without paying the indispensable tribute.

[Here Dr. Bash quotes another dream of a female schizophrenic patient, which is compared to the present case.][39]

It remains to be discussed how the seemingly missing lysis in the boy's dream has to be conceived. As mentioned at the beginning, the dream is rather a vision. No action takes place, but there is a confrontation, a juxtaposition, that does not directly call for a lysis. Or we could interpret his waking up with a cry of fear as a kind of lysis. We may well expect that his successive dreams will deal with the facts given here. It would probably be most salutary for the dreamer to try and bring about a solution of the conflict straight away, that he summon his courage and go through, instead of flinching from it as he does here. That he does not do it, however, is by no means a bad or even fatal omen, all the more so in that the possibility of slipping through is repeatedly offered in the dream.

In summarizing the psychological meaning of the dream, we may say: the six-year-old boy already has a partial consciousness of his situation, the transition from early infantile unconsciousness, collectivity, subjectivity, love and security within the family, and attachment to the mother, to a stage of budding consciousness, differentiation, objectivity, stepping out into the world, and disengagement from the family. In all this he is hindered by forces that are partly effective in his unconscious, but which he has not been completely unaware of. These forces rather confront him from the outside than develop out of his inside. It stands to reason that it is the mother who wants to hold him back in a primitive phase, *in utero*, so to speak. There is a way out of this danger, but it is not without risks. It is not practical just like that, because the right moment has passed. It requires a certain insight, above all the realization and use of the fateful moment in which, and in which alone, rescue is possible. This moment, however, recurs over and over again for the time being. The

---

[39] Square brackets in original (trans.).

431

child is not yet condemned to a necessarily pathological escalation of the situation, as we have seen it in the dream of the schizophrenic patient.

Professor Jung: So this is a dream that contains no activity but, as Mr. Bash has rightly mentioned, is actually an image, a confrontation. The dream is only an image that has been presented to him, so to speak. And this image now represents his situation, his critical situation, in which he is. Mr. Bash has quite correctly shown that the age between the fifth and the sixth year is a critical age, and I am glad that Mr. Bash has also consulted other psychological literature. Today there are very many objective descriptions of infantile psychology. Our *furor paedagogicus*, which we have chiefly directed at the child, has indeed been useful, although the interest is a bit pathological, generated so that the teacher need not deal with his own psychology. The human soul is something we only educate, but we are not interested at all in what it is!—Well, this is a critical age insofar as the child approaches school between the age of five and six. The child is no longer in the former unconscious atmosphere, but feels that he is approached by a world to which he has to adapt. Naturally, it is understandable at such a moment that a dream, which clearly shows the specific handicap, will appear, if the child is somehow not ready for this adaptational work. And this is what the present dream does. It shows the specific handicap of this person. Because we can say it in a few words: he is not yet born. He is still *in utero*. Mr. Bash has had the quite correct idea to interpret the boy of the same age as someone identical. However, this duplication does have a specific meaning in such a case: first of all, there is a mythological foundation of this duplication *in utero*. The primitives, for example, see the afterbirth as the "other." He is the brother, the twin, who is also treated like a child, because he is simply a differently shaped twin. He actually is one, only looks a bit different. That the placenta is the other is only a rationalization. The fact is that a human being always feels himself as two; the other is the shadow. We could also say: he still has a placenta with him, still has an umbilical cord to his placenta, because the shadow is what connects him to the dark world, that is, the unconscious.

432

We have to assume a considerable shadow, which, however, will show only when he steps into the light; otherwise, the shadow is invisible. In that case, the dreamer is the man without a shadow. As long as this dream is valid, he is the man without a shadow. Because he is not yet born, his main figure is still in the womb, in his shadow. Although he does exist on the outside, he is not the real one at all; he is half or something like that. The reason why he cannot come out is given in the dream: the *grids*. Now what could such grids be in reality, for a person who has not yet come out of the mother, but lives in complete darkness? What is described by two rotating grids? What can this mean to us? The grid of course is always something that prevents entering or exiting; teeth or clashing rocks would also make it awkward to slip through. So what is specific about the grids?

Participant: Probably it is the family itself?

Professor Jung: Yes, sure, but what are the grids? First of all: grids do not grow naturally; grids have been placed by somebody. Somebody has willfully played this devilish trick. If you think of the mother, you are absolutely correct. A witch, an evil power, has ingeniously placed these grids. But in what do they consist?

Participant: In prohibitions.

Professor Jung: Yes, instead of saying: "It is forbidden to climb through the window," we make a grille. This is a possible explanation. These are very concrete prohibitions, concrete obstacles; thus there is a positive resolve to block this passage. What can a mother do in this respect? What is the most favored means of a mother to block the birth canal?

Participant: To make you aware of threatening dangers.

Participant: To bring up moral pairs of opposites, good and bad.

Professor Jung: This is correct. But this is not so in our case. These grids have been placed by the witch, so that Hansel cannot get out of the oven; and if he gets out, she will pinch off his feet. The grids rotate, so that one could possibly go through, which is questionable, however. So the mother has to do something, which is expressed by the rotating grids. This is an opposition, in that you are quite right, a strange opposition. What kinds of opposites does the mother make?

433

Participant: She encourages him, and when he wants to do it she holds him back.

Professor Jung: Yes, it's along these lines.

Participant: Perhaps, on the one hand, she makes a special hero out of him, and, on the other, there is still the nanny in the room.

Participant: Or she can show him the world, but when he wants to get out, she'll say: you're still too little for that.

Professor Jung: Well, yes, on the one hand, a mother has a normal interest that the child grows up, develops, wants to get out, and becomes an honest and capable child; on the other hand, all this is forbidden in, oh, so many words. So, for instance, she gives him a long lecture that this and that is forbidden, yet she provokes him to do it after all. She slips him the opportunity. We can often see this when boys have become a little older. Then the mother might say: "Don't you ever dare to kiss a girl!" And then: "Don't you want to go to the party? Don't you see that all the others also go to the party?" This game is played thousands of times, with incitements and prohibitions. These are all mothers who do not think, but just hope, wish, and fear; they are always in the emotional state. They allure and seduce. But then it is crushed. One naturally can't get out in such a situation. I think that there is a specific agenda in this case, namely, that the mother wants a development as soon as possible, but then does not want precisely this because of the inherent dangers. These are obstacles a mother can erect to keep a child with her. Eventually a psychological attitude will develop in the boy that the only chance to get out is to catch the right moment. There are very well-behaved boys who only wait for the right moment, when the mother turns her back. Then something happens, but really something! Very often the children hurt themselves, even literally, by pulling down boiling water, or by playing tricks; to get the mother going, they climb on the highest trees and hope the mother will see them, but then they might fall to death.

Now this cave is clearly described as a uterus. And it is perfectly possible that this boy already knew that he had been in the mother's belly. The dream describes the inside of the belly. It says: hey, you are still in the belly of the mother. The rest is completely correct anatomically. There's one strange little detail: the way slopes down at first and then goes up. What does this mean for the mother, the one who has the belly? What does this mean for the whole situation? In which situation is the mother?

Participant: She is lying down.

Professor Jung: He is enclosed in the lying mother. When somebody is lying down, he or she is usually sleeping. He is simply enclosed in the mother. It is only a little detail. It could mean: the mother goes on lying down, meaning that she sleeps. The mother is unconscious.

Participant: This would prove that the mother makes the whole situation unconscious.

Professor Jung: This is the whole trick the mother plays. It is based on her unconsciousness.

At a Later Meeting of the Seminar

Professor Jung: We are still discussing the dream of the boy who is in his mother's belly and can't get out. One could speak of a rebirth, although it is not really a rebirth, but a second birth. What is the difference?

Participant: A second birth is not something new, but a prolongation of the first one.

Professor Jung: Yes, the first one was incomplete, and thus has somehow to be completed later. What is the actual rebirth?

Participant: A transformation.

Professor Jung: Yes, a total guarantee that all requirements have been met. Man is completely transformed by this rebirth. Where does it occur?

Participant: In the mysteries.

Professor Jung: Yes, we encounter it whenever we are dealing with mysteries. And of course it is also found in myths, and in which myths in particular?

Participant: In heroic myths.

Professor Jung: Yes, in most cases of heroic myths we find the rebirth symbolism, and why?

Participant: The hero has to be born twice in order to be a hero.

Participant: As a hero he is superhuman.

Professor Jung: Yes, at first he is a man, but because it is his fate to become a superman he has to be reborn as such.

And where is this idea demonstrated technically?

Participant: In the initiation rites.

Participant: In baptism.

Professor Jung: Yes, there the idea of the birth of the hero is once again realized. We also find the idea of rebirth in the form of a political institution. In Egypt the kings had to be born twice. In many temples there was a birth chamber,[40] in which the king was procreated again by the gods. There is an indirect indication for this. For Heracles, the two mothers are Alkmene and Hera. In the case of the latter it is an adoption. Hera offers him her breast and feeds him. He sucks so hard that the milk spurts out, thus creating the milky way. There is a painting by an Italian painter of the adoption of Heracles, on the occasion of the birthday of a duke of Ferrara, in the sycophantic, Byzantine style of the tyrannical courts. It shows the duke as Heracles, lying under the skirts of Hera. It has been seen as an Aphroditian amorous play. But it is the adoption of Heracles. The second mother stands for the great destiny, which can be favorable or unfavorable, just as in our case.

Participant: The godparents also belong here.

Professor Jung: Yes, "godfather" and "godmother"[41] are gods. There is a connection with the English word [to] beget.[42] They are already present at birth, to demonstrate that this child was born not only bodily and carnally, but was also procreated by the gods—for baptism itself is already the second birth. In former times adults were baptized.

Participant: In the Orthodox Church, the real parents are strictly forbidden to be present at baptism.

Professor Jung: This is very logical.

---

[40] This expression in English in the original (trans.).

[41] In the original: "*Gotte*" and "*Götti*," Swiss German for "godfather" and "godmother." In standard German (*Pate, Patin*; derived from the Latin *pater* = father) this connection is lost (trans.).

[42] This word in English in the original (trans.).

Participant: There also is a canon law that godfather and godchild must not marry.

Participant: Achilles is secretly brought to be baptized by fire.

Professor Jung: In Plutarch, too, Isis puts the child into the fire every night to make him immortal. Then the mother cries out, and Isis says: Now the whole rebirth is kaput.

In our case, too, this second birth shows the mythological motifs of a difficult passage. Mr. Bash has quite correctly compared this difficulty with difficult passages in mythology, as, for example, in the motif of the clashing rocks, which is found in several variations. It is also situated in the right place, although it is not a mythological rebirth. What is interesting about this passage is that there is obviously only one right moment at which it is possible. As you know, such right moments can also be found in fairy tales.

Participant: For instance, the search for mysterious caves that open only during Midsummer Night. Then one can enter, then it is possible.

Professor Jung: There are also revolving doors, where the door opens only once.

Participant: Another example is the dream of the "swinging ax."[43]

Professor Jung: Yes, there, too, it is one precise moment at which the passage is possible.

Participant: Midnight is also such a special time.

Professor Jung: Yes, such conditions exist, for example, for digging up treasures. The treasure blossoms every nine years, nine months, and nine days; in this night the treasure can be simply picked up from the ground. Then, the following night, it again falls into the earth, fourteen fathoms deep. This is called the blossoming of the treasure. It is a *kairós*, the appropriate, right moment at which this is possible. What does this mean psychologically?

Participant: To be constantly awake.

Professor Jung: Yes, if you do not want to miss the moment, you have to be absolutely attentive. You constantly have to be alert. This

---

[43] See volume 2 of the English edition (trans.).

means that a constant devotion is necessary, a particular exertion of consciousness. If something happens only at one particular moment, one has to be damn careful not to miss this moment. This is important for the healing of an unborn state. By exerting one's consciousness, by reflecting and paying attention, it is possible to get through at one particular point. It is a consciousness that is captured, and then at one point finds an advantageous moment to break through somewhere. Therefore, the *kairós* is stressed.

Another thing has still to be mentioned: Mr. Bash has drawn a connection between the blood-red color of the cavity and the symbol of the red color as such. This is always about something emotional. So he would be captured in an emotional state. Now it is generally a characteristic feature that a consciousness that is not yet born is always under the spell of emotions. How is this expressed in the teachings of the chakras?

Participant: The Kundalini is still below the diaphragm.

Professor Jung: Yes, where?

Participant: In the Manipura.

Professor Jung: Yes, in the solar plexus. This is an emotional center, because diaphragm and stomach are affected. The emotions affect stomach and liver. In case of anger, icterus, jaundice, can ensue. The emotional center is in the upper part of the belly, therefore, and if someone is still in the belly, not yet born, he is captured in an emotional state. And all persons who are still captured in emotions, and whose life is influenced and guided by emotion, are actually not yet born and still under the *Heimarmene*,[44] under the force of the astrological condition. Rebirth has not yet been achieved. Such a person is completely bound by fate; he is a victim of fate. Such a person then says: "But that's how I feel," or "I'm scared," or "I'm sad," or "I'm not in the mood"—and then there's nothing one can do about it. We can only achieve something if we put him into the mood for action, just like the primitives. We have to lead off the dance, so to speak, so that they get into the mood for doing something. You cannot treat emotional people other than by emotional means. Consciousness has not

[44] Greek, "fate"; Stoic concept (trans.).

438

yet risen above the diaphragm. As we know, there are still some three positions above the diaphragm. Let us dismiss the last one; one actually has to be half dead to reach it.

Participant: Couldn't the dream also be about the problem of a rebirth?

Participant: But this dream is actually about a neurosis.

Professor Jung: Rebirth means birth into another world. This birth in the dream, however, is a birth into the outer world.

Participant: What should we do with children who are so dependent on emotions?

Professor Jung: You have to remove them into an environment that exerts a different pedagogical influence, because you can't speak psychologically to the child at all. I remember a thirty-five-year-old doctor with a mother complex. I had to fight for two months with the man to convince him that he simply wouldn't get out of the mother if he remained at home any longer. After two months, he came and said he had been thinking and had to ask me something. And then he asked: "Do you really believe that I should live at another place?" Eventually he believed it. As a result, the mother fractured her femur. Then he had a dream: *He climbs on slippery grass, climbs up; the mother also wants to go up, she also wants to reach the top of the hill, as stubborn as ever. She slips and fractures the femur.*

Here you can see how things are connected. So this story took a very dramatic course. And when it took him so long to realize it, this was due to the fact that he could not risk the death of the mother. Because it could have taken the mother's life if he had gone away. It is a fact that mothers say: If you marry, I will do myself in. Such sons then feel responsible when the old witch has to beat it. He does love his mother, and if he has but the faintest idea that she risks her life, he won't be able to get away. It takes a desecrating move backward, a look away from the mother's Medusa head. But this is not nice.

Participant: Could it be the case that the upcoming school triggered this dream in the five- to six-year-old boy?

Professor Jung: Yes, of course. It then turns out that such an attachment is extremely inexpedient, because he will be insufficiently prepared for facing the exigencies of the outer world. If such a child is intelligent, he may cope with all the intellectual exigencies in school, but still won't achieve anything; he does not have the independence of personality. He is totally undermined by the mother. In the case of the doctor, the mother demanded that he tell her all about the analysis. He wrote down every word for the mother, so she always had him in her grip. Then I said: "This has to stop." And of course this was the straw that broke the camel's back. Fortunately, she didn't die. One gets so furious with such parents!

Participant: Even if she dies, she will still be living. It's completely useless. The mother will still always be there.

Professor Jung: Yes, dying is completely useless. As the mother of God, she will always crouch there and brood over the child. He will never get out. It's the same, of course, with the fathers. We must by no means think that it would end with death. What the other has done to us, we'll then do ourselves later. Everything remains in the same place, and one lives exactly as before. Many a bachelor is sitting in his apartment and nurses the Manes[45] of his parents, and is as constricted and inhibited as ever.

5. Dream of a Ten-Year-Old Boy of a Red Ball
PRESENTED BY PROFESSOR C. G. JUNG

Text: *I was playing in the room with my brother Meinrad. Suddenly a red ball appeared in the sky that came nearer to our house. I looked through the window. When the ball had come into the house, it opened and "God" came out. It was a shining triangle with rays, and in the middle there was a figure that looked like "God." But it was someone young, not an old man, and also not the Savior. He looked a bit like the picture in my Bible: the torso of a body with blessing hands in the triangle.*

Then I was playing in the garden. There I saw the end of the world. I was standing by in a meadow. The moon and the stars fell down on the earth. I watched that. Then I saw Jesus alone in the sky. There were no people. Then I came into heaven. It was a theater. There was a stage. Above, there was a floating cloud. And then there was a throne on the stage. I saw the Trinity on it (just like it is usually portrayed, as an old man, the Holy Spirit, and Christ). Then God had disappeared. A "spirit"

---

[45] Latin, the spirits of the deceased in ancient Rome (trans.).

440

*came. He had a green face. He scared me. I was still on the stage with him.
It was winter. I lunged out at the devil and dumped him into the snow.
Then I woke up.*

Professor Jung: Personally, I have to remark that this child has been
brought up as a Catholic. He lives in a city that is bombarded every
now and then at the present time, so he is suffering from the horrors
of war. Otherwise I know of nothing detrimental. Obviously, he has
been brought up very religiously. There is no exaggerated religious
atmosphere, however, but simply the ordinary Catholic one. And so
the boy has this dream.

Now to the beginning: he is in the room with his brother. Suddenly this red ball appears and comes near the house. What would
you conclude from that?

Participant: Shouldn't one think of bombs?

Professor Jung: Yes, one could think of a danger when the red ball
appears. The whole thing is not described like an air raid, however,
but like something completely different.

Participant: Martin Buber mentions the visions of a nun. There the
soul was seen as a shining globe.

Professor Jung: Yes, this is the deity. Ignatius of Loyola, too, had
such visions in which a globe appeared. This is the all-round, cosmic
being, the world soul, the *rotundum*, the round one. And what would
you say about the fact that the ball in the dream is red?

Participant: It is the emotional state in puberty that is approaching
him.

Participant: Isn't the red connected to what is devilish in the cosmos? Typhon is red. The cosmos approaches him red and bloody. A
bewilderment about the world is expressed by this. Then the meaning of the dream develops in the further course of the dream.

Professor Jung: This is absolutely correct. The color red is crucial
here. Red is the emotional color par excellence, the hot color. It is
the blood. Thus we may also assume that this approaching red ball is
something frightening.

Participant: There are fireballs, ball lightnings, also in reality.

Professor Jung: But this the boy does not know. It is a very rare phenomenon. What happens in this dream is something completely different. What imposes itself is portrayed as a ball, and this is a dubious, problematic phenomenon, something unknown. It is by no means a conventional appearance. The ball rather looks like a celestial body approaching earth. It is unusual, supernatural. Such a thing doesn't happen every day. The dream then says: God comes out; so this globe contains God. It contains the religious center that naturally emerges as God at first in the dream of this boy. From the following dream images you see that they really refer to his religious ideas, that is, the religious ideas serve to explain the strange phenomena to him.

In Ignatius of Loyola we find visions in which Christ allegedly appears to him. In one vision he also sees a snake with many eyes, which actually is not dogmatic at all. These are primordial images, which then are perceived in the religious images one happens to have. What follows next in the dream are all dogmatic images. First of all: God comes out. But it is not the figure of an old man at all, but of a shining triangle. This quite clearly is the ecclesiastical image: rays and the eye of God within. Here there is no eye within, however, nor an old man, but someone young. It is also not the Savior. What does that indicate?

Participant: It is a new religious image showing itself.

Professor Jung: We have to assume that the unconscious—in accordance with the undogmatic solution (ball) that is then perceived dogmatically—contains something undogmatic. Thus, this is not the old man and not the Savior, but a young man. The unconscious says: well, please, this is something different than what you think, not the eye of God, all-embracing consciousness, but a young man, a stranger. With this the unconscious prevails, as it has already shown with the help of the red ball: now comes something different. Although the young man in the triangle resembles the picture in his Bible—a torso with blessing hands—it is expressly stated that is not the Savior, but another religious figure.

Now a peripateia occurs in the dream. We can assume, can't we, that the unconscious has asserted itself so much that he can no longer

442

ignore it. He has to face it. And now he runs into the garden. What can we say about that?

Participant: He goes out of the house, out of the construction made by humans, into the garden, into nature.

Professor Jung: In any case, he runs away from the place of the vision, into a completely different environment. He leaves the consciousness of the vision and enters into a completely different situation. The view is now enclosed. And what does this enclosed consciousness refer to?

Participant: To the previous view.

Professor Jung: Yes, quite right: an inhabited house in which one is contained. It has separate rooms that contain something. This is the dogmatic form within which he perceives this new phenomenon. But then he is not able to perceive it completely. He can only roughly approximate it to Christ, and is now confronted, so to speak, with the unbearable fact that he has something new in these rooms that does not fit at all. It is now understandable that he leaves this room; one has to abandon it. The unconscious relocates him to the garden. What is the difference?

Participant: He is freer.

Professor Jung: Yes, but he is also fenced in.

Participant: He is freer toward the sky.

Professor Jung: Yes, there is no lid on top up there. Things can still develop further up until Sirius; if nothing can be done right and left, and backward and forward, there is still room upward until heaven. And now he sees the end of the world there. What does that mean?

Participant: If he accepted it, it would mean the end of what had existed until then. It is tantamount to the end of the world; it is a twilight of the gods.

Professor Jung: It is further elaboration of the novelty, of the new figure. This young man who appears here is the messenger of the end of the world. And what occurs outside is the end of the world. So who is this young man?

Participant: The Antichrist.

Professor Jung: Yes, in the end he could be the Antichrist. He

443

comes at the end. He comes just before closing time. Now the boy is already no longer in the garden, but on a meadow, again a bit farther away. Moon and stars fall down on the earth. Where does this image come from?

Participant: From the Apocalypse.

Professor Jung: Yes, obviously. You did hear that he has an illustrated Bible.

Participant: Aren't they thrown down from the tail of an animal in the Apocalypse?

Professor Jung: Yes, absolutely. The angel of destruction throws the stars onto the earth. "Then I saw Jesus alone in the sky. There were no people." What does that mean?

Participant: The people have defected.

Professor Jung: Yes, of course, all the people are gone. This means that the Lord Jesus is now left alone. The whole glory has disappeared.

Now the boy is further transported away. In a way, he has been removed from the room, from the narrow, defined place, into the garden, from there into the meadow, and now even into heaven. Now he is elevated into the heights. And this heaven appears as a theater.

Participant: It is a devaluation of the previous image.

Professor Jung: Yes, the old image of heaven is only that of a theater. Then the floating clouds and the throne: this goes back to the Holy Trinity as it is usually depicted. And finally God has disappeared. It is a devaluation. The theatrical tricks don't work. Then it says: "a spirit came." Now things really get going. And this spirit has a green face.

Participant: It is the spirit of the earth.

Participant: It is reminiscent of Meyrink's *The Green Face*.

Professor Jung: Which he hasn't read. It simply means that the spirit has a green face. Therefore we are free to take a further step: he is Al-Khidr, the Green One.[46] Who is this?

---

[46] Khidr, literally "The Green One," represents freshness of spirit and eternal liveliness, green symbolizing the freshness of knowledge "drawn out of the living sources of life." Khidr is associated with the Water of Life. Because he drank the water of immortality, he is described as the one who has found the source of life, "eternal youth." He is the mysterious guide and

Participant: An angel of God.

Professor Jung: He is the angel of the face, the visible Allah, the *deuteros theos*, the second god, a concrete god. As a human being, he enters into all things; therefore, he is also called the green one, because he is also in the vegetation.

During my journey in Africa, my headman[47] was a Sufi. He had been initiated by a sheikh. He explained the nature of Khidr to me: "You are walking on the street. There goes a man, and you know it is Khidr. How do you know that? Well, you read the Koran, and you will know it. Then you greet him: 'Salaam aleikum.' Then all your wishes will be fulfilled. At night you are sleeping, and then you see a white light. It does not smoke, it does not burn. It is no star, and you know: it is Khidr." And then he took a little blade of grass and said: "He can also appear as this."

He is a real Dionysus, an undivided and divided spirit, a life spirit in all living beings, which is always present and can assume all forms. The boy says in the report of his dream: "He scared me." What is frightening is the direct presence of God; this is frightening. "I was still on the stage with him"—thus, where the Holy Trinity is sitting, where Christian dogmatism is played, there he is with him. "It was winter."

Participant: Winter comes before spring.

Professor Jung: Yes, where Khidr sits there is no winter. The ground is covered by spring flowers. Where Khidr sits it is green, there the earth turns green. But here it is winter, because Khidr has just arrived. "I lunged out at the devil and dumped him into the snow." So, if it is not the Father, the Son, and the Holy Spirit, it has to be the devil! This is the same argument as in St. Anthony: he saw a great light at night, and spirits who said: "We have come to enlighten you." But he concluded that they were demons who tested him. So he packed his suitcase[48] and left. This is a story by Anatole France, by the way, not from the *Acta Sanctorum*.[49]

---

immortal saint in popular Islamic lore and the hidden initiator of those who walk the mystical path. He is a symbol of changeability, as further explained later (trans.).

[47] This word in English in the original (trans.).

[48] This word in English in the original (trans.).

[49] Cf. *Oeuvres complètes illustrées de Anatole France*, ed. Calman Lévy, vol. 4, pp. 526ff.

So the boy of this dream also comes to the conclusion: this has to be the devil. This dream has been dreamed at this very time: January 1940.

At a Later Meeting of the Seminar
Professor Jung: Last time we analyzed the dream of the ten-year-old boy and discussed various religious problems. I also told you a bit about that boy. Naturally, we cannot assume that this boy knew anything about the figure of Khidr, who is a not very well-known figure. I have also looked up the subject of "Islam" in Hastings, and "Chadir" is mentioned nowhere. From this you can see how little this figure is known. Coincidentally, in our regions he is known from the poem by Rückert about Chidher, the eternally young one who returns every five hundred years. Rückert took this story from the translation of a legend that was published in the 1820s.[50] It is by Al Qaswini, a Persian poet who lived around the year 900. He was a cosmographer who described the whole cosmology. So this Al Qaswini gives an account of Chadir, who is actually called the "Green One." He tells the story of a young man who has a friend, and this friend is Chadir or Khidr. (The pronunciation varies according to the various Arabic dialects; as you know, in the Semitic languages the vowels, but not the consonants, vary.) Now this young man loves his friend Khidr very much; the king hears about this friend, who tells such wonderful stories, and lets Khidr come to tell him a story. The result is that the king is so impressed that he tells him that he, the king, wants to be taught by him and follow him. Then Khidr says that he cannot do that.

There is a legend in the Koran in which Khidr appears, without being named. It is supposed that Khidr does not go back to a pre-Islamic figure, but is a purely Islamic one. It is not impossible, however, even likely, that this figure, as also stressed by Volz, comes from the Arabic syncretism,[51] that spiritual movement which has absorbed all

[50] *Deutscher Musenalmanach*, pp. 39ff (1830).

[51] Syncretism is the attempt to reconcile disparate, even opposing, beliefs and to meld practices of various schools of thought. It is especially associated with the attempt to merge and analogize several originally discrete traditions, especially in the theology and mythology of religion, and thus assert an underlying unity. In Islam, the Druzes integrated elements of Ismaili

446

the remains of antiquity. So there are Christian, Jewish, Greek, and certain Gnostic influences, as well as Persian and doubtlessly also Indian ones. In Islam in particular, where this figure belongs, in Islamic mysticism, many Indian influences can be found. So this figure comes from this ambience. It is not impossible, therefore, that Khidr is modeled on various other figures that we may then find under one name or another. We know, for example, of the connection to a pre-Islamic figure; the interpretation is that he is Elijah, who goes back to late Jewish syncretism. Moreover, there is a connection to Alexander the Great. Iskander (Arabic for Alexander) has a great tradition. The Alexander novel also appears in the Middle Ages. There are numerous legends about his great deeds. In the form of Dhulqarnein, the two-horned one,[52] he is the classical friend of Khidr, and is identified with him. This refers to the identification of Alexander with Jupiter Ammon, portrayed with two ram horns, and Dionysus, who also was two-horned. Khidr was seen as a vegetation god, as the green of the earth, which is revived after winter. In the dream of the boy, Khidr is also the green one who appears in the winter, and who is dumped into the snow by the boy because he believes him to be the devil. So here he is a slightly premature appearance of spring. The Koran does not mention Khidr by name, but contains his legend, which is the first version we have of it. The Koran places the story in the first decade of the seventh century. The Hidjra took place in the year 622.[53] Not long afterward, the suras came into existence. In the eighteenth sura, "The Cave" [Al-Kahf], you find the Khidr legend in a highly significant connection. There the legend of the Seven Sleepers is told, which essentially contains the idea that the seven gods,

---

Islam with Gnosticism and Platonism. Several of the Jewish Messiah claimants ended up mixing Cabalistic Judaism with Christianity and Islam. Sikhism blends Hinduism and Islam. The Bahá'ís follow a prophet whom they consider a successor to Muhammad, and recognize Jesus, Moses, Buddha, and Zoroaster, among others, as earlier prophets. Some have therefore considered it a syncretic faith (trans.).

[52] The aspect of Khidr-as-Friend is evident in the episode of Dhul-qarnein (or Zulqarnain), who in Islamic mysticism is equated with Alexander the Great ("The Two-Horned One") (trans.).

[53] The Hijra (also Hijrah or Hegira), or withdrawal, is the emigration of Muhammad and his followers to the city of Medina (trans.).

the planet gods, the ancient star gods, the seven Archons of the Gnosis,[54] have come to rest and sleep in the earth. They sleep for a long time, for many centuries, until they awaken to new life in a completely different time. The whole story, the whole content of the eighteenth sura, is quite dreamlike and strangely incoherent, just as the Koran as a whole is strangely incoherent. These are psychological stories that are interrupted by long moralistic reflections. Thus, the eighteenth sura is a conglomerate of all kinds of things.

There it says:

Moses once said to his servant, "I will not rest until I reach the point where the two rivers meet, no matter how long it takes." When they reached the point where they met, they forgot their fish, and it found its way back to the river, sneakily. After they passed that point, he said to his servant, "Let us have lunch. All this traveling has thoroughly exhausted us." He said, "Remember when we sat by the rock back there? I paid no attention to the fish. It was the devil who made me forget it, and it found its way back to the river, strangely." (Moses) said, "That was the place we were looking for." They traced their steps back. They found one of our servants, whom we blessed with mercy, and bestowed upon him from our own knowledge. Moses said to him, "Can I follow you, that you may teach me some of the knowledge and the guidance bestowed upon you?" He said, "You cannot stand to be with me. How can you stand that which you do not comprehend?"[55]

You see, this is the motif of teaching knowledge and not being able to follow.

What we learn from this and from the further course the story takes in the Koran, is that Khidr does things that are amazing and shocking,[56] but later find their explanation. This should indicate

---

[54] In late antiquity some variants of Gnosticism used the term *Archon* to refer to several servants of the Demiurge, the "creator god" who stood between the human race and a transcendent God who could be reached only through gnosis. In this context, Archons have the role of the angels and demons of the Old Testament (trans.).

[55] Sura 18:60–68 (trans.).

[56] This word in English in the original (trans.).

448

that Khidr, as an executive authority, is completely informed about the plans of God, and thus, with foresight and knowledge about things that are still going to happen, takes anticipatory measures, which are seemingly immoral, yet correspond to the plans of God.

Now this story continues in a certain way, and in a very strange one at that. For the talk moves on to Dhulqarnein, so to speak, who actually is a friend of Khidr, but who also appears to be identified with him. Quite abruptly, the text in the Koran says, still in the eighteenth sura: "The Jews will ask you about Dhulqarnein," which presupposes that a legend already existed, which saw Dhulqarnein and Khidr as one, or made Dhulqarnein a friend of Khidr.

We granted him authority on earth, and provided him with all kinds of means. Then, he pursued one way. When he reached the far west, he found the sun setting in a vast ocean, and found people there. We said, "O Zul-Qarnain, you can rule as you wish; either punish, or be kind to them." He said, "As for those who transgress, we will punish them; then, when they return to their Lord, He will commit them to more retribution. As for those who believe and lead a righteous life, they receive a good reward; we will treat them kindly." Then he pursued another way. When he reached the far east, he found the sun rising on people who had nothing to shelter them from it. Naturally, we were fully aware of everything he found out. He then pursued another way. When he reached the valley between two palisades, he found people whose language was barely understandable. They said, "O Zul-Qarnain, Gog and Magog are corruptors of the earth. Can we pay you to create a barrier between us and them?" He said, "My Lord has given me great bounties. If you cooperate with me, I will build a dam between you and them. Bring to me masses of iron." Once he filled the gap between the two palisades, he said, "Blow." Once it was red hot, he said, "Help me pour tar on top of it." Thus, they could not climb it, nor could they bore holes in it. He said, "This is mercy from my Lord. When the prophecy of my Lord comes to pass, He will cause the dam to crumble. The prophecy of my Lord is truth." At that time, we will let them invade with one another, then the horn will be blown, and we will summon them all together. We will present Hell, on that day, to the disbelievers. They are the ones whose eyes were too veiled to see My message. Nor could they hear.[57]

So this is the final word in the Koran on the essence of Khidr. This final part is interesting insofar as he appears in the role of a protector of the people, by building a dam against Gog and Magog. In the Old Testament (Genesis 10:2), Magog is mentioned as the name of a northern tribe. In Ezekiel (38:2ff.), Gog appears as the chief prince of the country of Magog. The Revelation speaks of "Gog and Magog" as if they were two peoples. In the first revelation it says: "And [Satan] shall go out to deceive the nations which are in the four quarters of the earth, Gog, and Magog, to gather them together to battle: the number of whom is as the sand of the sea. And they went up on the breadth of the earth, and compassed the camp of the saints about, and the beloved city" (20:8–9). This place between two paths is obviously the place of the center; the place of the center is Jerusalem. There is the center of the earth. And it is this center that he protects, and the two paths are those that enclose a valley and thus constitute a center. So this is a further contribution to the characterization of Khidr. Vollers gives the following summary on Khidr: "He is the never-tiring wanderer and teacher and counselor of pious people, the sage in things divine, the unexpected visitor who, however, denies unworthy people his visit, the immortal one."

You see that Khidr is a very strange figure; we actually cannot draw a direct parallel with any other figures. It is a very peculiar figure. What I told you last time about the contemporary religious practice of Muslims indicates that Khidr is probably most closely related to the widespread views on Dionysus in antiquity. For Dionysus is that vegetation god, that life god, life spirit, who is nothing but spirit, a whole, who appears in everything, however. This is how the dismemberment of Dionysus by the Titans was interpreted. By being torn to pieces by the Titans, Dionysus diffused into all things, so that all things contain Dionysus. Now, in the mystical view Khidr is able to appear in every form, and this naturally brings him closer to other views of a Gnostic nature, namely, that the Savior Himself is such a

[57] Sura 18:84–101 (trans.).

mutabilis, one who is able to change, one who goes through the heavens and takes one form or another, who goes up, unrecognized, through the orbits of the planets, and is not recognized by the Archons. Recently I read *Le Conte du Saint Gral*, a French account of the Grail legend. There it also says that Christ was so poor that the devil did not recognize him. This is also such a motif, because the Gnostics believed that Christ, too, had changed his appearance so that he was not recognized by the ruling planetary orbits. Now Khidr is also someone who can appear in many different forms; in particular he appears as a wanderer in various places, appears all of a sudden and causes all kinds of situations. For you can imagine that good old Moses really hit the roof when Khidr played such tricks. All that approximately describes the peculiar psychological factor represented by Khidr. For obviously he is an unconscious figure that causes all kinds of frightening things, that makes you think: "Now this goes awry, this goes all wrong," but then it turns out to have been exactly the right thing. So this is about all we can say about the essence of Khidr. I could still mention that, according to the commentaries, he also appears when Moses and Joshua ben Nun[58] return to the source of life. There they discover that somebody sits there on the ground, covered in a burnoose,[59] and all around him the ground turns green and is covered with flowers. There it also says: he sits on a green carpet, on the ocean. Again this is something that appears from the unconscious. In another version, the place on the ground or earth where he had sat is said to have turned into gold. All this expresses a sudden appearance from the unconscious, not understood at first, but then revealing itself as something of the highest value. As a matter of fact, this motif is already there earlier in the story, for they come to the source of life without knowing what it is. Only later, when they are already much more advanced, do they realize it. When Moses gets hungry and wants to eat fish, a drop falls from the source onto the fish, by which the fish comes to life again, jumps out of the basket into the brook, and from there goes to the sea again. There is a mys-

---

[58] Joshua ben Nun, of the tribe of Ephraim, successor of Moses, was the second person to lead the Jewish people in their early history (trans.).

[59] A hooded cloak worn especially by Arabs and Berbers (trans.).

terious connection between Joshua ben Nun, the fisherman's son, and the fish who jumps into the sea. This, however, would lead us into an analysis of this myth. This goes too far.

Now we come to the question: what does this mean for the boy, who is suddenly confronted with this strange dream vision by which his religious, dogmatic views are actually devalued?

Participant: One could imagine that the dream wants to say that now a great deal of incomprehensible things are happening. But somehow it would be the right thing.

Professor Jung: Well, only if this were indicated. But this is not indicated in the dream. We know it only from the Khidr legend. That is precisely why he defends himself against Khidr. He thinks he is the devil. And this could well be the case; if we didn't know anything about Khidr, we, too, might think this. Decent people don't have a green face. It still seems reasonable to suppose that this points to a natural spirit.

Participant: Does this spirit have anything to do with the devil?

Professor Jung: All natural spirits are devilish! Therefore, all things of nature have to be exorcized before sacred rituals so that the *admixtio diabolicae fraudis*[60] evaporates. Thus, for example, when an altar is consecrated, it has to be oiled with a spoonful of benediction oil, and then censed, sterilized in psychological terms, because evil spirits could be everywhere, and they have to be removed. Each thing of nature is false in a way. Even humans themselves are actually no good from the start. What dogma does the Church have on general corruption?

Participant: The dogma of original sin.

Professor Jung: Yes, the creation is mixed up with evil; it is corrupt. The pure cannot die; it is incorruptible; therefore, everything has first to be disinfected. Therefore man is distorted by original sin. If a child is not baptized, it will not be saved. What happens with these children?

Participant: They do not go into heaven, but into a preheaven. They do not see the face of God.

---

[60] Latin, "the admixture of devilish deceit, fraud" (trans.)

452

Professor Jung: Yes, that's correct. Contrary to popular belief, they don't rot in hell. But they are deprived of the *visio dei*,[61] and are in the hands of God's all-clement mercy. He certainly knows what can be done about these undeveloped human beings.

Participant: I know a man, half-Spanish, half-Swiss, whose two children are Catholic. They had been born in the hospital and were very weakly, and they were quickly baptized as Catholics so that they would not be buried outside the cemetery walls.

Participant: Should the figure of Khidr be understood as a compensation for the too-spiritual view of the Christ figure?

Professor Jung: This is a question one may really ask. Khidr is a natural spirit. He has a green face. But because of his relation to Dhulqarnein and Dionysus, as well as to Moses, who also has horns, he can also be seen as the devil. It is quite possible to see him as the devil; and due to the dogma of original sin, and also the whole relation with decayable nature, he is, as a natural spirit, something that corrupts. The devil, as we know, is a great corruptor; now, when this phenomenon appears in place of a devalued dogmatism, we have to conceive this as a compensatory relation. For he takes the place of the dogma that has become lifeless. The dogma no longer contains the *pneuma zoés*, the spirit of life, and then inevitably the natural spirit appears. As a matter of fact, what appears is always what had been discarded before; "The stone which the builders refused is become the head stone of the corner."[62] That is why the alchemists quoted this sentence over and over again, because they knew that something did not work out in the whole story, and that something still had to be found, that unknown healing motif which brings nature, the world, to perfection—and that perfection can only come out of nature. Thus the worship of nature and the mysterious statement about the philosopher's stone, which is also marked. In it the *benedicta viriditas* appears, the green spirit. This is Khidr.

Obviously, we have to assume that this boy, despite—or because of—his religious, very Catholic education, unconsciously already

---

[61] Latin, "the sight of God" (trans.).
[62] Psalm 118:22 (trans.).

senses something inanimate, so that something remains that attacks him now, and which, of course, he cannot but interpret as the devil. A child of this age, however, is naturally not yet a critic of the dogma; it just happens to him so. So, when this happens to a child, what else would you also take into account in such a dream?

Participant: Probably the criticism is already there in the environment.

Professor Jung: Yes, something has to be in the air, which this boy visualizes. So, this dream is a real war dream, isn't it, from serious times, and we may expect that the unconscious reaction to all these impressions will be quite faithfully reproduced in such a dream. And because the dreamer is actually still a child—a ten-year-old boy is actually still a child—we have to suppose that there is also something collective contained in this dream, that it is not merely individualistic, but a dream from which we could say that it is also true for many other people. We could say: just as this child simply reacts, this might perhaps happen everywhere; in other words, that similar dreams have been dreamed in many other places. So when the question is answered by the unconscious, well, what comes next, after this dogmatic image has withered?

Participant: A Khidr-like figure.

Participant: Isn't there a parallel with Faust, who had studied and yet feels empty, and then Mephistopheles comes, who also is a natural spirit?

Professor Jung: He studied what?

Participant: All existing sciences, and everything has become empty and futile; and then Mephistopheles comes just like that, who after all is a natural spirit. He loves to dance around with the witches.

Professor Jung: This is a primordial experience in alchemy. Mephistopheles is a natural demon, but a demon that has been distorted in a medieval way. He has taken over the role of the devil, although in fact he is simply a natural spirit.

Participant: He says, after all, that he always wants evil, but always creates good.[63]

---

[63] Goethe, *Faust 1*, verses 1335–36 (trans.)

454

Professor Jung: Exactly.

Participant: Couldn't we interpret this in a way that Christ has been abandoned by the humans, that the dogma is no longer human, that the relation has been lost?

Professor Jung: There is something to this, of course there is. Man has fallen a bit, and the Trinity is so far away. Think of the modern Protestantism in Karl Barth, in which God is *totaliter aliter*,[64] so that we cannot understand how a relationship could exist. If something is completely different, it can also no longer have an effect on me. The two of them have nothing to do with each other any longer. God has nothing to do with mankind, and mankind nothing with God.

A madman once thought that God would understand only the dead, and not the living. He then came closer to the world, but was so surrounded by miracles that it began to "wonder" in the world. The sun split in two and things unheard of happened. In the case of Schreber, too, we find the same idea, that God understands only something about the dead, but nothing about the living.

Participant: It is a reaction to the revival of paganism, to Wotan who was resurrected.

Professor Jung: Well, Wotan is another parallel. Wotan is a cousin of Dionysus. He also is the wanderer. Well, enjoy!

6. Dream of a Girl of Little Pigs and of Lice[65]
PRESENTED BY MARGRIT OSTROWSKI-SACHS[66]

Text: *I step out of the house and see two little pigs in a square, fenced-in little garden. They are very lean. "Oh, my poor little pigs; they nearly let you starve!" I cry out, take them on my lap, sit down at a table, and feed them with a spoon until they get all round. Then I see that the little animals are full of lice and begin to pick the bugs from them, but in the end I'm covered all over with them myself.*

Mrs. Ostrowski: The dream can be structured as follows:

Exposition:	The dreamer steps out of the house and sees the lean little pigs.

[64] Latin, "totally other" (trans.).
[65] Age of the girl unknown.
[66] Session of 10 December 1940.

455

Development:	The little pigs are taken onto her lap and fed until they are all round.
Peripateia:	She sees that the little animals are full of lice, which she wants to pick from them.
Lysis:	In the end, the dreamer herself is completely covered with them.
Dramatis personae:	The dreamer, the little pigs, the lice.
Time:	No age is given. According to the notes, this is a dream that has frequently occurred since childhood, at least twice a year; so we have to assume that this dream occurred until adulthood. Thus it would accentuate a problem, which was already important for the child, and has remained active and unsolved for many years.

As to the exposition: "I step out of the house and see two little pigs in a square, fenced-in little garden." The situation happens in front of the house, that is, in the place where contact with the outer world is made. So this will be about a process that did not develop out of the specific dispositions of the child, but rather out of the conditions of the milieu, probably not out of an external, open conflict, but out of unconscious tendencies or wrong attitudes in the educators. When we hear about a square, fenced-in little garden, we all naturally think what kinds of wonders might happen there, because inadvertently we think of the meaning of the rectangle in a mandala. Ample evidence has been given in the paper of Dr. Steiner that the garden is also "the place where something meaningful and important happens, the place where the task is found." Now the task seems to consist in taking care of the lean little pigs. Psychologically, this could mean to provide these little animals with the food they are entitled to in the menagerie of infantile psychic life. Before we determine this more precisely, we have to look at the amplifications for the *little pigs*. These are by no means only negative—as we experience in the age of fat rationing anyway. The young, rosy little pigs can actually be an appetizing sight; they are also considered to bring good luck and are, with a four-leaf clover in their snout, the bearers of the most hearty

456

wishes for the New Year on the greeting cards; and the expression "he really is a lucky pig"[67] also means to be very fortunate. I will still go into the specific nuances of luck, as represented by the little pigs, in more detail.

Preller writes that the pigs symbolically indicate a sexual relationship and the idea of rut and lustful fertility. The pig was sacrificed to Aphrodite in Greece and Cyprus and, according to Roscher, was also the sacrificial animal of Demeter and Persephone, particularly of the chthonic Demeter, in Hermione. There exists a relief in Eleusis with the pictures of the two goddesses and the Eleusinian pig sacrifice. In the Hermitage in Leningrad[68] there is a Cumaeic relief vase, on which a priest sacrifices a little pig. According to Preller, the constellation of the Hyads—their Greek name indicates humid rain stars—was also depicted as a herd of little pigs, because pigs love puddles. Something similar is reported by Scheffer in his legends of the stars around the antique world, namely, that the Hyads were represented by little piglets—just like the Pleiades—instead of delicate nymphs.

In his book *Das Tier in der Religion* [*Animals in Religion*], Fuhrmann reports that in some places in China it is believed that sluggish women are turned into wild pigs that ravage the rice fields. The peasant then puts some part of a handloom in his field (the sluggishness of the women was with regard to weaving), and the pigs no longer return. In *Deuteronomy*, pork is declared forbidden food: "ye shall not eat of their flesh, nor touch their dead carcasse" (14:8). The Koran also adopted the prohibition. From the Gospel you will remember the passage, in Mark 5:2–13, in which Jesus sent the unclean spirit of the possessed man—who said, "My name is Legion"—into a great herd of swine, which then ran violently down a steep place into the sea. Matthew 7:6, admonishes: "Give not that which is holy unto the dogs, neither cast ye your pearls before swine, lest they trample them under their feet, and turn again and rend you." Something similar to this statement of the Bible happened to the dreamer.

[67] Original: *der hat aber Schwein*—he really is a lucky devil (trans.).
[68] Now St. Petersburg (trans.).

According to Brehm, the most important features of swine that bear on this dream are their great fertility—they have ten to twenty young pigs—and their voracity! They have the teeth of a true omnivore. "Their voice," says Brehm, "is a special grunt, which expresses much sedateness, complacency, and coziness." Of the young pigs, he writes: "They are lovely, agile creatures that can enchant everybody." Jung writes in *Transformations and Symbols of the Libido*: "It is a particularly precious invention of Christian fantasy that the animal assigned to St. Antony is the swine, because the good old saint was one of those who were subject to the worst temptations by the devil."[69]

In summarizing this material, the main characteristics of the pig are: extreme fertility, laziness, rooting through the dirt, enormous voracity, obsessiveness, rut, grunting, coziness, and pleasure; in short: the primitive, instinctual world. Thus it is sung in Auerbach's basement: "We're feeling terribly fine, just like five hundred swine." These characteristics may be true for the little pigs of our dream to a somewhat lesser extent, because after all they are not fully grown swine, but piglets. The fact that there are only two little pigs seems to stress this more strongly.

Depending on the age of the dreamer, these little pigs are of a more or less harmless nature. It can often be heard how a child is told: "You're really a little pig,"[70] e.g., when the child spilled some cocoa on her dress or the tablecloth. When adults are given that name, its meaning can be less harmless.

The dreamer cries out: "Oh, my poor little pigs; they nearly let you starve!" Thus all the characteristics of swine are too little accentuated in the dreamer, it was not she, but "they," who let them starve—probably her environment, her parents, her educators. She did not know the delight to be allowed once to lick a plate with her tongue; she was not allowed to play with water and clay, nor to let off steam to her heart's content. On the street she certainly had to dutifully "hold hands," and was never allowed to step into the middle of the most beautiful puddles, even if they attracted her with almost mag-

---

[69] Not included in *Symbols of Transformation* (trans.).
[70] In the original in Swiss German: *"Du bisch es rächts Säuli"* (trans.).

458

netic force. We can often observe how children stride through the dirtiest ditches with the greatest pleasure, grind their boots into the dirt—that this work is highly important to them and, in any case, fulfills a deep-seated need. And because a well-behaved, sheltered, and dutiful child must not do any of this, because anything instinctual has been neglected and despised in her education, the characteristics of little pigs were nearly dead of starvation in our dreamer. It is surely her duty to feed the little pigs, to take care, that is, of these very primitive needs, or, in other words: sacrifices have to be made also to Aphrodite and the chthonic gods in the hierarchy of the soul powers, because otherwise they can make themselves felt in a very unpleasant way.

In the Institute for Child Psychology in London there is a special ward in which children, apparently without supervision, can play with clay and water; there not only babies, but also nervous children of ten to fourteen years, are allowed to secretly make up for what a mother had denied the child at the right time, out of a wrong attitude and her exaggerated love of cleanliness, order, and hygiene. In his book *Schwierige Schüler* [*Difficult Students*], Hans Zulliger, the Bernese teacher and psychologist, writes of a girl from a good family, who underwent a considerable change at the age of about nine, and showed a more than usual slovenliness and a striking indifference toward any cleaning procedures. Added to these peculiarities was an extreme craving for food, which made the girl devour amounts of food that stood in absolutely no relation to her stomach. She binge ate and then vomited pots of preserves, craved sweet as well as sour things, ate the leftovers in the fridge, stole cheese and sausages; her ravenous appetite was even satisfied with boiled potatoes as if they were delicacies. In a similar way, our dreamer may have tried to satisfy her needs. It may be assumed from her exclamation, however, that outwardly she used seemingly utterly harmless, sanctimonious methods. Usually the pig food is thrown into the trough or before the swine. But our girl takes the animals on her lap and treats them like her peers. She grossly exaggerates her care for the little animals. She does not care for her little pigs in a normal way, but behaves as if she were full of loving care for the little animals, feigning a very special sympathy for them. Perhaps she also blotches her exercise books in a seemingly harmless way—"it just so happened"; she seems to have made use of that veil of harmlessness. During puberty she would perhaps be offered other possibilities, perhaps she would show a special interest in books and would voraciously read certain bad literature, or look for certain passages in Schiller's plays that might satisfy her requirements. As an adult she might perhaps gloat over the little scandals in her immediate or larger neighborhood, or she might even be on a committee for fallen girls and there get the food for her own swine in social activity. Of course, her interest in these animals could also have taken more extreme forms, but this seems hardly to be the case here. After all, the pigs get all round. The tension in the dream increases: she sees that the animals are full of lice, and starts to pick the bugs from them, with the result that in the end she herself is completely covered with them. In the *Brockhaus*[71] it says among other things: "Lice are ectoparasitic, i.e., they live on their host, they are living blood-feeding insects, their mouth parts are pricking and sucking, the legs endowed with clinging organs. In the case of insufficient cleanliness they get out of hand, and there can be thousands of them in repulsive masses on a single victim. The constant itchiness can highly interfere with the general well-being, the frequent scratching may cause purulent spots on the skin, gateways for all kinds of germs."

In the context of our dream, it is particularly characteristic of lice that they occur in cases of insufficient cleanliness, and that they are blood-feeding, constantly itch, and bring germs to the body. If positive sides could still be found in the swine, none of them can be detected in the lice. The dreamer, however, even goes as far as to pick the lice from the pigs. Psychologically speaking, by being interested so instinctively, with such obstinacy, in such an abnormal way, in uncleanliness, in voracity, in muckraking, in dirt, grunting well-being, and in the primitive instinctual world, and so on, by all this she falls victim to ordinary parasites that proliferate in the case of such defects or such features. She is deprived of her strength and her tranquility, is exposed to all pathogenic influences, and is constantly plagued;

[71] Authoritative German encyclopedia (trans.).

460

the blood, the lifeblood, is sucked out of her; she is completely covered with bugs, she herself has become bugs, a parasite. Professor Jung writes in *Analytical Psychology and Education*: "Wherever an important instinct has been underestimated, an enormous overestimation has to be the result."[72]

The final result is very negative and unsatisfactory. The dreamer experiences what some proverbs say: she made her bed, and now has to lie in it. She jumped out of the frying pan into the fire; the apparently harmless affair got out of control. She gave the devil an inch, and he took a mile. She played with the fire and now is burning herself. Her fate is the same as that of the Sorcerer's Apprentice: the spirits that she's cited her commands ignore.[73]

The problem that awaited her was solved in the wrong way, and she was more and more entrapped in guilt and misery by the invisible, powerful laws. The carefully sheltered child, the well-educated daughter, notices this and that in her environment, at first quite savory, harmless, unclean things, some little "pigsties."[74] Precisely because she knows nothing or too little about them, she is much too interested in them. She is fascinated by them in such an uncanny way, so to speak, that she affectionately concerns herself with them, until she herself is completely possessed by the effects of this constant decline, as a result of the constant sustenance of these fantasies or activities. She has probably slipped into a neurosis, whose psychology completely corresponds to the Freudian model, and which has to be broken down for a longer period of time, until it will be possible, as Professor Jung has expressed it, to tackle constructively a new solution of the task, a correct integration of these animals into the balance of the human soul.

Professor Jung: This reminds us of the fairy tale of the frog and the princess.[75] Unfortunately, we do not know at what age this dream was first dreamed. It is one that recurred. The recurrence happened over many years. Mrs. Sachs has quite correctly assumed that this is

---

[72] C. G. Jung, *The Development of Personality*, CW 17, § 157 (ed.).

[73] From Goethe's poem "The Sorcerer's Apprentice" (1779) (trans.)

[74] Original: *"kleine Sauereien"*—some little mess or obscenity (trans.).

[75] The Grimm fairy tale "The Frog King or Iron Heinrich" (trans.).

about a difficulty that was triggered by a special environment. As far as I know this doesn't seem to be a neurosis; but the peculiar way of treating the little pigs exhibited by the dreamer points to something special. It is a bit exaggerated, this sympathy for these poor little pigs. True, it is not right to let these little animals famish, but it's a bit much to embrace them in such a way. The mother would probably say: You mustn't do such a terrible thing! The dreamer treats these piglets a bit too well in the dream. We have to assume that it is probably not so in consciousness, but that the attitude is perhaps a bit more careful there. We may perhaps surmise that the child is very well educated. So she has to compensate for this by dreaming of these little pigs. In the dream she then goes a bit too far. Eventually this can lead into some secret infantile misdeeds. In any case, this dream contains a very clear warning. Because what will happen to her if she cares so much for these little pigs that are covered with lice? She herself will become a little pig. Like the pigs, she is covered with lice, with parasites. The piglets actually then turn into parasites. What she cares for in these animals will become a habit in her, a vampire, a parasite, which sits on her and sucks her dry. But what do you make of the fact that the little pigs are in that fenced-in little garden?

Participant: In the fairy tale of the princess and the frog, the frog is in the well—but not as constricted as the piglets in the rectangular garden.

Professor Jung: Quite correct. It is a rectangular garden. These things are so trivial that we do not pay much attention to them. But the dream would not emphasize it if there weren't anything to it. What does it mean that she goes out of the house?

Participant: That she goes away from the parents' care.

Professor Jung: From her room. From her existence, where her parents are, from the area of human beings. People live there, and the world of her consciousness is also there. When she goes out of this, she goes into another area, where the pigs live. So there is a piece of nature, the garden, but it is fenced in and is real. One always has to prick up one's ears a bit when something is rectangular and fenced in, a fenced-in place.

Participant: It is a culturally important place.

462

Professor Jung: I'd say that now it is meant for the little pigs. Why are they fenced in?

Participant: So that they stay within their boundaries.

Professor Jung: Yes, of course. What disagreeable characteristics do they have?

Participant: They nuzzle the ground.

Professor Jung: Yes, just let your swine into your garden, and you will get a nasty surprise. The pig is an animal that can be allowed to run around a bit, but not too often; otherwise your garden will be devastated beyond recognition. So that's why pigs are fenced in, because they have such ravaging features, such messy eating habits. Now this is a completely natural image—a house in the country, a little garden, but there is also some exaggeration. Pigs are never in a little garden. Where they are, everything is churned up, dirty, and eaten up. Here the sentimentality already starts in the dream. Reality is different. Where pigs are there is a dark place.

Participant: When it says "in a little garden," then it probably will be indeed a little garden. They simply have been put there already.

Professor Jung: Yes, but in reality it simply can't be a garden. This is precisely the sentimentality in the dream—that it is a little garden. This is something incommensurable, a pig and a garden. Because then you will have a pigsty. This is what also happens in the dream. In the end she, too, is the louse. So, what is wrong about this?

Participant: The swine should be in the pigpen.

Professor Jung: Yes, of course; the pigs have broken into her garden. What does that mean?

Participant: The garden, that is flowers, feeling.

Professor Jung: Yes, the beautiful feelings; and then something stupid happened. You see, in the garden there are the beautiful roses and the little flowers, and now the little pigs are in it, so good-bye, little garden! What happened here is that a "pigsty" has sneaked into precisely the place where there should be nice feelings. What can that probably be? What psychological situation exists at home, as an educational influence? How come, instead of a little flower garden, the image of a little pig garden has risen in a child?

Participant: In this milieu the flowers, the feelings, are not cared for.

Professor Jung: Yes. In this milieu there is probably something that is responsible for the fact that, in the child, the little pigs have to secretly come into that place. Most of the time this happens when, as Dr. Fierz has correctly pointed out, a probably very emotional atmosphere prevails, an atmosphere of differentiated feelings, in which the rather unclean side is too heavily repressed. Naturally, this side then has to break into the emotional world more than ever, but unconsciously, from the backside, so that the feelings are all the more beautiful, more differentiated, the more a little "pigsty" is behind this.

Participant: Perhaps it is a puritan milieu?

Professor Jung: Yes, probably. Simply an increased, differentiated feeling. These are probably terribly orderly, nice people, who even exaggerate a bit, and bring up the child in a somewhat too clean way. As a boy I observed in school, for example, that the boys who were the greatest rascals had been raised terribly strictly at home. Usually these were boys from overly distinguished families. And they did the craziest things. When I went to school in the country, none of this happened. Nobody would have thought, for instance, of eating a live toad; the country boys never thought of anything sadistic. They got plenty of dirt on their shoes and hands, and the smell of the pigpen and cattle manure. They didn't need this.

Well, the little pigs ran into the garden because they also wanted to eat something. The first impulse of the child, to feed the little pigs, is perfectly okay, just a normal action to somehow satisfy that unclean side, and also to please it. In the English Löwenfeld Institute the children are given paint; they put their hands into it and smear it around with great delight. They also get paper that they may besmear completely. I saw the paintings they made. We can vividly imagine what a big relief it is for these children when they once are allowed to make a real mess with the paint. The child, however, has already been made a bit sentimental and makes a virtue out of necessity, because naturally the little pigs now have to be raised with very special loving care. It becomes a task, it becomes something eth-

464

ical, somehow beautiful; this, however—that it now has to be nice and be made lovingly—is too disciplined. And so that's why she gets the lice; she is stuck in the dirt more than ever because of her distortion of the feeling. For then the dirt has to prove to her how dirty it really is. And in the end she herself turns into such a little pig, so to speak. Now this is the transformation that shows what comes out of getting involved with pigs in this distorted way. For when she behaves nicely, she can't ever be nice enough, can she? For then it even becomes a virtue. And she can't ever be virtuous enough, can't ever be concerned about the little pigs, and that's precisely why she herself also becomes a pig.

Participant: In many dreams, it is witches who have got the lice, who are contaminated, and he who delouses them has to eat the lice and is then contaminated himself.

Professor Jung: Yes, the lice are vampires, often also spirits. When a child is born in the Caucasus Mountains, they take a louse from the grandfather's head and plant it on the head of the grandchild. By this the soul has been transferred, because in the primitive view the spirits always accompany us, buzz around us like bats or like vampires; they suck the blood from us. So when we get lice from pigs, for example, we have absorbed the pig spirits into us. The lice are the *familiares*[76] of the pig. If we concern ourselves too much with them, we take over the *familiares* and get the animal spirits ourselves. Now we come to the fact that there are two pigs. Why exactly two?

Participant: It is a special accentuation of the moment.

Participant: Like in the dream of the two giants. It means a development of consciousness.

Professor Jung: The double appearance of a symbol means "unconscious"; because two of the same cannot be distinguished from each other, and this means that one does not know if there is one or if there are two. It is indistinguishable. We can only discern that there are two of them, but not which two. When an unconscious content is about to become conscious, a part of it is conscious and a part unconscious, like something visible and something invisible. The motif

[76] Latin, "belonging to the family, close" (trans.).

always appears in the case of psychic contents that are about to become conscious. Therefore we always encounter the motif of the two in the case of such figures that stand at the border between two worlds. Messengers of the underworld mostly come in two. This of course is also the case at the border of consciousness. Actually, it is simply the dreamer's shadow in the form of an animal. But we still have to deal with the story of this little garden into which the pigs have come. We have already mentioned its naive meaning.

Participant: It could really be a mandala.

Professor Jung: It could really be a *temenos*. This can be a symbol of the self, that specially fenced-in place in which one should actually be contained. This is unconscious, of course, and projected onto a perhaps really existing little garden. In this garden there are living creatures. So this fenced-in place is apparently only an enclosure for animals. And this is now the unsightly aspect of something extremely important, because it is the self in the unconscious, in the form of an animal; the animal is still in it. You can find the same motif in my text in the *Eranos Yearbook 1937*, in which I have described the symbols of individuation,[77] where, for instance, a bulky living mass can be found. Also snakes and other animals are in it. This is also a kind of enclosure for animals.

Participant: The paradise is a rectangular zoo.

Professor Jung: Yes, the paradise is a zoo, and the humans are unconsciously in it. There is still another important symbolism in connection with the self. It has repeatedly been illustrated.

Participant: Buddha with a boar's head.

Professor Jung: This is a bit far-fetched. Nobody knows about that. True, in one of his avatars[78] Buddha has a boar's head, but I am thinking of something much more familiar to us.

Participant: The Evangelists.

Professor Jung: No, something very concrete. The birth of Christ, with the ox and the donkey in the barn—this is the enclosure. Because in reality the caves in Bethlehem are goat barns, cow barns.

---

[77] An enlarged version in C. G. Jung, *Psychology and Alchemy*, dream 18, in CW 12, §§ 183ff (ed.).

[78] Incarnations (trans.).

466

The birth cave is such a barn, as miserable a hole as all the others that can still be seen there, full of goats and all kinds of poultry. Christ is the symbol of the self and was born in the barn. So here we have the animal enclosure, and here of course we are coming to a deeper level of the dream. A collective symbol is thus behind it, and suddenly we begin to understand how much more there is actually hidden behind all that. It is a legitimate attempt to feed this animal in the *temenos* and thus lead it toward its development. But this is a problem that is not suited for childhood. It is an archetypal problem, as you can see, one that can't possibly be addressed in childhood. It is an archetype that comes nearer here, and which, by virtue of its fascination, can provoke—and has perhaps already provoked here—something that can have, or has already had, deleterious and harmful effects. Which?

Participant: A disintegration.

Professor Jung: Yes, a falling apart into a multiplicity of small elements. This multiplicity of small elements always indicates processes in the sympathetic nervous system. This is a slight dissociation, caused by the autonomy of the instincts. Thus, if animal instincts awaken and take possession of the personality, those elements, which should compose the human personality, drop to the level of the animal instincts, resulting in a disorder of the sympathetic nervous system, which often expresses itself in these multiplicities.

In the dream of a child that died young many of these dissociative phenomena can be found,[79] which were originally caused by a strong and inopportune appearance of the archetype.

Participant: It could also be a problem of the parents.

Professor Jung: Quite right. There is something in the milieu that does not correspond with nature, for example, a high-handedness, an exaggerated false distinction. This does not correspond to nature, and, therefore, the archetype of the unclean animal is constellated, and this appearance then brings about such a difficulty. For the child cannot answer the problem of this archetype. She is simply assailed

[79] Cf. C. G. Jung, *Der Mensch und seine Symbole*, pp. 69ff, where Jung discusses such dreams (ed.).

467

by it, and this is the secret reason why the little pigs then appear in the garden. Well, such a constellation can bring about the most incredible things in children, perversities or even very dangerous things, when they hurt themselves terribly or get into dangerous situations, because archetypes are constellated at the wrong time.

Participant: This is already contained in the symbol of the pig. The pig is the darkest and, in the Chinese zodiacal system, the last sign. There really has to be a big problem in the environment.

Professor Jung: In the East the pig means Avidya, the state of being unconscious. It also is a chthonic sacrificial animal. So there is a plethora of connections that confer special meaning on the pig. Although we naturally have to take all this into account, this brings us to an archetype a young child can't possibly deal with. The whole problem is impossible, and often possessions or strange perversion, which then assume a mythological character, result from such situations. So this is what lies behind the dream and is hinted at in it. What is interesting, however, is to know, in terms of the therapy, how strange archetypal connections underlie a simple dream. This is the basis that shows how important it is that nature be given its due, that an attitude or an educational method that does not force nature prevail in the parents. Otherwise certain archetypes will emerge out of nature, which take possession of the children and subsequently completely distort them. The children can, for example, develop into real devils, which means that they identify with the repressed contents.

Appendix
Dream Series of a Boy

First dream (age: 3 years, 10 months)

At night I flew away from you[1] and to the maidens.[2] The maidens had sent for me. Then we did some washing in a tub.

But I'm not flying to the maidens with wings, like the Christ Child, but like in an airship. One has to get into the airship on a pole, it has no doors.

Second dream (age: 3 years, 11 months)

Mommy, this evening I was [i.e., in the dream] with a woman; she had a child and a snow house. I wanted to slip into the snow house, then the evil "Stuttgarter" (originally a doll) looked into the window. I thought it was an evil daddy and got scared.

Third dream (age: 4 years, 11 months)

I've dreamed something weird (like Grittli[3]): I wanted to go and meet Helene, and bring her a little bird. I reached into a hedge and got hold of something disgusting: an animal that pinched, like a crawfish.

Fourth dream (age: 5 years, 4 months)

In the dream I saw a woman, an evil woman, and she was all made of iron. The woman was old. She had long scissors that were driven by a lit-

---

[1] The boy told all these dreams to his mother (ed.).

[2] Original: *Jungfrauen*, which can mean both "virgins" or "maidens" (trans.).

[3] Swiss female first name (trans.).

tle iron machine; made[4] like that [he makes the motions of kicking]. You, Mommy, were away shopping, and I was scared.

Fifth dream (age: 5 years, 4 months)

I dreamed that I lay on a platform with Veronika. Then a dog came and jumped on the cornice. We teased him and then jumped down the ladder from the platform. The dog ran after us, but we locked the parlor.

Sixth dream (age: 7 years, 9 months)

Mommy, I had a funny dream: there was a house on a river. I am standing[5] on the other side and can see everything. Two big men—I think giants—are there. They go on the roof and [from there] let a basket down into the water. Then they plop into the water themselves. There are waves in the water, because the giants are so big. They fished with the basket and filled it up, then they pull it out of the water.

---

[4] The subject of this sentence is missing in the original (trans.).

[5] The change in tenses is significant; by it the boy expresses his distance or closeness to the dream (ed.).

Bibliography

Abraham Eleazar (Abraham le Juif). *Livre des figures hiéroglyphiques* (seventeenth century). Manuscript no. 14765, Bibliothèque Nationale, Paris.

Ars chemica, quod sit licita recte exercentibus, probationes doctissimorum iurisconsultorum. Strasbourg, 1566.

Artemidorus of Daldis. *Symbolik der Träume.* Vienna, Pest, Leipzig: Hartleber, 1881.

Artis auriferae, quam chemiam vocant. 2 vols. [A collection of alchemical treatises by different authors.] Basel, 1593.

Aurora consurgens: Quae dicitur aurea hora. In *Artis auriferae*, vol. 1, pp. 185–246.

Avalon, Arthur. *Shri-Chakra-Sambhâra Tantra: A Buddhist Tantra.* Trans. Kazi Dawa-Samdup. Tantric Texts, vol. 7. London: Aditya Prakashan, 1919; reprint, 1987.

Bächthold-Stäubli. See *Handwörterbuch des deutschen Aberglaubens.*

Barlach, Ernst. *Der tote Tag.* Drama in five acts. Berlin, 1912.

Baumann, Hans. "Betrachtungen über die Symbolik der Pyramiden." In *Die kulturelle Bedeutung der komplexen Psychologie.* Berlin, 1935.

———. "Tier und Pflanze als Symbole." *Zeitschrift für Psychotherapie* 10, no. 3 (n.d.).

Beit, Hedwig von. *Symbolik des Märchens—Versuch einer Deutung.* Berne: Francke, 1952, 1971.

Benoit, Pierre. *L'Atlantide.* Paris, 1919; reprint, Paris: LGF—Livre de Poche, 1973.

Bergson, Henri. "Le rêve." *Bull. de l'Inst. gen. psych.,* 1901. In *L'Energie spirituelle.* 1919; reprint, Paris: Presses Universitaires de France, 1940.

Berthelot, Marcellin. *La Chimie au moyen-âge.* 3 vols. Paris: Imprimeries nationales, 1893.

———. *Collections des anciens alchémistes grecs.* Paris, 1887; reprint, Osnabrück: Zeller, 1967.

Bibliotheca Chemica. See Bonus, Petrus.

Blätter aus Prevorst. Ed. Justinus Kerner. Fourth collection. Karlsruhe, 1833; reprint, Berlin: S. Fischer, 1926; Frankfurt am Main: Insel Verlag, 1987.

Bonus, Petrus. *Bibliotheca Chemica Curiosa seu rerum ad alchemiam pertinentium thesaurus instructissimus.* Ed. Johannes Jacobus Mangetus, 2 vols. Geneva: Ritter & de Tournes, 1702.

Brehm, Alfred E. *Illustrirtes Thierleben—Eine allgemeine Kunde des Thierreichs [Brehms Tierleben].* Leipzig, 1864ff.

Buber, Martin. *Ecstatic Confessions: The Heart of Mysticism.* Martin Buber Library. Syracuse, NY: Syracuse University Press, 1996.

Buettner, Herman. *Meister Eckeharts Schriften und Predigten.* Translated and edited by Hermann Buettner. Jena: Diederichs, 1912.

Caussinus, Nicolaus. *Polyhistor symbolicus, electorum symbolorum et parabolarum historicarum stromata.* Paris, 1618; Cologne, 1632.

Chamisso, Adalbert von. *Peter Schlemihls wundersame Geschichte.* 1814; reprint, Berlin: Cornelsen, 1987.

Colonna, Francesco. *Hypnerotomachia Poliphili, ubi humana omnia non nisi somnium esse ostendit, atque obiter plurima scitu sane quam digna commemorat.* Venice, 1499. Bib. Class. Ravenna (Inc. 652). English translation online at http://mitpress.mit .edu/e-books/HP/hyp000.htm (14 March 2007). [F. Béroalde de Verville. *Le Tableau des riches inventions . . . qui sont représentées dans le songe de Poliphile.* Paris, 1600.]

Consilium coniugii de massa solis et lunae. In *Ars chemica,* vol. 3, pp. 48–263.

Corpus Hermeticum. See Hermes Trismegistus.

Cumont, Franz. *Textes et monuments figurés relatifs aux mystères de Mithra.* 2 vols. Brussels: H. Lamertin, 1896–99.

Cumont, Franz. *Die Mysterien des Mithra. Ein Beitrag zur Religionsgeschichte der römischen Kaiserzeit.* Leipzig: Teubner, 1911. *The Mysteries of Mithra.* New York: Dover Publications, 1956.

Dante Alighieri. *Divina Commedia.* Stuttgart: Neff, 1871–72. *The Divine Comedy,* 6 vols. Ed. Charles Singleton. Princeton, NJ: Princeton University Press, 1970–75.

De massa solis et lunae. See *Consilium coniugii.*

Dieterich, Albrecht. *Eine Mithrasliturgie. 2nd ed.,* Leipzig, Berlin: Teubner, 1910.

Dorneus, Gerardus. *Speculativa philosophia, gradus septem vel decem continens.* In *Theatrum chemicum,* vol. 1, pp. 255–310.

Eckhart, Meister. See Buettner.

Edda: Götterlieder und Heldenlieder. Trans. Hans von Wolzogen. Berlin: Verlagsanstalt für Vaterländische Geschichte, 1920.

Eisler, Robert. *Orpheus the Fisher.* Whitefish, MT: Kessinger Publishing, 1920.

Eleazar, Abraham. See Abraham Eleazar.

Encyclopaedia of Religion and Ethics. Ed. James Hastings. Edinburgh: T. & T. Clark, 1908ff.

Erman, Adolf. *Ägypten und ägyptisches Leben im Altertum.* 2 vols. Tübingen: H. Laupp'sche Buchhandlung, 1885. Reprint Hildesheim: Gerstenberg, 1987, 4th ed.

———. *A Handbook of Egyptian Religion.* London: Archibald Constable, 1907.

———. *Die Religion der Ägypter, ihr Werden und Vergehen in vier Jahrtausenden.* Berlin: de Gruyter, 1934. 2nd edition, Berlin: de Gruyter, 2001.

Evans, Ivor. *Studies in Religion, Folklore and Customs of British North Borneo and the Malay Peninsula.* Cambridge: Cambridge University Press, 1923.

Evans-Wentz, Walter Yeeling (ed.). *Das Tibetanische Totenbuch: Mit einem psychologischen Kommentar zum Bardo Thödol von C. G. Jung.* Zurich, Leipzig: Rascher, 1936. *The Tibetan Book of the Dead; or, The After-Death Experiences on the Bardo Plane,* according to Lama Kazi Dawa-Samdup's English rendering, by W. Y. Evans-Wentz. With foreword by Sir John Woodroffe. London: Oxford University Press, H. Milford, 1927. Reprint: *The Tibetan Book of the Dead; by W. Y. Evans-Wentz.* New York: Oxford University Press, 2000.

Fierz-David, Linda. *Der Liebestraum des Poliphilo: Ein Beitrag zur Psychologie der Renaissance und der Moderne.* Zürich: Rhein, 1947. *The Dream of Poliphilo, Related and Interpreted by Linda Fierz-David.* Trans. Mary Hottinger. New York: Pantheon, 1950.

Flournoy, Théodore. *Des Indes à la planète Mars: Etude sur un cas de somnambulisme avec glossolalie.* Paris, Geneva: Alcan, Eggimann, 1900. *From India to the Planet Mars: A Study of a Case of Multiple Personality with Imaginary Languages.* Ed. Sonu Shamdasani. Princeton, NJ: Princeton University Press, 1994.

France, Anatole. *Oeuvres complètes illustrées de Anatole France,* vol. 4. Ed. Calman Lévy. Paris: Calmann-Lévy, 1926.

Franz, Marie-Louise von. *Alchemy. An Introduction to the Symbolism and the Psychology.* Toronto: Inner City Books, 1980.

Frazer, James George. *The Golden Bough. A Study in Magic and Religion.* 12 vols. London: Macmillan, 1907, 1911; New York: Macmillan, 1922.

Frobenius, Leo. *Das Zeitalter des Sonnengottes.* Berlin: Reimer, 1904.

Fuhrmann. *Das Tier in der Religion.* Munich: Georg Müller, 1922.

Gilgamesch: Eine Erzählung aus dem alten Orient. Zu einem Ganzen gestaltet von Georg Burckhardt. Wiesbaden: Insel, 1955. English translation at http://en .wikisource.org/wiki/The_Epic_of_Gilgamesh (14 March 2007).

Goethe, Johann Wolfgang von. *Die Faustdichtungen.* Leipzig: Insel, 1942. *Faust 1 and 2.* Collected Works, vol. 2. Princeton, NJ: Princeton University Press, 1994.

Goethe, Johann Wolfgang. *Sämtliche Gedichte.* Zurich: Artemis, 1950.

Goetz, Bruno. *Das Reich ohne Raum.* Potsdam: Kiepenheuer, 1919. *Das Reich ohne Raum: Mit einem psychologischen Kommentar von Marie-Louise von Franz.* Zurich: Origo, 1962.

Grimm, Wilhelm Karl and Jakob Ludwig Grimm. *Kinder- und Hausmärchen* (KHM). Jena: Diederichs, 1922.

Grimm, Jakob Ludwig. *Deutsche Mythologie.* 4th ed., ed. Elard Hugo Meyer. 3 vols. Gütersloh, Berlin: Dümmler, 1875–78. *Teutonic Mythology.* 4 vols. London: Routledge, 2000.

Haggard, H. Rider. *Ayesha: The Return of She.* London: Ward Lock & Co., 1905.
———. Rider. *She: A History of Adventure.* London: Longmans, Green & Co., 1887. *Sie: Roman aus dem dunkelsten Afrika.* Jena: Hermann Costenoble, 1911.

473

————. Rider. *She and Allan*. London: Longmans, Green & Co., 1921.

————. *Wisdom's Daughter: The Life and Love Story of She-Who-Must-Be-Obeyed*. London: Hutchinson, 1923.

Hambruch, Paul, ed. *Südseemärchen*. Jena: Diederichs, 1916.

Handwörterbuch des deutschen Aberglaubens. Ed. Hanns Bächtold-Stäubli. 10 vols. Berlin: de Gruyter, 1927–42.

Hauer, Jakob Wilhelm. *Der Yoga als Heilsweg: Nach den indischen Quellen dargestellt*. Stuttgart: Kohlhammer, 1932.

Hermes Trismegistus. *Corpus Hermeticum*. In *Hermetica*, 4 vols., ed. Walter Scott. Oxford: Clarendon Press, 1924–1936. English translation at www.hermetic .com/texts/index.html (14 March 2007).

Herzog, Rudolf. *Aus dem Asklepieion von Kos*. Archiv für Religionswissenschaft, vol. 10. Ed. A. Dieterich. Leipzig: Teubner, 1907.

Hetzer, Hildegard. *Psychologische Untersuchung der Konstitutiou des Kinder*. Leipzig: Barth, 1937.

Hildegard von Bingen. *Wisse die Wege: Scivias*. Nach dem Originaltext des illu- minierten Ruppertsberger Kodex ins Deutsche übertragen und bearbeitet von M. Böckeier. Salzburg: Müller, 1956. *Scivias: Know the Ways*. Mahwah, NY: Paulist Press, 1990.

Hoffmann, E.T.A. *Der goldne Topf: Ein Mährchen aus der neuen Zeit*. 2nd ed., Bam- berg: Kunz, 1819. *The Golden Pot and Other Tales*. Oxford: Oxford Paperbacks, 2000.

————. *Die Elixire des Teufels: Nachgelassene Papiere des Bruders Medardus, eines Kapuziners*. Leipzig: Buchverlag fürs Deutsche Haus, 1908. *The Devil's Elixirs*. London: John Calder, 1963.

Horaz (Quintus Horatius Flaccus). *Oden und Epoden*. Leipzig: Teubner, 1899. Ho- race. *Odes and Epodes*. Cambridge. MA: Harvard University Press, 2004.

I GING: Das Buch der Wandlungen. Trans. and ed. R. Wilhelm. Jena: Diederichs, 1924. *The Complete I Ching*. Rochester: Inner Traditions International, 1998.

Ignatius Loyola. *Exercitia spiritualia*. In Sebastián Izquierdus; *Praxis exercitiorum spiritualium P. N. S. Ignatii*. Rome, 1695.

Janet, Pierre. *Les obsessions et la psychasthénie*. 2 vols. Paris: Alcan, 1903.

Jung, C. G. *Aion: Untersuchungenz zur Symbolgeschichte*. Part 2. Zurich: Rascher, 1951.

————. *Der Mensch und seine Symbole*. Olten: Walter, 1968.

————. *Dream Analysis (Notes of the Seminar Given in 1928–1930)*. Ed. William McGuire. London,: Routledge & Kegan Paul; Princeton, NJ: Princeton Univer- sity Press, 1984.

————. *Erinnerungen, Träume, Gedanken*. Ed. Aniela Jaffé. Zurich: Rascher, 1962. *Memories, Dreams, Reflections*. New York: Harper Collins Paperbacks, 1999.

————. *The Practice of Psychotherapy: Essays on the Psychology of Transference and Other Subjects*. 2nd ed., London: Routledge, 1966.

————. *The Psychology of Kundalini Yoga.* Ed. Sonu Shamdasani: Princeton, NJ: Princeton University Press, 1996.

————. *Wandlungen und Symbole der Libido.* Zurich: Rascher, 1925. *Symbols of Transformation.* CW 5.

Kerner, Justinus. See *Blätter aus Prevorst.*

Koepgen, Georg. *Die Gnosis des Christentums.* Salzburg: Müller, 1939.

Kubin, Alfred. *Die andere Seite.* Munich: Georg Müller, 1908. *The Other Side.* Dedalus: Langford Lodge, 2000.

Küster, Erich. *Die Schlange in der griechischen Kunst und Religion.* Gießen: Alfred Töpelmann, 1913.

Leisegang, Hans. *Die Gnosis.* Leipzig: Kroner, 1924.

Lévy-Bruhl, Lucien. *Die Seele der Primitiven.* Düsseldorf, Cologne: Diederichs, 1956. *The "Soul" of the Primitive.* New York: Macmillan, 1928.

Lincoln, Jackson Steward. *The Dream in Primitive Cultures.* London: Cresset Press, 1935.

Maehly, Jakob A. *Die Schlange im Mythus und Kultus der klassischen Völker.* Basel: Schultze, 1867.

Maier, Michael. *Symbola aureae mensae duodecim nationum.* Frankfurt am Main, 1617.

Maitland, Edward. *Anna Kingsford: Her Life, Letters, Diary and Work.* London: Redway, 1896.

Mangetus, Johannes Jacobus. See Bonus, Petrus.

Matthews, Washington. *The Mountain Chant: A Navajo Ceremony.* Fifth Annual Report of the U.S. Bureau of American Ethnology, 1883–1884. Washington, DC: Smithsonian Institution, 1887. Online at www.sacred-texts.com/nam/nav/tmc/index.htm (14 March 2007).

Mommsen, Theodor. *Römische Geschichte.* 3 vols. Leipzig: Reimer, 1854–56. Online at http://gutenberg.spiegel.de/mommsen/roemisch/roemisch.htm (14 March 2007).

Musaeum Hermeticum reformatum et amplificatum, omnes sopho-spagyricae artis discipulos fidelissime erudiens etc. Frankfurt am Main: Sand, 1678. See at www.levity.com/alchemy/musaeum2.html (14 March 2007).

Nietzsche, Friedrich. *Also sprach Zarathustra.* In *Nietzsches Werke,* 16 vols. Leipzig: Alfred Kröner, 1899. *Thus Spake Zarathustra.* Harmondsworth: Penguin Books, 1978.

Ninck, Martin. *Wodan und germanischer Schicksalsglaube.* Jena: Diederichs, 1935.

Novalis (alias Freiherr von Hardenberg). *Heinrich von Ofterdingen* (1802). Online at http://gutenberg.spiegel.de/novalis/ofterdng/ofterdng.htm (14 March 2007).

Peucer, Caspar. *Commentarius de praecipuis divinationum generibus.* Wittenberg, 1553 (printed 1596).

Pico della Mirandola, Giovanni. *Opera omnia.* Basel, 1557–73. *Ausgewählte Schriften.* Trans. A. Liebert. Jena: Diederichs, 1905.

Plutarch. *Über Isis und Osiris. Nach neuverglichenen Handschriften mit Übersetzungen und Erläuterungen.* Ed. Gustav Parthey. Berlin: Nicolaische Buchhandlung, 1850. *Moralia, Volume V, Isis and Osiris. The E at Delphi. The Oracles at Delphi No Longer Given in Verse. The Obsolescence of Oracles.* Cambridge, MA: Harvard University Press, 1936.

Przywara, Erich. *Deus semper maior: Theologie der Exerzitien.* 3 vols. Freiburg im Breisgau: Herder, 1938–40.

Rank, Otto. *Der Mythus von der Geburt des Helden.* Leipzig, Vienna: Deuticke, 1909. *The Myth of the Birth of the Hero.* Baltimore: Johns Hopkins University Press, 2004.

———. *The Trauma of Birth.* New York: Dover, 1993.

Rasmussen, Knut. *Neue Menschen: Ein Jahr bei den Nachbarn des Nordpols.* Berne: Francke, 1907.

Rochas, Albert de. *Die Ausscheidung des Empfindungsvermögens.* Leipzig: Altmann, 1909.

Rohde, Erwin. *Psyche: Seelencult und Unsterblichkeitsglaube der Griechen.* Tübingen: Mohr, 1907.

Rosarium Philosophorum. In *Artis auriferae*, vol. 2.

Roscher, Wilhelm H. *Ausführliches Lexikon der Griechischen und Römischen Mythologie.* 6 vols. and supps. Leipzig: Teubner, 1884–1937.

Ruska, Julius F. *Turba Philosophorum: Ein Beitrag zur Geschichte der Alchemie.* Berlin: Julius Springer, 1931.

Schaeder, Hans Heinrich. *Urform und Fortbildungen des manichäischen Systems.* In: Vorträge der Bibliothek Warburg 1924/25. Leipzig: Teubner, 1927.

Schiller, Friedrich von. *Wallenstein.* Stuttgart, Tübingen: Cotta, 1822–26.

Scott, Walter, ed. See Hermes Trismegistus.

The Serpent Power, Being the Shat-Chakra-Nirupana and Paduka-Panchaka: Two Works on Tantrik Yoga. Trans. from the Sanskrit and ed. by Arthur Avalon. London: Luzac & Co., 1919.

Silberer, Herbert. "Phantasie und Mythus." *Jahrbuch für psychoanalytische und psychopathologische Forschungen* 3 (1912): 329–400.

Steinthal, Hajim (Heymann). "Die Sage von Simson." *Zeitschrift für Völkerpsychologie und Sprachwissenschaft* 2 (1862): 129–78.

Theatrum chemicum, praecipuos selectorum auctorum tractatus . . . continens. Vols. 1–3, Ursel, 1602; vol. 4, Strasbourg, 1613; vol. 5, 1622; vol. 6, 1661.

Thurnwald, Richard. *Primitive Initiations- und Wiedergeburtsriten: Eranos-Jahrbuch, 1939.* Zurich: Rhein, 1940.

The Tibetan Book of the Dead. See Evans-Wentz, Walter Yeeling.

Upanishads: The Sacred Books of the East, vol. 15. Trans. and ed. Friedrich Max Müller. Oxford: Oxford University Press, 1900.

Visio Arislei. In *Artis auriferae*, vol. 1, §3, pp. 146–54.

Vollers, Karl. "Chidher." *Archiv für Religionswissenschaft* 12 (1909): 252ff.

476

Wells, Herbert George. *Christina Alberta's Father*. New York: Macmillan, 1925.

Wilde, Oscar. "The Picture of Dorian Gray." *Lippincott's Monthly Magazine*, 1890. *The Picture of Dorian Gray and Other Short Stories*. Harmondsworth: Penguin, Signet Classics, 1962.

Wilhelm, Richard, and C. G. Jung. *Das Geheimnis der Goldenen Blüte*. Zurich: Rascher, 1938. *The Secret of the Golden Flower*. New York: Causeway Books, 1975.

Winthuis, Josef. *Das Zweigeschlechterwesen bei den Zentralaustraliern und anderen Völkern*. Leipzig: Hirschfeld, 1928.

Zimmer, Heinrich. *Maya—Der indische Mythos*. Stuttgart: Deutsche Verlagsanstalt, 1936.

———. *Weisheit Indiens: Märchen und Sinnbilder*. Darmstadt: Wittich, 1938.

Zosimos of Panoplis. In Berthelot, *Collections des anciens alchémistes grecs*.

Zulliger, Hans. *Schwierige Schüler: Acht Kapitel zur Theorie und Praxis der tiefenpsychologischen Erziehungsberatung und Erziehungshilfe*. Bern: Huber, 1935.

Index

Two numbers in parenthesis indicate dream number, then seminar number.

479

The Collected Works of C. G. Jung

Editors: Sir Herbert Read, Michael Fordham, and Gerhard Adler; executive editor, William McGuire. Translated by R.F.C. Hull, except where noted.

(continued)

(continued)

(continued)

(continued)